THE SELECTED WORKS OF GORDON TULLOCK

VOLUME 8

The Social Dilemma

THE SELECTED WORKS OF GORDON TULLOCK

VOLUME 1 *Virginia Political Economy*

VOLUME 2 *The Calculus of Consent: Logical Foundations of Constitutional Democracy* (with James M. Buchanan)

VOLUME 3 *The Organization of Inquiry*

VOLUME 4 *The Economics of Politics*

VOLUME 5 *The Rent-Seeking Society*

VOLUME 6 *Bureaucracy*

VOLUME 7 *The Economics and Politics of Wealth Redistribution*

VOLUME 8 *The Social Dilemma: Of Autocracy, Revolution, Coup d'Etat, and War*

VOLUME 9 *Law and Economics*

VOLUME 10 *Economics without Frontiers* (includes a cumulative index for the series)

Gordon Tullock

THE SELECTED WORKS OF GORDON TULLOCK

VOLUME 8

The Social Dilemma

Of Autocracy, Revolution, Coup d'Etat, and War

GORDON TULLOCK

Edited and with an Introduction by

CHARLES K. ROWLEY

Liberty Fund
Indianapolis

This book is published by Liberty Fund, Inc., a
foundation established to encourage study of the
ideal of a society of free and responsible individuals.

The cuneiform inscription that serves as our logo and
as the design motif for our endpapers is the earliest-known
written appearance of the word "freedom" (*amagi*), or "liberty."
It is taken from a clay document written about 2300 B.C.
in the Sumerian city-state of Lagash.

Printed in the United States of America

Paperback cover photo courtesy of the
American Economic Review

Frontispiece courtesy of Center for Study of Public Choice,
George Mason University, Fairfax, Virginia

c 10 9 8 7 6 5 4 3 2 1
p 10 9 8 7 6 5 4 3 2

Library of Congress Cataloging-in-Publication Data
Tullock, Gordon.
The social dilemma : of autocracy, revolution, coup d'etat,
and war / Gordon Tullock; edited and with an introd. by
Charles K. Rowley.
p. cm. — (Selected works / Gordon Tullock ; V. 8)
Includes bibliographical references and index.
ISBN 0-86597-527-2 (alk. paper) — ISBN 0-86597-538-8 (pbk. : alk. paper)
1. War—Economic aspects. 2. Dictatorship. 3. Social choice.
4. Rent (Economic theory).
I. Rowley, Charles Kershaw. II. Title.
HB195.T84 2005
330.9—dc22

2004061542

LIBERTY FUND, INC.
8335 Allison Pointe Trail, Suite 300
Indianapolis, Indiana 46250-1684

CONTENTS

INTRODUCTION

The Social Dilemma: Of Autocracy, Revolution, Coup d'Etat, and War brings together Gordon Tullock's path-breaking contributions to the analysis of collective action under conditions of limited democracy and dictatorship. In these contributions, Tullock deploys public choice and rent-seeking analysis to explore, within the framework of rational choice, political market behavior that is based on conflict rather than on bargaining and thus behavior that results in wealth reduction rather than in gains-from-trade. This volume thematically organizes materials drawn from two of Tullock's books, namely, *The Social Dilemma: The Economics of War and Revolution* (1974) and *Autocracy* (1987).

The Intellectual and Historical Background

The Calculus of Consent was written during the dying years of the second, bipartisan Eisenhower administration.[1] At that time, the environment was conducive to the theory of politics, as put forward in *The Calculus of Consent*, that focused attention on the gains-from-trade available from well-functioning political markets and that challenged the winner-takes-all notion of conflict-based, two-party politics that had energized U.S. behavioral political science research throughout the preceding quarter of a century. Inevitably, as new theories often do, the new rational-choice theory of politics met with resistance, both in economics and in political science. Yet, by the late 1960s, the gains-from-trade model had established a respectable toehold in both disciplines.

The tranquility of the U.S. political marketplace then abruptly vanished as latent sociopolitical tensions rose to the surface.[2] The combat troops introduced into Vietnam by President Kennedy in 1963 led to a minor war under the administration of President Lyndon Johnson. The war continued without

1. James M. Buchanan and Gordon Tullock, *The Calculus of Consent: Logical Foundations of Constitutional Democracy* (Ann Arbor: University of Michigan Press, 1962).

2. See Charles K. Rowley, "The Reason of Rules: Constitutional Contract versus Political Market Conflict," *Annual Review of Conflict Knowledge and Conflict Resolution* 2 (1990): 195–228.

decisive military success throughout the first Nixon administration and ended in defeat for the United States during the second Nixon administration.

By the summer of 1974, with the Vietnam War, the assassinations of President John F. Kennedy, Robert F. Kennedy, and Martin Luther King Jr., and the resignation of President Richard M. Nixon in the wake of the Watergate scandal, the calculus of consent no longer seemed to be the glue that bonded Americans into mutually beneficial political harmony. The United States appeared to be closer to the "Hobbesian jungle" than at any time since Abraham Lincoln's controversial election to the presidency of the United States, in 1860.[3]

Buchanan and Tullock had clearly recognized such a possibility of constitutional discord in their 1962 book but had downgraded its relevance for the United States:

> Our analysis of the constitution-making process has little relevance for a society that is characterized by a sharp cleavage of the population into distinguishable social classes or separate racial, religious, or ethnic groupings sufficient to encourage the formation of predictable political coalitions and in which one of these coalitions has a clearly advantageous position at the constitutional stage.[4]

In so doing, Buchanan and Tullock chose to ignore both the nature of the founding of the U.S. Constitution, which was based on an enfranchised population comprising only white male property owners who constituted less than one-sixth of the adult population, and the racial schism exposed by the Civil War and reinforced by Reconstruction. That decision came back to haunt them during the long summer of 1974, as the Watergate investigations reached crisis point and as President Nixon contemplated whether to hide behind executive privilege and to challenge the checks and balances of the Constitution.

The responses of Buchanan and of Tullock to this perceived constitutional crisis diverged sharply. Buchanan, in his 1975 book *The Limits of Liberty*, rationalized the durability of the consent calculus in terms of the ever-present threat of Hobbesian anarchy should the Constitution break down, and thereafter, he focused almost exclusively on constitutional political economy.[5]

3. Thomas Hobbes, *Leviathan*, ed. M. Oakeshott (1651; Oxford: Basil Blackwell, 1946).

4. Buchanan and Tullock, *Calculus of Consent*, 80.

5. James M. Buchanan, *The Limits of Liberty: Between Anarchy and Leviathan* (Chicago: University of Chicago Press, 1975).

Tullock's contrasting response, in his 1974 book *The Social Dilemma*, was to acknowledge the Hobbesian nature of democracy and to switch from the gains-from-trade model to the reality of generalized prisoners' dilemmas, in which political actors find themselves locked into wealth-reducing circumstances by the nature of the noncooperative game, and by intractable holdout problems, even within the context of a constitutional republic such as the United States.[6]

Throughout history, the large majority of the world's population has lived under conditions of autocracy. Even from the beginning of the twenty-first century, a small majority (some 3.5 billion of a world population of 6.3 billion) still live under such conditions, if democracy is rigorously defined to require a full suffrage and fair elections, that is, to exclude oligarchies.

Although much has been written philosophically and descriptively about autocracy, Tullock was the first economist to apply the rational-choice model to analyzing systematically the behavior of individuals under such conditions.

Tullock is a keen student of the Greek philosophers Plato and Aristotle, neither of whose writings are particularly favorable to democracy. In *The Republic* Plato cites Socrates as stating that the best form of government, both in times of peace and in times of war, is timocracy, in which the king, chosen from the aristocracy, is well versed both in philosophy and in war and has a love of honor.[7] The second-best form of government is oligarchy, the rule of the few; the third-best is democracy, the rule of the people; and the worst is tyranny, "the most extreme pestilence that a city can have."[8]

In *The Politics* Aristotle adopts a somewhat less *judgmental* position among these forms of government. He explains that the terms "constitution" and "government" have the same meaning and that the government, which is the supreme authority in states, must be in the hands of the one, of the few, or of the many.[9] The "true" forms of government are those in which the one, the few, or the many govern with a view to the common interest. Whether of the one, of the few, or of the many, governments that rule with a view to the

6. Gordon Tullock, *The Social Dilemma: The Economics of War and Revolution* (Blacksburg, Va.: Center for Study of Public Choice, 1974).

7. Plato (427–347 B.C.), *The Republic*, in *Great Dialogues of Plato*, ed. E. H. Warmington and P. H. Rouse (Markham, Ont.: New American Library), 118–446.

8. Ibid., 342.

9. Aristotle (384–321 B.C.), *The Politics*, ed. Stephen Everson (Cambridge: Cambridge University Press, 1988).

private interest are perversions. Thus, the perversions are as follows: of kingship, tyranny; of aristocracy, oligarchy; and of constitutional government, democracy.

When comparing the true forms of government, according to Aristotle, kingship is the best, followed by aristocracy and then by constitutional government. Among the perverted forms of government, however, democracy is best, followed by oligarchy and then by tyranny. Because, as we shall see, Tullock analyzes all forms of government as pursuing the private interest, democracy, in his estimation, holds a fragile advantage.

Writing almost two millennia later, Hobbes, in *Leviathan*, evinces a much more favorable portrait of government by the one, should such government be conducted in the common or the private interest. Hobbes is obsessed by the idea of the dissolution of authority—of the disorder that results from the freedom among individuals to disagree about what is just and unjust and with the disintegration of the unity of power that he views as inevitable once individuals begin to contend that power must be limited.[10]

The ultimate goal that motivates individuals, according to Hobbes, is pursuit of peace, not of liberty. The ultimate evil to be avoided at all cost is anarchy, which he views as a return to the state of nature. Hobbes describes a state of nature, the first objective condition, in which human beings, de facto, are equal. Being equal by nature, they are capable of inflicting the greatest of evil on each other, namely, death. To this is added the second objective condition, scarcity of goods, which causes individuals all to desire the same thing.

This combination of equality and relative scarcity generates a permanent state of reciprocal lack of trust, which induces all to prepare for war and to make war, if necessary, rather than to seek peace: "So that in the first place, I put forward a general inclination of all mankind, a perpetual and restless desire for power after power, that ceaseth only in death."[11]

According to Hobbes, there is only one way to make the laws of nature effective and to make human beings act according to their reason and not their passions: the institution of the irresistible power of the state. To exit the state of nature and to establish civil society, individuals must enter into a universal and permanent covenant. Because individuals cannot be trusted to honor any contract among themselves, they must all consent to give up their own power and to transfer it to one person. This person will have as much power as is necessary to prevent any individual from harming others.

10. Hobbes, *Leviathan*.

11. Ibid., 24.

Individuals acquire a fundamental obligation as a consequence of this *pactum subiectionis* (pact of subjection), namely, an obligation to obey all the commands of the holder of the shared power. This "covenant of union" is an agreement in which all parties agree to subject themselves to a third party who does not participate in the contract. The third party thus combines the supreme economic power (*dominium*) and the supreme coercive power (*imperium*). "There is no power on earth" (says the verse from the Book of Job that describes the sea monster Leviathan) "which is equal to it."[12]

Tullock is enough of a Hobbesian to recognize this logic. While not necessarily endorsing *Leviathan* on moral grounds, he understands why societies sometimes prefer autocracy to any other form of government, knowing that no other form of government can feasibly survive and that anarchy, therefore, is the only realistic alternative.

Tullock's writings on autocracy, war, revolution, and coups d'etat commenced at the end of a troubled first three-quarters of a dangerous twentieth century. The First World War had devastated most of Europe, autocracy and democracy alike. Regicide in Russia was followed by the imposition of a socialist dictatorship. Germany descended from the weak democracy of the Weimar Republic into the powerful dictatorship of Hitler's Third Reich.

The Great Depression of the 1930s led many intellectuals (including many economists in Britain and the United States) to support dictatorship (left or right) over democracy. The Second World War exacerbated the collapse of European civilization as the Soviet Union extended its hegemony throughout much of central Europe. Once again, many economists in Britain and the United States looked enviously at the supposed economic success of the Soviet Union and looked hopefully for the collapse of the capitalist democracies.

In 1975 some three-quarters of the world's population lived under conditions of dictatorship. This is the historical backcloth against which Tullock tuned his rational-choice model into the analysis of the workings of autocracy.

Gordon Tullock's Contributions to the Literature

Part 1, "The Roots of the Social Dilemma," brings together three papers that analyze, from the rational-choice perspective, individual behavior in societies characterized by conflict as well as by cooperation.

12. Job 41:24.

"The Roots of Conflict" sets the scene by centering attention on redistribution rather than on gains-from-trade as a primary source of political-market interaction between individuals and groups. In such conflict conditions, where a coercive solution is eventually imposed either through private mechanisms or through the political process, individuals invest resources wastefully in an attempt to defend their own property or to seize the property of others.

"The Cooperative State" uses Hobbes's notion of the state of nature, in which all individuals endlessly predate upon each other, to identify the prisoners' dilemma that underpins such a destructive pattern of behavior.[13] Tullock points out that all societies that have risen above the level of barbarism deal with potential theft, fraud, and robbery by varying combinations of three methods. First, some resources are put into passive protection in the form of locks and barred windows. Second, some resources are put into personal retaliation. Third, some resources are placed within a central apparatus (government) designed to inflict penalties on criminal behavior. The third method, at least in principle, is the rationale for the cooperative state.

"The Exploitative State" questions the degree of generality of the cooperative state in which individuals seek gains-from-trade through cooperative bargaining. Tullock focuses attention on the exploitative state, in which a small minority of individuals maximizes its private returns through exercising a monopoly of force over the large majority. Even such dictatorships often provide benefits to the majority, unavailable in the state of nature. Usually, though not always, the exploited majority would prefer to live within a cooperative rather than in an exploitative state.

Part 2, "The Goals and Organizational Forms of Autocracy," brings together six papers that explore the varying objectives and institutional structures of governments that fall under the broad rubric of autocracy.

In his introduction to *Autocracy*, Tullock points out that there had been almost no scientific analysis of dictatorships since Machiavelli in the early fifteenth century.[14] Yet historically, and still in the late twentieth century, dictatorships had been and were the dominant form of government. Under the general term "autocracy" Tullock distinguishes between dictatorships by hereditary rulers of kingdoms and empires on the one hand and nonhereditary dictatorships on the other. He distinguishes autocracy from feudalism

13. Hobbes, *Leviathan*.

14. Niccolò Machiavelli, *The Prince* (1514; London: Penguin Classics, 1981).

and democracy, arguing that the latter forms of government provide more individual freedom than is typical of any autocracy. He also distinguishes between totalitarian and authoritarian autocracies and places all communist dictatorships in the former category.

"The Uses of Dictatorship" investigates the goals of autocrats. Tullock notes that power is never absolute and that autocrats do not enjoy complete freedom to satisfy their personal desires. Always they are concerned to secure themselves against would-be challengers. Hereditary monarchs tend to be more secure and, therefore, are less constrained than dictators. In all cases, autocrats use their power to seek personal wealth. Many autocrats, dictators as well as monarchs, seek to secure the succession. Some seek to implement policies that they believe will be beneficial for subjects. Successful dictators, unlike monarchs, tend to be highly intelligent and ambitious and so pursue their policies more efficiently. They enjoy luxurious, if insecure and potentially short, lives.

"Becoming a Dictator" focuses attention on the methods whereby existing dictators are ousted and whereby nondictatorships are subverted into dictatorships. Because they desire to avoid being displaced, dictators rarely attempt to secure a dynasty. Tullock explores, with a wealth of contemporary examples, the mechanism of the coup d'etat as the most successful route to the top for ambitious and highly placed members of a dictator's entourage.

"The Problem of Succession" provides a rational-choice evaluation of how aging autocrats approach the issue of their succession. Tullock explains the reluctance of such dictators to name an heir in terms of their fear of assassination by the named heir and his associates. He notes the tendency for dictators to appoint an advisory body that becomes responsible for determining the succession once he dies. This system was deployed by two autocracies, namely, the Catholic Church and the Soviet Union, both with considerable success in avoiding assassinations of their respective leaders.

"Democracy and Despotism" centers discussion on the instability of government forms. The chapter chronicles the lengthy history of the transition of autocracies into democracies, sometimes as a consequence of foreign intervention, often as a consequence of internal struggles. It also focuses on examples of democracies transitioning into autocracies. Tullock concludes that autocracy is the equilibrium condition.

"Monarchies, Hereditary and Nonhereditary" chronicles the instability of monarchies, including that of England, before the hereditary principle was firmly embedded. The evolution of monarchies from nonhereditary to hereditary rule typically is accompanied with increased internal stability and economic advancement. According to Tullock, modern scholars do not engage in a serious rational-choice analysis of the respective merits of monarchy and democracy.

Part 3 of the volume, "Revolution and Its Suppression," brings together five papers that apply the rational-choice model in analyzing a variety of methods utilized historically to overthrow existing governments and a variety of methods adopted by governments historically to suppress such insurgencies.

"Revolution and Welfare Economics" casts empirical doubt on the relevance of the romantic notion of revolution, in which a downtrodden population rises up spontaneously to eject a hated despot and to introduce an economically and politically superior new order. Insurgencies are rarely concerned in practice with establishing an efficient democracy. Indeed, insurgencies typically replace despotism with despotism or democracy with despotism. The goal of insurgents is to redistribute the political and economic spoils of victory to themselves, not to redistribute them to the downtrodden masses. Overall, insurgencies generally lower the wealth of a nation.

"The Paradox of Revolution" utilizes Mancur Olson's logic of collective action to evaluate potential revolutionary behavior.[15] Because the general benefits of a successful revolution are public goods, rational individuals will underprovide revolutionary inputs unless they perceive additional strictly private benefits. Thus, any public-good products of revolution must be byproducts of such private incentives. Tullock develops a simple formal model to explain this paradox.

"The Economics of Repression" shifts attention to the methods whereby rational dictatorships repress insurgencies. Tullock develops a model to demonstrate how a dictator can repress a popular uprising much more easily than an attempted coup d'etat. The model focuses on the importance of incentives (negative as well as positive) to inform on potential insurgents as a basis for repressing an uprising.

"'Popular' Risings" suggests that successful popular uprisings against an autocrat are largely figments of romantic historians' imaginations. Almost all

15. Mancur Olson, *The Logic of Collective Action* (Cambridge: Harvard University Press, 1965).

successful overthrows of autocracies occur as a consequence of either coups d'etat or foreign intervention. The so-called French Revolution and the so-called Russian Revolution are examples of the former, and the so-called American Revolution is an example of the latter. Tullock supports his hypothesis with numerous historical examples.

"Legitimacy and Ethics" attempts to explain how dictatorships that are considered evil by outsiders (for example, Hitler's Third Reich and Stalin's Soviet Union) nevertheless are accorded legitimacy by their own subjects. Tullock raises the bar for his explanation by defining legitimacy as support for a regime against the best interests of those who provide such support. Tullock's explanation is based on an interesting theory of human evolution that allows man to be rationally indoctrinated.

Part 4 of the volume, "The Coup d'Etat and Its Suppression," consists of three papers that explore in some depth the nature of the coup d'etat and the rational approach to its prevention.

"Coup d'Etat: Structural Factors" defines the coup d'etat as a split within the government, usually involving the military-police establishment. Tullock suggests that, whereas the optimal course for citizens confronted with the possibility of a popular uprising is to remain neutral, this is not so for members of the military-police elite when confronted with a potential coup. Choosing sides is the optimal strategy in such circumstances.

"The Theory of the Coup" poses the question, Which side should senior members of a dictatorship choose when a coup is contemplated? Tullock makes use of the concept of a "focal point," drawn from game theory, to explain how decisions to join a coup are made in practice under conditions where open discussion is too costly. He also examines the nature of the decision-making process that leads entrepreneurs within an autocracy to initiate an uprising designed to replace the existing leadership.

"Coups and Their Prevention" explains how an autocrat retains power, given the pervasive incentives for senior members of his government to rise up against him. Tullock argues that a widely utilized strategy is that of killing or exiling all potential coup leaders, even when this strategy implies a weakening of his own military-police organization. In addition, Tullock outlines two other mechanisms whereby the dictator can hold on to power: that of continually changing the elite so that no single individual can build an effective opposition network and that of always soliciting advice but never accepting unsolicited advice. In all these respects, the autocrat who reads and comprehends the advice of Machiavelli is well placed to survive in office.

Part 5, "The Economics of War," comprises four papers that apply the rational-choice model to the analysis of war.

"International Conflict: Two Parties" directs attention to formal international warfare in a bipolar system. Tullock models the conflict in terms of two countries to outline the predictable strategic behavior of competing nation-states. He demonstrates how an autocracy might behave aggressively at a net expected cost to the nation as a whole where there are positive gains to the dictator. He shows that nations that commit themselves to defensive but not to aggressive strategies (for example, the United Nations in the case of Korea, and the United States in the case of Vietnam) place themselves at a serious strategic disadvantage. He evaluates alternative mechanisms whereby two nations may avoid conflict. Throughout, Tullock maintains an unwavering judgment that international conflict is driven by rational calculations.

"Agreement and Cheating" reveals why it is difficult for two potentially hostile countries to negotiate effective mutual disarmament treaties, even when both parties recognize the economic benefits of such arrangements. Tullock identifies two important impediments, namely, the difficulty of negotiating a comprehensive treaty that eliminates all avenues of evasion, and the mutual suspicion that the other party will unilaterally renege on the treaty. He explores mechanisms whereby nations can overcome these impediments, thus resolving the prisoners' dilemma problem that plagues international diplomacy.

"Three or More Countries and the Balance of Power" explores the enhanced prospects for limiting international conflict in a multipolar world. Tullock outlines the balance of powers principle deployed by the European powers from the sixteenth century onward as a means of preventing the emergence of a European superpower. He notes that the principle was not designed to prevent international conflict but, more conservatively, to prevent single-country dominance by an explicit mechanism of strategically changing coalitions. Tullock ends with a gloomy recognition that the advantages of the balance of power principle have been largely eroded, from the mid 1950s onward, with the emergence of the bipolar model now predicated on the overwhelming nuclear superiority of the United States and the Soviet Union.

Tullock's "Epilogue to *The Social Dilemma: The Economics of War and Revolution*" reemphasizes that the investment of resources in conflict is frequently rational from the standpoint of individuals even though it leads to a net waste from the standpoint of society.

In this volume, Tullock reaches out well beyond the confines of mainstream economics to apply the rational-choice model to fundamentally important issues of autocracy and of war and peace. In so doing, he uses techniques of public choice to open a fruitful area of research. By downgrading the relevance of romantic and utopian thinking, and by introducing a much-needed dash of realism, Tullock provides a wake-up call for all individuals who cherish and seek to defend individual liberty.

CHARLES K. ROWLEY

Duncan Black Professor of Economics, George Mason University

Senior Fellow, James M. Buchanan Center for Political Economy, George Mason University

General Director, The Locke Institute

PART I

THE ROOTS OF THE SOCIAL DILEMMA

THE ROOTS OF CONFLICT

The primitive view of trade included the belief that the profits of one party must necessarily come from losses of the other. Indeed, although I have called this view primitive, it is widely held today. A rather similar view is frequently held by analysts of politics. In this view, politics is about power, and power is so defined that an increase of power to Mr. *A* must carry with it a reduction in the power of Mr. *B*. In a way, the foundation of modern economics was a realization that profits from economic transactions may be mutual. It is quite possible (in fact, it is generally true) that both parties are better off after an economic transaction than they were before. Economists, however, have not normally drawn the conclusion that there are no grounds for conflict between the parties to a bargain. Clearly, the distribution of the profits between the two parties is still a matter upon which they have directly conflicting interests. Nevertheless, economics has concentrated upon those aspects of the transactions between different persons that are mutually profitable.

Political scientists have recently come to realize that there may be gains-from-trade in politics, too. All parties may be benefited through the establishment of a suitably designed constitutional government. Further, there may be changes in the design or in the activities of an existing government that benefit everyone. However, the profits of these government activities may be distributed in different ways, and there is a clear conflict among the parties with respect to these different distributions. Indeed, if we use the ordinary definitions of economic and political spheres, redistribution among the parties to some political transaction may well proceed in a mutually disadvantageous manner. A transfer from *A* to *B* may take place in such a way that *B* receives less than *A* gave up.

If I have the power to extract a transfer from you, I would normally take the transfer in the most efficient way—as a direct switch of purchasing power. This would make you worse off and me better off, but we would remain on the Paretian frontier. There may be institutions, however, that make such an efficient transfer impossible. Under these circumstances, I may be driven to an inefficient transfer method, with the result that what costs you $10 benefits

Reprinted, with permission, from *The Social Dilemma: The Economics of War and Revolution* (Blacksburg, Va.: Center for Study of Public Choice, 1974), 1–8.

me \$5. Both of us would have been better off had you bribed me with \$7.50, but the institutional structure may make this bribe impossible.

In a way, this book will be devoted to a consideration of this unfortunate type of transfer. Economics has traditionally studied the benefits of cooperation. Political science is beginning to move in that direction. Although I would not quarrel with the desirability of such studies, the fact remains that conflict is also important. In general, conflict uses resources; hence it is socially inefficient, but entering into the conflict may be individually rational for one or both parties. If this is so, we will be in a prisoner's dilemma and society will be worse off than if it were possible to avoid this situation. The social dilemma, then, is that we would always be better off collectively if we could avoid playing this kind of negative-sum game, but that individuals may make gains by forcing such a game upon the rest of us. There are institutions that will reduce the likelihood of being forced into such a game, but these institutions cost resources, too. Our well-being, thus, will always be less than it would be if somehow we could avoid the problem. Still, the problem is unavoidable—at least in our present state of knowledge. Pretending that it does not exist is likely to make us worse off than conceding its existence and taking rational precautions.

Let us consider a traditional problem. Suppose we have a two-person society composed of Mr. *A* and Mr. *B*, and they currently have some level of wealth and income. Some event occurs—technological discovery, change of taste, etc.—which makes it possible for the two parties to gain between them \$10. The result of this event is that they are no longer on the Paretian frontier, or, putting it differently, they are now off the contract locus. Traditional economics has pointed out that they now have an incentive to reach some agreement to obtain this \$10. This agreement will, among other things, provide for the distribution of the \$10 between them. Traditional economics, however, has primarily devoted its attention to pointing to the incentives for reaching agreement, and has given relatively little attention to the problem of deciding upon the distribution of the profit between the parties. This book will turn to the other problem: distribution.

The two parties, in traditional terminology, "bargain" in order to determine the apportionment of this profit. This bargaining will in part be an example of what I will refer to as "conflict" in this book. The real world activity of "bargaining" involves two separate activities: first, the attainment of the \$10 profit for the two parties and, second, the determination of its distribution. These two activities are carried out at one and the same time by one and the same operation. This book will differ from traditional economics in dealing mainly with the second activity—the distribution problem—rather than the first—the efficiency problem. This, of course, does not imply that the two actions are normally separated. We simply wish to concentrate on one aspect.

Bargaining, insofar as it is directed to the determination of the distribution of the profit, absorbs resources. Further, the resources are absorbed from both parties. As a result, the net outcome of the bargaining is apt to be that instead of a \$10 gain to be divided between the two parties, the actual net gain is, let us say, \$9. Much of this book will be devoted to the investment of resources for the purpose of obtaining distributional gains, and mechanisms that may be adopted to reduce the amount of resources "invested" in this mutually canceling activity. For the time being, however, let us leave the problem and go on to another.

The distribution problem is important not only with respect to new profit opportunities but also with respect to existing resources. It is true that we characteristically discuss this matter under the rubric of "redistribution"; but "redistribution" is as likely to cause differences of opinion between those who lose and those who gain as is "distribution." Let us return to our two-man society and assume that Mr. *A* would like to receive not only all of the \$10 profit from the efficiency improvement but also \$5 of Mr. *B*'s initial endowment. He feels he can get it because he is bigger than Mr. *B*. Under these circumstances, Mr. *B* would presumably make appropriate calculations and decide whether or not to resist. Once again there would be offsetting investments of resources by the two parties; and once again good social policy would indicate that we should try to minimize this mutual canceling of resources in conflict.

Put very briefly, the theme of this book is that situations will frequently arise in which *A* wants what *B* has. This will lead to investment of resources by *A* to get *B*'s property and by *B* to defend it. Regardless of the outcome of the conflict, the use of resources for this purpose is offsetting and therefore inherently wasteful. Social contrivances for reducing such investment of resources are, on the whole, desirable, although there may be cases where it is more efficient to place no institutional restrictions on such conflict. Two areas in which this type of conflict can occur, revolution and war, will be the main subject of this book. In each case, we will outline the characteristics of the struggle and discuss methods (insofar as they exist) to minimize its cost.

Because such conflict involves prisoner's dilemma games, it will never be possible to totally eliminate, but careful thought and rational design of institutions may civilize it.

Peter Gay, in his study of the Enlightenment, said that

> The prosperity of reason in the eighteenth century was less the triumph of rationalism than of reasonableness. Reason and humanity were easily confounded, and an instance of one was often taken as an instance of the other.[1]

He quotes Diderot as saying, "Reason has grown refined, and the nation's books are filled with its precepts. The books that inspire benevolence in men are practically the only ones read."[2] This attitude survives to this day. There is a tendency to assume that reason and ethically correct or humanitarian sentiments are one and the same thing. To say that violence may be rational seems to some people a contradiction in terms. Obviously this usage of terms is one that anyone who wishes may adopt. For myself, I prefer to use the word "rational" for those acts that might well achieve the goals to which the actor aims, regardless of whether they are humanitarian, violent, etc. My preference in this matter cannot be imposed on other people; but, since I am writing this book, I am free to use words in any way I wish, as long as I warn the reader. Thus, in this book the word "rational" will not carry with it any overtones of morality or humanism.

This discussion of definitions is necessary because unfortunately this book is largely devoted to certain matters that many intellectuals regard with considerable abhorrence. Violence, threats of force, coercion, and the deliberate infliction of harm upon people will be discussed. They will not be the only subjects of the book, but they will be a large part. Further, I will not mention these subjects only to deplore them. It is one of the themes of this book that, under certain circumstances, people may *gain* from the use of these unfortunate practices. I share the general feeling that these activities on the whole are undesirable from a social standpoint, but it seems essential to recognize their frequent individual rationality if we are to design social instrumentalities which have some chance of civilizing them.

To make a very brief digression on linguistics, I will find it necessary in this book to use a number of words that are emotionally loaded. This is not be-

1. Peter Gay, *The Enlightenment: An Interpretation*, 2 vols. (New York: Alfred A. Knopf, 1966–69), 2:29.

2. "Fils naturel," Act IV, scene 3. *Œuvres*, VII, 68.

cause of any desire on my part to do so, but because they are the only suitable words in the language. For example, "theft" obviously carries very strong negative implications. So far as I know, there is no other word carrying the same meaning that does not also have these implications. Thus I cannot discuss this subject without using emotionally loaded words. The same will apply to "violence," "coercion," and indeed "conflict" itself. On the other hand, for many people "transfers" and "redistribution" have emotional loading in the other direction; i.e., they are thought to be desirable. Once again, so far as I know there are no words to replace them which are free of emotional overtones. Granted this restriction of the English language, I hope that the reader will bear with me and realize that when I say, for example, "theft is a transfer," I am simply attempting to make a statement of analytic significance and not convey approval or disapproval.

As an example, consider the word "coercion." If I point a gun at you and say "your money or your life" and you give me your money, it is reasonable to say that you have been coerced. On the other hand, at the moment I am filing my income tax for the past year, and I assure you that the only reason I am making this payment is that I am coerced. Most of us regard the payment of taxes as desirable and robbery as undesirable. Nevertheless, the word "coercion" carries a negative implication. The negative connotations of "conflict" and "violence" are even stronger. Conflict and violence have been conspicuous parts of human history, however, and I hope to demonstrate that they are amenable to economic analysis. I shall also try to demonstrate that the individuals engaging in conflict and violence are not necessarily behaving irrationally, although they are normally playing a negative-sum game and would be better off if some way could be worked out to avoid the prisoner's dilemma in which they find themselves.

The area which I am about to enter is one that excites a great deal of emotional feeling; nevertheless it is worth examining. Further, it seems to me that it will be worthwhile for the reader to avoid (insofar as possible) emotional involvements raised by these words and concepts. Definition of terms is frequently either unnecessary or simply a display of scholarship. However, there are good reasons why I must be particularly careful with respect to the meaning of words. The words I wish to use will be used in a manner that is somewhat, although not radically, different from their normal usage.

The first term is "conflict," which I shall define as a situation in which two or more parties find themselves with opposing interests, and in which they devote resources to partially canceling attempts to achieve their opposing goals. This definition is not particularly unusual, but in many cases transactions between individuals have some elements of conflict and some elements of cooperation. The traditional example is the bargaining process. Very large net resources may be invested in attempting to get a good price. I am on the Board of Directors of a very small corporation which currently has under consideration the purchase of another very small corporation in order to take advantage of a tax loss. This negotiation cannot be completed before the beginning of 1971, and, as a result, about 20 percent of the tax loss will disappear under the current internal revenue rulings. Thus, the net return to the two parties taken as a group would be higher if there were an immediate agreement. On the other hand, both parties feel that showing anxiety would lead to a shift of the terms against themselves and therefore are unwilling to attempt to expedite the process. The net effect is a pure loss arising from the conflict portion of what is basically a cooperative transaction.

"Transfer" is very simply defined: It means the shifting of wealth or income from *A* to *B* under circumstances where *A* does not feel that he has benefited by the transaction. Note that this is a very wide concept. For example, my payment of taxes meets this requirement even though I might be fully in accord with the present government and feel that all of its activities are desirable. This would be because I, like most taxpayers, would realize my nonpayment of taxes would have substantially no effect on the total provision of services to me; hence, I would prefer to receive the government services without paying. For each dollar I pay, I receive something like $0.0000005 in benefits and transfer to my fellow citizens $0.9999995. Since Samuelson's initial articles on this subject, we have realized the solution to the apparent paradox. I agree with my fellow citizens that we shall all be coerced into making these payments, because the consequence to me from all of us being coerced is better than the consequence of all of us being free to pay or not to pay. An arrangement under which my neighbors were coerced and I was not would, of course, be even better, but it seems unlikely that I will be able to reach that nirvana.

There are many other examples of transfers in our society. Theft is clearly an example, as is a transfer of funds from the wealthy to the poor if done by coercion.[3] Note, however, that ordinary charity is not an example of transfer in this definition. If I make a gift to Mr. *B* voluntarily, I do so because for one

3. And, of course, transfers of wealth from the poor to the wealthy à la urban renewal or the California university system are also examples.

reason or another I prefer to do it.[4] Thus, although he is better off, I am not actually injured by the transaction. Hence, in a rather technical use of language that we will be using in the remainder of this essay, this is not a transfer. In other respects, however, our terms will be very closely in accord with general economic usage. "Transfer payments" in the national income accounts are not defined as broadly as the expenditures which we intend to list as transfers; but I think most economists would agree that the word "transfer" in itself would fit situations in which I pay money to support a police force that benefits me but, much more importantly, also benefits other people.

The words "distribution" and "redistribution" will be used more or less synonymously with "transfer." For example, bargaining involves both a co-operative movement to a Pareto superior point and a noncooperative quarrel about distribution. "Redistribution" will be used, in accord with common practice, as indicating a purely noncooperative change in wealth and income from the status quo to some other arrangement. An example of this is the government program which taxes the poor by increasing the price of bread in order to benefit wheat farmers.

Conflict is to be expected in all situations in which transfers or redistribution occur and in all situations in which problems of distribution arise. In general, it is rational for individuals to invest resources either to increase the transfers they will receive or to prevent redistribution away from them. Thus, normally any transactions involving distribution will lead to directly opposing resource investments and so to conflict by our definition. Occasionally this might not be so. One can imagine some person subject to a tax who is so convinced that there is no possible way of avoiding it that he does nothing except pay. Most people, however, try to avoid taxes, and the government finds it necessary to employ resources in reducing this evasion.

One particularly important use of resources in conflicts with respect to transfers are those resources used to get the government to undertake or stop some particular line of activity. Governments do not, in general, simply go

4. Economically this takes the form of including the well-being of other persons in your own preference function. For a good deal of discussion of the subject, see Harold M. Hochman and James D. Rodgers, "Pareto Optimal Redistribution," *American Economic Review*, 59 (September, 1969): 542–57; and Paul A. Meyer and J. J. Shipley, "Comment," *American Economic Review*, 60 (December, 1970), 988–90; Richard A. Musgrave, "Comment," *ibid.*, 991–93; Robert S. Goldfarb, "Comment," *ibid.*, 994–96; and Hochman and Rodgers, "Reply," *ibid.*, 997–1002.

about the world doing either good or evil. Normally, if the government decides to transfer money from *A* to *B*, it will be because Mr. *B* has exerted sufficient political influence to initiate the transfer, and Mr. *A*'s political influence proved insufficient to stop it. Thus, resources were invested in causing and attempting to prevent this particular transfer even if Mr. *A* makes not the slightest effort to evade the tax once it has been imposed.

As we have defined them, conflict, transfer, distribution, and redistribution are not unambiguously good or bad things. One can be in favor of the conflict on one side and not on the other. To fight for the right is good and to fight for the wrong is bad; but fighting itself is essentially neutral. It is the object toward which it is aimed that gives it desirability or undesirability. Similarly, transfers can be desirable or undesirable. Most readers of this book would probably regard a heavy tax upon people with high IQs as undesirable. It would, of course, be a perfectly clear-cut example of a transfer. Once again, we must judge transfers not in terms of any intrinsic presumption that redistribution is good or bad, but in terms of the individual transfer. Further, the transfers and/or the conflict will normally appear to be good to some people and bad to others. If a burglar steals some of my money, I assume that he is satisfied with the transaction. Naturally, I object to it. Similarly, a wealthy man who finds himself taxed for the benefit of the poor may resent it, although the poor probably like it.

Our last two terms—"violence" and "coercion"—are similarly neutral. Whether they are desirable or undesirable must be decided in terms of the individual cases and the words themselves carry no particular connotation of good or evil. "Violence" is the use of force upon another person or his property. It may be reciprocal. It will normally injure, perhaps only mildly, the person upon whom it is applied. Since the satisfaction gained by the person applying the violence is usually very small and is frequently negative, it is clear that if we could somehow arrange societies so that compensation payments were undertaken to avoid violence, it would usually be possible to make the payments in order to avoid a given act of violence.[5]

Violence, however, may be very desirable from the standpoint of the individual engaging in it. This is not because he likes violence in itself (few people do), but because the consequences of engaging in violence are desirable from his standpoint. For any individual, the use of violence may well be the most effective use of his resources, either to enrich himself or to maintain his pres-

5. Prize fights are examples of spectators compensating individuals for undergoing violence.

ent situation. Government agencies themselves frequently find it necessary to use either violence or the threat of violence. Violence is normally used not to physically cause a person to do something, but as part of a threat mechanism. The victim is threatened with further violence if he continues resisting, and the injury he has already received, in essence, simply improves his information about likely future developments.

By its simplest definition, "coercion" is the threat of violence in order to get some person to do or cease doing something. Thus the policeman tells you to come along and holds his club at the ready in order to coerce you to walk with him to the police station. The knowledge that there are police cars moving through the neighborhood reduces the likelihood of burglary, etc. I should like, however, to use the word "coercion" a little more broadly to include compelling people to do something or to refrain from doing something by threats of unpleasant consequences without specifying that these be violent. Threatened violence is normally part of the situation, but it may not be proximate.

For example, the Internal Revenue Service gets my taxes not by threatening me with violence in any direct sense, but by levying on my bank account in the event I do not pay them. However, if my banker refused to accept the levy (and I imagine a bank advertising such a policy would be extremely profitable), they would arrest him. Once again, this would probably mean that he would simply be called upon by a couple of FBI men who ask him to go with them to the police station. The threat of violence that is implicit would probably not develop into explicit acts. He would go to the police station and eventually spend some time in prison and might never be hit at all. If, however, he refused to go to the police station and there were not enough FBI men present to carry him, he would find himself subject to violence. Further, if he breaks discipline in the prison, he is likely to find himself subject to violence. In a sense, then, I am coerced into paying my taxes because my banker may be coerced into accepting a levy by the threat of imprisonment, and the banker would be coerced into entering the prison by the threat of physical violence. Thus, although violence is a part of the chain, it is not a very close one.[6]

There is in economics a very difficult, almost philosophical, question as to what is the difference between a transaction that involves coercion and any ordinary bargain. Let us suppose that I offer to sell you something. Being

6. I am reminded of my favorite quotation from Captain Peter Blood: "Coercion, I see no coercion: you have a perfectly free choice. You can sign that paper or be hung."

satisfied with the arrangement, you purchase it from me. This is an ordinary economic transaction. It would be so even if you were dying of thirst in the desert and what I offered to sell you was water. On the other hand, in a recent kidnapping case the victim was buried alive in a box. The kidnappers then sold information on the location of the box to the victim's parents for $500,000. Both situations are bargains. There is a simple distinction, however. In the case of the kidnapping, the kidnappers first imposed a reduction in utility and then sold its cessation. The latter bargain is an ordinary economic transaction, but this need not concern us. In the case of the water in the desert, I did not put you into your position of thirst. Thus in one case the criminals began by sharply reducing their victim's satisfaction, and in the other did nothing of the kind.

THE COOPERATIVE STATE

One of the oldest techniques of economic analysis is to assume a society in which some institution does not exist, introduce the institution, and then deduce the difference that it makes. I will follow this technique in this chapter; but it should be emphasized that there is no implication that at some time in the ancient past, man lived in a "state of nature" which resembled the institutions with which I shall start. Indeed, insofar as we can tell, man developed from an ape which was already social. In other words, our predecessors lived in small bands whose social coherence depended to a considerable extent upon inherited behavior patterns. As they became closer and closer to man, their brains increased in size and efficiency and presumably the instinctive component of their behavior declined, while the learned and rational component increased. Hobbes' "war of all against all" was *not* part of human history, although we can make use of it for analytical purposes.

It is well known that "theft is the oldest labor saving device." In spite of this, even the most efficiency-dominated of us are opposed to theft. The reasons are obvious, but let us go through them. Consider a society in which theft is completely unrestricted; i.e., no resources of any sort are devoted to preventing theft. Another way of saying this is that property does not exist as a legal category. Under these circumstances, it is almost always true that the most highly profitable "investment" of resources is to take something from your neighbor. Therefore, we anticipate that very few resources would be put into productive activity—i.e., providing something that probably will be stolen immediately on being produced, and very large resources would be put into searching out opportunities for theft.

Production of anything becomes, in essence, production of a public good. If I produce a bushel of grain, I have no more probability of benefiting from that bushel of grain than any other person in society. Although it is no doubt true that only one person consumes any particular handful of grain, the grain is *ex ante* a public good. The usual theorems concerning public goods apply, and we anticipate very little production of grain. Over time, the population probably falls to the point where it is sufficiently thinly distributed so that the resources invested in walking to my neighbor's property in order to find

Reprinted, with permission, from *The Social Dilemma: The Economics of War and Revolution* (Blacksburg, Va.: Center for Study of Public Choice, 1974), 9–16.

out whether or not he produced a bushel of grain I can steal is in marginal adjustment with producing a bushel of grain myself. At this point, the population becomes stable. Fortunately, most human societies have realized that the situation described above is a dangerous one and have taken steps to prevent it. It is true that some social philosophers have urged that people be given what amounts to free access to resources, but, so far as I know, no one has ever actually put such ideas into effect on a major scale.[1]

Let us, therefore, consider the use of resources to prevent theft. As a first stage, let us assume that individuals attempt to protect their property themselves. Note in this case that the question of whether a "taking" is theft or not is defined by the legal system in the society. For simplicity, we will assume simply that individuals try to protect what happens to be under their control at the moment, and not inquire whether they have obtained it by productive activities or by seizure. Further, we shall begin by discussing the situation where the protection against theft is entirely by passive means—locks, walls, and similar devices that make theft hard but which do not place the potential thief in danger. Use of a system of threats or reprisals will be dealt with later.

With this simple change, any good ceases to be a public good and becomes a private good. I have three possible areas in which to allocate resources: (1) production of something, let us say wheat; (2) provision of suitably secure storage for the wheat; and (3) attempting to get into someone else's storage area in order to get his wheat. Note that if I do obtain his wheat, I then use resources to guard it.

Only activity (1) increases the total amount of wheat in society. Activities (2) and (3) are very likely costly, but over society as a whole they offset each other. I budget my time so that the marginal return of production of wheat, protection of wheat, and stealing other people's wheat is identical. The size and prosperity of the population, however, is determined by the resources spent in producing wheat.

Under these circumstances, all existing individuals are better off if more effort is devoted to producing more grain. It is possible that one individual exists whose special capacities for theft are so much greater than his abilities to raise grain that he is better off under the free theft system, but on the whole

1. The early period of the Soviet government in Russia was in part an effort to do just this. After the experiment failed, it was renamed "War Communism" and blamed on the war. Even during this period, however, many direct allocations of resources were made by the government. The Red army, for example, was not required to let anyone who wished take its guns.

this is unlikely. In this connection, it should be noted that passive protection against theft in most cases is technologically a more onerous and difficult task than theft itself. Protection against theft must cover all possible approaches to the protected object; whereas the person engaging in the theft need enter on only one. For example, one method of protection from theft is use of a guard. Unless the guard is on duty 24 hours a day, he might as well not be there. The thief, on the other hand, needs only a few moments to carry out his enterprise.

The problem is a many-sided prisoner's dilemma. Everyone is better off if no one engages in theft; hence, no one must invest resources into guarding against theft. On the other hand, if other people do not devote resources to guarding against theft, then the returns to me from thievery are extremely high. As in most prisoner's dilemma cases, the establishment of a control apparatus that forces people to follow the cooperative course of action is desirable. The individuals presumably are willing to pay some finite fee for this service.

Before considering possible organizations to prevent further theft, however, let us consider two other special problems connected with theft in the situation where individuals use only passive means to protect their property. The first of these is the possibility of fraud. Let us suppose that I build a storehouse and a stranger informs me that he has invented a very superior lock that he is willing to install on the door of my storehouse. After some chaffering about his fee, I agree to let him install the lock, and I go about my business while he is doing so. Instead of installing the lock, he removes the grain from the storehouse and proceeds to find another sucker.

In this particular case, I could protect myself from having this happen to me very often by only dealing with people whom I know. The con man has to move from one place to another frequently. Nevertheless, once again it is a nonoptimal situation. I must devote some resources to checking the accuracy of information given to me by people who have various proposals. On the other hand, they are using resources to produce deceptive proposals. Further, honest persons who are genuinely trying to sell me a superior lock must invest resources in convincing me that they are indeed honest. Once again, we have a many-party prisoner's dilemma.

The other special case concerns the use of violence. We can assume a society in which individuals protect their grain in part by being willing to fight for it, and in which one of the ways of obtaining grain is to (again) fight for it with the current possessor. This was, in fact, an important way of obtaining and protecting property in the Middle Ages. Let us then imagine that Mr. *A* has some grain and Mr. *B* would like to have it, and that for various reasons the most efficient method of obtaining the grain from Mr. *A* is the use of violence. This might be because it is locked in a secure storeroom to which Mr. *A* has the key, or because Mr. *A* is standing in front of the grain, or for any one of a large number of other reasons.

An outside observer simply sees the two men fighting, and then the winner in possession of the grain. Looked at from the standpoint of the contestants in the fight, however, the matter is a bit more complicated. If I have been fighting with someone else for some time and have already suffered injury, the injuries are essentially sunk-cost. There is no reason why they should affect my future activity. At all times I should weigh the present discounted value of the injuries I anticipate from continuing the fight, and the likelihood that my opponent will permit me to take the grain. In a sense the part of the fight that is already over simply improves my state of information with respect to the injuries I am likely to receive in the future. Mathematically, I take the value of the grain discounted by the probability that I will be in possession of it at the end of the fight, and then subtract from this value the likely injuries I will receive during the remainder of the combat. If the result is positive, I should keep on fighting; if negative, I should give up.

Note, however, that I may be able to provide suitable information so that my opponent is not interested in the fight to begin with. If it is obvious from the very beginning that he will lose, it is unlikely that there will be any violence. Thus, the better prepared I am to fight, the less likely it is that anyone will suggest that I do so. It is, of course, possible to avoid fighting by simply announcing in advance that you will not fight to defend your food supply. Historically, a certain number of groups have done this. They can be divided roughly into three groups. The first of these are people who live in remote underdeveloped areas and have very little that anyone wishes to take. Some such primitive tribes have succeeded in surviving. The second category are people who, in fact, have been exterminated. Normally, of course, people who have announced that they will not use violence do in fact, use violence when they are subject to despoliation. Einstein's quick conversion from pacifism to advocacy of preventive war is an example.

The third class of people who refuse to engage in violence are those who live in a society which will use violence to protect them. It is not at all dangerous to be a believer in nonviolence in the United States. The police and the courts stand ready to use violence against anyone who attempts to take your property. The objector to violence is free to express disapproval of this use of violence if he wishes. He may even vote against appropriations for the police force if he wishes. His disavowal of the use of violence is safe because the society in which he lives will protect him even if he does not give overt approval.[2]

To repeat, however, there is no reason why people who wish to do so cannot avoid all fighting by accepting despoliation. On the other hand, their survival is doubtful. Those people who wish to retain control of things that are now in their hands, however, are well-advised to prepare for the use of violence.[3] But even if one is prepared to defend his property through use of violence, the outcome may not be totally predictable. In these circumstances, both parties could be made better off by an agreement in advance in which a transfer is made from the person now in possession to his proposed assailant of an amount that properly discounts the probabilities. Thus, if it is thought there is a one-in-five chance that the assailant can seize the property, immediately transferring to him 20 percent of the property without any fighting would benefit both parties.

Such precombat settlements, however, offer a strong encouragement for people to take up the activity of threatening violence. If it is known that I normally pay off, then I may expect a very large number of people to go into the business of coercing me. Once again, the margins would all be matched: people would invest money in threatening me to the point where the return was equal to the return of other activities. Of course, I could invest money in raising the apparent cost of actually being attacked until this reduced the amount of payment I have to make, but the loss could still be very large.[4]

In many ways, the best solution to the above problems would appear to be some mixture of fighting and paying off. Thus, if I regularly defend my grain store by fighting long enough so that anyone who attacks me would

2. In an appendix to my book *The Logic of the Law* (New York: Basic Books, 1971), I recommend that individuals who wished to disavow the use of violence for their protection be permitted to refrain from paying their share of the taxes for the protective services and receive no protection. I would predict that in practice few people would take advantage of this privilege, and those who did would rapidly change their minds.

3. Whether they are their *property* or not, of course, depends on the legal system.

4. George Stigler, in discussing a proposal that criminals be bribed not to commit crimes, pointed out that the total cost would probably be very much less than the cost of maintaining a police force. He also pointed out (and this is an ingenious way of putting the point above) that the basic problem is identification. If we paid criminals not to commit crimes, then we must have some way of telling who the genuine criminals are. It would be to the advantage of almost anyone to claim to be a criminal and to collect the funds for not committing crimes, even if he had no intention of committing any crime.

suffer at least some injury and only then compromising with him, the cost to him is always higher than the cost if I pay before the fight begins. The exact mix of combat and payment would be a matter of calculation. As an example, it seems likely that the Finnish army's defense of Finland in the fall of 1939, followed by an agreement, led to a much better outcome for Finland than would have been obtained had Finland not demonstrated a willingness and ability to inflict quite significant costs on her monster opponent.

Note, however, certain characteristics of violence and threats of violence. The first is that violence is in itself seldom a method of getting anything done or of protecting anything. Unless the violence leads to the death or incapacitation of the person upon whom it is worked, it is sunk cost to him and does not affect his future behavior. What he is actually concerned with is the threat of future violence, and the violence that has already been imposed upon him is simply information on its likelihood and magnitude. The reason a criminal accompanies a police officer to prison is not that the officer has hit him with a club, but that he fears that he *will* be hit. But this threat nature of the use of violence means that the use of violence to deter some particular activity need not be coincident in time or place with the activity. For example, I could announce that I propose to inflict a severe beating on anyone who removed the grain.

If the threat was believed and if the pain inflicted by the beating was likely to be greater than the benefit of eating the grain, no one would steal the grain. Further, violence is simply one way of inflicting unpleasantness. There are others. Locking them up is an example, and in our modern world this is our major reliance. It should be obvious, however, that although we can (within limits) inflict a given amount of unpleasantness upon a person as easily by locking him up as by beating him or inflicting some other kind of physical injury, the act of locking him up is hard to manage unless there is at least some threat of the use of violence at that point. If we wish to physically restrain an individual and remove him to a prison without in any way injuring him,[5] we will probably need three or four policemen for each person so restrained. Further, it is almost certain that the policemen themselves would be somewhat injured in the process if the prisoner resisted vigorously. Thus, it will be necessary to pay them a large enough salary to compensate for the probability of physical injury. Most taxpayers are not willing to hire the very large police force necessary to physically carry the prisoners if the prisoners simply

5. Whether this removal is preliminary to trial or after trial makes no difference at the moment.

"go limp." This is simply an expression of popular references and not any higher ideal.

The common method of removing a person to prison under present circumstances is to threaten him with violence in the sense that he will be hit by a club or perhaps have his arm severely twisted if he does not cooperate with the police officer. If everything goes well, no actual violence is used. The individual is aware of the fact that the policeman uses violence if necessary, and that once he gets to the prison he receives, or at least has a finite chance of receiving, an additional sentence for resisting arrest if he does not come along peacefully. Thus, a police force that is well known to be willing to use violence may seldom actually use it.

It should be realized, however, that this is not because there is no violence inherent in the system, but simply because the threat of the use of violence is so highly credible. A suitably administered system of punitive imprisonment for those persons who make it hard for the police to take them to jail would probably have much the same effect; although, as I have mentioned, it would be more expensive because it would require more policemen. A threat to physically remove you to jail in a gentle manner and then to give you an additional year if you have kicked three policemen in the shins en route is not credible, unless there are enough policemen present to carry out the action. The threat to break your skull with a club if you do not come quietly is quite credible if there is one large policeman with a heavy club present. The latter method is cheaper.

Absence of much use of police violence for making arrests has deceived a great many casual observers. Since they do not normally see the police hitting people they have arrested, they can come to the conclusion that violence is not necessary. The implicit threat is not visible. Hence, standards may develop among the general community that make it likely that the police would be very heavily criticized and, in fact, subject to disciplinary action when they do use violence for arresting people who have political influence.

But to return to more formal analysis, the protection of my property by threatening to beat up people if they take it can be simply a personal threat on my part. As such, the question of whether this is better than building a very strong storehouse is essentially a technological matter. There is, however, a third technological possibility. It is possible for a central agency to undertake the apprehension and infliction of some sort of penalty upon people who take grain. Here again, whether this is more efficient is a technological matter, but experience seems to indicate that this is indeed an efficient process.

	D.S.	S.
D.S.	10 10	18 2
S.	2 18	4 4

NO POLICE

	D.S.	S.
D.S.	8 8	4 7
S.	7 4	4 4

POLICE

FIGURE 1
Three-dimensional matrix

All societies that have risen above the level of barbarism deal with potential theft, fraud, and robbery by some combination of the three methods listed above. Some resources are put into passive protection such as locks and barred windows; some resources are put into personal retaliation. And, last but not least, resources are put into some kind of centralized apparatus for inflicting unpleasantness upon people who are believed to have committed this type of "crime."

In Figure 1 I have shown the payoffs to be expected from stealing, designated as *S*, and not stealing, designated as *D.S.* under two sets of institutions. In one the police exist, and in one they do not. It is clear under the nonpolice situation that *A* and *B* face a prisoner's dilemma and will end up in the lower right-hand corner where the payoff is very low, with each attempting to steal the other's property. The upper left-hand corner is, of course, a very much superior location, but the standard prisoner's dilemma arguments indicate that it is unobtainable, particularly in a society of many people.

The decision to establish a police force moves society to the second matrix. In this matrix it is assumed that the police force costs resources; hence, the gain made from production is subject to a tax, and the payoff for not stealing is only eight instead of ten. On the other hand, the police force makes the properly discounted payoff from stealing itself generally low. Thus individuals are not motivated to steal, and the don't-steal column dominates the steal column for both parties. There is, of course, a net social loss to society as opposed to being in the upper left-hand square of the no-police matrix. This is the social cost of maintaining the apparatus of enforcement.

In essence, Figure 1 shows a three-dimensional two-party game matrix. It differs from the ordinary matrix of this sort only in that moving from the no-police to police matrix involves joint action, rather than individual action. This joint action is undertaken in order to eliminate the prisoner's dilemma problem and, hence, moves the net outcome of society from the lower right-hand corner of the no-police matrix to the upper left-hand corner of the police matrix. Clearly this is a social gain.

So far as I know, no society has ever relied exclusively on those protective methods that do not involve threats of violence. There is no intrinsic reason why this could not be done, but the expense would be very great and most societies prefer a certain amount of violence (particularly since a credible threat of violence makes the actual use of violence unnecessary) to the really gigantic cost of going without it.

THE EXPLOITATIVE STATE

It would be pleasant to be able to say that modern police forces, and indeed governments in general, are the result of a general acceptance of this line of reasoning. Unfortunately, there is another and equally plausible explanation. Let us suppose there are some people in the community who are exceptionally adroit in the use of violence. In our present community there are the professional criminals and, in particular, that subset called "organized crime." Suppose similarly talented people in our "lawless" society. These people find that simply going about the community and seizing property is nonoptimal. Presumably they can, if they are very talented, intimidate the community so that no one makes any effort to prevent them from seizing property. They have what is technically termed a "monopoly of force." On the other hand, with random seizure of property it is irrational on the part of the citizens of the community to produce very much to be seized. In consequence, the pickings are slim.

If we examine the activities of racketeers, we find that to some extent they deal with exactly the same problem. One of their "rackets" is "protection" in which they, in essence, agree not to injure people in return for payment. In other words, they apply negative incentives—just like the Internal Revenue Service. This could well lower the satisfaction of the average citizen from that which exists in the society in which anyone can steal. It may be thought that it would be impossible for this band of criminals to actually reduce the consumption of the citizens of the country because, in such primitive conditions, presumably everyone is living on the Malthusian edge, and the citizens simply die if their consumption is reduced.

In Figure 2 on the vertical axis we show leisure, and on the horizontal axis the production of some food grain. The technical production function is shown by line P_{RW}. If there is no theft or other transfer in society, the individual shown produces at point 0, consuming 0_L leisure and 0_F in food. Assume, however, that we are in a primitive society in which theft is not banned. Under these circumstances, the individual faces another production P_{FK} that represents that part of the grain he can retain, granted he produces a given amount of grain. Under these circumstances, he is forced to a lower

Reprinted, with permission, from *The Social Dilemma: The Economics of War and Revolution* (Blacksburg, Va.: Center for Study of Public Choice, 1974), 17–25.

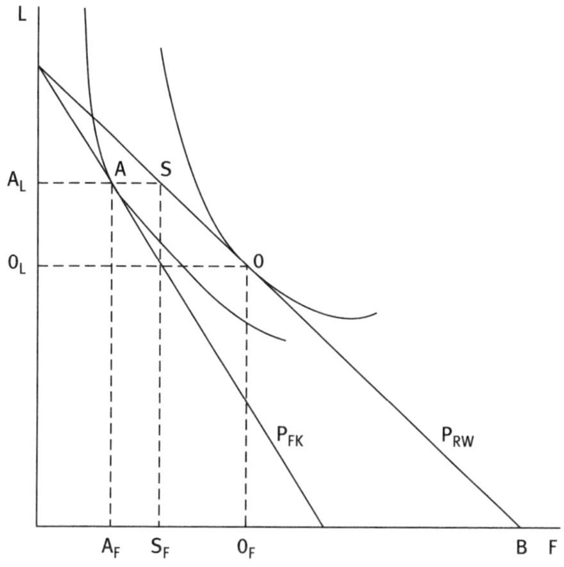

FIGURE 2
Welfare costs of theft

indifference curve. This indifference curve is tangent to the line P_{FK} at point A, and the individual will consume A_L leisure and A_F in food. Note, however, that the individual is actually producing more food than he consumes. The amount A_FS_F is stolen under our institutional structure. In order to simplify the diagram, assume that our particular individual does not engage in theft himself, presumably because he finds that he can receive a higher return on his labor in producing grain than in attempting to steal it. There will, of course, be other people in society with the converse set of production possibilities, but they will be ignored in the remainder of this example. In the real world, we anticipate that most people under these circumstances engage in *both* production and theft, but diagramming this situation would require three dimensions and hence we simplify here.

The cooperative government discussed in the last chapter aims at getting as close to point 0 as possible. Granted the need to put resources into police activities, the individual actually faces a tax that lowers P_{RW} and therefore cannot quite obtain 0; but clearly he gets to a higher level of indifference than his present one without any government. Assume, however, an exploitative state. Even if we assume that the amount of food A_F the individual is consuming is the bare necessity to keep him alive, there is still a large profit available. By threats of death, the state forces the individual into the corner solution at point B. At this point, he consumes no leisure, has A_F in food consumption, and pays a tax of the food represented by that segment of the horizontal axis between A_F and B. The individual is at a lower level of indifference than in the case in which there was no government. Clearly he is in a vastly lower state of satisfaction than in the situation where there was what we have called cooperative government.

Historically, it seems unlikely that most governments have exploited their citizens in this way. In fact, I think that if we assume that a despotism is establishing order in an area where at least relative disorder previously existed, it has a tendency to split the gains with its subjects. This benefits both parties—the despot and his subjects. It probably benefits the despot more. A Malthusian situation existed in most of the world until quite recently, however. This means a rise in population until per capita income falls to its previous level.

Such an organization is able to make a very large income from an economy. They can compute the tax rates to maximize returns. This is not, in general, the objective of modern public finance analysis of taxes, but at one time there was a discipline—"camaralistics"—which devoted itself solely to the maximization of the revenue of the state. Clearly one can plan a tax system in order to maximize the return, over time, of the apparatus of force which extracts the taxes. Equally clearly it will probably be wise for the apparatus of force to invest a certain amount of its tax revenue into public facilities that will increase the total tax base, and to make certain that other people are not engaged in use of force, threats of force, fraud, or theft to take property from people within the area in which this organization operates.

We thus have two "models" of government. One is a cooperative venture by individuals to reduce the extent to which they are compelled to play a negative-sum game.[1] Facing a prisoner's dilemma, they turn to coercion of each other to behave in a "cooperative" manner. The other model is that of an exploitative group that simply has the power and is attempting to maximize the returns it can obtain by the use of this power. Some elements of each of these models are present in almost any real government. Some governments, many South American and African dictatorships, for example, are

1. Needless to say, there is no argument here that government should not also do other things. Indeed the provision of any public good can be argued for on exactly the same grounds.

fairly close to the exploitative model. Nevertheless, for reasons to be canvassed below, they may, in fact, provide a genuine benefit to their subjects.

At the other extreme, a well-functioning democracy comes fairly close to the model of a cooperative arrangement. It deviates mainly in two respects; first, the bureaucracy is normally a powerful pressure group and therefore uses the government to transfer funds from the rest of the community to itself. The importance of this factor, of course, varies from government to government. Second, certain other pressure groups make use of the government to transfer funds to themselves. One does not have to be opposed to such transfers to realize that they cannot, in any true sense, be referred to as cooperative activity by all members of the community. They are a coerced transfer from some members of the community to others. To repeat, it is quite possible to be in favor of this type of coercion, but we should at least recognize that it is not cooperation.

Let us, however, return briefly to the exploitative model and inquire as to why it is usually stable. The first reason, of course, is that such states can be expected to devote considerable resources to preventing *private* crime. Theft by outsiders reduces the tax returns to the state. The state, in order to continue to exist, must keep on hand a very considerable apparatus for the application of coercion and violence, and it may as well use it on competing criminals. Second, the well-functioning coercive state, like the Russian state today, has an elaborate apparatus to make it very dangerous for members of its coercive apparatus to conspire among themselves. Further, it pays them very well and makes it very clear that they are superior in status. At the same time, it sees to it that they are equipped in such a way that a few of them can readily deal with large-scale popular uprisings. In spite of this apparatus, however, its power is not infinite, as the Russian state has discovered in recent years. It may find itself making concessions to the people who superficially appear to be completely under its control. The general level of courage among the population, the probability that the government enforcement apparatus will mutiny, and the level of compensation paid to the enforcement apparatus are all variables in determining how much pressure can be put upon the common people. The revenue that can be derived by such a government appears from historic experience to be very large.

One of the problems, and at the same time one of the assets, of an exploitative state is a controlled ideology. It sometimes happens that the band of people in control of such a state will find that their views as to this world or the next are quite different from that of the average subject. If this is so, this special ideological mission of the governing group may make it harder for them to be overthrown in the sense that they have greater inherent cohesion and less tendency to schism. On the other hand, it may make it more likely that they will be overthrown because they may attempt to impose their point of view on the rest of the population, and this may lead to opposition over and above the opposition that comes from "exploitation." For example, Mao Tse-tung's government in China generated a major crisis for itself in the "great leap forward." The genesis of the "great leap forward" lies in certain ideological views held by Mao Tse-tung on the best method of producing grain. It turned out these ideas were wrong, and very general starvation occurred in China.[2]

Most of us would much prefer "cooperative" government to the exploitative model. Simple preference does not rule the world, however. If there is a group of people in society who would like to organize a Mafia-type government (and it is likely that all societies contain people of this sort) and the remainder of the population is not willing to use violence to stop them, then they will succeed. Nonviolent resistance on occasion has been successful against people of sensitive conscience. Unfortunately, not everyone is of this sort, and, hence, violence or threats of violence are necessary to stop some people. In well-functioning democracies a very strong potential for violent opposition to any group attempting to seize control exists, but is not obvious in day-to-day politics. Since the subject of revolution and coup d'état will be discussed later, we can defer further consideration of this point.

The problem of determining optimality under these circumstances is extremely difficult. Assume a simple community that is producing two goods, X and Y, as shown in the left, or production, half of Figure 3. At the beginning it is producing them according to the production frontier shown by line 1. The reason for this, of course, is that the individuals spend a good deal of their time trying to steal their neighbor's property and protecting their own goods against theft; hence, the total net product of X and Y is low. As outside observers, we deduce that the introduction of a centralized police force and the consequent reduction in resources devoted to theft and protection from theft will permit the society to produce X and Y according to production

2. It is hard to tell what happened during this period, but the best calculations seem to indicate a population deficit of 20 million people. For the most part, of course, these deaths occurred among the very old and the very young. There probably were also a very large number of spontaneous abortions caused by inadequate food for pregnant women.

frontier 2. Unless we value theft and protection against theft independently, we will presumably recommend that they establish a police force.

When we turn to the right half of Figure 3, the distribution diagram, the problem loses its simplicity, however. Here we assume that the community consists of two people, *A* and *B*, and that the production shown by line 1 on the production half of the figure can be distributed between them at any point shown by line 1 of the distribution half. Point 0 on the production half corresponds to point 0 on the distribution side. *B* is somewhat better off than *A*.

Shall we, then, communicate to them our knowledge that the establishment of a centralized police force will move them to a higher production frontier? At first glance, this question may seem foolish, but let us think about it a little bit. The particular technological improvement we are suggesting is the establishment of a "monopoly of force" which can compel people who do not carry out its orders to undergo some type of punishment. The distinction between passively protecting your own goods and having a police force protect them is very largely that the police force is able to impose retribution on the persons who either steal or attempt to steal your property after they have done it. Such an organization may also be in a position to

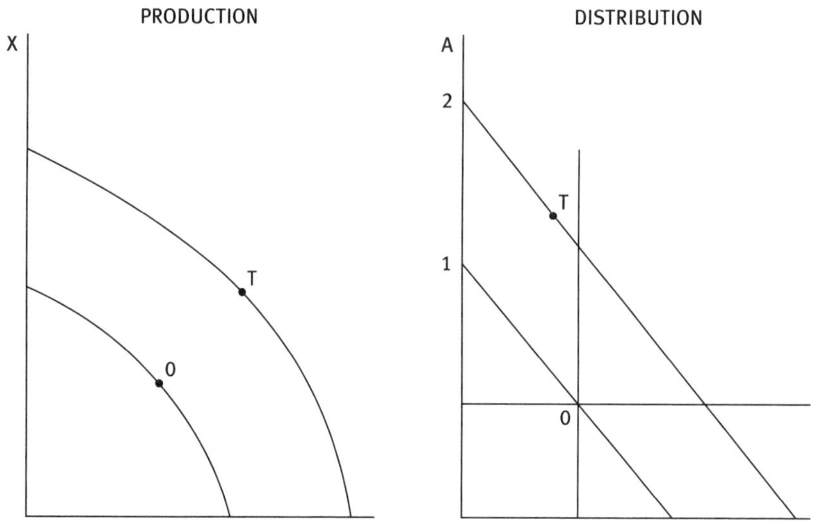

FIGURE 3
Non-Paresian production increase

effect a redistribution of income toward itself by the same means. Let us suppose that if we communicate the knowledge of this possible technology to this society, *A* will establish a monopoly of force under his own control and use it to move society from point 0 to point *T*.

Clearly, from the traditional economic point of view, this is not a Pareto-desirable move, because at least one party is made worse off. He will not be compensated, not because he could not be compensated, but because *A* does not want to compensate him and has the power to refrain from doing so. On the other hand, there clearly has been an increase in the physical product of society. The change in distribution shown on the distribution half of the diagram corresponds with the change of desired goods production from 0 to *T* on the production side. It is quite possible that all goods will be produced in larger quantities after this technological change than before. The improvement might be very large, perhaps even a doubling or tripling of GNP.

In most societies people introducing new technology are permitted to inflict injury on those who have invested resources in old technologies made obsolete by the new. The normal rationalization for this policy is, of course, that there are very many new technologies introduced at any given time, and over any individual's lifetime his probable gain from the introduction of new technology is greater than his probable loss from the obsolescence of his resources caused by these new technologies. That this is persuasive is clear; but it is also clear that it is not conclusive. For example, shall I be permitted to tear down your house without compensating you, because I have thought of a better use for the land? I presume most people would agree that the answer to this should be "no."[3] Similarly, in our present case I think most people would say either that the change would not be desirable or, at least, that they find it a difficult problem. Clearly, it does injure one person, although the total national product is increased so that it would be possible to compensate *B*, even if we know he will not be compensated.

So far, I have not discussed the possibility that the establishment of the police force be subject to veto. Normally, in talking about Pareto optimality we assume that any individual can prevent a change from occurring until he has been appropriately compensated. I have not included this in our present discussion because it is obvious that no one can prevent the establishment of a force strong enough to compel him, unless he himself has a strong force at his command. In any event, often a strong force can be created without

3. These matters are discussed much more completely in Gordon Tullock, *Private Wants, Public Means* (New York: Basic Books, 1970).

attracting notice until it is too large to be compelled to disband. One is reminded of Edward Teller's remark that the nuclear club has no blackball mechanism. However, let us assume a slightly different situation; i.e., let us assume that we, as outsiders, are in a position to prevent the members of this society from establishing a police force until they have unanimous agreement—until all have been compensated, in other words.

In order to discuss this problem, let us turn to Figure 4, where once again society starts at point 0. The possible distributions of the total product with a police force are shown by line 2. We are in a position where we can compel the individuals to bargain and reach agreement, if they are to adopt a police force. The question is whether we should do so. Surely this bargaining will take a certain amount of time and absorb resources. The present discounted value of different points along the productivity frontier, therefore, is not the frontier itself but the present discounted value of income streams in the future. This should both discount the probability that maximum physical productivity will be reached at different times, depending on the institutional structure we permit them to use, and the direct resource consumption in the bargaining process.

Let us assume that we simply inform them of the possibility of a monopoly of force and observe what happens. One anticipates that either *A* or *B* will set up such a force and move up to the frontier shown by line 2. He may,

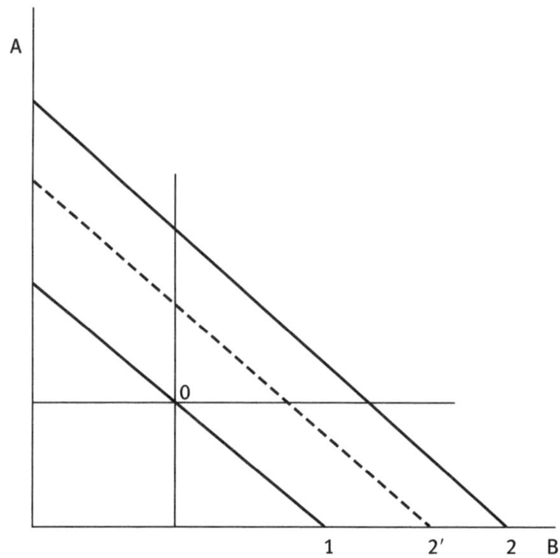

FIGURE 4
The costs of agreement

however, adopt a location outside the Paretian triangle. If, on the other hand, we require that they reach unanimous agreement, then it is likely that the bargaining process will take quite some time; hence, the present discounted value of the improvement follows the dotted line 2′. Setting up a monopoly of force without requiring everybody's agreement is likely to be much faster than setting one up *with* everyone's agreement; hence, the total present discounted value of future income streams (measured in physical goods) will be higher.

It is by no means obvious that we will choose to compel parties to reach unanimous agreement in this case. Here we have a conflict between a fairly straightforward method of computing total physical output of the society and the welfare requirement that no individual person be injured. We have combined a transfer with an improvement in efficiency and therefore have entered an area with which the Paretian apparatus does not purport to deal. Unfortunately any decision as to whether an exploitative state is better than no state or better than a cooperative state *after* a delay depends on our ability to solve this problem. It is not at all clear that present-day social science provides us with any tools that will even approach it.

Historical evidence seems to indicate that the average person prefers the despotism to a state of no government. The evidence, however, is quite obscure. It is certainly true that the earliest governments of which we have any positive knowledge were despotisms of one sort or another, and that despotisms have remained the dominant form of government of the human race ever since. This may not indicate, however, that individuals in "a state of nature" preferred an immediate despotism to a cooperative state after considerable negotiation. It may simply indicate that it is relatively easy for an entrepreneur to establish a despotism and then keep it in power, regardless of the desires of the average person. Decisions as to types of government are clearly public goods, and a citizen who is unhappy about the present type of government may not wish to run the gigantic private cost of facing up to the forces of repression maintained by that government in order to confer a public good upon the population as a whole. Thus it may be that the apparent dominance of despotism in history does not represent a line of reasoning of the sort which we have been discussing in the last few pages, but simply the technical efficiency of forces of repression together with the fact that formal government is a public good; hence, one would not anticipate that most citizens would put very much energy into attempting to improve it. All of these matters will be discussed in greater detail in the next few chapters devoted to revolution and coups d'état.

PART 2

THE GOALS AND ORGANIZATIONAL FORMS OF AUTOCRACIES

INTRODUCTION TO GORDON TULLOCK'S *AUTOCRACY*

Most governments in the world today are dictatorships of one sort or another.[1] In spite of this fact there has been almost no scientific analysis of this form of government since Machiavelli. Scholars such as Karl Loewenstein and Carl Friedrich have written learned and perceptive[2] studies, but they are essentially contributions to political philosophy, not to Public Choice. This book is intended to take the first steps towards filling the gap.

I have chosen to call it "autocracy" instead of "dictatorship" because I also want to discuss kingdoms and empires. The difference between a dictatorship and a kingdom is, as far as I can see, simply that the kingdoms tend to be hereditary. I should like to emphasize the word "tend" because disputed successions are by no means uncommon. We English speakers, in essence, descend from what was probably the most unstable monarchy in Europe, with undisputed succession for three generations almost unknown.[3] Most other monarchies in Europe were somewhat stabler, but still, there was the Fronde in France[4] and the wars of Austrian and Spanish succession.[5]

Reprinted, with kind permission of Kluwer Academic Publishers, from *Autocracy* (Dordrecht and Boston: Kluwer Academic Publishers, 1987), 1–15. Copyright 1987 Martinus Nijhoff Publishers, Dordrecht.

1. Dahl estimates about 80% of present-day governments. Robert A. Dahl, *Polyarchy Participation and Opposition* (New Haven: Yale University Press, 1971), 202; see also his table 5.3, p. 67.

2. Not always perceptive. In 1946 Loewenstein expected the early overthrow of Franco (Karl Loewenstein, *Political Reconstruction* [New York: Macmillan, 1946], 152). Presumably, my book will also show clouds in my crystal ball if it is read forty years from now.

3. Between 1400 and 1900 there was only one case of undisputed succession involving three or more monarchs in England—the Hanoverian line, from George I to Victoria. There were major risings against the Hanoverians in 1715 and 1745, and George III lost both one-third of his kingdom and the real power of the dynasty. See A. W. Ward, G. W. Prothero, and Stanley Leathes, eds., *The Cambridge Modern History*, vol. 13, *Genealogical Tables and Lists* (New York: Macmillan, 1911), tables 1–4.

4. "Fronde" is a word used to refer, collectively, to two open revolts in France in the seventeenth century. The first revolt, which was led by the Parlement of Paris and joined by many

In the actual government, however, there is not all that much difference between a hereditary ruler and a dictator.[6] There are differences, and they will be discussed below, but they clearly belong in the same family of governments. The word "autocracy" encompasses both.

This form of government, as I said, is the dominant one in the world today. Further, more of the world is now ruled by such autocratic governments than, let us say, twenty-five or thirty years ago. It is dangerous to base predictions on historic trends, but since 1914, on the whole, democracy has become a less significant form of government, and dictatorships more important.[7] The situation is highly unstable, however. At the time I prepared the final draft of this book there were only six dictatorships in Latin America, possibly an historic low. In the few months between then and the final

of the old nobility, occurred in June 1648. It was inspired by what was perceived to be the financial excesses of the Italian-born finance minister Jules Magarin. This revolt quickly collapsed. The second revolt occurred in 1650 and was again led by the old nobility and their private armies. Plagued with infighting and shifting allegiances, this revolt ceased in 1653. See Jerome Blum, *The Emergence of the European World* (Boston: Little, Brown, 1966), 224–25, and Jerome Blum, Rondo Cameron, and Thomas G. Barnes, *The European World: A History*, 2d ed. (Boston: Little, Brown, 1970), 235–37, 269.

5. The War of the Austrian Succession (1740–48) occurred after Maria Theresa's claim to the Hapsburg throne was disputed by Philip V of Spain, who considered himself a more suitable heir. Eventually Spain, France, Saxony, Bavaria, Prussia, and Great Britain were involved (with Austria, of course). See R. Ernest Dupuy and Trevor N. Dupuy, *The Encyclopedia of Military History, from 3500 B.C. to the Present*, rev. ed. (New York: Harper and Row, 1977), 630–37. The War of the Spanish Succession (1701–14) resulted from England's and Holland's objecting to the inheritance of the Spanish throne by a grandson of Louis XIV of France (ibid., 617–27).

6. The word "king" has two meanings in modern parlance. Firstly, a pleasant, powerless man like the present King of Sweden. Secondly, somebody like William the Conqueror (r. 1066–87; see Norman F. Cantor, *The English: A History of Politics and Society to 1760* [New York: Simon and Schuster, 1967], 62), or Louis XIV (r. 1661–1715; see Pierre Goubert, *Louis XIV and Twenty Million Frenchmen* [New York: Vintage, 1972], who actually rules as well as reigns. Sweden is as democratic a state as the United States. The fact that the Swedes rather enjoy spending some of their resources maintaining certain ceremonies in downtown Stockholm is of no more importance in determining the form of their government than are the elaborate ceremonies that the Marine Corps performs at the Iwo Jima monument every Tuesday during the summer in determining the American form of government.

7. Predictions are particularly hard here. In 1959 Tad Sculc wrote a book entitled *Twilight of the Tyrants* (New York: Holt, Rinehart and Winston) which dealt with South America. As we now know, *Tyranny Resurgent* would have been a better title for that date.

proofing, the number went up to seven. I hesitate to guess how many there will be when you read it.[8]

But having said that autocracy is the commonest form of government, I should like to briefly discuss two other forms of government, mainly because that is the easiest way of limiting what I mean by autocracy. Governments that depend on voting of some sort or that are feudal are not autocracies. I am not at all sure there may not be forms of government other than these three, but these make up the overwhelming majority of all historic governments. Indeed, autocracy by itself is the dominant form of government, and most governments that are not autocratic are either feudal or electoral. As we shall see, however, there are intermediate stages between these three forms of government.

It is common for most people to think that their own experience is universal, and it is common of most countries and areas to think that their history is universal history. It happens that the Western European area was essentially feudal for at least five hundred years. From this a great many people, including Marx, have come to the conclusion that feudalism is a necessary stage in development.[9] As a matter of fact, feudalism is quite rare in the world; the only other clear-cut case that I know of is Japan. Perhaps the Rajputs were a third, and Mycenaean Greece a fourth.[10]

It is particularly astonishing that the myth that feudalism is universal could arise, since one of the great periods of feudal history was the Crusades, in which the feudal lords attacked centralized nonfeudal Mohammedan kingdoms[11] either in alliance with, or sometimes opposed to, the centralized Byzantine empire.[12] In fact, centralized Mohammedan, Byzantine, Persian,

8. Albert O. Hirschman began a survey of the problem: "The point of departure of any serious thought about the chances of democracy in Latin America must surely be pessimism." "On Democracy in Latin America," *New York Review of Books*, April 10, 1986, p. 41.

9. See J. K. Ingram's discussion, "Karl Marx," in *Palgrave's Dictionary of Political Economy*, vol. 2, ed. Henry Higgs (London: Macmillan, 1925), 705.

10. On the form of feudalism in ancient Greece which developed between 1200 and 800 B.C., see W. G. Forrest, *The Emergence of Greek Democracy, 800–400 B.C.* (New York: World University Library, 1979), 45–46.

11. Or Turkish tribes, in some cases. The first Crusade (1096–99) attacked the Seljuk. See Dupuy and Dupuy, *Encyclopedia of Military History*, 311.

12. In fact, one Crusade (the fourth, 1195–1200) had as its object the conquest of Constantinople and is generally considered to have constituted, for all practical purposes, the death knell of the Byzantine empire. See Ibid., 380–82.

Chinese, and Indian kingdoms paralleled the feudal epoch. Much more of the human race lived under these systems than lived in feudal Europe or feudal Japan. The Rajput case, which I mentioned as possible feudalism, is somewhat later than the European feudal period.[13] Most of India, however, was not part of this Rajput feudal confederacy, but was a set of independent despotic states which were, for a short period of time, united under the rule of the Great Mogul, also not feudal.[14]

The feudal system was a complex blend of different powers. In theory the king was surrounded by a group of nobles who each held territory from him, who were loyal to him, and who subinfeudated this territory to lower nobles. In practice, anyone who reads the history will realize that the degree of loyalty to the king was distinctly limited. Further, the system in Europe was complicated by the existence of another very great power, the Church, and the further existence of a large number of free cities.[15]

Lord Acton, no mean judge, thought that the thirteenth century was the highest point in human freedom.[16] The immediate thought one has when hearing this is that he was crazy, but actually he had a not bad argument. He pointed out that the existence of quite a number of powers meant that any individual had a great deal of bargaining power in dealing with someone who nominally was his superior. A peasant, legally, was bound to the land. As a matter of fact, if he became annoyed with his lord, he could decamp quietly at night feeling fairly confident that about twenty miles down the road there would be another lord who would welcome him because he needed additional peasants to operate his land.[17] There were, of course, also the Church and the free cities, both of which would offer him protection.

13. Japanese feudalism lasted much longer than European feudalism and, in fact, started later also.

14. The Rajput princes retained their feudal system under the Moguls. In fact they provided most of the Mogul cavalry.

15. See Douglass C. North, *Structure and Change in Economic History* (New York: Norton, 1981), 126–29.

16. See Gertrude Himmelfarb, *Lord Acton* (Chicago: University of Chicago Press, 1968), 82–84.

17. Douglass C. North and Robert Paul Thomas state that "would-be founders of new manors had to seek out peasants aggressively, even to the point of limiting their own powers by offering grants and privileges to entice potential emigrants . . . Peasants who succumbed to

This is, of course, not the standard historical picture of this era, but new economic historians have pretty much demonstrated that the average peasant could, if he wanted, change lords.[18] An overlord, meeting with Parliament in London and passing vigorous laws to prohibit peasants from leaving their land and to prevent lords from accepting strange peasants, might at the same time be writing to his steward, encouraging him to accept any peasant who came along.

In Japan, the peasants were not as free as they were in Europe, but it was nevertheless true that the small scale of the land held by any given feudal lord meant that movement was possible. Further, the control of the feudal lord was by their superiors, and the Ashikaga who preceded the Tokagawa were able to exercise little or no control. The Tokagawa, in fact, were an intermediate station between autocracy and feudalism, but a rather different intermediate station than that found in Europe as the feudal system gradually changed, during the Renaissance, into despotism.[19]

This definition of feudalism is not quite the ordinary one, although very close. A great many people think that feudalism is just an earlier state of society, and by that definition, of course, almost everything that is not modern and Western is feudal.[20] Marxists have, of course, contributed a great deal to this definition, with serious debates as to whether the Ching dynasty in China was or was not feudal.[21] Traditional histories of China did refer to the Chou dynasty as feudal, and it may have been in its earliest days. By the time that it becomes actually part of history, however, it is clear that the Chou emperor was a shadowy figure with no real power. The individual "feudatories" were actually independent monarchs whose governments within their own

---

the lure of the frontier could either purchase their freedom from their lord, have it purchased for them by the lord, organizing a new manor, or steal away in the night. It is clear that large numbers of them followed one or another of these paths to the frontier" (*The Rise of the Western World: A New Economic History* [London: Cambridge University Press, 1973]).

18. See ibid., 25–37.

19. See Blum, *Emergence of the European World*, 64–72, and Lynn Thorndike, *The History of Medieval Europe*, 3d ed. (1917; Boston: Houghton Mifflin, 1949), 576–612.

20. See the account of this debate in Richard J. Smith, *China's Cultural Heritage: The Ch'ing Dynasty, 1644–1912* (Boulder: Westview Press, 1983), v–xi.

21. See Roy Hofheinz Jr., *The Broken Wave: The Chinese Communist Peasant Movement* (Cambridge: Harvard University Press, 1977), 3–9.

territories were despotic and not feudal.[22] It was not, for example, like the government of the medieval Holy Roman Emperor in which the great feudatories who held from the emperor had their own feudal retainers and did not have direct control over the bulk of the land which was within their kingdom or dukedom.

The earlier, possibly feudal, government in ancient Greece in which Menelaus, the King of Men, led an army to the siege of Troy, is relatively little known. It was destroyed by the Dorian invasion.[23] When the night of the Greek Dark Age receded, a series of independent city-states resulted.[24]

Western feudalism, of course, died with the development of the Modern Age. It was ended in France and Spain by the kings establishing complete power over the lords, and in Germany and Italy, with the lords becoming independent rulers, with the nominal emperor simply a ceremonial figure.[25] England had a unique solution to this problem, a sort of compromise. This compromise was, of course, of immense importance for the development of democracy in the Western world. Unfortunately, I know almost nothing about the Rajputs. As far as I can see, they retained their feudal organization right down to the end of the Mogul dynasty and could even be said to have continued under the British Raj, albeit the individual rajas were immensely restricted in their power at that time.[26] This book is not about feudalism, and we will discuss feudalism only occasionally, when we are discussing possible transitions between it and despotism.

Democracy is also not the subject of this book, but I am compelled to deal at some length with a more general category of government, of which democracy is a member. Specifically, if the government proceeds through votes

22. See Rushton Coulborn, ed., *Feudalism in History* (Hamden, Conn.: Archon Books, 1965), 54–58 and 65–71.

23. See Forrest, *Emergence of Greek Democracy*, 10; A. R. Burn, *The Pelican History of Greece* (Great Britain: Penguin Books, 1984), 56–60.

24. See Forrest, *Emergence of Greek Democracy*, 45; Burn, *Pelican History of Greece*, 56–83, is a compact account of the Dark Age.

25. As a matter of fact, during most of this time, the nominal emperor was also the ruler of Austria-Hungary and, hence, "the most powerful single lord." But his control over what actually went on in, say, Brandenburg was probably no stronger than that of the Russian emperor, Brandenburg regarding, in practice, both of them as foreign sovereigns.

26. The Rajput nobility were forced to sign a treaty with the British governor-general which substantially restricted their powers (see Thomas Joseph Edwards, *Military Customs*, 5th ed. [Aldershot: Gale and Polen, 1961]).

by a considerable number of people, I shall call it an "electoral system." Dahl has coined another word "polyarchy,"[27] which I would prefer to my "electoral system" if he had not given it a meaning which is different from mine, but close enough to cause confusion if I used it.

Democracy is, of course, an example of an electoral system, but there are others. A Greek city-state, for example, emerges from the Greek Dark Age governed by a council of about thirty heads of noble families. They make decisions by voting, but we would hardly call this a democracy. Such "electoral systems" will be referred to from time to time because they are historically important. Normally the electoral systems which are discussed in this book will not be democracies, because the franchise is limited. The word "democracy" will be reserved for governments in which the entire sane and noncriminal adult population can vote. I am simply trying to separate off despotic forms of government.

Thus, with this definition, Athens had an electoral system in spite of the fact that there was widespread slavery and a number of people, foreigners in residence, who were not permitted to vote.[28] But also, those Greek states which were referred to as oligarchies would be electoral, because they also depended on the votes of a considerable number of people, even if not a large part of the population.[29] Similarly, Venice, Béarn, and most of the city-states used the electoral system. Modern Israel and South Africa are also electoral, although in both cases a considerable number of the residents of the geographic area are not permitted to vote.[30]

Note that my definition of "democracy" is stricter than the normal one. For most writers, "democracy" is defined by the number of voters being large. Exactly what "large" means in this definition is not very clear. Anthony Downs[31]

27. Dahl, *Polyarchy Participation and Opposition*.

28. See Forrest, *Emergence of Greek Democracy*, 48ff.

29. Ibid., 98–101.

30. The number is, of course, very much larger in South Africa than in Israel. Israel has a Jewish population of about 3.5 million and an Arab population of about 1,650,000. Of the latter, about 1.15 million live in the area conquered by Israel in 1966 and cannot vote. There are about 5.4 million whites with full franchise, and about 18 million blacks and Asians with either restricted or no franchise in South Africa. See James Dunnigan and Stephen Bay, *A Quick and Dirty Guide to War: Briefings on Present and Potential Wars* (New York: William Morrow, 1985), 48–49, 170–71.

31. See Anthony Downs, *An Economic Theory of Democracy* (New York: Harper and Row, 1957), 23–24.

feels that universal adult suffrage is necessary for the usage of the word "democracy."[32] Both the Downs definition and mine rule out almost all historical examples. England was never a democracy until the end of World War I. Indeed, there were practically no democracies before World War I and certainly none before 1850. Washington and Jefferson were not democratic statesmen, nor was Pericles. Caesar did not overthrow Roman democracy. Most people do not put such extreme limitations on the use of the word "democracy," but the exact size of the necessary number of voters is blurred. Fortunately this book is not about democracy, so I don't have to solve the problem.

I must here make a few more rather rough distinctions within the autocracy category. Firstly, there is currently in the literature a good deal of talk of totalitarian, as opposed to authoritarian, governments. These terms aren't necessarily clear, but it is clear to anyone who looks at the data that it's easy to tell a certain class of governments—most of which in the present-day world are communist—from the others. I shall use the word "totalitarian" for those governments where the government actually makes a strong effort to control all aspects of the lives of its subjects. Present-day Russia and China are obvious examples.

It is an open question whether the type of ancient hydraulic civilization described in Karl Wittfogel's *Oriental Despotism*[33] was or was not, as Wittfogel thought it was, the logical predecessor of modern communist states. Certainly these governments exerted a great deal of power over their subjects, but it's also notable in most of them that the local villages were self-governing and used essentially democratic methods to govern themselves. Wittfogel explains this in terms of the declining marginal return on administration, i.e., that the government knew that if it tried to control everything, its control would disintegrate in the outer reaches of the government apparatus.[34] The problem is of great historic interest, but no great importance for our purposes. We can distinguish quite readily between modern totalitarian governments and other dictatorships.

32. He has a footnote in which he says that possibly not letting women vote would not deprive the nation of the right to be called democratic (23).

33. See Karl Wittfogel, *Oriental Despotism: A Comparative Study of Total Power* (New York: Vintage, 1981).

34. See Gordon Tullock, *The Politics of Bureaucracy* (Washington, D.C.: Public Affairs Press, 1965), 137–65, for a formal elucidation of the point.

Consider, for example, Spain during the heyday of Franco. This was clearly a rather inefficient, badly run dictatorship. It was not, however, totalitarian in the sense that Russia was. Franco made little effort to interfere with the private lives of his citizens. He did not, during most of the time that he was dictator, even have a death penalty. Further, throughout the time that he was dictator, foreign newspapers and magazines were reasonably available in Madrid.[35] After the first few years of Franco's reign, there were not even very many political prisoners in Spain, although, of course, there always were some.[36] This is radically different from the government of Stalin or even the government of Gorbachev.

In this respect, Franco is relatively typical of the average African, South American, or Asiatic dictator of the present day. We will discuss this kind of situation in great detail throughout the book, so there is no point in elaborating here. The dominant form of autocracy has been the nontotalitarian type presented by Franco, Lee of Singapore, or Mobutu of Zaire. I've chosen those names, incidentally, with animus aforethought. Zaire is surely one of the worst-governed countries in the world, and Singapore one of the best. They both fall, however, within our category of standard dictatorships.

There are, of course, some intermediate stages between autocracy and various other forms of government. We all know the history of the development of English democracy, which essentially came out of feudalism rather than out of autocracy. Looking around the world today, however, we find a number of governments which I am going to call "limited autocracies." They are places like the Philippines under Marcos, South Korea, and Mexico, where you have a pretty clear-cut dictator,[37] but there is also an elected legislature. This legislature, like the legislature of George II in England,[38] usually is elected by methods which would not meet with the approval of the ACLU, but nevertheless it is not completely dependent on the ruler. Its relationship to the ruler is also rather unclear. It is clear that the ruler is not controlled by

35. By "foreign" here I mean things not written in Spanish. Franco apparently felt that people who could read foreign languages either could be trusted or, perhaps, were not controllable. See Paul Johnson, *Modern Times: The World from the Twenties to the Eighties* (New York: Harper and Row, 1983), 607, on the restricted tyranny of Franco's dictatorship.

36. Ibid., 608.

37. In Mexico he rules for only six years and then has to appoint his successor and retire.

38. See Lewis B. Namier, *The Structure of Politics at the Accession of George III* (London: Macmillan, 1957).

the legislature in the same way that Margaret Thatcher is controlled by the House of Commons in England, but it's also clear that the legislature does put some checks on the power of the ruler. This intermediate form of government will be discussed at some length later.

The intermediate stage between feudalism and autocracy will not be discussed very much in this book mainly because I don't know very much about it. Historians of the gradual switch of both France and Spain from feudal monarchs to "enlightened" despotism may be able to shed some light here.

The intermediate stages between feudalism and the electoral system may, or then again may not, be important. We know almost nothing about what happened during the Greek Dark Age after the previous probably feudal society had been destroyed by the Dorians.[39] The conversion of Japanese feudalism and Rajput feudalism into democracy came essentially through outside influences. This leaves us with England.

It is not at all clear exactly what happened there. The Wars of the Roses killed a good many feudal lords, and they were succeeded by the strong Tudor monarchs, who clearly proposed to wipe out what was left of the power of the lords.[40] One of their tools, a rather minor one, was the House of Commons.[41] Elizabeth, the last Tudor, died without issue.[42] The throne went to the king of Scotland.[43] The House of Stuart became involved with some of the nobility and the House of Commons in what is called the English civil war.[44] It should be pointed out that it was, in this case, the king who revolted rather than the House of Commons. The king went to Oxford to raise his standard, and the only permanent professional military force, the navy, remained loyal to the House of Commons in London.[45] Essentially, however, the war seems to have been fought on religious grounds.[46] The immediate outcome was the establishment of a much stronger monarchy under Crom-

39. See Forrest, *Emergence of Greek Democracy*, 45.

40. See Giles St. Aubyn, *The Year of Three Kings: 1483* (New York: Atheneum, 1983), 11–15.

41. Ibid., 16. There is a myth that the Commons had been a significant part of the government in the Middle Ages.

42. See Cantor, *The English*, 807.

43. Ibid., 809–10.

44. See Maurice Ashley, *The Greatness of Oliver Cromwell* (New York: Collier Books, 1966), 93ff.

45. See Dupuy and Dupuy, *Encyclopedia of Military History*, 511.

46. See Ashley, *Greatness of Oliver Cromwell*, 43ff.

well, but he died leaving matters in the hands of a weakling son, and a constitutional monarchy was established.[47] What we can make of this for our present purposes isn't obvious. It is clear, however, that the period from, let us say, the return of Charles II through George III's insanity[48] was a period of what we have been calling "limited autocracy," i.e., a very strong ruler who nevertheless has to put up to some extent with the votes of an elected body which he does not completely control.

The reader will, no doubt, by now have gotten the general idea of what this book is about, but also a feeling that the boundaries are rather vague. Vagueness seems to be inherent in the subject matter. It's easy enough to produce very sharp definitions and divisions, but if you do, you'll find that the world doesn't seem to divide up that way. It seems to be easier and more efficient to accept the vagueness of our historic evidence and work forward from there.

Another problem is the nature of the historical evidence I will use. It will, unfortunately, be mainly anecdotal. This is not because I would not like more sophisticated methods, but because the neccessary data for their use are not available. Further, granted the diversity of autocracies, collecting such evidence would require knowledge of quite a number of languages. I have been unable to undertake the task, but I hope this book will lead other scholars to begin the work. As some help in empirical testing of my theories, I have put in an appendix at the end which lists hypotheses which could, in theory, be tested. I hope other scholars will take up the challenge.

Now a few words about the remainder of the book. I have said that dictatorship or some type of autocracy is clearly the dominant form of government both in the world today and throughout history. Western history, it is true, had occasional upsurges of electoral governments, but in earlier centuries these were followed by the restoration of autocracy. Although that does not prove it will happen this time, it still must be accepted as a statement about history up to now. It is therefore important to understand this, the commonest form of government.

The organization of the book may impress the reader as a little bizarre. I will begin by discussing how an existing dictator remains in power. He faces essentially three potential sources of danger. The first of these are the

47. Ibid., 350–58.

48. On Charles II's return in 1660, see Dupuy and Dupuy, *Encyclopedia of Military History*, 556. On George III's insanity, see Cantor, *The English*, 892.

high officials of his own regime. Most dictators are overthrown by higher officials of their own regime, simply because the higher officials want to promote themselves, with at least one of them becoming the new dictator. If the reader has doubts about this I suggest that he consult the *New York Times Index* for the previous six months or so and check the number of cases in which dictators have been overthrown. In most cases the persons overthrowing them will be either officials or former officials in the government which was overthrown. The consequence is simply the establishment of a new dictatorship.

Normally a new dictatorship will announce that it's going to have different policies, but the policy changes are usually modest. In fact, the whole policy change between dictatorial regimes is rather similar to the policy change when the party in power changes in a democracy. In both cases there is a lot of talk about what changes will be made, but mainly the changes turn out to be modest. Occasionally, in both, quite radical changes will be made. As a democratic example, we may take Franklin Roosevelt in 1933.

The second most frequent cause of the overthrow of a dictator in recent years has been foreign intervention. Over the long sweep of history, however, foreign conquest has been the most common source of the termination of dictatorial power. It has not been very important in the last forty years, but this I believe represents a peculiarity of that historical period. This was a time when the United States dominated the world. The United States has a rather irrational objection to "aggression." It is true that Israel and India were permitted to annex pieces of their neighbors.[49] But during most of this period any other country attempting to grab neighboring real estate would have had trouble with the United States. Apparently one of the results of the Vietnamese War is that this is no longer true. Qaddafi has been permitted to seize a substantial (and apparently worthless) piece of the Sahara.[50] The Vietnamese government conquered Laos and Cambodia, Indonesia took Timor, and Russia has invaded Afghanistan, all without anything except expressions of pain and surprise from the United States. The current rather bloody war between Iran and Iraq started with an Iraqi effort to invade Iran, and when that failed, it developed into an Iranian effort to conquer Iraq.[51]

49. See Johnson, *Modern Times*, 305, 481. India seized Portuguese Goa in 1961, an event largely ignored in the West (outside of Portugal).

50. See Dunnigan and Bay, *Quick and Dirty Guide*, 132.

51. Ibid., 72–75.

Once again, the American reaction has been pretty largely simply expressions of pain and surprise. Naturally, the U.N. has done nothing about any of these things. The basic difference is that the U.N. doesn't even show pain and surprise. It seems likely that we can expect a good deal more of this kind of thing in the near future.

The last, and in many ways least likely, way in which a dictator may be overthrown is by a genuine popular uprising. This is rare, not only in my own opinion but in that of most people who have seriously looked into the matter. "Armed insurrection in some form or other is the classic method of making a revolution, and . . . it is bound to imply a clash with professionally trained troops equipped with all the gear of scientific warfare. History shows that, in the last resort, success or failure hinges on the attitude which those armed forces of the status quo government will take toward an insurrection . . . Whatever government or party has the full allegiance of a country's armed forces is to all intents and purposes politically impregnable."[52] This is quoted with full endorsement and approval by Johnson.[53] If full allegiance to a country's armed forces is rare in the study of actual overthrows of dictatorship, it is very common in the romantic literature. The Bastille was actually taken by a regiment of regular infantry, but the legend claims that it was a Paris mob.[54] It is true that the King of France, like the Shah of Iran, felt that his troops should not fight and, hence, left himself rather defenseless.[55] The Napoleonic dynasty took a different position. Napoleon I became ruler of France to a very considerable extent because he was the only general in the French army who was willing to order cannon to fire grapeshot into the Paris mob. Napoleon III converted himself from prince-president of France to emperor in part because he led a cavalry charge into the grandchildren of the victims of his uncle's grapeshot. Although popular uprisings are rare, they are not totally unknown. It can, however, be said that they occur only when, for

52. See Katherine C. Chorley, *Armies and the Art of Revolution* (London, 1943), 11, 16. Also see Karl Marx and Friedrich Engels, *Selected Works*, vol. 1, *The Class Struggles in France 1848 to 1850* (Moscow: Progress Publishers, 1969), 136. "Let us have no illusions about it: a real victory of an insurrection over the military in street fighting, a victory as between two armies, is one of the rarest exceptions."

53. See Chalmers Johnson, *Revolutionary Change* (Stanford: Stanford University Press, 1966), 102.

54. See Francis Charles Montague, *The History of England, from the Accession of James I to the Restoration (1603–1660)* (London: Longmans, Green, 1920), 164.

55. The Shah also, in the last eighteen months of his reign, stopped torturing people.

one reason or another, the military machine is immobilized. The matter will be discussed in greater detail later.

There will then be a discussion of the apparently irrelevant subject of ethics. This concerns the fairly obvious fact that some dictators, even some of the worst of them, seem to have convinced their subjects that there is an ethical duty to support them. The subject is related, of course, to the traditional political science discussions of "legitimacy." How and why ethical importance can be attached to an existing regime, or for that matter to someone who wants to overthrow it, is an important subject and will be given a chapter by itself.

Having discussed the problems a dictator faces in holding his job, we will discuss how he selects policies and administers them. We will then turn to what an ambitious man who wants to overthrow the dictator should do. It is, in a way, looking at the problem of maintaining power from the other direction. In the final section of the book we will turn to some technical problems, such as how a dictator can arrange a reasonably peaceful succession to himself without providing an opportunity for someone to kill him; the intermediate stages between dictatorship and democracy, which are quite common in the present-day world; and why very small voting bodies normally develop into dictatorships.

As one final introductory note, I think that I should explain my view of dictators. At a recent conference two scholars, both of whom are emotionally much more antagonistic to dictatorships than I am, denounced me for having an unduly low opinion of dictators. Basically, they thought of dictators as people who had acquired dictatorial power for the purpose of implementing certain policies. The policies were ones that they disliked, hence their strong emotional aversion to the dictator. What they objected to about my attitude was that I thought that dictators were people who acquired power essentially because for personal reasons they preferred being dictators to being lower-ranking officials. Policies in my view were then adopted largely, not entirely, but largely, in terms of their effect on the dictators' careers rather than in terms of their intrinsic desirability.

It can be seen that in this case I am simply carrying over what I might call the "public choice view" of politics. Anthony Downs is frequently quoted as having said, "Political parties do not seek power in order to select policies: they select policies in order to seek power." This has been the general view of most people in the public choice movement. It is, in a way, one of the more radical differences between public choice and traditional political science. We think politicians are like the rest of us, in that most of the time, not always, but most of the time, they seek their own advantage. We can buy reasonably good cars not because the car manufacturers have our interest at heart, although to some extent they do, but basically because they want to make money. Similarly, if we have a choice of policies offered by different political groups, this is because those political groups are seeking political power and hope to use the policies as incentives to collect our votes in the case of democracy.

The basic advantage of a democracy is that those people who seek power must seek power by attempting to please a majority of the voting population. Dictatorships are ruled by people who seek power and must please other people, but the people who must be pleased are a much smaller group.

This is, indeed, different from the normal attitude towards politics, both democratic politics and dictatorial politics. Nevertheless, I think it is also realistic. If a dictator comes from a society where most of the people who could affect his future are firmly convinced of the truth of some political proposition, he is likely to accept it because that is the way to power. His convictions are, however, rarely deeply held and can be changed very rapidly if there is a political gain to be obtained from it. Lyndon Johnson and George Wallace were not, of course, dictators, but both were at different times in their careers in favor of keeping the blacks firmly down and of civil liberties for blacks. In both cases they made considerable political gain from the switch. Similar startling changes of position will be found in the careers of most dictators.

It may be that in taking this point of view, I am, indeed, being unjust to the dictators, but I think not. Dictators may follow extremely bad policies when looked at from our value system. The normal reason, however, is not that they are devoted to those policies on ideological grounds, but that they think that those are the policies most likely to permit them to obtain and maintain power.

I should not close this chapter, however, without making one point clear. This is a book about dictatorship. It is not a book advocating dictatorship as a form of government. The average person in our society knows of dictatorships, or autocratic governments, only that they are bad things. I don't deny that they are bad, but they are very common. We should try to understand them. This book is dedicated to that end.

THE USES OF DICTATORSHIP

So far, we have talked about how the dictator keeps his power, but have said little or nothing about why he should want that power. What can he do with the power? The first thing to be said here is that the dictator is far from having absolute power. He is, undeniably, the single most important man in the society in which he operates. But he is far from being the mythical absolute ruler of all he surveys.

He must always remember that he can be overthrown. To take but one obvious example, he can hardly order his personal guard all shot while he is surrounded by them. The rise of the Turkish empire depended very heavily on the Janissaries, but by 1800, the Janissaries had become a severe burden upon that empire. The Padishah decided that they had to be eliminated and succeeded in getting rid of them, but it took a long, careful conspiracy. Indeed, it is, on the whole, odd that he got rid of them rather than they getting rid of him.[1]

It is not only his personal guard; the dictator, after all, is only one man. He is surrounded by a large number of people, and if he succeeds in either annoying them or giving them the impression that he is weakening, he will probably be removed. Thus, his decisions are always subject to fairly severe constraints. These constraints are not of the sort we think of as constitutional, i.e., that somebody can literally veto his action without removing him from power.

The president of the United States is restricted in what he can do, because Congress may choose not to pass acts he suggests nor appropriate money for things he wants to do. Further, the Supreme Court may decide that various of his actions are unconstitutional. These restrictions, however, are of a totally different nature from the possibility of throwing him out, and in fact the procedure for getting rid of the president is tedious and difficult, and only

Reprinted, with kind permission of Kluwer Academic Publishers, from *Autocracy* (Dordrecht and Boston: Kluwer Academic Publishers, 1987), 115–30.

1. By the summer of 1826, the Janissaries were a powerful force, basically independent of the Sultan. Mahmud II prepared an ambush for the Janissaries in which hidden cannons decimated their ranks with grapeshot: This was the culmination of an elaborate conspiracy which might easily have failed. See Lord Kinross, *The Ottoman Centuries* (New York: Morrow Quill, 1977), 456–57.

twice in our history has it been even tried. On the other hand, the frustration of his policies by the various other branches of the government is a common everyday operation.

The reverse is true with a dictator or king. It's very hard to prevent him from doing what he wants, provided he concentrates on it.[2] A dictator can, however, be removed, and this has been the historical experience of most dictators. Further, removal is normally not into a peaceful retirement, although he may well escape abroad. There have been, indeed, some dictators who were able to return to their countries after a period of time and be reasonably safe and happy there. On the whole, however, the ex-dictator faces the major risks of being killed, imprisoned, or forced to spend the rest of his life abroad. Death by torture is by no means unknown.

Thus, every time a dictator does anything, he must keep in mind the prospect that it will weaken his position. Note that this, once again, is not like constitutional restrictions, in that his power is restricted by rules which are supposed, on the whole, to lead to it being wisely and virtuously exercised. It is, of course, not at all obvious that the restrictions which we impose on constitutional democratic officials have that effect, but that is the intent.

The dictator, on the other hand, has to worry not about the policy outcomes of his decisions, but about their effect on other high officials and on other powers in his government. Returning to his personal guard, it may be large and overpaid, but he is unwise to briskly reduce it or cut its salary. He may shift officials out of jobs for which they are well suited into jobs for which they are not well suited simply because it is safer for him. He may in various ways sacrifice the welfare of the state for his own continuance in office. He can also find it necessary to "invest" by reducing his own living standard in order to increase his tenure in office.[3]

With this much said about the restrictions on the power of the dictator, we can now turn to what he can do with what power he has. We should divide this use of his power into two categories. The first is the use of his power for his personal aggrandisement, his own living standard either while he is dictator or after he has been forced to flee the country. Securing the succession for his family is another "personal" gain which many rulers have apparently valued.

2. Passing whims on his part can frequently be bypassed in various ways.

3. A dictator will normally have a living standard which is sharply higher than that of anyone else in the government. Conspicuous displays of truly great wealth, however, are unusual too.

Secondly, there is the carrying out of government policies which he thinks are desirable. Both of these are areas where he can use his power. But, of course, as we have said again and again, he is limited by the fact that he may get thrown out as dictator if he does either one too vigorously. Let's begin with his own living standard. No one who has visited Versailles or that vast complex of palaces that dominates the center of Peking will have any doubt that rulers have devoted a great deal of money to their own living standard. For another instance: Buckingham Palace is a massive building. Communist rulers seem to do very well by themselves. In the last case, they are very secretive about their conditions of life, but rumors hold that they live very well indeed.[4]

In one case, a Communist ruler's living standard is known to have been very high. Marshal Tito, during the later part of his life, deviated from the ordinary Communist practice by having a good deal of the budget of Yugoslavia published. The ministry which dealt with his various houses had a larger appropriation than the ministry of interior.[5] Since this is a Communist country where the ministry of interior maintains the secret police, this shows an extremely high consumption level. Arab rulers have, of course, also developed extremely high living standards in recent years, and most South American dictators live well too. There are occasional exceptions in South America, and indeed there are even occasional South American dictators who, when they are overthrown, appear not to have very much in the way of outside resources.

President Rhee of Korea, after twenty years of rule, was finally overthrown. It turned out at this point that he had laid away so little in the way of resources that he and his wife, in essence, lived on charity in the latter part of their lives. This does not mean that they were poverty stricken. They lived as permanent house guests of a wealthy Korean businessman in Hawaii. But they clearly had not laid aside vast amounts of money in a Swiss bank account.

The problem with a high living standard is that it's not obvious that it helps a ruler stay in power. It has been argued many times that royal rulers surround themselves with pomp, ceremony, and luxury because in a way this gives people who meet them the idea that they're important and powerful. There is, undeniably, something of this sort of effect for royal dynasties and to a lesser

4. On the very affluent life-styles of Soviet rulers—palaces, unlimited open bank accounts, etc.—see Michael Voslenskii, *Nomenklatura: The Soviet Ruling Class, An Insider's Report*, trans. Eric Mosbacher (Garden City, N.Y.: Doubleday, 1984), 225–28.

5. I do not read Serbo-Croatian, so I am accepting the word of Professor Svetosvar Pejovich here.

extent for dictators. But the idea that the dictator is wasting the taxpayers' money is a little hard to avoid. When he tells the army or his guard, or for that matter the higher ranking officials in his own government, that it's impossible to raise their incomes, they are apt to, at least subconsciously, feel that perhaps if he had one fewer palace they could have more money. Further, the more money spent on the dictator, the more there is to be divided among other high officials if they conspire together to overthrow him. Thus, on the whole, personal expenditures are probably negative factors in a dictator's survival. This does not, of course, mean that he will not make them, merely that he regards them as expenditures in two senses. One, they use the taxpayers' money, and two, they to some extent reduce the period of time that he will be dictator.

A special form of expenditure is, of course, foreign bank accounts and foreign investments.[6] Indeed many South American dictators seem to put a good deal of money into domestic investments. The apparent reason for the domestic investment rather than foreign is that the return, as long as the man is dictator, tends to be very high because he can in various ways bend government policy so as to make these investments profitable. A road apparently built solely for the convenience of the country estate of the current dictator of Chile is merely one of many examples.

It should be pointed out, however, that this way of benefiting himself—i.e., building up his local investments by having the government do things which improve their value—once again has a cost, in that it makes it less likely he will stay and provides greater rewards to anyone who throws him out. Indeed, investments in his own country are particularly likely to provide a reward to the individual or group who replaces him, because they can always confiscate them.

Foreign investment is safe in the sense that the dictator is unlikely to lose it if he succeeds in getting out of the country. Further, foreign bankers are accustomed to this particular business and can be depended on to hold the money and keep the investments a secret. They hope also to have the business of the successor. Thus, the exact size of the funds the dictator has will not be known. It is thought, for example, that Batista had about a quarter of a

6. It is extremely interesting to make an effort to approximate the foreign investments by dictators in the modern era. Thus banks are unlikely to make their books open to the investigator, but examination of how well the dictator lives after he leaves, when he gets away, would be a suitable substitute.

billion dollars[7] at the time that he was first removed. It is also thought that he stole relatively little during his second term as dictator, probably because he already had enough. Perón is thought to have taken a full half-billion dollars when he left Argentina. Certainly in both of these cases they lived well in retirement. The Somoza and Trujillo families seem to have invested enough money within their countries so that the amount they could take abroad was not in the same category as the two I have given above. Nevertheless, no one regarded them as likely to become objects of charity.

Lenin, when he was ruling Russia, in the early days, apparently put aside a significant collection of jewelry which was to be used for the specific purpose of supporting the higher ranking Communists in the event they were driven out of Russia.[8] Since this jewelry was actually kept in the Kremlin, it is not obvious they would have gotten it out, but on the other hand, a deposit in a foreign bank in his case was probably not feasible.

But these are merely a small smattering of examples. Anyone who even glances through the literature will pick up many more. One thing that dictators do is put money abroad, another thing they do is use money to build up their current living standard in their country, and they many times invest money domestically. It's interesting that kings and emperors are less likely to do this. Apparently they feel sufficiently secure in possession of their offices so that they do not think it necessary to provide for the contingency of their being overthrown. This has meant that in a number of cases kings and their close relatives have been driven into poverty or found themselves dependent on the charity of either refugees from their own country or foreign governments who think that they may be useful for political purposes in the future.

But all of this is familiar. Though it may excite some indignation, it will not surprise. Any dictator would, of course, realize that he can make money out of the job but that the job is risky, and the more money he makes out of it, the more risky it is. He must balance these various requirements against each other, and different dictators have chosen different exchange rates.

7. In 1946 dollars.

8. In 1919 or 1920, Lenin's secretary saw records of a large cache of diamonds secreted in the Kremlin for use by Lenin and his immediate entourage should they fall from power. See Nikolai Tolstoy, *Stalin's Secret War* (New York: Holt, Rinehart and Winston, 1981), 58. Merle Fainsod, *Smolensk under Soviet Rule* (Cambridge: Harvard University Press, 1958), 157, reports that in 1922 a large hoard of gold was hidden in Smolensk for use by the Bolsheviks should they be forced to flee abroad.

Let us now turn to the other area: control over policy. The first thing to be said about this is that there is really relatively little evidence that dictators have very strong ideas about policy. Most of them have risen to their rank by a series of complex political maneuvers either within the military machine, in which they had to get promoted, or in other parts of their governments. In a few cases they have been able to rise to positions outside the government from which they then overthrew the government, but in all cases, this rise in rank to the position of dictator has required the ability to adapt very quickly to other people's views on policy.

There is a partial exception here. The ruler may have risen to power in part because of his espousal of some particular ideology. Khomeini and Lenin are examples. Such a ruler is unlikely to abandon his ideology, although Franco abandoned his original ideology when it became obvious it was a handicap rather than an asset. Usually these ideologies are flexible enough so that they put little real restraint on the dictator. Lenin and Khomeini are, of course, examples of this. In these cases, belief in the ideology and use of it to stay in power are intermingled. Operationally we cannot determine which is the stronger.

This book is supposed to deal with both dictators and hereditary rulers. As we said above, the hereditary ruler normally feels a good deal more secure, and he normally has attained his position without the necessary devious political maneuvering which has dominated the early life of the potential dictator. Thus, we might expect such kings to have more interest both in high living standards and in imposing their policy ideas on societies. With respect to the high living standard, I don't think there is any doubt that hereditary kings do live better than dictators on the whole. But when we turn to policy, the matter is nowhere near so clear. Hereditary kings frequently do not seem to have as much control over their governments as do dictators. I believe that the explanation is the high living standard. A young man brought up in the extremely privileged position of heir to the throne is likely to develop not only very expensive tastes in terms of money but also tastes for entertainment which are expensive in terms of time. Given the choice between a day's hunting or a day in the office, a king is far more likely to choose the day's hunting than is a dictator. This is in part the result of his upbringing, but also in part the fact that he does feel more secure.

But turning to policy, it's necessary to avoid a misapprehension. The fact that a king or dictator very commonly may be able to change policy does not necessarily mean that his government will be extremely oppressive.

Those who have read Sterne's *Sentimental Journey*[9] know that the "journey" was undertaken by two Englishmen in ancien régime France. They were mildly inconvenienced because a war between the two countries broke out as they were about cross the Channel, and hence, the traffic was interrupted for several days. On arriving in Paris, they set out to see the sights. Several days after they arrived, their landlord told them that the police had been around and wanted them to get the proper documents since they were, after all, enemy aliens. They went to Versailles and saw an official whom they convinced should give them the documents because they were Shakespeare's countrymen and then continued their sightseeing. This is not the kind of government that one associates with deep oppression.

Indeed, had Louis XVI been a more oppressive king, he probably would not have had his head cut off. He actually organized the elective bodies which eventually executed him. He was in the process of further cutting restraints on public expression when the revolution broke out. There was not one genuine political prisoner in the Bastille when it was taken.[10]

Once again, Francisco Franco is a fairly good example of the dictator, and Louis XVI a less than normally intelligent example of the hereditary monarch. Neither ran a good government, but neither can be regarded as a terrible oppressor.[11]

Turning then, once again, to the dictator, not the hereditary king, the first thing, as we have noted, is that he has had to climb the greasy pole to get to his position. This has normally occupied his full attention, and he has risen not by good judgement as to what policies the country should adopt, but by good judgement as to what policies are likely to get him ahead and who can, and who cannot, be trusted. It is true that once he gets to the top he has a little breathing spell and more power. He can, if he wishes, implement policies which are different from those which he inherited. Most dictators do

9. Sterne, Laurence, *A Sentimental Journey through France and Italy* (London: Simpkin, Marshall, Hamilton, Kent, 1937).

10. There were seven prisoners in the late Spring of 1789. Four were forgers; one was a mentally unbalanced Irishman who alternately believed himself Julius Caesar and God and was accused of being a spy; another, also deranged, was suspected of being involved in a plot to assassinate the king; and the last was a young man imprisoned at the request of his family for incest. See Christopher Hibbert, *The Days of the French Revolution* (New York: Morrow, 1980), 72.

11. On Franco's relatively benign dictatorship, see Paul Johnson, *Modern Times: The World from the Twenties to the Eighties* (New York: Harper and Row, 1983), 608–9. On Louis XIV, see Hibbert, *Days of the French Revolution*.

to some extent change previous policies, and some of them change them quite considerably. Pinochet in Chile and Lenin in Russia are examples. Lenin, of course, changed them further than Pinochet.

But if we look at democracies, we find that they also sometimes change policies very sharply. Bismarck's invention of the welfare state occurred essentially because he wanted to win an election.[12] As I have said, the difference between democracies and dictatorships in policy is hard to document, but this is partly because both democracies and dictatorships do follow very many different policies. James Madison and Franklin D. Roosevelt were both American presidents, but it would be hard to find anything much that their policies had in common. For a more recent example, there are indeed similarities between the policies of Mao Tse-tung and Deng Xioping. Nevertheless, it's fairly obvious that Deng changed policies sharply when he took power.[13] But, then, so did Abraham Lincoln when he became president. Clement Atlee and Margaret Thatcher were both British prime ministers, and both instituted significant changes in policy. Atlee's were more severe than Mrs. Thatcher's; still she too made significant changes.[14]

Thus, the fact that dictators may make considerable changes when they come to power does not mean that their policies are radically different from those of democracies. Democracies also may make considerable changes. New democracy, that is a democracy which is set up after the overthrow of a king or a dictator, in particular, is apt to make significant changes, as the former military rulers of Argentina are now discovering. Lincoln actually started a war by his changes.[15]

12. Bismarck instituted his national social insurance scheme to limit the political gains of the pro-union and pro-welfare-state social democrats. See Hajo Holborn, *A History of Modern Germany: 1840–1945* (Princeton: Princeton University Press, 1982), 291–93. He also may have wanted to provide some centralized structure to the German empire, which at that time was a very loose federation.

13. After Deng came to power in 1978, the Peking *People's Daily* apologized to readers for "all lies and distortions" it had carried during the Mao era. On this and the movement away from central planning under Deng, see Johnson, *Modern Times*, 966.

14. When Atlee came to power in 1945, he wanted Britain to disarm, decolonize, make friends with Russia, and build a welfare state. See Johnson, *Modern Times*, 966. On the policy changes brought about by Thatcher, see Paul Hare and Maurice Kirby, *An Introduction to British Economic Policy* (London: Wheatsheaf Books, 1984).

15. Actually, the American Civil War was precipitated by secession of the Southern states in *anticipation* of Lincoln's policy reorientation.

But in the average case, the policies don't seem to be very much different. Both dictators and democracies normally go along without too much change in policy, although they sometimes make radical changes. In both cases, the policies pursued, both before and after radical changes, seem to be drawn from the same sample, at least statistically.

Why is this? We've already pointed out that the dictator has to be a person who is deeply concerned with rising in power; he has to be intelligent; he has to be ambitious. He doesn't have to be a profound scholar of economics, and so far as I know, none of them ever has been. Plato, it will be recalled, nearly lost his life because he thought that rulers should be philosophers.[16] There was indeed later a philosopher-emperor, Marcus Aurelius. It's rather hard to find any great improvement in Roman policy that came from his philosophy.[17]

What we see then is an intelligent, ambitious man without very much background in the science of government insofar as there is such a thing. He has risen by a series of difficult maneuvers which prove he clearly is intelligent but not that he has firm ideas as to what policies should be. As dictator, he must always concern himself seriously with the prospect that he'll be overthrown; i.e., keeping power is highly important to him. This is true even if he is consciously attempting to reform the society, because he can do so only if he keeps power. If we look at dictators, we frequently find that they announce that they have some kind of general reform in mind, but the reforms seldom seem to be even coherent, let alone brilliant.

A dictator, then, will spend much of his time worrying about being replaced, and much of his choice of policy will turn on just exactly that fear of being replaced. Almost any policy proposal is apt to be judged by him firstly in its likely effect on his personal security and only secondly in terms of its ultimate success. Further, by training and experience he is very good at judging the effects of policy on his security and normally has very little ability to judge the policies in terms of their probable social outcomes.

16. Plato apparently incurred the wrath of the Syracusan despot Dionysius I by lecturing him on his philosophical responsibility. See Francis M. Cornford, introduction to *The Republic of Plato* (New York: Oxford University Press, 1945), xxvii.

17. William Grampp, *Economic Liberalism*, vol. 1 (Chicago: University of Chicago Press, 1960), 98, argues that the stoic philosophy of Marcus Aurelius offered no unambiguous principles of guidance to rulers or anyone else; its principal structure was basically "do whatever is necessary."

For example, a proposal to permit private competition with a national airline, with the national airline being permitted to survive only if it can meet that competition, is apt to be judged not in terms of its economic efficiency but on its effect on his survival.[18] It may not seem to have much to do with a possible coup, but surely there will be officials who will be irritated by being put under competitive pressure, and there will be employees who face at least a theoretical risk of losing their jobs, and there will be socialist-minded intellectuals who feel that, per se, the government-run airline is better than the private one, and hence the private one shouldn't be permitted to exist. None of these is likely to be a major minus to the dictator, but they are all minor minuses. Most dictators, in fact, have decided upon a nationalized airline rather than private competition.

There is here, of course, another matter. The private interests may be paying off the dictator or high officials. In the old days of royal governments this was done quite openly.[19] A guild, asking for monopoly of, let us say, paving streets in London, would point out that they were particularly loyal, competent, and honest and that they were willing to pay the king a certain amount every year. Another guild would appear, urging that it was also loyal, competent, and honest—in fact, more so than the first guild—and that it was willing to pay even more. This, in essence, put the matter up to bid. I suspect that a great many dictators do the same kind of thing, although it isn't done in the open-ended, aboveboard way characteristic of mercantilist England.

Note that in this case the funds given are not necessarily used to build up the dictator's Swiss bank account. The kings of England used some of these funds to maintain the army and provide other public expenditures. Admittedly, a great deal of them were used to support the court.[20] It would be

18. Pinochet actually adopted a somewhat similar program. He permitted any foreign airline that wished to fly into Chile and charge whatever fares they wanted. It turned out that the Chilean airline was in fact able to improve efficiency and meet the competition.

19. See Tollison and McCormick's work on mercantilism: Robert E. McCormick and Robert D. Tollison, *Politicians, Legislation, and the Economy: An Inquiry into the Interest-Group Theory of Government* (Boston: Kluwer, 1981); Robert B. Ekelund and Robert D. Tollison, *Mercantilism as a Rent-Seeking Society: Economic Regulation in Historical Perspective* (College Station: Texas A&M University Press, 1981).

20. A great deal of money was spent by kings to bribe members of Parliament. For example, George II spent over £117,000 on bribery in 1734. See Lewis B. Namier, *The Structure of Politics at the Accession of George III* (London: Macmillan, 1957), 195.

easy for a dictator who did not have a good grounding in economics, practically none do, to believe that a group of "patriotic" men who proposed to, let us say, monopolize copra exports from the Philippines and pay out of their profits a very large sum of money either to the government or to the dictator himself were in fact public benefactors. The dictator may have great difficulty distinguishing between this institution and simply taxing copra exports. Certainly, the highly paid experts who are provided by the potential copra monopolist will not enlighten the dictator. Further, it is unlikely that the potential free market in copra will be able to hire such expensive lobbyists.

In this, of course, the situation is much the same as in a democracy or, for that matter, in a hereditary monarchy. In all cases there will be highly paid and skilled lobbyists, different lobbyists for the three forms of government, of course, who are pushing for various policy changes which are in the private interest of special interest groups. If we look at history, in all three of these cases such private interests have frequently succeeded.[21]

It should be noted that both with dictatorships and with democracy the lobbyist activity does not necessarily involve corruption but may. In other words, they may depend on persuasion or on payment. It is likely that payment is commoner in the case of a dictatorship than in the case of democracy. Leaving the moral issue aside, in both cases, if there is persuasion, it will partly take the form of indicating that the new policy is a good policy, and partly that it is politically wise, in the sense that it would lead to political support. The dictator, like the democratic politician, must balance these requirements against each other. There are direct payments to be made that also should be taken into account.

We have so far been talking about various pressures that influence a dictator in making policy decisions. If the policy decision is how much he should spend on his palace or on his bodyguard, then history indicates that, on the whole, dictators are apt to choose very large bodyguards and large palaces. Occasionally there are individuals, like Stalin, with rather spartan tastes. In the case of Stalin, of course, his rather spartan tastes in furnishings was much

21. I have a paper, which will be published in an upcoming book, in which I argue that the reason for the development of the general freedom in England was, in essence, that the English government was incapable of establishing these specialized monopolies, because of a constitutional weakness in its structure. This is, of course, for the period from the English civil war to, let us say, 1800. For the next century, they seem to have been convinced that an open economy was a good idea.

more than counterbalanced in budgetary terms by his paranoia, which led to an extraordinary bodyguard.[22]

But this desire to use your power to benefit yourself is a very natural trait, and we need not explain it particularly. Further, the need to offset it to some extent in order to avoid giving too much temptation to other people to replace you is also obvious. Note that the procedure followed by most Communist dictators, living very well but concealing their living standard from the bulk of their subjects, is not really very helpful in this regard. The very elaborate special facilities that are available for the higher-ranking Communists in Russia, for example, are, firstly, known to other high-ranking Communists, the most dangerous enemies they have, and, secondly, depend on a very large number of low-ranking Russians such as guards and servants. Thus, although the average Russian probably knows nothing about the special facilities, the Russians who are most likely to be in a position to do something nasty to the dictator do know.[23]

Turning to general policy again, it has been pointed out that the man who rises to dictator normally does not have very strong policy positions. There are occasional cases in history, Lenin and Khomeini come immediately to mind, where a dictator has been very deeply involved in one particular ideological position before he becomes dictator.[24] He's likely to stick to that ideology. It should be pointed out, however, and once again Lenin and Khomeini are excellent examples, within this ideology they are likely to make a number of changes which benefit them in terms of power. Khomeini's political theory is quite unknown in previous Shia writing, and, indeed, he seems to have actually "modernized" Shia political thought partly to make it conform, to some extent, with democracy but even more to make it such that his position of power would be very much greater than that of any previous ayatolla.[25]

22. About 15,000 NKVD troops were permanently stationed in Moscow as Stalin's bodyguard. See Tolstoy, *Stalin's Secret War*, 52.

23. Periodically the privileges of certain high-ranking Communists became publicized in the USSR, apparently by opponents in various power struggles. For example, a dramatic "corruption" scandal took place in 1970 when the lifestyle and real income of the First Secretary of Azerbaijan were revealed by a rival, who subsequently received the lucrative post himself. See Michael Voslenskii, *Nomenklatura: The Soviet Ruling Class, An Insider's Report*, trans. Eric Mosbacher (Garden City, N.Y.: Doubleday, 1984), 190.

24. On Lenin, see Sheila Fitzpatrick, *The Russian Revolution* (New York: Berkley, 1982), 23–26. On Khomeini, see Shaul Bakhash, *The Reign of the Ayatollahs: Iran and the Islamic Revolution* (New York: Basic Books, 1984), 19–27.

25. See Bakhash, *Reign of the Ayatollahs*, esp. 32–51.

Lenin was somewhat the same type of person. Reading his biography, I cannot avoid the impression that he honestly believed that the world was going to eventually enter the great Marxist Utopia and, hence, that the only real issue politically was who would be head of it. He was always willing to do almost anything in the way of damaging prospects of Communist control, such as splitting the party, if it only benefited Lenin's position within the Communist movement.[26] Thus, even these two individuals who seem to have a fairly strong ideological position clearly bent the clear ideology to their own ambition.

Nevertheless, there is some possibility of a dictator simply exercising policy judgement in terms of what he wants. After all, he probably is very interested in power and likes to exercise it for its own sake. He is likely to take advantage of his position, not only to build himself a spectacular palace, but to flatter his ego by giving orders which people have to carry out. He is unlikely to give orders that people have to carry out if he thinks that they have a possibility, even a small possibility, of leading to his being overthrown. In many cases he can avoid that possibility. Further, he may think that it's necessary to occasionally run a bit of danger in terms of longer-run safety.

It should be said here, however, that not only does he worry about his own safety, human nature suggests that he's apt to also want to be liked. Most human beings do. He would like to be liked by the people immediately around him and by other people too. Thus the dictator would, other things being equal, prefer to be the favorite of public opinion. It is true that he frequently will have difficulty in determining whether he is or isn't, but he may try to improve his status with the public by doing things that they will approve of as well as by increasing the level of torture in his dungeons.

Hussein, the current dictator of Iraq, has featured a number of times in this account, and we have here a clear example. After his ghastly miscalculation in the early part of the war with Iran, when he realized that he was in real trouble, he increased sharply the degree to which opponents of his were arrested and tortured. He also, at the same time, increased his subventions to the Shia church in Iraq, the church which contains the majority of the population and which he had previously rather moderately suppressed.[27] Both of these measures were sensible.

26. See Johnson, *Modern Times*, 51–57.

27. On Hussein's various repressive measures, see Phebe Marr, *The Modern History of Iraq* (Boulder: Westview Press, 1985), 303–5.

It has sometimes been argued, incidentally, that a dictator who decides to make concessions to public opinion—i.e., do things he thinks will make him popular—had better increase his level of repression at the same time. The populace, and, for that matter, members of his own government, are apt to take concessions made by him to any group, and particularly the public, as signs of weakness and hence try to replace him. In the long run, the concessions may pay off in terms of greater security, but their short-run effect may well be the reverse. The short-run negative effect can be canceled out by increased repression.

The problem here is that the individual dictator attempting to use his power for policy purposes may, in fact, have little or no policy effect. There are several reasons for this, the first of which is that he may in fact be trying to increase his popularity with various groups. This would mean that he would tend to select policies that are favored by other people. As we have said above, it's likely that the dictator does not have very strong policy preferences of his own; if he had, he would not have risen to high rank. So using his policy power to (a) get the satisfaction of giving orders and (b) make friends is likely to be something that he thinks is a good idea.

Further, when he does try to do something which is "good," regardless of its effect on the people around him, he has a problem in that he probably doesn't know what is "good." He is normally not a trained economist or political scientist; he isn't even, as a general rule, capable of recognizing a good economist from a poor one. He is likely to simply pick up whatever ideas happen to be current and fashionable in his society and apply them. Thus he is very likely to adopt policies which would have been adopted by a democracy or, for that matter, the preceding dictator whom he overthrew. This is probably the reason that it is statistically so extremely difficult to tell dictatorships from democracies by their policy output. There is a great deal of variance in the policy output of both dictatorships and democracies, and it tends to occupy much the same issue space simply because to a large extent it depends on the same collection of basic ideas, fads, foibles, etc.

As general summary, the advantage to the dictator of being dictator is that he is able to get his desires carried out to a quite large extent. His desire for security cannot ever be fully satisfied; in other respects he can have a very high living standard. Not as high as a hereditary monarch, but still very high. He has considerable power to see to it that the people around him at least express friendship and admiration for him, and he can do various things which will make it likely that the populace will like him, at least to some extent.[28] His desire for admiration can also have considerable effect on what we might refer to as the grand policy of his country. Normally, however, he won't have very strong ideas as to what that should be and is apt to end up giving orders which are rather similar to those which would be given by any other dictator or, for that matter, passed by a democratic legislature. Looking at it briefly, it's a good life but apt to be a short one.

28. The Shah, after he was overthrown, pointed out that the serious rioting against him had started in a town in which six months before he had been welcomed by gigantic and enthusiastic crowds.

BECOMING A DICTATOR

So far we have devoted our attention mainly to what happens after dictators get in power. We now turn to how they get power. This may seem a perverse way of dealing with the problem, since obviously they become dictators before they are faced with the problem of retaining power, but for analytical reasons it's easier. The basic problem faced by a young man who wants to be dictator is the existing dictator himself. Hence, unless we are fairly well informed about the defenses that that dictator may have, we're not in a position to discuss the rise to rank of such a man as Sgt. Doe[1] of Liberia.

As I trust the previous chapters have convinced the reader, the life of a potential dictator is not an easy one. He runs a very large risk of being neutralized or even killed. Further, even if he is successful in overthrowing the existing dictator, the chances that some colleague of his will become the successor rather than he himself is by no means zero. We closed the last chapter on the dictator by pointing out that he lived an insecure life even if a luxurious one. The man trying to overthrow the dictator does not have a high current living standard to set off against the even greater risks. He is, in essence, making an investment, laying his life quite literally on the line in hopes of a better future.

Because of this extremely risky aspect of the matter, it is not likely that very many who eventually become dictators started out in life with that as a conscious objective. Probably they simply were attempting to rise to high rank in the existing system, but then later took advantage of opportunities that opened up.

A rise to high rank normally means literally rising in the governmental hierarchy, whether on the military side or the civilian.[2] Sometimes, however,

Reprinted, with kind permission of Kluwer Academic Publishers, from *Autocracy* (Dordrecht and Boston: Kluwer Academic Publishers, 1987), 131–50.

1. General Samuel K. Doe assumed the presidency on April 12, 1980, following a predawn coup by army enlisted men. The existing regime was charged with the general crime of "rampant corruption" by the attacking soldiers, and the raid produced the death of then Liberian head of state Tolbert. *New York Times*, April 13, 1980, p. 1.

2. African dictators who are civilians are commoner than those who are military men. In South America, the reverse is true. See Lucy Mair, *African Kingdoms* (Oxford: Oxford

the rise can be completely outside the formal government. Granted the history of China, probably every single bandit chief in the last five hundred years has dreamt at least faintly of eventually becoming emperor. Chang Tso-lin in the 1920s came very close.[3] Historically Nurhachi and Genghis Khan each started out as something between a bandit leader and the leader of a tiny tribe, in both cases mustering fewer than ten fighting men.[4] Although neither himself became emperor of China they both built powerful dynasties which eventually conquered China. In the case of Genghis Khan, of course, he also conquered much of Europe and the Middle East.[5]

University Press, 1977), and Christian P. Potholm, *The Theory and Practice of African Politics* (Englewood Cliffs, N.J.: Prentice-Hall, 1979); and Andrew Wheatcroft, *The World Atlas of Revolutions* (New York: Simon and Schuster, 1983), respectively. In African societies, apparent control over environmental threats (drought, disease, etc.) rather than military opponents has often served as the catalyst for a rise to power. In Rwanda, for example, tribal rulers have been popularly held "to have ritual powers; they controlled the weather, causing the rain to fall at the right time and not in excessive quantities, and they combated disasters such as locust invasion. Such powers were . . . an inseparable element in the quality of chiefliness" (Mair, *African Kingdoms*, 25; see also Potholm, *Theory and Practice*, 28–31).

3. Chang Tso-lin, a well-known warlord of northern China, dominated the region of Manchuria from 1920 to 1928. At times he ran the area virtually as a distinct country, independently negotiating treaties with foreign governments. For example, he conquered Peking (1925–26) and claimed the title of Grand Marshall of China, despite the fact that southern China was not under his control. Revolutionary forces from the south toppled him from power in the "Northern Expedition" (1928) (James E. Sheridan, *China in Disintegration: The Republican Iraq in Chinese History, 1912–1949* [Stanford: Stanford University Press, 1975], 61–65. See also James E. Sheridan, *Chinese Warlord, the Career of Feng Yu-Hsiang* [Stanford: Stanford University Press, 1966]). It might be noted that there is some dispute about whether Chang himself was a practicing "bandit," or was merely "accused of banditry only because the local defense unit he commanded was not part of the regular military establishment" (Sheridan, *China in Disintegration*, 63).

4. On Nurhachi's modest beginnings, see W. Scott Morton, *China: Its History and Culture* (New York: Lippincott and Crowell, 1980), 138–39; Witold Rodzinski, *The Walled Kingdom: A History of China from Antiquity to the Present* (New York: Free Press, Macmillan, 1984), 156; Fredric Wakeman Jr., *The Fall of Imperial China* (New York: Free Press, Macmillan, 1975), 75–79. Temuchin (Genghis Khan's originally given name) "came from a family of hereditary leaders but had to work long and hard to reach a position of power, since his father had been killed [when Temuchin was] a boy" (Morton, *China*, 116).

5. See R. Ernest Dupuy and Trevor N. Dupuy, *Encyclopedia of Military History, from 3500 B.C. to the Present*, rev. ed. (New York: Harper and Row, 1977), 336–45; Oddvar Bjorklund, Haakon Holmboe, Anders Rohr, and Berit Lie, *Historical Atlas of the World*, map 42 (1962;

But these are exceptions. More normally, a potential ruler rises in a functioning government of some size. He may, of course, eventually, like Napoléon, massively expand that government,[6] but it is rare that he literally starts with nothing and then acquires great status by military means. Rising within a government structure is a far commoner first step. It was, of course, the way Napoléon rose.

Although rising within the government structure is the normal route, there may well be a major deviation. The current dictator of Uganda, Milton Obote, was put in power by Nyerere, the dictator of Tanzania.[7] There are a number of other people in the present-day world who have achieved dictatorial power in the same way. Kim Il Sung of North Korea entered North Korea in the baggage train of the Red Army.[8] With quite clever maneuvering between the Chinese and the Russians, he has actually succeeded in obtaining the status of an independent dictator.[9] Such a man as Jaruzelski of Poland, on the other hand, although, of course, appointed by outsiders, cannot really be regarded as a dictator. He is more akin to a provincial governor.[10] At best his

---

New York: Barnes and Noble, 1980). So efficient were Genghis Kahn's techniques that they were carefully studied by German staff officers before World War II (Alfred Crofts and Percy Buchanan, *A History of the Far East* [New York: Longman Green, 1958], 39).

6. "Absolutism" is a term frequently used to describe the extent of government controls under Napoléon Bonaparte's rule as emperor of France (1804–15). For details of the economic and social regulations he instituted, see A. W. Ward, G. W. Prothero, and Stanley Leathes, eds., *The Cambridge Modern History*, vol. 9, *Napoléon* (New York: Macmillan, 1906), 141–42; Jerome Blum, Rondo Cameron, and Thomas G. Barnes, *The European World: A History*, 2d ed. (Boston: Little, Brown, 1970), 494–97, 503–4. Napoléon went so far as to regulate, for example, the numbers and types of theatrical companies each city and town was to be allowed (Ward, Prothero, and Leathes, *Cambridge Modern History*, vol. 9, 129–30).

7. See *New York Times*, April 4, 1981, p. 3; *New York Times*, April 29, p. 5; *New York Times*, June 14, 1984, p. 25; *New York Times*, July 1, 1981, p. 5.

8. His return by rail followed a period (beginning in 1943) of extensive indoctrination in the Soviet Union; see Han Wookeun, *The History of Korea*, trans. Lee Kyung-shik (Honolulu: East-West Center Press, 1970), 499.

9. See Han, *The History of Korea*, 500–504.

10. See Harold D. Nelson, ed., *Poland: A Country Study* (Washington: U.S. Government Printing Office, 1983), 290, 291; M. K. Dziewanowski, *Poland in the 20th Century* (New York: Columbia University Press, 1977), 233–36; Norman Davies, *Heart of Elrode: A Short History of Poland* (Oxford: Clarendon Press, 1984), passim; Hélène Carrére D'Encausse, *Confiscated Power: How Soviet Russia Really Works* (New York: Harper and Row, 1980), 343–46.

status would be that of one of the Indian rajas in the days of the British empire.[11] He has a good deal of power to deal with local matters as long as he doesn't do anything which offends his masters too much. Kim Il Sung, on the other hand, really has a good deal of genuine independence.[12]

In the former French empire, the French government has been keeping people in power, or putting them in power, for some time.[13] Nyerere himself was temporarily overthrown a number of years ago, but that was back in the days when the British maintained an aircraft carrier in the Indian Ocean, and a British expeditionary force with great promptness put him back in power. The whole thing was over within twenty-four hours.[14]

I've chosen to talk about this particular situation using only present-day examples, but anybody who is at all familiar with history knows that it is a fairly common phenomenon. Further, people appointed from outside quite frequently have genuine independence. They're usually appointed by the outside power rather than the outside power directly taking over the government, because there is some reason why the outside power does not want to take over the government. In the case of the Communist empire in Eastern Europe, of course, the Russians did want to control its empire, but thought that for political reasons there should be at least some kind of thin camouflage over that control.[15]

Nyerere, on the other hand, clearly does not himself want to run Uganda. He'd be delighted to have a government there which is strong enough so that it doesn't require any support from him. Of course he does not want an unfriendly government there, but basically he doesn't care very much what goes on inside Uganda and is quite willing to establish an independent power.[16] But one must be careful not to exaggerate here. Milton Obote, the present

11. On the British Raj in India, see Lawrence Henry Gipson, *The British Empire before the American Revolution*, vol. 5, *Zones of International Friction: The Great Lakes Frontier, Canada, the West Indies, India, 1748–1754* (New York: Knopf, 1942), 231ff.

12. See Han, *The History of Korea*, passim.

13. See James Dunnigan and Stephen Bay, *A Quick and Dirty Guide to War: Briefings on Present and Potential Wars* (New York: William Morrow, 1985), 130–38.

14. See Paul Johnson, *Modern Times: The World from the Twenties to the Eighties* (New York: Harper and Row, 1983), 528.

15. Ibid., 76–77, 710–11.

16. *New York Times*, August 26, 1981, p. 1, provides a summary of the last three successive Ugandan regimes that Nyerere has had a hand in installing.

dictator of Uganda, is the third one appointed by Nyerere, who became unhappy with his two previous choices.

More normally, the outside power which has established somebody as dictator has at least some idea as to what he should do, and may take action if he doesn't but will give the dictator a great deal of freedom. The Communist puppet rulers are decidedly an exception from the norm.

Note that the person who is brought in from outside to be a dictator is, in most cases, somebody who has risen to quite high rank inside the government to which he eventually becomes dictator and then has had difficulties which lead him to flee abroad. The old-fashioned international law principles of asylum under which political enemies of your neighbors were given protection within your borders started not out of humanitarian motives but precautionary ones. It was always helpful to have somebody within your borders who could get support within your neighbors' country in the event you had difficulty with them. The younger brother of the emir now ruling your neighbor was as much a part of your armament as a division of infantry.

A recent illustration of this concerns the Ayatollah Khomeini. He was expelled from Iran and promptly went to Iraq, which had very bad relations with Iran. He had been there a number of years in a position of respect and with a reasonable income until Iran and Iraq's relations improved. As part of his moves to improve relations with the Shah of Iran, Hussein, the dictator of Iraq, simply deported the Ayatollah. Khomeini has never forgiven him.[17]

All of this is typical and represents the traditional view of the asylum institution. It is not infrequent that an ambitious young man will rise to high rank in his own government, find it necessary to hastily go abroad, and later return to become dictator either directly, with the support of a foreign army, or by organizing a coup or revolution from his foreign refuge without much in the way of aid from the foreign country concerned.

To repeat, this route to power normally requires acquiring in one way or another a position of considerable prestige and general importance within the country before taking off for foreign climes. Further, if the individual is to be an effective dictator he must retain considerable influence within the country so that when he returns (whether he returns with a foreign army or

17. Iraqi president Ahmad Hasan al-Bakr expelled Khomeini from his country (to Paris) in early October, 1978 (R. F. Nyrop, ed., *Iraq: A Country Study [Area Handbook for Iraq]*, American University Area Handbook Series [Washington, D.C.: American University, 1979], 215).

at the head of a group of his own supporters) he will be able to set up a government of which he in fact is dictator. He must be both effective inside his own country's governmental machine and a good diplomat in dealing with foreigners. Fortunately, as a rough rule of thumb, the same set of personal attributes which will lead to success in one area will lead to success in the other, so this is not too difficult a task.

The person who has fled the country and is now engaging in intrigues to come back has a number of disadvantages because of his foreign location. He has at least one advantage: he can openly state his desire to overthrow the government and install himself as dictator.[18] An individual who stays within the country and attempts to rise to high rank does, in general, conceal his ultimate ambitions. Since coups far more commonly originate from officials within the government than from exiles abroad, it's obvious that this disadvantage, although real, is not overwhelming.

There is another way to the top which does not involve working one's way up through the bureaucracy, whether military or civil, but it's a very unusual one. We have not yet turned to the problem of succession to the dictator, but as a general proposition, rulers do not like to have anybody around them who is their official successor. The reason is that they quite reasonably regard such an official successor as a risk to themselves. In consequence, it is frequently true that there is no official "crown prince" in any given dictatorship.[19]

Death of a dictator under these circumstances provides an opportunity for many ambitious men, and it is by no means obvious that the one who wins will always be somebody who is a high official in the regime. The previous dictator may have been carefully weeding out all people who he thought were strongly aggressive from his higher officials, with the result that there's no one there who really is capable of holding his own against a strong outsider. Dr. Francia, of Paraguay, was in some ways the worst of a absolutely awful array of dictators that ruled South America in the early nineteenth century.[20] When Francia died, Lopez, a complete outsider, turned out to be in a better position to seize control than anyone else.[21] There have been occasional cases where somewhat the same thing has occurred while the dictator was still

18. It might be better for him to say that he proposes to overthrow a government and install a democracy; I doubt that very many people are deceived.

19. There are, of course, notable exceptions to this rule. See the *Washington Post*, June 27, 1985, p. 1, on the relevant transfer of power in North Korea.

20. See Dupuy and Dupuy, *Encyclopedia of Military History*, 814.

21. Ibid., 910–11.

alive. This is however, though possible, not a very common phenomenon. In any event, the outsider who comes in by this route has to engage in much the same kind of behavior as an insider would.

Another kind of government outsider is the leader of some nongovernmental but powerful group, most commonly, a tribe or possibly a subnation within a country. In this case his rise to power normally takes the form of actual fighting. This is on the whole uncommon historically, simply because the existing dictator, knowing that there are these risks, does his best to see to it that there's no one in that kind of position. I say it's uncommon, but that's not to say that it never exists. What I would call the romantic revolution, people rising up under wise and noble leaders to overthrow a corrupt dictatorship, would be a special example of this kind of thing, but it seems to be extremely rare historically.

We're thus left with the normal way in which somebody rises to a dictatorship in South America, Africa, and other places: a coup or attempted coup, which we observe in South America, Africa, and Asia with such regularity. Note that this coup normally is set off by fairly high members of the regime. Note, also, that it is more likely to turn out to be an attempted coup than a coup, if we look at the actual figures. There is another, even more common, phenomenon in which the dictator announces that there was a plot and punishes the "plotters" but in which there is at least some doubt that anything happened at all. Dictators are apt to be extremely suspicious men and may well misinterpret innocent activity for a plot. They also may feel that they want to get rid of certain of their officials and find that inventing a false plot is a good way of doing it. Certainly most of the high officials killed by Stalin were not plotting against him, and the Doctors' plot,[22] which he apparently was in train of setting off when he died, was also imaginary.[23] Since he was paranoid, it's possible he believed in the plots, but it's certainly equally possible that he simply regarded them as a convenient tool for suppressing suspicious activity.

Having risen to a high position, one might simply aim at succession to the existing dictator when he dies or, as occasionally happens, retires.[24] Sadat, of

22. See Nikolai Tolstoy, *Stalin's Secret War* (New York: Holt, Rinehart and Winston, 1981), 354.

23. Ibid., 51–57, provides an account of the extreme precautions Stalin took to avoid attempts on his life.

24. Sometimes when the leader retires he will be apt to set up a democratic government rather than a dictatorial one. This will be dealt with below. President Omar Torrijos Herrera

Egypt, is an example,[25] as is Joaquín Balaguer, president of the Dominican Republic after Trujillo.[26]

It is notable that these two people, and, as far as I know, the other cases where the same kind of thing has happened, were in the position of official followers of the existing dictator[27] because they were thought to be harmless. They had risen to high rank as "yes men" in the case of Sadat and Joaquín Balaguer. Moi, as a member of a minor tribe, was thought not to have an adequate political position.[28]

As it turned out, all three of these people were actually strong personalities. When the dictator was gone, they turned out to be rather competent and strong people. In the case of Balaguer, this is particularly remarkable, because after the death of Trujillo, he ruled as a democratic leader, with the elections in which he was elected subject to very extensive foreign observation. His previous record certainly would not have led most observers to expect this. He had been so completely devoted to Trujillo that when Trujillo decided to spend two years as a Dominican Republic ambassador to the United Nations, he appointed Joaquín Balaguer president of the Dominican Republic.[29] This took a great deal of apparently justified faith on the part of Trujillo that Joaquín Balaguer was completely under his control.

---

of Panama, for example, retired as head of government in October, 1978, and was immediately replaced by President Arístides Royo (R. F. Nyrop, ed., *Panama: A Country Study [Area Handbook for Panama]*, American University Area Handbook Series [Washington, D.C.: American University, 1980], 136). Despite his official retirement, however, Torrijos retained a large share of supreme power in his country until 1980 (133).

25. Upon his death by heart attack on September 28, 1970, Egyptian president General Gamal Abdel Nasser was smoothly followed by his successor, then vice president Sadat. Sadat was installed as president the following day. See David Hirst and Irene Beeson, *Sadat* (London: Faber and Faber, 1981).

26. Rafael Trujillo resigned as president of the Dominican Republic on April 1, 1962, and was succeeded by his handpicked vice president, Dr. Joaquín Balaguer in August of that year (Robert D. Crassweller, *Trujillo: The Life and Times of a Caribbean Dictator* [New York: Macmillan, 1966], 273, 375–77). Trujillo assumed the presidency of another institution, the Central Bank, during his reign. By no mere coincidence were outstanding loans of $38 million borrowed by Trujillo's sugar company suddenly "repaid" at about the same time (380).

27. Also Moi of Kenya.

28. See Crassweller, *Trujillo*, 375.

29. Ibid., 377.

This route to power is certainly one which could be successfully followed by only very few people. Historically it is not particularly common. Sadat, Balaguer, and Moi are exceptions. Normally, when a dictator dies, there's no official successor, and we have an undignified squabble for power. Once again, the problem of succession and ways of avoiding this squabble will be discussed below.

Normally, an existing dictator is overthrown in a coup or civil war. The people who overthrow him are high, although not necessarily the highest, officials of his own government. In most cases the dictator does not last a very long time—five years would probably be par for the course—although there are individuals who last twenty or thirty years. Sometimes they go on and set up a dynasty. In the more normal case, however, most of the high officials were also at least medium-high officials in the government of the current dictator's predecessor and rose to their high rank as a result of the overthrow of the predecessor. Thus everybody, the dictator and all of his officials, are fully aware of the possibility of such a coup.

We will not here discuss the early period of the rise to prominence of somebody who starts in the government apparatus at the bottom. I've written a previous book[30] on rising in the bureaucracy, and so I will assume that the reader can turn to that one, or for that matter, to any one of the large number of books on this general topic, if he is curious. Rising in a dictatorship where the dictator is periodically removed by somebody else is, of course, somewhat different than rising in a more peaceful bureaucracy. The principles, however, are the same. I will not trouble the reader here with repetition. It's only when the bureaucrat gets to a fairly high rank that the special problems of coup and potential coup begin to impinge on his career prospects.

A high-ranking official in South America, Africa, or Asia can feel fairly confident that during his career there will be one or, perhaps, many cases of attempted coup, successful coup, and those cases where the dictator decides to denounce a plot even if there is no actual plot there. Further, he can feel fairly confident that the existing dictator will, in any event, be sufficiently nervous about his inferiors so that he shifts them around a good deal.

Under the circumstances, he has to develop a sort of general policy with respect to such coups, and this policy, of necessity, must contain a fairly large component of opportunism. That he should not join a coup which seems

30. Gordon Tullock, *The Politics of Bureaucracy* (Washington, D.C.: Public Affairs Press, 1965).

foreordained to failure, but should join one that is certain to win, is obvious. The problem with this rule, however, is that he is unlikely to be particularly rewarded for joining after it becomes clear who is going to win. The high payoffs are for the people who enter into a coup in the early days, before it's obvious who will win, or who loyally support the dictator against a coup when it is not at all obvious that the coup will lose. Thus, both careful calculation and a willingness to take major gambles are necessary for the successful official at this rank.

Once again, the life is a luxurious one, although, of course, not as luxurious as the dictator's life, and a risky one. There's no reason for us to feel sorry for these high-ranking officials in such dangerous positions, because after all, they've chosen their own career paths. Nevertheless, it's easy to see why in most of these dictatorships there are a fairly large number of highly talented men who strenuously avoid all political activity. The businessman who finds it necessary to regularly pay large bribes to government officials may rather resent paying the bribes. He is probably aware, however, that the government officials to whom he pays the bribes sometimes change abruptly. He is normally not personally interested in joining in this highly paid lottery.

There is another problem with respect to the coup: even if the coup is successful, it's by no means obvious at the time that it is organized and carried off, who will end up at the top. Prime Minister Benyoussef Ben Khedda was the man who basically ran the revolution against the French in Algeria. He also signed the final treaty with them. He almost immediately lost power and eventually died in an Algerian prison. Many people who have been involved in the kind of high politics that involves a coup have had similar histories.

Note that there's no safe way out of this problem. There's no conservative way of simply holding your position without joining in the squabble on either one side or the other. Even though you may have been neutral and hence made no enemies, whoever wins will want to reward his faithful followers. Thus, you may be removed, not because anybody particularly dislikes you, but because somebody else wants to be secretary of the treasury.[31]

31. This is, of course, characteristic also of democratic politics. He who follows the policy of neutrality in a presidential election is unlikely to retain his job. Secretary Forrestal, of course, was a very prominent example. On the career of James V. Forrestal, Secretary of Defense (1947–49), see, for example, Robert C. Batchelder, *The Irreversible Decision, 1939–1950* (New York: Macmillan, 1961), 197ff.

As a rough rule of thumb, anyone who rises to really high rank must be planning on following a rather opportunistic course of action. This may in fact be one reason for refusing promotion. I was told by a member of the British Intelligence Service that in Russia under Stalin you normally found that the brightest and most competent man in any given factory was not the manager, but the deputy. He normally had refused several opportunities to acquire the much larger prestige and income of a manager because it also involved a much larger chance of going to Vorkuta.

But we are interested in the people who actually do make it to the top, and that necessarily means we must be interested in only people who do try. Of course, many of the people who try don't make it, and the man entering into this particularly risky way of making a living must be aware of the fact that the odds are against him.

The problem is, of course, particularly difficult because everyone will be watching him with the intent of guarding against him. The dictator is worried about cliques and powerful men immediately under him. The people immediately under the dictator are looking for allies but not for superiors. In other words, they hope to rise in the world by a coup and, on the whole, would like to become the new dictator themselves. They look for supporters and, in general, do not look for a position as a supporter of someone else. There is, of course, an exception to the latter category among people who feel that at the moment, in any event, they have no chance to be dictator. Hence, for them, simply a promotion, either through helping install a new dictator or eliminating a plot so that a number of their superiors are removed by an existing dictator, is a sensible course of action.

One thing that is frequently discussed in this area, and which I believe is almost never found in reality, is a carefully laid plot. The trouble with a carefully laid plot is that too many people have to know about it. Even discussing a coup with one or two persons is dangerous. On the whole, the high-ranking politician must try to get into a position where he can quickly assume a position of control or, at the very least, take a position on one side or another of a coup without first constructing an apparatus which could betray him.

There is an exception to the above rule in those cases in which coup and attempted coup are perfectly ordinary parts of life, as, for example, in South America. It seems likely that most South American armies are so accustomed to coup that the potential of overthrowing the government or supporting it would be a rather ordinary topic of conversation in the officers' mess. Although this is true enough, the very highest military officers had better not engage in this kind of conversation. It's not possible for the dictator to get rid of the bulk of the junior officer corp, but he can always make his chief of staff the ambassador to Australia.

What the ambitious man should attempt to do is to convince all of the other high-ranking officials that he is a very competent man. Competence in this case does not mean necessarily that they would regard him as a good lawyer, even though his present position may be a legal one. It means that they think of him as a man who is good at intrigue, tough, aggressive, and likely to win.

At the time that he is attempting to develop this reputation among his co–high officials, he should be trying to convince the dictator that he is really not a significant menace. This looks impossible, and certainly it is very hard. Nevertheless, to the dictator, the ambitious man only has to look like a man of average safety, and to the other high officials—all of whom have been selected by the dictator for having only this rather limited amount of ability—more likely to win than anyone else.

If possible, the individual should develop relations with others such that they are apt to, on the whole, accept his leadership. Once again, this is a dangerous matter, because it may tend to frighten the dictator. Trying to convince the dictator that you are a complete "yes man," and the other officials of the dictator, that you're a tough man who is likely to win in a fight is an extremely difficult task.

Let it be said here that success may be dangerous. The number of generals who have been removed from office and possibly killed because they have been conspicuously successful, and hence threaten the dictator and king, is very large indeed. This is the reason that traditional kings always led their own armies. They might not be very good generals, but at least they can trust themselves. The switch to using professional generals, first in France and then in the rest of Europe, was one of the harbingers of the restriction of royal power. Hitler, Stalin, and Mao Tse-tung all commanded their own armies.[32]

32. In the case of Mao Tse-tung, this was rather concealed. In China, the position of a general is not one of great prestige, so he always maintained an opium-sodden senile wreck of a professional general called Chu Teh as the formal commander of the army. He, himself, was chairman of the committee that dealt with the army. No one in the army, however, was deceived by the arrangement. Possibly some intellectuals outside were. When Chu Teh assumed the post of Commander of the People's Liberation Army in 1969, he was eighty-four. On Mao's effective control of the army, see Jurgen Domes, *The Government and Politics of the People's Liberation Army* (Boulder: Westview Press, 1985), 113.

We earlier talked about the desirability of rotation and collective responsibility on the part of dictators who are attempting to keep the possibility of a coup or revolution down. Looked at from the standpoint of the man trying to rise, these are clearly elements which impede his rise. It should be kept in mind, however, that they also impede the rise of anyone else. He is competing with the existing dictator for power, but he is also competing with other higher officials for the succession. The measures taken by the dictator, which make it harder for him to overthrow the dictator, handicap the others just as much as him. He suffers no differential disadvantage.

But if he cannot engage in plotting, and if building up a personal train is difficult, what are the things he can do? Clearly, he must convince other people that he would be a suitable replacement without frightening the dictator. Since everyone whom he must convince knows the danger of frightening the dictator, they are apt to calculate correctly that a man who appears to be a total "yes man" may in fact be very strong and independent.

The final act in any plot to overthrow the dictator is a coup, or what is in South America called a "pronunciamiento." It is simply a statement, apparently backed by great force, that the dictator is to be relieved of his power because he is corrupt and, above all, weaker than the man or group making the statement. The pronunciamiento is, almost of necessity, sudden and not very well prepared, because preparations will almost certainly come to the attention of the dictator.

This last is not absolutely certain. There appear to be some dictators who come to the conclusion that they simply cannot win and, hence, don't remove the dangers to themselves. Caetano, in his memoirs, says he read Spinola's book, spending an entire night doing so, and in the early morning, when he put the book down, realized that his dictatorship was going to fall. Why he did not take steps immediately to neutralize Spinola, and in fact made him chief of staff, is obscure. It may be simply that he, himself, was a rather weak man. He had, of course, acquired the throne when Salazar became incapable.[33]

33. Professor Marcelo Caetano took over as the new prime minister of Portugal on September 25, 1968, after Salazar suffered a stroke (September 6) and could no longer perform the duties of that office. See Hugh Kay, *Salazar and Modern Portugal* (New York: Hawthorn Books, 1970), 413–16; A. H. de Olivera Marques, *History of Portugal* (New York: Columbia University Press, 1972), 223–24. Salazar's condition and the subsequent change in power were brought on by a freak accident: a chair collapsed under him, and his head hit the ground, producing a blood clot in his brain (Marques, *History of Protugal*, 224).

But this is very unusual. Normally a dictator would have simply removed Spinola on realizing that he was a danger.

A pronunciamiento is, of course, dangerous. Normally, it requires seizing control of at least some part of the communication network and using this for the statement. Anything can go wrong at this time. The second earl of Essex failed to a considerable extent because the horses didn't arrive on time.[34] The generals' plot against Hitler in 1944 terminated when a lieutenant colonel refused to believe orders from his superiors and made contact with Dr. Goebbels, with the result that the appropriate orders were not transmitted.[35]

More commonly, however, the pronunciamiento is at least made public, and there is an immediate counter-pronunciamiento by the dictator. If the dictator himself can be seized, which is sometimes possible, either through the connivance of his guard or the overwhelming of the guard by other military units, this will normally finish the matter off, although there may be a counter-coup by people who at least appear to be in support of the dictator, but who probably are more accurately described as enemies of the first group who want to have another man as dictator.

In all of this, the odds are on the side of the dictator himself, simply because the communication procedures are always better on his side. In other words, it's easier for him to give the impression that he will win than it is for his opponents to give the impression that they will win. To say that the odds are rather on his side does not, of course, mean that he will always win, and indeed he doesn't.

Sometimes all of this goes wrong, but not wrong in the sense that the coup is simply put down; wrong in the sense that the coup succeeds in getting control of significant military forces, but not enough to take over the country as a whole immediately. The result can then be a long-lasting civil war. This is the way the Spanish civil war of the 1930s started,[36] and there have been a great

34. On Robert Devereux, second earl of Essex, his failed attempt at a coup to install himself as king (February 8, 1601), and subsequent execution by Queen Elizabeth I, see Blum, Cameron, and Barnes, *European World*, 171; or William H. Harris and Judith S. Levey, eds., *The New Columbia Encyclopedia* (New York: Columbia University Press, 1975), 893.

35. It's also sometimes said that the fact that General Beck turned up for the coup wearing civilian clothes rather than a uniform was of some significance. In any event, of course, the fact that Hitler had not actually been killed would probably have scuppered it even if these other difficulties had not occurred. See Constantine FitzGibbon, *20 July* (New York: Berkley, 1956), 90.

36. See Johnson, *Modern Times*, 321ff.

many South American civil wars fought along these lines. The English civil war of the seventeenth century was another example: the king left London, raised his standard in rebellion, and attracted enough military support to hold much of the country but not all, and therefore, too, there was a full-dress war.[37] As can be seen, the problems from the standpoint of the man who wants to rise are very difficult. Further, so far, in any event, I have been unable to find any good generalizations or testable hypotheses about the matter. Economists know the so-called random walk hypothesis regarding the stock market, which holds that all available information is already incorporated in the market price, with the result that that price or its recent movements have no predictive value. Something vaguely like it is important in the situation we have been describing. The dictator probably knows as much as anybody else does about his immediate inferiors. Thus, if one of them appears to be in a position where he might be able to overthrow the dictator, this probably indicates that the dictator is about to get rid of him. Outside predictions of the future such as this are extremely difficult. The main point of my discussion above is to point out that predictions from the standpoint of an insider are at least as difficult. Further, if he wants not only to predict, but to take steps to improve his position, it is even more difficult.

As we have said above, life at these elevated ranks is risky business, but the compensation is apparently high enough so that many people are willing to take the risk. Looking at it not as competitors for power, but as outside analysts, however, we can rarely if ever hope to know either what is going to happen or even, in any certain way, what in fact did happen. Retrospective accounts of this kind of intrigue by different participants normally differ a good deal. It is likely that this comes not from any desire on the part of the various memorialists to lie about the matter, but from the fact that they themselves didn't quite know what was going on. The situation is one where everyone is engaging in devious maneuvers and attempting to conceal at least part of his maneuvering from everyone else, with the result that the true story is seldom known.

37. Actually two full-dress wars; there was an intermediate period of peace. On the other hand, the restoration of the Stuarts after the death of Oliver Cromwell was a more classical and quick affair, with substantially no military opposition. See Norman F. Cantor, *The English: A History of Politics and Society to 1760* (New York: Simon and Schuster, 1967), 412–33; G. M. Trevelyan, *History of England*, vol. 2, *The Tudors and the Stuart Era* (Garden City: Doubleday, 1953), 184–98.

We've talked about this vague area where technical hypotheses are impossible. I would like to now turn to one specific detail of the process where I believe I can make a prediction as to what will happen with quite a high degree of accuracy. Sometimes the result of the overthrow of a ruler or, for that matter, his death, will not be his immediate replacement by another dictator, but by a small group of people called, in South America, a "junta." The hypothesis which I think would survive most tests is that this junta will gradually change into a dictatorship by one person, normally a member of the original junta, although occasionally the process of change will involve the introduction of outsiders to the original junta in replacement of various members who are leaving, and one of those will win.

The historical evidence that this is what does happen in South America is overwhelming. Indeed, so far as I know, only the recent Argentine military government avoided this fate. In that case, the junta remained a junta throughout the entire period, with the result that strictly speaking one cannot call it a dictatorship. There was usually one member of the junta who was more important than the others, but no one ever really acquired complete control, and indeed, members of the junta retired in a rather routine way from time to time and were then replaced by other high-ranking military officers.[38] This is an extremely unusual event, and I know of no other case. A more common procedure is the shrinkage of the junta to one man.

The same thing, by the way, will be found in Communist countries. After the death of Lenin, there was a period in which the politburo of the party actually was powerful and was only gradually replaced by Stalin.[39] After Stalin's death there was a small group: first three and then five members ruled collectively while Khrushchev was maneuvering into absolute power.[40] When Khrushchev himself was overthrown, there was once again a collective leadership, although not for very long, since Brezhnev, in this case, was able to establish complete power very quickly.[41]

38. See John Paxton, *The Statesman's Yearbook: 1983–1984* (New York: St. Martin's, 1983), 90.

39. See Sheila Fitzpatrick, *The Russian Revolution* (New York: Berkley, 1982), 98–102.

40. On the development of the collective leadership between Stalin's death in March, 1953, and Khrushchev's assumption of effective control in early 1955, see Basil Dmytryshyn, *U.S.S.R.: A Concise History* (New York: Scribner's, 1984), 265–73.

41. Although about a year and a half separated the coup against Khrushchev in October, 1964, and Brezhnev's appointment as General Secretary of the Communist Party in March–April, 1966, the latter had assumed an increasingly dominant position in the collective

It's hard to say what has been happening since the death of Brezhnev, since Andropov and Chernenko died so quickly. Gorbachev has not yet ruled for very long.[42] One would suspect, however, that with time this custom will become one in which the period of collective leadership is extremely short indeed. This is simply because all of the members of the collective leadership will have noticed previous cases in which it became a single-person dictatorship and, hence, will anticipate that and take steps to either become the dictator or become the supporter of the dictator right away.

Among Communist states the phenomenon is not confined to Russia, of course. The same thing happened in China after the death of Mao.[43] Other Communist countries are mainly not genuinely independent, and who is dictator is presumably decided in Moscow. Provincial governor might be a better term than dictator. Albania and North Korea, which are rather independent, have not yet had a death of the ruling dictator,[44] and I regret to say that I simply don't know very much about the history of Yugoslavia since Tito died. Developments there are extremely complicated and don't seem to follow any particular fixed pattern.[45]

Empirically, the junta characteristically shrinks to one man, but how can we explain this theoretically? The following theory I actually developed on my own before looking into much of the empirical literature, although I must admit I knew that the juntas became dictatorships quite commonly in South America. In a way, it is thus halfway between an ad hoc explanation of previously known data and a hypothesis which I tested by looking up more South American history.

---

leadership, beginning within a month of Khrushchev's ouster, and shortly thereafter he was, for all intents and purposes, the sole leader. See Dmytryshyn, *U.S.S.R.*, 334–36.

42. Andropov died in February, 1984, after a fifteen-month rule. See the *Washington Post*, July 28, 1985, p. 1, for details on the recent regimes of Andropov and Chernenko.

43. What was essentially a collective leadership arose after Mao's death in 1976, in which Hua Kuo-feng emerged as "first among equals" as the chairman of the Chinese Communist Party. But by late 1980 another member of this collective leadership, Teng Hsiao-ping, assumed effective control after defeating Hua in a bloodless power struggle. Interestingly, Teng refrained from naming himself chairman. See Domes, *Government and Politics*, 116–76.

44. Albania's dictator, Enver Hoxha, did recently expire, and he handpicked (before death, of course) his successor, Ramiz Alia. See *Washington Post*, August 8, 1985, p. A27.

45. Since Tito's death, Yugoslavia has remained nominally without an acknowledged individual ruler, with the politburo ostensibly forming a collective leadership. On the decisions leading to this post-Tito organization, see Stankovic, 1981, 104–10.

The theory is really quite simple. Suppose we have a group of five men who are currently ruling a country by some voting process. Each of them presumably would prefer to be dictator. Suppose that one[46] decides to take action to make himself dictator. Either he succeeds, in which event the junta has been condensed to one man, or he fails. If he fails, the remainder of the junta have their choice of removing him from the junta[47] or leaving him in. If they leave him in, they're obviously simply asking for further plots of the same sort, either by him or by other members of the junta who notice that there's no cost to such plotting. If they remove him, on the other hand, they have shrunk the junta by one man.

This means each of the others is now stronger, but it also means each of the others now feels he has a better chance of succeeding in becoming a sole dictator. It is true that they could remove the plotter and bring somebody else in from outside—and occasionally that has been done—but this involves a failure on the part of the majority of the junta to take advantage of an opportunity to improve their power. To bring somebody in from outside, who is intended to be formally a member of the junta but who is actually inferior to the existing members, is a possibility. Historically, however, such outside members have on occasion turned out to be strong enough so that they are genuine risks to their sponsors. It can be seen that this process would tend, over time, to lead the junta to become just one man through the gradual exclusion of individuals who had failed in plotting, or the success of an individual who had not.

There is another possible route to the same conclusion. Suppose again a junta of five, and suppose that three of them form a caucus. A caucus, of course, has to first make up its own mind as to what should be done, and in essence, if the group is still voting, it will itself become the dominant group. In other words, the real junta has shrunk from five to three. Within these three, there are apt to be two who tend to vote with each other more often than each with the third, and that involves a still further reduction in size. All of this, once again, makes it more likely that some individual will take over either as a result of the gradual shrinkage of the effective ruling group within the junta or through taking advantage of the strong position to remove the remainder of the junta.

Altogether, a small voting body in control of the government does not seem a stable situation. Note that it is different from a committee within a

46. Possibly two.

47. Perhaps by that most permanent of methods, a firing squad.

legal structure. The board of directors of a corporation which appoints an executive committee does not jeopardize its own potential control, since the courts would enforce any decision of the majority of the board against that committee. Within a group ruling an absolute government, however, there is no external court to enforce such a rule. Thus, small groups tend to reduce to one.

Earlier I defined democracy in a situation where quite a large number make decisions by voting. I didn't give any absolute number, but discussion of the condensation of the junta will explain what I had in mind. A group of five or six hundred people voting can readily afford to throw out some subset which attempts to overthrow the voting body. This would be true even if that subset were quite large. Thus, historically, such large voting groups have tended to be relatively stable, whereas the small ruling group, the junta, has tended to rather rapidly turn into a dictatorship.

In this chapter we complete our discussion of the internal functioning of a dictatorship. I wish that I had been able to provide a more rigorously testable theory, but what you have now read is what I have. To repeat what I've said before, I hope that this will inspire other people to do the research which eventually will produce a rigorous theory of dictatorship.

Regardless of that point, there are a number of aspects of a dictatorship's dealings with society which we have not yet dealt with. In a way, we have been talking about the micropolitics of the dictatorship and will now turn to the macropolitics.

THE PROBLEM OF SUCCESSION

So far we have dealt with dictators who are insecure with people who are trying to replace them. Dictators do grow old, however, and their replacement, upon death or, rarely, upon retirement, is a real problem. As we shall see below, the long-run solution to this problem is usually the development of a hereditary ruler whom we call "king" or "emperor" rather than "dictator." Before turning to this problem, however, we should examine the more general situation in which a tradition of passing the throne through one line is not yet established.

Consider then a dictator who is getting elderly and realizes that he is not long for this world. We shall begin by assuming that he is not proposing to retire, although he may wish to lighten his work load to some extent by shoving some of his responsibilities onto someone else. We also assume that he is, in fact, concerned about the status of his country after he dies. Note that this concern doesn't have to be very strong. Most of us are, to some extent, interested in the public good, but more interested in ourselves. The dictator, presumably, normally hopes that his country will continue running well after he is dead, but he is likely to give this hope and the actions it requires less priority than the actions required to avoid assassination.

The basic problem that the dictator faces here is that if he formally anoints a successor, he gives that successor both strong motives for assassinating him and reasonable security that he will get away with it. Obviously the sooner the successor becomes dictator in his own right, the better—from his standpoint—and shortening the life of the current dictator is an obvious way of speeding up the succession. Secondly, and this I believe is more important, there is always the possibility that the current dictator will change his mind. A man who has spent the bulk of his life in one of these dictatorial polities and who has observed the dictator continuously engaging in the type of protective activity we have discussed above, would feel relatively little security in his position as an official successor. He may remember the time when he had been minister of war and suddenly found himself ambassador to France. A similar sharp change, with somebody else becoming official successor, is surely something which he thinks is reasonably likely.

Thus he has a strong motive to get rid of the current dictator. Assassination is the short way. It may be possible to arrange exile or even a forced retirement. But, in any event, the anointed successor now has strong motives to get rid of the man whom he will succeed. Let it be said here that the successor is not the only person who has these motives. If the other courtiers around the dictator are convinced that this particular man in fact will be the successor, then they begin planning their own maneuvers, on the theory that they will spend much more of their lives under the rule of the successor than under the rule of the current dictator.

The position of the current dictator, in essence, goes down, and that of the potential successor rises, and any sign of bad health or weakness on the part of the dictator is likely to make this even stronger. The brother of the current dictator of Syria was in a quite strong position, although he had not officially been anointed as successor. The dictator then had a heart attack and spent a considerable period of time under medical attention. His brother apparently thought that this indicated that he would shortly be in power, and it seems likely that many other people thought the same thing and took measures to ensure his succession. The dictator then recovered, and the brother was exiled to Switzerland.[1] He was lucky; a more common procedure, particularly in Syria, would have been to kill him.[2]

So much for the motives. I earlier said that the successor is safe in carrying out the assassination. The basic reason for this is simply that he will be in charge of the investigation. He will be in a position to maintain that the dictator either died naturally, was killed by somebody else, or was killed by his successor under circumstances where that is justifiable. As a general rule, no one will say him nay.

1. By his actions at the time of his illness, President Hafiz al-Assad himself seemed uncertain about the desirability of appointing his brother (one of six) Rifaat as his temporary successor (*New York Times*, May 17, 1984, I27 : 1). Rifaat, a powerful figure in his own right, was later exiled to Switzerland (*New York Times*, July 17, 1984, I4 : 1; October 31, 1984, I6 : 3; and November 27, 1984, I8 : 4).

2. For Syrian law on assassination attempts, see, for example, A. R. Kelidar, "Government and Ideology," in *The Syrian Arab Republic: A Handbook*, ed. Anne Sinai and Allen Pollack (New York: American Academic Association for Peace in the Middle East, 1976), 47; R. F. Nyrop, ed., *Syria: A Country Study (Area Handbook for Syria)*, American University Area Handbook Series (Washington, D.C.: American University, 1979), 222.

This fact is the reason that one can rarely be sure that kings who are succeeded by one of their children have in fact died of natural causes. In my opinion, Louis XIV simply died, as an elderly man very commonly will, with collected diseases of old age. If Louis XV, actually a great grandchild, or one of the courtiers who hoped to benefit from Louis XV, had poisoned him, however, we would never know.

Actually if you look over history, the number of times that a king is known to have been killed by his eldest son is by no means trivial. I frequently say that this is the commonest cause of death of kings.[3] I haven't actually counted up the cases. If we could add those cases in which the king is killed by his son or by one of his confederates, but where the son then covers up the assassination, we might get a much larger number.

Note that the designated successor is not the only risk here. Once the courtiers begin shifting their loyalty from the king to his successor, there inevitably will be some of them who feel they will be better off under the successor than under the current ruler. They do not have the protection from being punished from an assassination that the successor himself will have, but, nevertheless, it is unlikely that the successor will track down with great vigor any rumor or report that his predecessor was, in fact, killed instead of having a heart attack. Even if he does know about the matter, he may decide not to proceed further, because, after all, he has gained a great deal by the killing.

It isn't even necessary for courtiers to do anything directly. Those members of the entourage of the dictator who are responsible for his personal security may simply become a little careless. It should be said that this technique might not pay off, since if outsiders succeed in assassinating one dictator, it is, on the whole, unlikely that the captain of his guard will become the captain of the guard of his successor. The captain of the guard is unlikely to be punished, and he might well expect that the new dictator would be grateful and would eventually give him some job of importance that did not give him the opportunity to be careless with the new dictator's security.

Looked at from the standpoint of the dictator then, it's dangerous to have an official successor. Even if we look in democratic politics, we observe this kind of thing. In the United States it is required that a president have a vice president. If the president dies and the vice president succeeds, then various procedures (they have changed from time to time over the history) provide

3. At least of those kings for which there is a regularly established succession, with the eldest son succeeding. There will be more on this below.

automatically for a further succession. It's notable that as a general rule, relations between the president and his vice president have been poor. This is not, I think, because the president suspects the vice president of trying to assassinate him, but because both the president and the vice president are aware of the fact that the vice president will gain a great deal if the president dies. This is not the foundation for a firm friendship.

As a result of this, in other democratic countries usually either there is no official successor at all or there are efforts made to keep the official successor in a relatively subordinate position. Before Nixon, the vice presidency was normally thought of as a job which was given, in essence, to an unsuccessful politician. In the musical *Of Thee I Sing*,[4] the vice presidential candidate is a figure of fun. At one point, he says he doesn't want to be vice president because he thinks his mother will object, and he is assured by the professional politican to whom he is talking[5] that she will never find out. Keeping the vice president in a position of subordination, as I say, has been the tradition.

In the case of the United States, this changed with Nixon, and since then vice presidents have had a fairly good chance of being permitted to run for the presidency on their party's ticket after the president in office completes two terms. It is possible that this change simply reflects the constitutional amendment which made it impossible for a president to have more than two terms.[6]

Another possibility is simply Mr. Nixon's ability to convert a dead-end job into an important job. Certainly his relations with Eisenhower were never very close nor were those of Nixon himself with Agnew.[7] In both cases, there

4. Written by George Gershwin in 1931. See Charles Schwartz, *Gershwin: His Life and Music* (New York: Da Capo Press, 1979), 212ff; Gilbert Chase, *America's Music* (New York: McGraw-Hill, 1955), 628–29.

5. Who has previously mistaken him for a waiter.

6. The two-term presidency limitation appears in section 1 of the Twenty-second Amendment to the Constitution and was adopted in 1951. See Henry J. Abraham, *The Judiciary: The Supreme Court in the Governmental Process*, 5th ed. (Boston: Allyn and Bacon, 1980), 237–38, for a text of the amendment.

7. The Nixon-Eisenhower relationship was not improved by Eisenhower's refusal to designate Nixon publicly as his preferred running mate in the 1952 and 1956 presidential elections (Arthur Larson, *Eisenhower, the President Nobody Knew* [New York: Scribner's, 1968], 8). See also Dan Rather and Gary Paul Gates, *The Palace Guard* (New York: Harper and Row, 1974), passim, but particularly 74–75, on Nixon and Eisenhower. On Nixon's relationship to Agnew, see Rowland Evans Jr. and Robert D. Novak, *Nixon in the White House: The Frustration of Power* (New York: Random House, 1971), 312–13, 402; Rather and Gates, *The Palace Guard*, 128, 255, 281.

was an effort by the president in office to get his vice president to drop out of the election for the second term. In both cases, this took the form of offering him a high cabinet post, and in both cases, when that was turned down, the president decided that the political cost of forcing the man out was greater than the benefit.[8] Johnson, of course, kept Humphrey in a position of extreme subordination, but then that was his habit with all of his inferiors.[9]

In some parts of the world we observe the same kind of thing. President Rhee of Korea is frequently referred to as a dictator, but I think this is too simple. He did run elections in which, on the whole, the votes were honestly calculated, he did have a reasonably free press, and the legislature normally was dominated by his political opponents.[10] It is notable, however, that when I was in Korea he had as his vice president[11] the only prominent politician in Korea who was older and more dilapidated than Rhee himself. The only time I ever saw the vice president, he had his hat on backwards.

Eventually, of course, President Rhee, becoming very old, did decide on a successor. Yi Ki-Pung appears to have been fairly loyal and, in fact, killed his family and committed suicide when President Rhee was overthrown.[12] It is notable that in the other form of government, parliamentary democracy, where the prime minister is not compelled to have an official successor, no prime minister has chosen to arrange one. There is no official successor to

8. Fred I. Greenstein, *The Hidden-Hand Presidency: Eisenhower as Leader* (New York: Basic Books, 1982), 234, discusses the (reconsidered) attempt by Eisenhower to eliminate Nixon from the presidential race; on the similar case of Nixon and Agnew, see, for example, Rather and Gates, 281.

9. See Vaughn Davis Bornet, *The Presidency of Lyndon B. Johnson* (Lawrence: University Press of Kansas, 1983), 320–21; Robert A. Caro, *The Years of Lyndon Johnson: The Path to Power* (New York: Knopf, 1982), 230, 234.

10. The use of free elections and the extent of opposition-party power during Rhee's presidency in South Korea (1919–60) are noted in Nena Vreeland et al., *Area Handbook for South Korea*, 2d ed., American University Area Series (Washington, D.C.: American University, 1975), 28; Richard C. Allen, *Korea's Syngman Rhee* (Rutland, Vt.: Charles E. Tuttle, 1960), 101ff, 205ff.

11. The constitution had been copied after that of the United States, where Rhee spent such a large part of his exile. Rhee's vice president was Lee Si-yong. For a history of the modeling of the Korean constitution along the lines of the Constitution of the United States, see Vreeland et al., *Handbook for South Korea*, 143–49; Allen, *Korea's Syngman Rhee*, 218.

12. The president, who had no children, had formally adopted Yi's son. Rhee's immediate successor was Yun Boseon. His reign lasted only nine months and was cut short by General Park Chung Hee. See Vreeland, *Handbook for South Korea*, 28ff.

Mrs. Thatcher of Great Britain, Kohl of Germany, or whoever at the moment happens to be prime minister of Italy, for example. Once again, the danger here would not be that the successor might assassinate the prime minister but that his appointment would change the structure of power so that the successor would be in a position where his replacement of the prime minister would be a real possibility. Most politicans in this circumstance have chosen not to take the risk.

This, by the way, is also true of most dictatorships. Appointing a formal successor is rare. Further, it normally occurs only very late in the life of the existing dictator. Even then, dictators frequently change their successors. It is notable that Hitler, when he decided to make a noble gesture at the outbreak of the war and appoint the persons who would replace him if he were killed, chose Hess, who had substantially no chance of developing enough support within the machine so that he could replace Hitler.[13] Mussolini and

13. In September, 1939, Hitler appointed Hermann Göring his first successor; Rudolf Hess, his second in line (Alan Bullock, *Hitler: A Study in Tyranny*, rev. ed. [New York: Harper and Row, 1964], 547–48). A few years later, however, before his death in April, 1945, Hitler asked Admiral Karl Dönitz to succeed him in order to show "his disillusion with his generals" (T. L. Jarman, *The Rise and Fall of Nazi Germany* [New York: Signet, 1961], 304). (Hess had defected to Scotland in May, 1941. See Bullock, *Hitler*, 643.) With Dönitz designated President and Supreme Commander, the chancellorship went to Joseph Goebbels, and the position of Party Minister to Martin Bormann (Jarman, *Rise and Fall*, 304; Bullock, *Hitler*, 795ff).

A "weakest-successor" rule has apparently emerged (in a somewhat modified form) in the Soviet Union: "[I]n the struggle for power inside the Central Committee [over] the post of Secretary-General . . . the contestant with the best chance is neither the strongest nor the ablest. The prize usually goes to the least able and most harmless-seeming member of the politburo" (Michael Voslenskii, *Nomenklatura: The Soviet Ruling Class, An Insider's Report*, trans. Eric Mosbacher [Garden City, N.Y.: Doubleday, 1984], 255). The possible motive? "Politburo members find it easier to have as weak a Secretary-General as possible. A quite human characteristic: Life is easier when you have a weak boss" (367). Voslenskii notes, however, that "In the countries of eastern Europe, the rules of the political game and of making a career differ from those of the West. An ambitious Western politician must attract attention and try to stand out of the ruck, since his advancement depends on the favor of as large as possible a proportion of the active members of his party or the electorate as a whole. A rising politician in Eastern Europe must stake everything on the goodwill of the [current] Secretary-General, and, if not the support of, the absence of opposition from, other leading figures. He must therefore concentrate on not standing out of the ruck, on not drawing attention to himself; he must create the impression of being innocuous and even rather dumb in the eyes of his colleagues. That was how Stalin, Khrushchev, Brezhnev, and later Chernenko rose to the top" (263). Gorbachev may be an exception to the rule.

Franco, of course, never had successors.[14] It is rumored that in the early days, the Franco regime was consciously modeling its government after that of Facist Italy.[15] They asked the Italians what the arrangements were for the replacement of the current dictator (Franco had been a soldier and probably was willing to consciously contemplate his own death). They were unable to get either a specification of what would happen when Mussolini died or even a clear statement that there was no such provision.

As a somewhat amusing aside, in the late forties, when I was a student at the University of Chicago, there were, of course, a certain number of students who were Communists, and a number of them were attempting to conceal their affiliation. This was also true in 1951 and 1952, when I was studying Chinese at Cornell and Yale. I discovered a simple test. Most of my acquaintences were much interested in politics, particularly foreign politics. I would ask who they thought would succeed Stalin. The "secret" Communists were unable to even discuss the question. I don't imagine this would have worked with more serious Communists, who presumably would have been given some kind of dispensation, so I never suggested this test to the FBI.

If we look at people who have risen high in a dictatorship and then succeeded in replacing the dictator when he died, we are apt to find people like Sadat or Moi, who must have seemed to the dictator completely safe.

On the relative benefits (and costs) of appointing "weak" successors, see also Gordon Tullock, *The Social Dilemma: The Economics of War and Revolution* (Blacksburg, Va.: University Publications, 1974), 72ff.

14. Mussolini had three sons, Bruno, Romano, and Vittorio, all of whom were for a time available as potential successors. Unfortunately, the first was killed in a car accident, while "Vittorio had been interested mainly in films, Ramon in Jazz, and it caused their father much grief that they took after their mother and lacked serious intellectual interests. Vittorio was now egged on by various friends and relations to play a part in politics, and his father, by encouraging the ambition of these 'princes of the blood,' showed poor judgement" (Dennis Mack Smith, *Mussolini* [New York: Knopf, 1982], 310).

15. Jerome Blum, Rondo Cameron, and Thomas G. Barnes, *The European World: A History*, 2d ed. (Boston: Little, Brown, 1970), 943: "In 1936 General Francisco Franco led a revolt against the government . . . Franco, who reorganized the Falange party, created by Primo de Rivera, on the model of Mussolini's Fascists and Hitler's Nazis, and proceeded to establish a reactionary authoritarianism that outlasted by far its model." See also Shlomo Ben-Ami, *Fascism from Above: The Dictatorship of Primo de Rivera in Spain, 1923–1930* (Oxford: Clarendon Press, 1983), passim.

Sadat, after all, was a total yes-man as long as Nasser was alive.[16] Moi was a member of a minor tribe and did not seem to have adequate political backing.[17] Thus their apparent weakness was one of their qualifications for their positions.

But even here, they are exceptional. Most dictators do not even have a single person who is a relatively prominent candidate as their successor, because they regard it as dangerous. Even an apparently spineless yes-man cannot be permitted to occupy this kind of position. Clearly, Sadat, Moi, and Balageur were all men of really great talent, because they succeeded in concealing their ambition, determination, and intelligence from the dictator whom they served. They were probably put in their relatively prominent positions not because the dictators thought they would be suitable successors, but because the dictators thought that they, like Hess, clearly were not suitable successors, and that by their mere occupation of the prominent positions they would prevent the more likely successors from being in positions where they could damage the dictators during their lives.

So far, in discussing the succession, in essence, I have been saying that the wise dictator doesn't make any arrangements for succession. He tries to avoid clear-cut straightforward succession procedures. Thus the actual succession, once he dies, will be a quick outburst of intrigue, with possibly some violence, in which a number of potential candidates maneuver for position. This maneuvering may possibly take the form of the junta discussed above, but it also may not.

Take an open variant of this kind of thing. In the first part of the T'ang dynasty of China, the death of an emperor led to a small civil war fought in the capital city by the adherents of his sons. Sian was repeatedly burned down as part of this fight.[18] One of the sons won; the others lost.[19]

16. See, for example, R. Hrair Dekmejian, *Egypt under Nasir* (Albany: State University of New York Press, 1971), on the relationship between Nasser and Sadat. On Nasser's relationship to his predecessor, Mohammed Au, see Anthony Nutting, *Nasser* (New York: Dutton, 1972); Jean LaCourture, *Nasser: A Biography* (New York: Knopf, 1974).

17. Moi's tribal beginnings are indicated in Norman N. Miller, *Kenya: The Quest for Prosperity* (Boulder: Westview Press, 1984), 28.

18. Sian, also called Ch'ang-an, Ching-chao-chun, and Hsi-an-fu, was the western capital of China at the beginning of the T'ang dynasty (618–907). See William L. Langer, *An Encyclopedia of World History*, 5th ed. (Boston: Houghton Mifflin, 1972), 145, 363.

19. The first emperor of the T'ang dynasty, Li Yüan, was succeeded by his son, Li Shih-min, and created the title "T'ang T'ai Tsung."

A number of African tribes have this procedure worked down to almost a formal ceremony. In the cases of both T'ang China and these African tribes, the king is, of course, polygamous and has a number of children. This formal civil war has nothing whatsoever to do with efficient transmission of power, but it does mean that the current ruling emperor or tribal ruling chief has little to fear from any individual among his children.[20]

A somewhat similar arrangement was used by Turkish Padishah in the latter days of the Turkish empire. In this case the Padishah normally executed all of his brothers, and his sons were kept in a special palace-prison until he died. At the time he died, there would be a quick squabble in this palace-prison from which only one son would emerge alive. This procedure initiated by Selim the Grim pretty much eliminated intrigues for the throne during the reign of any particular Padishah. It also, of course, produced a rather bizarre collection of Padishahs.

All three of the above examples are cases of hereditary succession rather than the nonhereditary succession we have been discussing so far. All three of them, however, show in an overt way the kind of struggle that does go on after a dictator dies when there is no clear-cut procedure for replacing him. They are, in a way, an open and rather exaggerated model of what happens anytime when a dictator dies and there's no procedure for replacing him.

As we have said above, the most likely outcome of all of this is hereditary succession, preferably a hereditary succession that is more peaceful than the ones we have just described. There have, however, been some cases of reasonably successful governments in which the succession problem has been solved for at least a period of time.

The son ruled from 600 to 649. His reign began "after a brief struggle with rival claimants [his brothers]" (R. Ernest Dupuy and Trevor N. Dupuy, *The Encyclopedia of Military History, from 3500 B.C. to the Present*, rev. ed. [New York: Harper and Row, 1977], 239). His battle for succession was won on July 4, 626, the day "Li Shih-min murdered his brothers" (Arthur F. Wright and Denis Twitchett, eds., *Perspectives on the T'ang* [New Haven: Yale University Press, 1973], 246). See also ibid., 19; and Wang Gungwu, *The Structure of Power in North China during the Five Dynasties* (Stanford: Stanford University Press, 1963), 203; Woodbridge Bingham, *The Founding of the T'ang Dynasty: The Fall of Sui and Rise of T'ang, A Preliminary Survey* (New York: Octagon Books, 1970), 119–20; Langer, *Encyclopedia*, 363ff.

20. "In African kingdoms it was exceptional for succession rules to designate a single individual; in the majority of cases a choice was made between a number of eligible candidates, and in some of them the contest was expected to be one of armed force" (Lucy Mair, *African Kingdoms* [Oxford: Oxford University Press, 1977], 121; see also 122–31).

The oldest of these is the Roman adoptive emperors. The reader will recall that Gibbon thought that the century of their control was the high point in the history of mankind. Eventually the throne became hereditary.[21] Normally the Roman empire was strong, peaceful,[22] and prosperous during this period.

The procedure was fairly simple and straightforward. Each of these emperors except the last, Marcus Aurelius, had the misfortune to have no son.[23] They therefore associated with themselves as an adopted son a prominent official, usually a military man, to succeed to the throne. The procedure seems to have been quite peaceful, and there are not even rumors of murders in

21. William G. Sinnigen and Arthur E. Boak (*A History of Rome to A.D. 565*, 6th ed. [New York: Macmillan, 1977]) point out that the rule for hereditary succession was not formally instituted and imposed, but was simply tacitly adopted and used by a succession of emperors during this period (432). Chester G. Starr (*The Roman Empire, 27 B.C.–A.D. 476* [New York: Oxford University Press, 1982]) offers a possible rationale for the adoption of such a rule: "Such a pattern made it legally easier to pass on the ruler's personal estate or *patrimonium*, which was already extensive under Augustus and was enlarged by bequests and additions from the property of condemned political criminals. Although later rulers sometimes made gifts of land to favorites, mistresses, or wives, the *patrimonium* of the emperor tended to become even larger as aristocrats were sent to the block" (38). Cf. Bertrand de Jouvenel, *On Power: Its Nature and the History of Its Growth* (Boston: Beacon Press, 1962), 327ff.

22. Peace was not universally enjoyed, however, and on occasion, there was even some confusion about the identity of the peacekeepers: "Although imperial literature has frequent praises of the imperial peace which safeguarded travel 'from the fear of bandits' attacks,' realities did not always correspond; and travellers faced dangers especially if they strayed off main routes. Disguised by the conventional eulogies of the empire as bringing order and security there bubbled in reality a caldron of violence and sudden death as men settled their differences outside the law and preyed on the weaker. Lucius, the hero of Apuleius' picaresque *metamorphoses*, found brigands aplenty in Macedonia, and his group was almost attacked by villagers with fierce dogs and stones until it could prove that it was not a band of robbers. Marcus Aurelius, as crown prince, jestingly wrote . . . that he and his companions in the vicinity of Antoninus Pius' royal villa were mistaken as robbers by shepherds, whom they charged on horseback and scattered—the shepherds may not have thought it as amusing" (Starr, *The Roman Empire*, 118–19).

23. Marcus Aurelius had the misfortune to have a son. During this period (98–161) of the Roman empire (27 B.C.–A.D. 493), "[p]hysiological accident produced the series of 'good emperors'—Trajan, Hadrian, Antoninus Pius—none of whom had sons; the last of this group, Marcus Aurelius, however, did, and Commodus duly became emperor (at age 16), ruled badly, and was strangled on the last day of 192" (Starr, *The Roman Empire*, 39). See also Sinnigen and Boak, *A History of Rome*, 320.

order to acquire the throne. It must be said, however, that in a number of cases, the new emperor had rather resented his predecessor. This is particularly clear in the case of Hadrian with Trajan.[24] Also, it appears that the emperor and his adopted son were rarely in physical proximity. Whether this was important or not, I don't know.

It will be noted here that once the man had been legally adopted, it was hard, even if not impossible, for his newly found father to get rid of him. Further, the procedure normally occurred in such a way that with ordinary life expectancy it was obvious that the newly adopted son would have twenty years or so of reign even if he didn't do anything about his adopted father's life expectancy. Nevertheless, this seems to be an exceptional procedure and, as far as I know, has never been copied.

There is something that looks vaguely like it, a new invention, actually, of this century. The Mexican government, since the 1930s, has had a dictator who reigns for six years and then appoints his successor and withdraws.[25] A priori I would have said that this was not a likely system to succeed, but so far, in any event, it has. Further, this system was copied by Brazil. The only basic difference was that Brazil had a four-year term instead of a six-year term. Here again, it seems to have been quite successful,[26] although it has now been abandoned. The Brazilians, of course, had the system for a much shorter period of time than the Mexicans and also were never willing to go to quite such extremes in eliminating opposition as were the Mexicans.[27] Mexico hasn't followed the Brazilian precedent and abandoned the system, but the current president of Mexico was "elected" in an "election" in which the opposition was actually permitted to campaign to some extent.[28]

24. "Trajan and Hadrian were personally incompatible, since the late emperor had not distinguished the younger man by granting him much power during his own lifetime" (Sinnigen and Boak, *A History of Rome*, 314).

25. Martin C. Needler, *Mexican Politics: The Containment of Conflict* (Stanford: Hoover Institution Press, 1982), 8, 85, 89–93. See also Roderic A. Camp, *Mexico's Leaders* (Tucson: University of Arizona Press, 1980), esp. 15–66.

26. See, for example, Riordan Roett, *Brazil: Politics in a Patrimonial Society* (New York: Praeger, 1978).

27. Ibid., 76ff. See also Kenneth F. Johnson, *Mexican Democracy: A Critical View*, 3d ed. (New York: Praeger, 1984), 12, on Mexican opposition parties and their treatment by those in power. Georges-André Fiechter, *Brazil since 1964: Modernization under a Military Regime, A Study of Interactions of Politics and Economics in a Contemporary Military Regime* (New York: John Wiley, 1975), offers an overview of twentieth-century political developments in Brazil.

28. Aiza, *Washington Post*, July 16, 1985; Needler, *Mexican Politics*, 58. But cf. Robert E. Scott, *Mexican Government in Transition*, rev. ed. (Urbana: University of Illinois Press, 1964),

To repeat what I said with respect to the previous system: this does not seem to be in any sense a stable way of running a government, and I am very surprised that it has lasted as long as it has. There may, however, be underlying structures which have not yet been discovered which make this feasible.

297ff, and J. A. Hellman, *Mexico in Crisis*, 2d ed. (New York: Holmes and Meier, 1983), who notes, for example, that "even today, the [Mexican] president is rarely challenged publicly. A ban on direct criticism of the president in the Mexican press is enforced by the state monopoly on the supply of newsprint. Since 1935, a government agency has set the price and allotted quantities of paper to each publication . . . Newspapers and magazines critical of official policy are often forced to buy paper on a black market or 'borrow' from sympathetic periodicals against the day when those publications may incur the hostility of the regime . . . The Christmas season is made particularly jolly for both Mexican and foreign journalists by the arrival on their doorstep of huge baskets of liquor and gourmet foods sent by government and party figures. But perhaps the most subtle form of control of the press is exercised through the use of the government's advertising budget, which constitutes the bulk of paid advertisement in many publications. For example, until government advertising was withdrawn in 1982, *Proceso*, a weekly men's magazine which attempts to maintain a clearly independent editorial line, received $117,000 from newsstand sales and subscriptions and $53,000 from the government publicity and propaganda carried in its pages each week . . . Historically, the relationship between the PRI (Institutional Revolutionary Party, headed by the President of Mexico) and its official opposition was so close that the parties were often referred to as a 'kept' opposition. Indeed, in some cases opposition parties were financed by the government itself . . . Ballot stealing, strong-arm pressure at the polls, and electoral fraud of every description contribute to the official party's electoral preeminence . . . The corruption of the electoral process in Mexico is so well documented that few people take the final statistics without a large serving of salt . . . [O]pposition parties have never achieved more than the status of pressure groups" (127–28, 129).

Another difference here is that the Mexican president and other higher officials seem to have stolen much more money than the Brazilian ones. I am at a loss to explain this difference. *Washington Post*, June 8, 1984, C15c; *Washington Post*, September 8, 1984, E53c. Kenneth Johnson observes that "in the colonial period of Mexican history there was less corruption and more respect for civil liberties than in present-day Mexico," and concludes that "people in Mexico accept fraud, terrorism, even bodies lying in the street with no public show of pity, as facts of life. This sounds very much like a war of all against all, in which almost everyone is certain to lose" (*Mexican Democracy*, 3).

Brazilian political corruption has, of course, also been widespread (for example, Clarence H. Haring, *Empire in Brazil: A New World Experiment with Monarchy* [Cambridge: Harvard University Press, 1958], 170, 171); but bureaucratic waste and inefficiencies appear to be an even larger problem. Robert T. Daland (*Exploring Brazilian Bureaucracy: Performance and Pathology* [Washington, D.C.: University Press of America, 1981]) suggests that "[t]he picture is not simple incompetence derived from clientelistic patronage appointments—though we should not minimize this element. There is a whole class of do-nothings (*ociosos*) in the

I think that it is worth serious thought by anyone interested in dictatorial governments.

The third system for peaceful succession has been successful for quite a long period of time. The dictator appoints a voting body which, while he is dictator, advises him. He is free during this period of time to change its membership if he wishes. Upon his death, this voting body elects someone, usually, but not necessarily always, one of its members, as his successor. This successor then acquires the same dominance over the voting body as the man who originally appointed it.

This system has been used by the Catholic church for a thousand years;[29] although one would be hard put to argue that there have never been difficulties in this particular chain of rulers, it has worked fairly well. There have been a number of cases in which there was more than one pope elected by different colleges of Cardinals.[30] Although the succession, on the whole, has been

---

bureaucracy. Some do nothing because they are incompetent. Some do nothing because they are protected by their patron, and have job security without the effort of working for it. Still others do nothing because they are not permitted to . . .

"A young lawyer obtained a technical position in the ministry of education upon finishing his studies. After some delay, during which he was given no instructions whatever as to his job, he sought out his supervisor and asked what needed to be done. The supervisor replied that he should wait and instructions would be forthcoming later.

"After several repetitions of this exchange, the idealistic young man became restive about accepting his monthly check without earning his pay. He then went to his supervisor with various suggestions for projects which by law it was evident should be undertaken. The boss became positively threatening, and warned the employee that he should terminate the pressure to engage in actual work if he wanted to keep out of trouble. So the employee gave up, and decided to enter a career in civil engineering, which he did with a scholarship from the Ministry, . . . and went into the private sector as a successful engineer" (216–17).

29. In the early days of the church, the pope was elected by popular voting in Rome. The College of Cardinals' control is thus more recent than the papacy itself (Elizabeth Lynskey, *The Government of the Catholic Church* [New York: P. J. Kennedy, 1952], 93–94). See also Leopold von Ranke, *The History of the Popes during the Last Four Centuries*, vol. 2 (London: G. Bell and Sons, 1913), 5–19. Bishops also were originally elected by the laity. See Henry Chadwick, *The Early Church* (New York: Penguin, 1976), 165.

30. The election of "multiple" popes occurred in 1378, beginning a period of papal history known as the Great Schism (1378–1417). Following the death of Pope Gregory XI, the college appointed two "popes," Urban VI of Rome and Clement VII of Avignon. Such multiple appointments continued to occur until the early fifteenth century and were in each instance usually resolved by a meeting of the Cardinals to determine the "true" pope. Occasionally,

peaceful and has produced a group of fairly successful rulers, it does have a tendency to select elderly men.

This system has been copied by the Soviet Union. Its not clear whether this is conscious or whether they simply accidentally fell into the procedure.[31] In any event, since the death of Lenin, the politburo has played more or less the role of the College of Cardinals. It should be pointed out that in the early days, for example, right after the death of Lenin, establishing one-man control took some time.[32] The same was true in the second succession crisis after the death of Stalin. When Khrushchev was overthrown,[33] there was an immediate successor who possibly had engineered the overthrow. On Brezhnev's death, of course, the succession was almost instantaneous,[34] and the same was true at Andropov's death, although in the latter case apparently his

---

a "pretender-pope," or antipope, such as Benedict XIII, would persist in asserting his papal authority despite the Cardinals' decision. For a brief synopsis of events, see Langer, *Encyclopedia*, 299ff.

31. See, for example, Bohdan Harasymiw, *Political Elite Recruitment in the Soviet Union* (New York: St. Martin's, 1984); Ronald J. Hill and Peter Frank, *The Soviet Communist Party*, 2d ed. (Boston: Allen and Unwin, 1983). I believe that it has also been copied by a number of minor churches in various parts of the world, but I don't know enough about them to be certain. Many churches, such as the Mormons or the Mennonites, are governed by a board of elders who do indeed tend to be very old, but most of them do not have a single ruler at the top of that board. See Thomas F. O'Dea, *The Mormons* (Chicago: University of Chicago Press, 1957), 160ff, 176ff, for a discussion of the internal organization of the Mormon church; on the Mennonite system, see, for example, John A. Hostetler, *Amish Society*, rev. ed. (Baltimore: Johns Hopkins University Press, 1968), 13.

32. Harasymiw, *Political Elite Recruitment*, 86; Blum, Cameron, and Barnes, *European World*, 923–24. As Michael Voslenskii (*Nomenklatura: The Soviet Ruling Class, An Insider's Report*, trans. Eric Mosbacher [Garden City, N.Y.: Doubleday, 1984], 255) points out: "The public in the West often hears about 'struggles for power in the Kremlin' and wrongly associates these with the idea of perpetual differences of opinion and dramatic debates similar to those that enliven Western parliaments. Nothing of that sort takes place in the Central Committee. There is a long-drawn-out affair involving lying in wait for years, in the course of which intrigues develop of a subtlety probably inconceivable to Western politicians."

33. I know of no direct parallel to this in the history of the Catholic church.

34. See Voslenskii, *Nomenklatura*, 370ff. He notes: "The probability of Andropov's getting the Secretary-General job became significant; it was noticed even by a computer. In 1981 a computer at Iowa University predicted who Brezhnev's most likely successor would be. The result was, given the variables—age (sixty to seventy years) and nationality (Russian) . . . limited to one person. That was Andropov" (377).

death was concealed for a few days.[35] Chernenko's death, similarly, seems to have led to an immediate succession by a much younger man.

The tendency to move towards gerontocracy is, of course, particularly conspicuous in the Soviet Union because the early rulers, Lenin and Stalin, were members of almost the same generation. Four of the rulers since then can be regarded as more or less contemporaries.[36]

Note, however, that this tendency to move to an elderly ruler is not invarying. The current pope is by papal standards a young man.[37] Further, Gorbachev is also a relatively young man.[38] Note that in both cases, however, that "relatively young" means somewhere in their 50s. In a more competitive system, such as the other kind of dictatorship, in which people fight their way up the greasy pole, or for that matter, in democracy, the top rulers tend to be younger when they first take control.

The advantages of this system, from the standpoint of the dictator who is interested in obtaining control thoughout his life and arranging a relatively peaceful succession so that at least to some extent his work will be continued, are obvious. The voting body can be made large enough so that the members of it can exercise, on an individual basis, supervision over all parts of the government and so that no one of them has very much power. In addition, the individuals within this group find some difficulty in conspiring, because they regularly, day in and day out,[39] discuss matters in an environment in which

35. Voslenskii (ibid., 381ff), discusses Chernenko's succession to Andropov's position as Secretary-General.

36. See Jerry F. Hough, *Soviet Leadership in Transition* (Washington, D.C.: Brookings Institution, 1980), esp. 150–56; Voslenskii, *Nomenklatura*, 263ff. Actually, there have been six rulers since Stalin: Georgy Malenkov who ruled for a brief and politically turbulent period (1953–55), Nikita Khrushchev (1955–64), Konstantin Ustinovovich Chernenko (1984–85), and the current secretary-general, Mikhail Gorbachev.

Though "contemporaries," recent Soviet rulers have tended to replace "old" policies with those more reflective of their own "political style and policy preferences." See Archie Brown, "Leadership Succession and Policy Innovation," in *Soviet Policy for the 1980's*, ed. Michael Kaser (Bloomington: Indiana University Press, 1982), and V. Bunce, *Do New Leaders Make a Difference? Executive Succession and Public Policy under Capitalism and Socialism* (Princeton: Princeton University Press, 1981).

37. Pope John Paul II was fifty-eight years old upon election in 1973, the youngest pope to be elected in this century (*New York Times*, October 17, 1978, p. 16).

38. Gorbachev was a relatively young man of fifty-four when appointed; at the time, the youngest member of the politburo (*Washington Post*, March 12, 1985, A1c).

39. Actually there is only one official politburo meeting a week, on Thursdays (Voslenskii, *Nomenklatura*, 264)—perhaps to avoid scheduling conflicts with the Secretariat, an equally

it would be very hard to conceal from the dictator any cliques that seem to be developing. The dictator is not absolutely secure under these circumstances—Khrushchev, after all, was thrown out—but he is reasonably secure, and the succession so far has not involved open violence.[40]

Note that the system works best when the members are indeed elderly. The reason for this is very simple. If the current dictator is elderly, it is obvious that one doesn't have to wait too long for his replacement. Thus the ambitious man has no strong motive for fighting his way up right now. Further, with this large collection of people, all of whom can anticipate some kind of promotion in the not too distant future through the death of the dictator, it's harder to promise promotion as a bribe for support. Last but by no means least, the dictator can remove a member of the politburo and replace him by somebody else without significantly changing the dynamics of the process. We do not have to worry about the condensation of the junta here.

Although this system does have advantages, as far as I know, the Catholic church and the Communist Party of the Soviet Union are the only places where it is used. It is, of course, quite possible that China will move to this system. After all, if we had observed the Soviet Union right after Stalin achieved power, we would not have been able to predict the eventual outcome. China has just gone through its first succession crisis in as disorderly a way as did Russia during its first succession crisis in the 1920s.[41]

---

powerful committee partly composed of politburo members which meets on Wednesdays (Hill and Frank, *Soviet Communist Party*, 68). But the members do have a lot of outside contact: "A less formal, but frequently used and vitally important communication channel is the telephone: it is in constant use at a local level, between officials and officers of the district or city committee and primary organization secretaries, economic managers, and so forth. Central Committee meetings are reported in summary to the press, but presumably these accounts for mass consumption are amplified in private conversation to party workers and, as appropriate, the mass membership, through the PPOs (Primary Party Organizations), where they may be discussed. Information internal to the party's affairs—on party finances, for example, or in how to conduct the party's affairs—is kept essentially private" (Hill and Frank, *Soviet Communist Party*, 81).

40. Though, of course, not for everyone. In the Soviet Union, "there is likely to be a rapid turnover of elite personnel. This will have a number of effects, including making certain categories of people very happy, others sad" (Harasymiw, *Political Elite Recruitment*, 190).

41. See David W. Chang, *Zhou Enlai and Deng Xiaoping in the Chinese Leadership Succession Crisis* (Lanham, Md.: University Press of America, 1984), for a discussion of Communist China's recent succession crisis.

The three communist ruling parties which are independent, North Korea, Albania, and Yugoslavia, do not seem to be following this process. Tito has been dead for quite a while now, and Yugoslavia has not yet developed a dictator or this kind of politburo control.[42] Once again, of course, this would be the first succession crisis, and we can't deduce too much from it. In the case of North Korea, the first dictator is still alive, but there seem to be arrangements for keeping the throne in the family.[43] In semi-independent Romania, the same thing seems to be taking place.[44]

Perhaps there are other ways of arranging a peaceful succession without jeopardizing the current dictator, but the number of instances which could be given of regular institutional structure for this sort of thing is very limited.

42. "One possible solution, which seems the most obvious to commentators accustomed to Kremlin-gazing, would be for a new strong man to emerge. There are, however, no obvious personalities in Yugoslavia today fitted to play this role. Party leaders have always tended to be identified with their republics, and the trends in party organization since the sixties have strengthened this attitude, so any aspiring heir to Tito is hindered by the likely resistance from other republics . . . There is no doubt that the army is an important force in Yugoslav politics, well represented in the party; and General Nikola Ljubici has been minister of offices. If there were a really serious nationalist crisis, then it is possible the army would back a strong man to reimpose and maintain order. There is not at present any evidence, however, that the army aspires to exercise controlling power. Therefore, it seems likely that the republican party bosses will be forced to resolve their disputes by compromise, as Tito envisaged, and to cooperate in a genuinely collective leadership. The virtually confederal nature of the Yugoslav state, and the federal elements in the party organization itself clearly conduce to this kind of solution. So it is possible that Yugoslavia after Tito will, as in many other respects, diverge from the standard communist party pattern, and avoid one man dominance" (April Carter, *Democratic Reform in Yugoslavia: The Changing Role of the Party* [Princeton: Princeton University Press, 1982], 256–57). See also Steven L. Burg, *Conflict and Cohesion in Socialist Yugoslavia: Political Decision Making since 1966* (Princeton: Princeton University Press, 1983), esp. 326–35.

43. On current plans for the succession of forty-two-year-old Kim Jong Il by North Korean president, seventy-three-year-old Kim Il Sung, see Azia, *Washington Post*, August 7, 1984; *New York Times*, July 9, 1985. According to North Korea's constitution (1972), "Although he is to be elected every four years by the Supreme People's Assembly, to which he is theoretically accountable for his conduct in office, there is no explicit constitutional limitation on his tenure, nor is there any ambiguity about the fact that he is not actually accountable to any governmental authority . . . the Constitution is silent on the question of presidential succession" (Vreeland, *Handbook for South Korea*, 160, 161).

44. See T. Gilberg, "Politics and Social Development in Rumania," *Current History* 83 (November 1984): 375–94.

I would not like to claim that I have discovered all of them, but I don't think there are any very conspicuous examples which I have missed.

As we have said above, however, commonly hereditary succession is the ultimate outcome. We, as people of European ancestory, tend to think of hereditary succession as succession by the eldest son. This is not necessarily the system used in other cultures. You may recall that Marco Polo went to China by land, but came back by sea. The reason that he did so is that in Mongolian law, the youngest son succeeded his father. Kublai Khan was not the youngest son, and the youngest son living in Mongolia led a revolt which broke the gigantic Mongolian empire into halves. It was not safe for Marco Polo to return across the Gobi Desert as he had come.[45]

This is not, of course, the only case of succession by somebody who is not the eldest son. I mentioned above cases in which succession actually involved a sort of war among the possible successors (in the case of the Turkish institutions, a very small war confined to one palace prison). There are other cases. The Ch'ing dynasty of China was perhaps the strongest dynasty that China ever had.[46] The basic reason for this, I believe, was that in the early days the succession was not to the eldest son. The emperor selected from among his children the one that he thought should succeed. Since, as a polygamist ruler, he always had quite a large number of sons, the early emperors were all men of exceptional capacity. Unfortunately, they were living in China, and the Chinese view that the eldest son should inherit was eventually adopted, resulting in a set of weak emperors.[47]

I could name other examples. The basic reason the pharaohs of Egypt normally married their sisters was that succession in Egypt was through the female line.[48] The current prince of Monaco succeeded his father while his father was still alive.[49] Altogether, hereditary succession is not necessarily eldest son to eldest son.

45. See Marco Polo, *The Travels of Marco Polo* (New York: Grosset and Dunlap, 1931); Blum, Cameron, and Barnes, *European World*, 49; Langer, *Encyclopedia*, 383–84.

46. See, for example, Lawrence D. Kessler, *K'ang-hsi and the Consolidation of Ch'ing Rule, 1661–1684* (Chicago: University of Chicago Press, 1976); Jonathan D. Spence, *Emperor of China: Self-Portrait of K'ang-hsi* (New York: Knopf, 1974).

47. See Langer, *Encyclopedia*, 575–79, 909–16; Kessler, *K'ang-hsi*, 167ff.

48. As, for example, noted in Leonard Cottrell, *The Warrior Pharaohs* (New York: Putnam's, 1969), 14.

49. Prince Rainier III, current ruler of Monaco, is in turn preparing *his* son, Albert, to succeed him in the not too distant future (*New York Times*, February 17, 1984).

Even if we confine ourselves to areas where the succession is supposed to be eldest son to eldest son, uniform peace is by no means insured. In the first place, lines do run out; i.e., there is no son of the current ruling king, and there is no near relative who seems a reasonable replacement. The Uffizi, in Florence, was a gift to the city of Florence left in her will by the last of the Medici.[50]

We could go on. Hereditary succession is certainly not a guarantee of peaceful succession. The obvious example of this, of course, is the Wars of the Roses in England. It started when a potential heir to the throne, although not necessarily the most likely heir, overthrew the existing king. It continued for years and years and years, being mainly a war between close relatives.[51] The end product, Henry VII, was a man who actually had no Plantagenet blood in his veins.[52] The long and bloody Hundred Years' War between England and France was set off when the king of England decided that he was the legitimate heir to the recently deceased king of France.[53] Those of you who have seen Shakespeare's *Henry V* are familiar with the English claim that descent could go through the female line in France because the Salic Law of Succession, which banned such succession, did not apply in France. Shakespeare does not tell you that if female succession was permitted, there were around a dozen people who had better claims to the throne than Henry V. All of them were French.[54]

50. The Uffizi, an art gallery containing a "mass of pictures, statues, bronzes, rare gems, and other works of art," was donated "to the state of Tuscany forever, in the person of the new Grand Duke and his successors" by Anna Maria Ludovia (1667–1743), "The Last of the Medici," shortly before her death (G. F. Young, *The Medici* [New York: Modern Library, 1930], 740. See also 736–47).

51. See H. A. L. Fisher, *The History of England from the Accession of Henry VII to the Death of Henry VIII (1485–1547)*, vol. 5 of *The Political History of England*, 12 vols. (1906; Kravs Reprint Co., 1969), 1–24; Edward P. Cheyney, *A Short History of England*, rev. ed. (Boston: Ginn, 1918), 269ff; Dupuy and Dupuy, *Encyclopedia of Military History*, 419–23.

52. See J. D. Mackie, "The Early Tudors, 1485–1558," in *The Oxford History of England*, ed. G. N. Clark, 47–50, 656a (Oxford: Clarendon Press, 1957); Fisher, *History of England*, 1–15.

53. Desmond Seward, *The Hundred Years War: The English in France, 1337–1453* (New York: Atheneum, 1978).

54. See Blum, Cameron, and Barnes, *European World*, 225. On Salic Law of Succession, see Langer, *Encyclopedia*, 296. G. B. Harrison, *Shakespeare: The Complete Works* (New York: Harcourt, Brace, 1952), reproduces Shakespeare's "The Life of King Henry the Fifth" (732–72).

All of this is merely to point out that hereditary succession does not guarantee a peaceful succession of the throne from father to son over untold generations. Nevertheless, it seems to be more peaceful than other methods. I can think of two examples, Byzantine history and the history of the Mamluks in Egypt, both running about a thousand years.[55] It is clear that things on the whole ran better during those periods of time, usually not more than three generations in which they did indeed have hereditary succession, than in those periods of time in which they fought about the succession. Popular devotion to the "legitimate" king may have been quite sensible. The common people had little or nothing to gain from a civil war and a great deal to lose. Unfortunately, there almost always is at least one person who can gain from it.

In any event, historically hereditary succession to the throne has been the commonest form of government. This does not mean that every succession is undisputed, merely that most of them are. England, with disputed successions in roughly every third generation, is an exceptionally disturbed country. Since most of us think of our history as English history, this exceptional disturbance may appear to us to be characteristic of hereditary monarchy. Actually I think every fifth time would be a better rough average.

This has been a discussion of the historical record of hereditary monarchy and not an explanation of why it is indeed quite a common form of government. Why do hereditary monarchs tend to replace dictatorships, which are not hereditary? Why do we observe today dictators of North Korea and Singapore obviously planning for hereditary succession and the last dictator of Haiti as being, in fact, the hereditary successor to his father?[56] Why was the house of Somoza as successful as long as it was,[57] and for that matter why did

55. On the Byzantine empire (324–1453), see Cyril Mango, *Byzantium: The Empire of New Rome* (New York: Scribner's, 1980). The Mamluks (or Mamelukes) of Egypt are discussed in Ramsay Muir (*A Short History of the British Commonwealth*, vol. 2, *The Modern Commonwealth [1763 to 1919]* [Yonkers-on-the-Hudson, N.Y.: World Book, 1924]), passim; and J. R. Harris, *The Legacy of Egypt*, 2d ed. (Oxford: Clarendon Press, 1971), 461–66.

56. Jean-Claude Duvalier succeeded his father, Dr. François Duvalier ("Papa Doc"), following his death in 1971 (*New York Times*, February 1971; *New York Times*, April 23, 1971, 1:2). He occasionally expressed a nominal interest in democratic elections beginning in 1987 (*Washington Post*, July 7, 1985). In light of his father's brutal regime and practices (Bernard Diederich and Al Burt, *Papa Doc: The Truth about Haiti Today* [New York: Avon, 1969]), these reforms were not considered serious proposals.

57. Anastasio Somoza Debayle finally resigned under fire as president of Nicaragua in July, 1979 (*New York Times*, July 18, 1979).

it take direct intervention by the American government after the death of Trujillo to prevent his son from remaining in control of the family hacienda?[58]

The first thing to be said is that from the standpoint of the father-son pair, the situation is a little easier than the relationship between a dictator and one of his officials. Secondly, and this is actually an important matter, the son is apt to be at least twenty years younger than the father. Thus he has a reasonable chance of a fairly long personal reign even if he waits until his father dies. It is not, of course, true that this has always worked out well. Louis XIV and XV both outlived their children.[59] Muhammad Ali, founder of the dynasty of Egypt which was only replaced by Nasser, lived long enough so that he and his extremely talented son had a relationship of almost mutual hatred at the end.[60]

Nevertheless, as a rough rule of thumb, the eldest son is wise to simply wait for his father to die. He knows this, his father knows that he knows this, and concern about assassination by the son is less in a hereditary successional arrangement than if the designated successor is a high-ranking official of the existing regime. Note that I say *less*. I have already expressed my opinion that

58. See, for example, John Bartlow Martin, *Overtaken by Events: The Dominican Crisis from the Fall of Trujillo to the Civil War* (Garden City, N.Y.: Doubleday, 1966); Robert D. Crassweller, *Trujillo: The Life and Times of a Caribbean Dictator* (New York: Macmillan, 1966), 261ff.

59. Louis XIV's death in France in 1715 "brought his five-year-old great grandson Louis XV to the throne" (Blum, Cameron, and Barnes, *European World*, 390; see also 454; Edward Armstrong, "The Bourbon Governments in France and Spain," in *The Cambridge Modern History*, ed. A. W. Ward, G. W. Prothero, and Stanley Leathes, vol. 6, *The Eighteenth Century* [New York: Macmillan, 1909], 120ff; Louis Kronenberger, *Kings and Desperate Men: Life in Eighteenth-Century England* [New York: Random House, Vintage Books, 1942], 4–5). Following Louis XV's death (of smallpox) in 1774, Louis XVI, his grandson, became king at the age of twenty (462).

60. Afaf Lutfi al-Sayyid-Marsot (*Egypt in the Reign of Muhammad Ali* [Cambridge: Cambridge University Press, 1984]) notes that Muhammad Ali and his son Ibrahim (one of Ali's thirty children) "closely resembled each other physically, although morally they were very different and clashes between father and son were to become frequent later on . . . Clashes over the promotion of Egyptians to the rank of officers broke out between the two men; [as well as] clashes over policy and tactics" (83). See also ibid., 223ff, 254ff; Bernard Lewis, *The Arabs in History* (New York: Harper and Row, 1966), 167. Ibrahim died in 1848, while his father was still living (Ahmed Abdel-Rahim Mustafa, "The Breakdown of the Monopoly System in Egypt after 1840," in *Political and Social Change in Modern Egypt: Historical Studies from the Ottoman Conquest to the United Arab Republic*, ed. P. M. Holt [London: Oxford University Press, 1968], 300). On Ibrahim's military accomplishments, see Gabriel Baer, "Social Change in Egypt," in *Political and Social Change in Modern Egypt: Studies from the Ottoman Conquest to the United Arab Republic*, ed. D. M. Holt, 139 (London: Oxford University Press, 1968).

a careful count would indicate that murder by the eldest son was the commonest cause of death to kings in those areas where the eldest male succeeds.[61]

As another aspect, there usually is a certain element of affection between father and son, and that means that both would get at least some satisfaction out of the satisfaction of the other.[62] There is an interdependence of utility functions here even if it is very far from a complete interdependence. This also makes it less likely that the son will murder his father. The fact that this is less likely means that the father will worry less about the matter, and hence this again makes this method of succession more likely.

As a final item while we are talking about reasons why sons may be designated as successors, it's hard for the father to switch under these circumstances. He, after all, has only one eldest son, and many kings had, in fact, only one son. If he becomes suspicious or annoyed with the current crown prince, he can hardly simply appoint somebody else as his eldest son. It is true that if he has other children, he could kill his son; many kings have. But this is an extreme measure.

The result of all of this is that the father has greater confidence in his son, and that in turn means that the son has a much weaker motive for murdering his father than would the designated successor if the designated successor was simply a high official of the regime.[63] This again means that the father can trust his son more than he can trust other people.

I mentioned above that the adoptive emperors and their adopted successors seem to have rarely been fairly close to each other. It is a rare, but not

61. This would, of course, depend to some extent on how you classified other forms of death. I am sure it is not commoner than "natural death," but if natural death is subdivided among the diseases my generalization, I think, would follow. Oscar Jaszi and John D. Lewis (*Against the Tyrant: The Tradition and Theory of Tyrannicide* [Glencoe, Ill.: Free Press, 1957]), for example, note that following the collapse of the Roman empire (during which "the practice of assassination became almost a political institution"), "political murder of this sort was characteristic also of the period that followed the German Migrations. The closest ties of nature are here disregarded; fratricide, the murder of the nearest relatives, becomes an everyday event. This situation lasted until the strong rule of the Carolingians enforced a certain order and unity" (152). See also William L. Langer, *An Encyclopedia of World History*, 5th ed. (Boston: Houghton Mifflin, 1972), 161.

62. Also dissatisfaction out of the other's misfortune. David's son Absalom (not the eldest son) revolted against his father and drove him out of Jerusalem. When Joab led the king's army against Absalom, he was ordered by David to see that no harm befell Absalom. Nevertheless he killed him, and David was thrown into deep grief (2 Samuel 19).

63. Or, like Absalom, merely one son among the many of a polygamous father.

unheard of, precaution for a ruler to appoint his son as viceroy in some distant and not militarily important province on the ostensible theory that he needs to be trained in rulership.

An even more common precaution, however—and this may be one of the reasons that hereditary monarchs tend not to be terribly good rulers—is simply to provide the son with a great deal of entertainment. The son can be provided with substantially any number of fine polo ponies, beautiful concubines, swimming pools, etc. This normally will not cost the king a very high percentage of his nation's GNP, and it may provide the child with enough distraction so that he's not seriously concerned with immediate succession. Unfortunately, this kind of training is unlikely to make him a good king.

These are reasons why the king may prefer his son as a successor. We also have to explain why the son is able to, in fact, seize control after the death of his father. Indeed, if we look at history we will find a number of cases in which a legitimate heir seized power even though he was not designated. When Queen Elizabeth died, she had not designated an heir.[64] James of Scotland was, however, a clear example of a suitable king and took over with no difficulty. Similarly, on the death of the reigning king of France (which led to the Hundred Years' War), in France itself, a quite distant relative of the existing king was peacefully accepted as the legitimate successor.[65] These, of course, are cases in which a dynastic tradition already existed. Movement to hereditary succession when it has not previously existed is not obviously the same thing. We can, however, find one very conspicuous example of this. Julius Caesar was not king of the Romans, but he certainly dominated the country.[66] On Caesar's assassination, Augustus, a young man who at the time must have seemed to have substantially no positive qualities except his relationship to Caesar, immediately became a member of the Triumvirate. Later, partly because he was a member of Caesar's family and partly because it turned

64. Blum, Cameron, and Barnes, *European World*, 171. At her last illness she is reported to have placed her hands above her head, and this was taken as indicating that she wanted the crown to go to the only potential who was already a king, James of Scotland. It seems likely to me that the people who interpreted her gesture this way were already partisans of James.

65. See, for example, Langer, *Encyclopedia*, 297–303; Seward, *The Hundred Years War*, passim.

66. See Theodor Mommsen, "The Old Republic and the New Monarchy, 46–44 B.C.," chap. 33 of *Rome, from Earliest Times to 44 B.C.*, vol. 3 of *The History of Nations*, ed. Henry Cabot Lodge (New York: Collier, 1928), 362–96.

out that he was a very talented intriguer, he became emperor and established a dynasty.[67]

A number of Greek tyrants were successful in placing their sons on their thrones. Usually in these cases, however, there was a more definite designation than had occurred in the case of Augustus.[68] Note that I've had to go back to very ancient history to find examples of this kind of thing. The history of the nineteenth century was the history of the replacement of absolute rulers of one sort or another by democracies.[69] The twentieth century has shown a good deal of movement in the other direction,[70] but in general this, as of now, has had such a short running time that a general tendency towards a particular method of succession has not yet had time to establish itself.

But to return to our main subject, why is the "legitimate" heir usually a son in particularly good position to succeed his father? In order to answer, we go back to our earlier discussion of the work of Schelling and the Schelling point.[71] Higher-ranking courtiers all would, of course, like to be the new dictator themselves, but all of them are aware that only one will win. Thus, although they are looking at the main chance always, they're also very interested in backing whoever they think will win. Under these circumstances, as Schelling has pointed out, conspicuousness is apt to be a strong argument. The coalition is apt to form behind the son simply because he is a very conspicuous individual. Being conspicuous it is likely that each politician thinks that other politicians will be attracted to him. Therefore, since other politicians will be attracted to him, I had better join him myself. All politicians

67. On the relationship between Julius Caesar and Augustus, see Stefan Weinstock, *Divus Julius* (Oxford: Oxford University Press, 1971), passim, but esp. chap. 13, "Kingship and Divinity," 270–86.

68. For a history of the Greek tyrants, see Bernadotte Perrin, trans., *Plutarch's Lives* (Cambridge: Harvard University Press, 1968), and Paul Turner, *Selected Lives from the Lives of the Noble Grecians and Romans*, vols. 1 and 2 (Carbondale: Southern Illinois University Press, 1963).

69. See, for example, Langer, *Encyclopedia*, pt. 5, passim; Blum, Cameron, and Barnes, *European World*, chaps. 11–29; A. W. Ward, G. W. Prothero, and Stanley Leathes, eds., *Cambridge Modern History*, vol. 11, *The Growth of Nationalities* (New York: Macmillan, 1909). See also Barrington Moore Jr., *Social Origins of Dictatorship and Democracy* (Boston: Beacon Press, 1966).

70. Langer, *Encyclopedia*, parts 6 and 7; Blum, Cameron, and Barnes, *European World*, pt. 4; Johnson, *Modern Times*.

71. Thomas Schelling, *The Strategy of Conflict* (Cambridge: Harvard University Press, 1980), esp. 113–15; see also Tullock, *The Social Dilemma*, 75ff.

feeling this way, the conspicuous person, in this case the legitimate heir, has a great advantage and will probably win.

Note that this would be particularly true if the legitimate heir was also a man of very considerable capacity. But that is by no means obviously true in most cases. Biologists are familiar with "regression to the mean," under which characteristics which are sharply away from the average of a given species tend to be less strongly represented in the next generation. The original dictator, who climbed the greasy pole, is undoubtedly of very considerable capacity; his son may not be. Further, his upbringing very likely has been one which gives him a strong feeling that he has a right to rule, but no great capacity to do it well.

Note that I am not alleging that hereditary rulers of countries are totally unfit, but merely that, in general, they are not the particular residents of the country whom a divine judge would select as the best rulers. Perhaps from the standpoint of the country as a whole, hereditary succession's principal advantage is that it avoids civil wars at the death of the dictator and indeed makes it unlikely that anyone other than his legitimate heir will make any effort to assassinate him. Succession is apt to be peaceful, at least most of the time, and that is surely a boon even if not an infinite boon.

But if this is, in my opinion, the likely outcome of the present situation in most countries, it certainly is not the current situation. Disorderly succession, putsch, coup d'etat, and in South America in any event, an alteration of dictatorship and democracy seem likely near-term predictions, even if the long-term prediction would be hereditary monarchs.

DEMOCRACY AND DESPOTISM

This book is primarly about absolute rule; hence, I have given very little attention so far to democratic governments. In my other books on democratic governments, I have normally paid no attention at all to despotic governments. Nevertheless, there are situations which are sort of between democracy and dictatorship, and there are other analyzable situations in which a democracy is changing into a dictatorship, or a monarchy into a democracy. This chapter will discuss these situations.

In current usage, "democracy" is normally confined to systems where all adults are permitted to vote.[1] Historically this situation was almost unknown before the twentieth century. Governments in which there were voters, however, did exist in those times. In Athens, for example, the full citizens conducted their affairs in an extremely "democratic" manner, but they were only a minority of adult inhabitants.[2] In the England of George II, the House of

Reprinted, with kind permission of Kluwer Academic Publishers, from *Autocracy* (Dordrecht and Boston: Kluwer Academic Publishers, 1987), 175–207.

1. Israel is an exception to this rule, since it is normally counted as a democracy in spite of the fact that West Bank Arabs are not permitted to vote for the Israeli government. Sometimes they are permitted to choose their own officials for local government organizations. See James Dunnigan and Stephen Bay, *A Quick and Dirty Guide to War: Briefings on Present and Potential Wars* (New York: William Morrow, 1985), on the limited political rights allowed West Bank Arabs by the Israelis; see also "West Bank Arabs Have Rarely Felt So Cornered," *New York Times*, August 11, 1985, p. E5.

2. As C. M. Bowra points out: "By the end of the eighth century hereditary kings had almost ceased to count in Greece . . . and [were] replaced by written constitutions, which gave power to . . . oligarchies and democracies . . . the first of which . . . meant the rule of nobles . . . A democracy, on the other hand, claimed that its government was in the hands of the whole free male adult population. This was a later growth than oligarchy and was always less common" (*The Greek Experience* [New York: New American Library, 1957], 82; see also William G. Forrest, *The Emergence of Greek Democracy 800–400 B.C.* (New York: McGraw-Hill, 1966), 65–66. A relatively small electoral class was also the case in Sparta's "democracy": "In speaking of 'Democractic' elements in the Spartan Constitution, one must of course remember that the citizens as a whole were a ruling class fiercely tyrannizing over the Helots [Greek populations conquered by Sparta] and allowing no power to the *Perloeci*," free inhabitants of Laconia (Sparta's capital) who had no political power (Bertrand Russell, *A History of Western Philosophy* [New York: Simon and Schuster, 1945], 97).

Commons clearly was an important part of the government and carried on its affairs by voting, but it was selected by rather odd procedures and was far from the most important part of the government.[3]

In order to deal with these cases, I am using the term "electoral system" for all cases where voting is a significant part of the governmental process. Democracy, in its modern meaning, thus becomes a special type of "electoral system." We can classify electoral systems in terms of how closely they approximate democracy, with the Holy Roman empire at one extreme and the United States in 1900[4] very close to the other.

Before discussing electoral systems, however, I must make a brief digression to deal with a phenomenon which is frequently referred to as partially democratic but which in fact is simply an aspect of some dictatorial governments. This is the "one-party state." Its origin is simple. A good many of our current dictatorships developed out of democracies or countries which were well on the way to democracy. In a number of cases, the dictatorship began as a party struggling for control in a democracy. Take Lenin, for example. I'd not like to call Russia as it existed during most of his life a perfect democracy, but it had at least some electoral aspects, and during most of his life before 1917, he was a party leader rather than an official of the government. All of

3. See, for example, Louis Kronenberger, *Kings and Desperate Men: Life in Eighteenth-Century England* (New York: Random House, Vintage Books, 1942), 200–211; Diana Spearman, *Democracy in England* (New York: Macmillan, 1957), 1–7, 52–59. Of course, as Ramsay Muir (*A Short History of the British Commonwealth*, vol. 2, *The Modern Commonwealth [1763 to 1919]* [Yonkers-on-the-Hudson, N.Y.: World Book, 1924]) points out, "All the Government proposals were carried by overwhelming majorities. And this was due not merely to the fact that corruption was employed on a wholesale scale—on a scale far more lavish than Walpole even dreamed of—but still more to the fact that most of the country gentlemen in the House of Commons were quite content that the King should control the Government, and had no quarrel with his policy . . . And there is no reason to suppose that in thus accepting the new regime the two Houses of Parliament ran counter to public feeling in the country at large. The King himself and the policy he pursued were by no means unpopular . . . If an election on quite democratic lines could have taken place at any time between 1770 and 1777, it is probable that the party which supported the King's policy would have obtained a majority quite as large as that which it enjoyed under the anomalies of the old representative system" (16).

4. Women could not vote. It wasn't until 1920, when the Nineteenth Amendment was passed, that they could, and, of course, in Great Britain universal suffrage began in 1918 when women over thirty were enfranchised. This was lowered to twenty-one a decade later. See, for example, Bernard Grum, *The Timetables of History: A Horizontal Linkage of People and Events* (New York: Simon and Schuster, 1979), 471ff.

his loyal followers were members of the party. That, when he seized control, he would put his followers, the members of that party, in all the positions of power that he could was, of course, obvious. There was also no reason why he should have formally dissolved the party, and he did not.[5]

He simply made all the other parties illegal, retained his own party in power, and called it a one-party state. Insofar as there was any direct motive in this, it probably was a desire to camouflage the dictatorship under a democratic patina, but a remarkably thin one. As time went by the Communist Party in the Russian state actually developed independent power, not as a party but as, in essence, a personnel control arm of the state. It was in part a propaganda agency for the state and in part an organization which controlled, through the nomenklatura, its personnel.[6] Presumably, its advantage

5. See, for example, Sheila Fitzpatrick, *The Russian Revolution* (New York: Berkley, 1982), 27, 29. Of course, as Paul Johnson (*Modern Times: The World from the Twenties to the Eighties* [New York: Harper and Row, 1983]) points out, "Lenin astutely made the greatest possible use of the spurious legitimacy conferred upon his regime by the Soviets . . . [H]e carefully operated at two levels[:] . . . on the surface was the level of constitutional arrangements and formal legality. That was for show, . . . the deep structures of a real power: Police, army, communications, arms. [On 12 November 1917] the elections proceeded with the Bolsheviks merely one of the participating groups. It was the first and last truly parliamentary election ever held in Russia" (64). Lenin formally dissolved the parliament on January 6, 1918 (see ibid., 71–72, for example). Today, of course, "from the initial decision to hold elections on a particular day through the selection, nomination and registration of candidates, right through the count and post-election scrutiny of the ballots, the [communist] party is involved, . . . making 'authoritative suggestions' . . . , and leading the propaganda campaign, designed to get the voters to the polls and to refrain from voting against the one approved candidate in each constituency by crossing out the name . . . Nothing is left to chance or spontaneity . . ." (Ronald J. Hill and Peter Frank, *The Soviet Communist Party*, 2d ed. [Boston: Allen and Unwin, 1983], 110–11). See also Ronald J. Hill, "Patterns of Deputy Selection to Local Soviets," *Soviet Studies* 25 (1973): 196–212; Ronald J. Hill, "The CPSU in a Soviet Election Campaign," *Soviet Studies* 28 (1976): 590–98; Derek J. R. Scott, *Russian Political Institutions*, 4th ed. (London: Allen and Unwin, 1969), esp. 97; Roger A. Clarke, "The Composition of the Supreme Soviet, 1958–66," *Soviet Studies* 11 (1967): 53–65; Everett M. Jacobs, "Soviet Local Elections: What They Are, and What They Are Not," *Soviet Studies* 22 (1970): 61–76; Everett M. Jacobs, "The Composition of Local Society," *Government and Opposition* 7 (1972): 503–19; Jerome M. Gilison, "Soviet Elections as a Measure of Dissent: The Missing One Percent," *American Political Science Review* 62 (1968): 814–26, esp. 820; Theodore H. Friedgust, *Political Participation in the U.S.S.R.* (Princeton: Princeton University Press, 1979).

6. Bohdan Harasymiw, *Political Elite Recruitment in the Soviet Union* (New York: St. Martin's, 1984), gives a discussion of personnel and recruitment policies with respect to membership in

for such dictators as Stalin and Khrushchev depended largely on providing an alternative channel which could be used to divide the government officials below them. More traditional governments without such a single "party" had used other methods for the same purposes.

Russia is the oldest "one-party state" in existence, and there has been a rather intermittent tendency for membership in the party to expand. I would predict that assuming things go on as they are, in fifty to seventy-five years they will make everybody in Russia automatically a member of the party just as eventually the Roman emperors made every resident of the empire a citizen.

The Soviet Union is not the only one-party state. Mussolini and Hitler both rose to power as political leaders and in both cases retained their former party. In neither of these two cases did this party have quite as much influence as the Communist Party of the Soviet Union, but still it was, in both cases, part of the control apparatus.[7]

In Franco's case, he, of course, took over the government as a military man from the outside, but there was one party which proclaimed its devotion to him and which was given one-party status. In this case it seems fairly clear that Franco never really trusted the Phalange, which had no great real importance.[8]

---

the nomenklatura and Communist Party. See also John A. Armstrong, *The Politics of Totalitarianism: The Communist Party of the Soviet Union from 1934 to the Present* (New York: Random House, 1961); John H. Miller, "The Communist Party: Trends and Problems," in *Soviet Policy for the 1980s*, ed. Archie Brown and Michael Kaser, 1–34 (Bloomington: Indiana University Press, 1982); Jerry F. Hough, *Soviet Leadership in Transition* (Washington, D.C.: Brookings Institution, 1980); Michael Voslenskii, *Nomenklatura: The Soviet Ruling Class, An Insider's Report*, trans. Eric Mosbacher (Garden City, N.Y.: Doubleday, 1984); Hélène Carrére D'Encausse, *Confiscated Power: How Soviet Russia Really Works* (New York: Harper and Row, 1980), 16ff, 70ff, 139–49, 320–22.

7. On Hitler's use of the Nazi party, see Alan Bullock, *Hitler: A Study in Tyranny*, rev. ed. (New York: Harper and Row, 1964), passim; see also T. L. Jarman, *The Rise and Fall of Nazi Germany* (New York: Signet, 1961), 79–94, 133–68. The Fascist Party established on March 23, 1919, by Mussolini as a means for gaining political control of Italy is discussed in Johnson, *Modern Times*, 95–96, 97–103. Indeed, as Johnson notes, in his use of the Fascist Party, Mussolini "did not make any of Lenin's obvious mistakes. He did not create a secret police, or abolish parliament. The press remained free, opposition leaders at liberty. There were some murders, but fewer than before the coup. The Fascist Grand Council was made an organ of state and the Blackshirts were legalized, giving an air of menace to the April 1924 elections, which returned a large fascist majority. But Mussolini saw himself as a national rather than a party leader. He said he ruled by consent as well as force" (100).

8. The suggestions seem correct that to Franco, "the army was the only truly national

The parties in most of the other one-party states are even less important than the Phalange was under Franco. Their history is usually the history of a party leader who led his party during a period in which the colonial power was withdrawing and who has, like Lenin, seen no reason for demolishing the party when he comes to power.

Nevertheless, the party in most cases is more decorative than anything else. A prominent man in the government, or for that matter outside the government, is apt to be a member of the party for the same reason that a businessman in a small town in the United States is a member of the Rotary Club. Further, it probably is as important and has somewhat the same function as the Rotary Club except that most of them do not have as much purely social importance as the Rotary Club.

In a small town in the United States we would be quite surprised to find anyone of prominence who was not a member of the Rotary Club; in a small African dictatorship we would be rather surprised to find anybody of importance who was not a member of the party. In both cases, however, the actual levers of power lie elsewhere. Mugabe of Zimbabwe is currently attempting to cement his power and as part of that is talking about establishing a one-party state. By one-party state, he simply means he is going to get rid of all the political power of his opponents. Any member of that one party who thinks that the party is in control of Mugabe rather than vice versa will find that he has made a mistake.

Note that in this case, as in the case of most African one-party states, the party itself is not an instrument of control. It is in essence a society which the people who exercise the control are normally members of. Once again, its resemblance to the Rotary Club is much greater than its resemblance to the Communist Party of the Soviet Union in let us say the 1920s.

But this has been a digression. The main point of this chapter is to talk about those situations in which democracies or dictatorships change into one another and to discuss a very interesting intermediate situation.

---

institution, ancient, classless, non-regional, apolitical, incorrupt, disinterested. If it was oppressed, it mutinied . . . ; otherwise it served." Franco "hated politics in any shape" and "exploited the two insurrectionary movements, the Phalange and the Carlists, amalgamating them under his leadership, but their role was subservient, indeed servile" (Johnson, *Modern Times*, 331). See also Shlomo Ben-Ami, *Fascism from Above: The Dictatorship of Primo de Rivera in Spain, 1923–1930* [Oxford: Clarendon Press, 1983], 396; and Andrew Wheatcroft, *The World Atlas of Revolutions* [New York: Simon and Schuster, 1983], 114–17, on Franco's military takeover.

The first thing to be said is that autocratic governments changing to electoral systems, let alone democracies, have historically been uncommon. The average reader of this book, whose knowledge of history tends to be concentrated on the recent West, may not realize that this is true, because that was a period in which democracy spread over Europe. But nevertheless, if he looks at the long sweep of history, it clearly is a fact. Most autocracies are succeeded by other autocracies. Succession of an autocracy by an electoral system is much less common than a change of dynasty.

On the other hand, if we look again at the long sweep of history, we will find cases in which autocracy became electoral. We will also find cases in which electoral systems succumbed to dictatorship. The most common explanation in both cases, of course, is foreign conquest, with a conqueror who imposes his own system of government. In the great days of Athens, Athens conquered a number of other Greek city-states, and in each case imposed upon the conquered city[9] an electoral form of government.[10] This electoral government was, of course, in most cases subordinate to a superelectorate in Athens. In this case, the governments replaced were, in general, by the rather lax standard presented in this book, already electoral, but with a much more restricted franchise. The governments which replaced what the Athenians called "democracies," when Sparta and, later, Thebes became dominant, were called at the time "oligarchies."[11] Using the terminology of this book, we

9. When it didn't sell all the citizens into slavery.

10. See Forrest, *The Emergence of Greek Democracy*. He notes that the Athenian empire "is often described as a savage and selfish tyranny . . . But although Athenian enthusiasm may have led her occasionally to impose or at least encourage democracy when it was not wholly necessary . . . to a considerable extent in fact, the ally remained autonomous . . . If Athenian rule was . . . harsh and unpopular . . . , it is curious how few of Athens' subjects were anxious to exchange it for Spartan freedom; most of the allied contingents in Sicily preferred to face almost certain death beside the Athenians than to accept an offer of safety from the Syracusans; curious that when revolts occurred they were nearly always the work of dissident oligarchs while the people were often prepared actively to support the return of the Athenians; even more curious how many former members of the Empire were ready to join a new Athenian confederacy in the fourth century after less than thirty years' experience of Spartan freedom" (39). See also S. N. Eisenstadt, *The Political Systems of Empires* (New York: Free Press, 1963), 106.

11. On the Theban period in Greece (371–355 B.C.), see R. Ernest Dupuy and Trevor N. Dupuy, *The Encyclopedia of Military History, from 3500 B.C. to the Present*, rev. ed. (New York: Harper and Row, 1977), 43; William L. Langer, *An Encyclopedia of World History*, 5th ed. (Boston: Houghton Mifflin, 1972), 77; C. W. C. Oman and G. Mercer Adam, *Greece*, vol. 2 of *The History of the Nations*, ed. Henry Cabot Lodge (New York: Collier, 1928), 426–51.

would call them "electoral," but with a much smaller electorate. They were still governed by voting, but only a quite small group was permitted to voter.

To continue then with the foreign conquest matter, the Romans, in general, set up electoral systems as the local government wherever their armies spread.[12] This did not mean that Rome itself was electoral, although at the time of its greatest expansion it was.[13] Macedonia, of course, never was even remotely democratic. Neither were the successor kingdoms which continued to use electoral local governments. The replacement of hereditary kingdoms in Gaul or Asia Minor by self-governing local structures of the overarching Roman empire was presumably a movement in the direction of democracy even if the movement did not go very far.

Note that this would not have been true with respect to the former Carthaginian empire, since Carthaginians also were electoral.[14] Indeed, in the period just before the Roman conquest, the Mediterranean was infested with city-states which had elected governments usually with a rather restricted group of electors. Rome partially conquered and partially extended this system but converted it into a system of local self-government.[15] As in the United States, with time, the local governments became less and less important, and the central government more and more so. Unlike the United States, of course, the central government was by this time a despotic and frequently chaotic monarchy.[16]

12. And, indeed, also the Macedonians. See, for example, William G. Sinnigen and Arthur E. Boak, *A History of Rome to A.D. 565*, 6th ed. (New York: Macmillan, 1977), 59ff, 62ff, 97ff; Theodor Mommsen, *Rome, from Earliest Times to 44 B.C.*, vol. 3 of *The History of Nations*, ed. Henry Cabot Lodge (New York: Collier, 1928), 62–73. On the Macedonians, see Langer, *Encyclopedia*, 91–92.

13. Sinnigen and Boak, *A History of Rome*, 133ff.

14. To a certain extent, though ruled by "merchant Princes," the Carthaginian state was nonetheless controlled in part by popular assemblies which were at liberty to "freely discuss and oppose matters brought before them." However, the assemblies' "agendas" were determined by a council of elders who decided just what these "matters" might be (Herbert J. Muller, *Freedom in the Ancient World* [New York: Harper and Row, 1961], 104).

15. Sinnigen and Boak, "Conquest of the Mediterranean, First Phase: 264–201 B.C.," chap. 8 in *A History of Rome*, 96–116; and chap. 9, "Conquest of the Mediterranean, Second Phase: 200–167 B.C.," 117–27. See also Mommsen, *Rome*, pt. 2, "Conquest of the Mediterranean States, 264–133 B.C.," 89–168.

16. Edward Gibbon, *The History of the Decline and Fall of the Roman Empire*, 7 vols. (London: Methuen, 1914), 1:vff; Sinnigen and Boak, "The Public Administration under the Autocracy," chap. 23 in *A History of Rome*, 431–50.

More recently, the European states have had somewhat the same phenomenon. During the period of the French Republic, electoral institutions were imposed all over Europe, and a good many aspects of them, elected parliaments, juries, etc., remained in existence through the Napoleonic empire.[17] As a result of this experience, and possibly of other factors, the nineteenth century was a period in which monarchies gradually shifted to what we will call "limited autocracies" and then became either republics or what I think should be called "decorative monarchies," like the present situation in Sweden.

These nineteenth-century electoral governments were among the greatest conquerers in world history.[18] They certainly deserve to be ranked with Rome and the Macedonians. Their empires were not originally electoral, but as time went by, the European countries controlling them gradually began moving towards electoral institutions for their colonies. At the same time, of course, they were expanding the franchise at home, with the result that most

17. As Leo Gershoy, for example, summarizes the process, "In that part of Europe which lay closest to France, the guiding impulse [of the first republic (1792–1804)] had been in 1792–1793 to liberate the enslaved peoples . . . [C]ivilians and generals alike were imbued with the consciousness of their country as *La Grande Nation*, superior as well as victorious and entitled by the laws of nature to the natural frontiers that her armies had gained . . . people of the annexed and incorporated territory continued as before to pay for benefits received. The privileged aristocracy, both law and secular, had been dispossessed by 1799; the feudal and mandrinal regimes, totally uprooted. The sale of nationalized property was proceeding briskly. Careers were open, within the salutary limitations imposed by the occupying liberators, to the talents of the home population. To be sure, old grievances still rankled: omnipresent French civil and military officials, periodic requisitions of food and material, military service obligations, and sporadic religious persecution. But the people were free, practicing more or less popular sovereignty. Time, the great healer, was working, aided by his assistant, the pocketbook, to reconcile the old with the new" (*The Era of the French Revolution, 1789–1799: Ten Years That Shook the World* [Princeton, N. J.: Van Nostrand, 1957], 93). See also ibid., 57–58, 70–101; cf. Jerome Blum, Rondo Cameron, and Thomas G. Barnes, *The European World: A History*, 2d ed. (Boston: Little, Brown, 1970), 480–91, 515, 604.

18. Of course, the industrial revolution these countries were experiencing at the time produced technological advances which contributed to the development of weapons and, as a result, enhanced their military capacities. See William H. McNeill, "The Military Impact of the French Political and the British Industrial Revolutions, 1789–1850," chap. 6 in *The Pursuit of Power: Technology, Armed Force, and Society since A.D. 1000* (Chicago: University of Chicago Press, 1982), 185–222; and chap. 7, "The Initial Industrialization of War, 1840–84," 223–61. See also D. K. Fieldhouse, "The Colonial Empires after 1815," pt. 2 in *The Colonial Empires: A Comparative Survey from the Eighteenth Century*, 2d ed. (London: Macmillan, 1982), 177–371.

of them became full democracies with universal adult suffrage in the early twentieth century.

The ultimate outcome in the colonies was depressing. They were all given independence with democratic institutions, but most of them switched back to autocracy fairly quickly. The degree to which they retained electoral institutions after independence seems to be roughly correlated with the amount of experience they had with such institutions under the colonial regimes. The prospect for democracy, or, indeed, any kind of electoral institutions in these areas, seems poor.

The most famous military extension of democracy, of course, was the imposition of democratic regimes on about half of Germany and all of Italy.[19] In Japan the existing electoral system was changed to full democracy by giving women the vote and lowering the voting age.[20] The House of Peers was also abolished.[21] All three of these countries had had extensive experience with electoral institutions in earlier years.

These are all cases in which democracy came as a result of outside intervention, and I don't think that we need to concern ourselves very much with them. It's obviously possible for a powerful military system to impose a form of government on nations it conquers. Determining whether these democracies will last a long time is not easy. In most cases the democracy established as the empires withdrew collapsed almost immediately. Nevertheless, I think we can simply recognize here that democracy can be spread by military force and historically has been on a number of occasions.

I ignore cases in which a democratic country simply expanded itself, as, for example, the United States and Canada moved into Indian areas which had previously been subject to a rather chaotic system which was not obviously either electoral or despotic and, indeed, was not obviously even a government. In Latin America, of course, the Spaniards seized a number of well-organized kingdoms, but this did not change the form of government.[22] It was one autocracy replacing another.

19. These campaigns are described in Dupuy and Dupuy, *Encyclopedia of Military History*, 683–88.

20. In 1945. See Langer, *Encyclopedia*, 1344–45.

21. See, for example, Johnson, *Modern Times*, 179–90, 719ff; Langer, *Encyclopedia*, 1344–45, describes various constitutional changes in modern Japan's government.

22. See, for example, Fieldhouse, "The Spanish and Portuguese Empires in America," chap. 2 in *Colonial Empires*, 11–33; and chap. 5, "Myths and Realities of the American Empires," 84–99.

But these are cases in which electoral governments have conquered other areas and imposed their form of government on them. There are also cases, of course, where despotisms have conquered countries with electoral systems and imposed their form of government. This is, I think, rarer, not because it's any less probable, but simply because electoral systems themselves are rarer. If Ligny had gone the other way, and the European kingdoms had reestablished the monarchy in France, only one government would have changed form. Since Ligny was won by the French Republic, and it then proceeded to win a number of other battles, it was able to change the government in many countries.

There are, however, a good many cases historically, where electoral systems have been taken over. All of the Greek city-states fell under the suzerainty of the Macedonians, who, in general, permitted electoral local self-government.[23] Nevertheless, clearly such places as Athens became, in essence, states in a larger despotic kingdom.[24] Similarly, many, although not all, of the electoral city-states which were set up in the Middle Ages succumbed to conquest by autocratic neighbors. Mostly conquest meant they were annexed, but in some cases an independent dynasty was established.[25] Once again, this is not a matter of great interest. It is clear that, for example, both Hitler and Stalin could impose their systems on Czechoslovakia once they had occupied it. Nevertheless, as I have said above, it seems most likely that the commonest single reason for a country's ceasing to be a despotism and becoming electoral is conquest by a country which itself is electoral. Similarly the commonest reason for a country's moving from electoral government to despotism is seizure by a neighboring despot. Although this is true enough, it's not very interesting. Neither autocracy nor electoral systems could have originated in this way.

As far as we know, the earliest governments, the ones we find in Mesopotamia, Egypt, and China,[26] were all despotisms.[27] Further, as far as we can

23. Bowra, *The Greek Experience*, 77; see also Forrest, *The Emergence of Greek Democracy*, 42.

24. Muller, *Freedom in the Ancient World*, 221–22; Langer, *Encyclopedia*, 78; Oman and Adam, *Greece*, 471–520.

25. Langer, *Encyclopedia*, pt. 3, sec. C, "The Later Middle Ages," 287–391; Blum, Cameron, and Barnes, *European World*, 27, 31ff; Cyril Mango, *Byzantium: The Empire of New Rome* (New York: Scribner's, 1980), 46–59, 60, 220.

26. Until we decipher Indian script, we cannot be sure whether this was true there also.

27. See, for example, Robert Silverberg, *Empires in the Dust: Ancient Civilizations Brought to Light* (New York: Chilton, 1963), passim; Langer, *Encyclopedia*, 27–34; Archibald Henry Sayce, *Ancient Empires of the East*, vol. 1 of *The History of Nations*, ed. Henry Cabot Lodge

also tell, the same situation existed everywhere else in the world, except possibly in central Europe. Further, there seems to be no evidence that any of these governments ever became electoral except by foreign conquest.

We have mentioned that Alexander and his heirs imposed self-governing city-states all over their empire, which included Mesopotamia and Egypt and indeed much else. In the late nineteenth and early twentieth centuries, of course, these areas came temporarily under the control of democratic states from outside, and in some cases this led to short intervals of domestic democracy.[28] Lebanon, where democracy was most successful, has for the last ten years been living through a genuine political nightmare. They still have an elected government, but that government is not able to govern.[29]

There is one exception to this rule for early states. For reasons that are not clear, the Phoenicians seem to have lived in a set of city-states. Their internal government was electoral, apparently with a very narrow electorate. Nevertheless, they did not, strictly speaking, have kings.[30]

Exactly why the Phoenicians and their great colony Carthage had this form of government, we do not know. It certainly was not in all ways a particularly

---

(New York: Collier, 1928). The Sumerian government did have some aspects which can be interpreted as electoral.

28. The short-term duration problem of "ready-made and superimposed" Western electoral regimes in this area of the world has been noted and examined in Bernard Lewis, "The Impact of the West," chap. 10 in *The Arabs in History* (New York: Harper and Row, 1966), 164–78.

29. As Johnson observes, the chances for long-run political stability in Lebanon were, of course, quite poor from the beginning (*Modern Times*, 703).

30. Sayce, *Ancient Empires*, 125. Silverberg (*Empires in the Dust*) suggests that it is in fact "wrong to refer to this land of the Phoenicians as a 'nation.' Even using the name 'Phoenicia' to describe the area is somewhat inexact. There never was a Phoenician nation under one government. What existed was a group of independent cities, bound loosely together by ties of commerce and language and kinship" (127). See also ibid., 146–47. "The government of the several states was a monarchy tempered by an oligarchy of wealth. The king seems to have been but the first among a body of ruling merchants, princes and powerful and wealthy chiefs. In time the monarchy disappeared altogether, its place being supplied by suffetes or 'judges,' whose term of office lasted sometimes for a year, sometimes for more, sometimes even for life" (Sayce, *Ancient Empires*, 124). Sayce states that though "successor royalty was abolished for a time, and the Tyrians elected suffetes or judges" (125) . . . On Hiram of Tyre (969–936 B.C.), see also, for example, Langer, *Encyclopedia*, 47–48. In Carthage, "There were also kings at first. But by 400 B.C. the hereditary monarchy had given way to a system involving two annually elected magistrates, a senate of 300 members appointed for life, and another assembly of 104 members whose role is unclear" (Silverberg, *Empires in the Dust*, 147). In fact, "Carthage never

pleasant government. Human sacrifice of children was in fact a major phenomenon, just as their Roman enemies' propaganda said it was.[31]

To offer my own opinion here, I believe that the Phoenicians were descendants of the peoples of the sea, an invasion that swept over most of the Middle East in about 1500 B.C. They were part of that same great wave of barbarian invasion which, over a period of five or six hundred years, made such a gigantic change along the northern coast of the Mediterranean.[32] In my opinion, and I emphasize that this is merely my opinion,[33] they differed from the Dorian Greeks, or the tribes who eventually established Rome, mainly in the fact that the very dense populations in the Middle East meant that in general they were absorbed by the natives and adopted native governmental techniques. The Phoenicians would then be a minor outpost that stuck to their older forms to at least some extent.

The rest of this wave which came in at about that time destroyed Cretan and Mycenaean civilization.[34] It inaugurated the Greek Dark Age, and these Dorian conquerors seem to have set civilization north of the Mediterranean back very sharply.[35] Nevertheless, when Greece comes out of the Dark Age,

---

founded a real empire. In Spain and Africa, the Carthaginian colonies seem to have been under direct political control of the mother city, but the other western Phoenician cities in the Mediterranean were only slightly affiliated with Carthage" (Silverberg, *Empires in the Dust*).

31. As Blum, Cameron, and Barnes (*European World*) state, "Moloch demanded the best and dearest that the worshipper could grant him, and the parent was required to offer his eldest or only son as sacrifice, while the victim's cries were drowned by the noise of drums and flutes. When Agathocles defeated the Carthaginians, the noblest of the citizens offered in expiation three hundred of their children to Baal-Moloch . . . The priests scourged themselves or gashed their arms and breasts to win the favor of the god, and similar horrors were perpetrated in the name of [the goddess] Ashtoreth. To her, too, boys and maidens were burned, and young men made themselves eunuchs in her honor" (9).

32. See, for example, Sayce, *Ancient Empires*, 117–36; Oman and Adam, *Greece*, 27ff, 18ff; see also Silverberg, *Empires in the Dust*, 130ff.

33. I offer my opinion here with little false modesty, because no one else knows much about the matter either. For an easily readable but nevertheless authoritative account of what little is known, see N. K. Sanders, *The Sea Peoples: Warriors of the Ancient Mediterranean*, rev. ed. (London: Thames and Hudson, 1985).

34. See, for example, Forrest, *The Emergence of Greek Democracy*, 45; Silverberg, *Empires in the Dust*, 131, 135–55.

35. The Greek Dark Age (1200 B.C. to approximately 800 B.C.) followed the "First massive Greek colonial movement" by the Dorians coming down from Asia Minor. Cities were destroyed and trade was cut off. "The Greeks became illiterate and were reduced to small local communities" (Langer, *Encyclopedia*, 60–61). See also Oman and Adam, *Greece*, 51ff.

it is no longer a country of many petty kingdoms, but a country of many petty governments which were electoral. They are usually called oligarchies or aristocracies.

We don't know very much about what happened in the Italian peninsula. There do not seem to have been any literate people there when the invaders arrived. Once again, however, this area does come into history about the same time as the Greeks recover from the Dark Age.[36] At the time, there were a number of states with basically electoral institutions.

Note that in all of these cases, the electoral institutions might possibly include a king or, in the case of Sparta, two kings.[37] These, however, would be people who were deliberately elected, as was the man who is carried in our history as the first king of Rome, or, if they were hereditary, whose powers were sharply restricted. We don't know as much about this area as we do about the later German invaders of Europe, but it seems likely that their institutions were similar.

We know a little more about the Germans partly because their institutions were described by Roman historians and partly because remnants of them existed well into relatively modern times. Nizhni Novgorod, for example, seems to have been governed by this traditional method.[38] Alexander Nevsky, who beat the Teutonic Knights and surrendered to the Mongols without fighting, is an example of the kind of leader who was referred to as a "king" by the Roman historians talking about Germany.[39]

36. In fact, it was Greeks setting up city-states who first began noticing the place. See Bowra, *The Greek Experience*, 20.

37. As Russell describes it, "The constitution of Sparta was complicated. There were two kings, belonging to different families, and succeeding by heredity. One or other of the kings commanded the army in time of war, but in time of peace their powers were limited. At communal feasts they got twice as much to eat as anyone else, and there was general mourning when one of them died" (*History of Western Philosophy*, 96–97). Forrest (*The Emergence of Greek Democracy*) summarizes the double monarchy as "a strange institution which the Spartans traced back to the twin sons of an early leader but is more probably to be explained by some earlier compromise and coalition of rival Dorian groups" (128).

38. Langer (*Encyclopedia*, 185, 258–59, 331–33, 341–42) describes the early political history of Novgorod, a city in Russia originally established by the Swedes (A.D. 862), later dominated by German traders as a commercial center (A.D. 1150–1250), and eventually conquered and made a territory of Russia by Ivan III (The Great) (A.D. 1478). In the eleventh century, "The assembly of freemen (*Vieche*) reached its fullest development" (259) as a political system in Novgorod.

39. On Alexander Nevsky (1220–63), Russian military leader and Grand Prince of Novgorod, and Vladimir, after 1252, see, for example, Dupuy and Dupuy, *Encyclopedia of Military*

The Germanic institutions were simple.[40] The basic governmental agency of these German tribes was an assembly of the entire population. They, of course, were not gigantic tribes in general. This assembly might, or then again might not, elect a king. Normally, these kings were members of the same family, but there was no regular rule of succession within that family.[41] Further, there was no requirement that the tribe have a king.[42] If someone was elected king he remained king until he died, but the tribe might not decide to elect anyone else at that time. The basic role of the kings was war leader, and they were completely subordinated to the folkmoot, but of course, during wartime it only rarely met.[43]

The invasion of the Roman empire meant that these tribes were, in essence, at war for very considerable periods of time. As a result, the kings appear to have been able to convert the institutions I have described above pretty much into genuine kingdoms in which they had hereditary succession and true control. Bits and pieces of the control of the folkmoot, however, did remain. Further, of course, many bits and pieces of the former Roman structure which involved elected local governments remained, and, of course, the church itself retained a number of electoral aspects.

Thus in the Middle Ages one found city-states with electoral governments, "national" voting bodies, which might have some control over the king (usually very little), and the local Catholic Cathedral might have a

---

History, 178; Langer, *Encyclopedia*, 258–61, 340. See also Blum, Cameron, and Barnes, *European World*, 47–48. Nevsky became, in effect, a "vassal of the mongols" from 1240 to 1263, following their successful conquest in Russia.

40. I follow mainly J. B. Bury, *The Invasion of Europe by the Barbarians* (New York: Norton, 1967), here.

41. More precisely, there were two distinct types of supreme rulers possible under the Germanic system, and tribes which had no monarch "had an officer who was called the graf. The graf had functions and duties corresponding to these of the king," but with one noteworthy difference: "The graf was elected by the assembly, and the assembly might elect anyone they liked. The king was likewise elected . . . , but in his case their choice was limited to a particular family, the royal family. In other words, the king was hereditary, and the grafship was not" (ibid., 13).

42. Ibid., 12, 13.

43. In fact, "The presence or absence of a king might almost be described as a matter of convenience; it had almost no decisive constitutional importance. In every German state, whether there was a king or not, the assembly of the freemen was sovran . . ." (ibid., 12; see also 14–15).

"chapter" which elected its own officers.[44] The emperor was commonly an elected official, albeit elected by a very narrow suffrage, and the pope was throughout an elected official, originally elected by the people of Rome in a rather disorderly assembly and later by the College of Cardinals.[45]

It would be hard to argue that these electoral institutions were of fundamental importance until modern times. There were, however, two reasons to believe that governments might once again become electoral. Firstly, education in Europe depended very heavily on Greek and Latin,[46] and hence almost all people who could read and write were aware of the existence of the previous electoral systems. Further, they tended to look back on these periods as high points of civilization, and on their current situation as, in every respect except religion, inferior.

Secondly, there was that rather mysterious state, England.[47] From the time of Simon Montfort onward, kings of England, rather irregularly called councils of their lords and of the country squires meeting in two houses.[48]

44. More commonly, of course, it was subject to direct control from some superior. See, for example, Leopold von Ranke, *The History of the Popes during the Last Four Centuries*, vol. 2 (London: G. Bell and Sons, 1913), 3ff, on the development of papal authority during this early period. On the movement towards centralization of the authority of the Roman church, see Sinnigen and Boak, *History of Rome*, 381, 480–85.

45. George H. Sabine (*A History of Political Theory* [New York: Henry Holt, 1950]) comments that "in constitution making the Papacy led the way by the establishment in the second half of the eleventh century of an orderly process of election by the clergy, to replace the older informal kind of election which often made a Papal election the plaything of the petty Roman nobility or of imperial politics" (211–12).

46. Charles Homer Haskins (*The Rise of Universities* [Ithaca: Cornell University Press, 1957]) notes that "it was almost wholly as formulated in a few standard texts that the learning of the ancient world was transmitted to mediaeval times" (28). See also ibid., 66ff.

47. I believe that some of the Scandinavian countries, particularly Sweden, had a development rather similar to that of England, but I must admit I don't know much about them.

48. J. D. Mackie ("The Early Tudors, 1485–1558," in *The Oxford History of England*, ed. G. N. Clark [Oxford: Clarendon Press, 1957], 562–67) describes relations between the monarchy and Parliament during this time. "In 1539, following the constitutional separation of Parliament into the two Houses, King Henry VIII nevertheless 'packed' parliament judiciously before it met; he was ready with a programme, and he 'managed' the debates . . . It is, however, uncertain how far the process of 'packing' went . . . Parliament was not a 'lion under the throne' which roared when the king pressed the hidden spring. It was, however, susceptible to 'management' and Henry understood 'management' very well" (ibid., 437). See also H. A. L. Fisher, *The History of England from the Accession of Henry VII to the Death of*

In fact, the level of power of these groups was never very clear, but England was a very disorderly country in any event in those days, with the crown frequently in dispute.

Nevertheless, from the time William of Orange became king of England, England began winning wars and also, apparently, began to become the most economically developed country in Europe. This led to a tendency to copy English institutions, particularly in France, where Voltaire and Montesquieu led the intellectual movements which eventuated in the French Revolution. At the time of the French Revolution, substantially everybody in France, apparently including Louis XVI, was in favor of a constitutional monarchy modeled after that of England. Of course, things didn't work out that way.

We've been discussing constitutional monarchy, in the meaning which that term was understood by Montesquieu and George II. But in any event, with the American Revolution and French Revolution, modern republican governments were born.[49] In the nineteenth century the electoral system, mainly with quite large, if not universal, electorates, rapidly spread all over Europe, partly, of course, owing to the armies of the French Revolution and, quite seriously, also through the armies of the French empire, since Napoleon also, at least in theory, believed in constitutional monarchy.

In the meantime, in England, George III had gone insane,[50] and the government of England had become almost entirely a parliamentary government

---

Henry VIII (1485–1547), vol. 5 of *The Political History of England*, 12 vols. (1906; Kravs Reprint Co., 1969), 434–35.

49. As one British scholar writes, "The American war had profound results on the nascent democratic movement because it roused strong opposition to the activities of George III and because so many people sympathized with the revolt of the colonies. 'No taxation without representation' was certain of a cordial response on this side of the Atlantic. There was also a feeling that the defeat of the colonies would have encouraged the King in his suspected designs on the constitution . . . Englishmen no longer congratulated themselves on the superiority of their institutions to those of other countries. The French Revolution was so spectacular that the similarly disturbing example of the United States is now forgotten, but it was very important," particularly in its economic effects: "Every year that democratic government existed in the United States it became a more damaging contrast to the Government of England. Many manufacturers had business contracts with the United States, as for example Cobden and the Radical manufacturers of Leicester . . . Everyone who was dissatisfied, the middle class, the working men, the dissenters, naturally asked why a system which worked in one country [the United States] would not work in another" (Spearman, *Democracy in England*, 48, 68).

50. See H. W. V. Temperley, "The Age of Walpole and the Pelhams," chap. 2 in *The Cam-*

with little or no royal influence. It was, however, a parliament the upper house of which was purely hereditary and still very powerful, and the lower house of which was elected by a set of bizarre institutions under which, for example, the House of Pitt owned in fee simple absolute six seats.[51] Conversion of this system to modern English democracy was the result of a series of reform movements running from about 1830 on, and it's hard to say whether they were copying the United States, the Continent, or pioneering. Indeed, the motives which led the people in control of England at that time to gradually give up their control step by step are not particularly clear. It looks very much like intellectual conversion to the democratic ideal as well as to free trade and limited government.[52]

In the twentieth century, democracy, which probably peaked in 1914, began a long slide which we hope will not continue. In 1914 there were only two countries, Thailand and Ethopia, that did not at least have some kind of an elected legislature with at least some power.[53] It is true that in the northern part of South America and Central America democracies tended to pop

---

bridge Modern History, ed. A. W. Ward, G. W. Prothero, and Stanley Leathes, vol. 6, *The Eighteenth Century* (New York: Macmillan, 1925), 69–73; J. M. Rigg, "Great Britain (1956–93): The King's Friends," chap. 14 in Ward, Prothero, and Leathes, eds., *The Cambridge Modern History*, vol. 6, 423ff; see also, on the derangement of King George III, Martin J. Griffin, "Great Britain (1756–1793): The Years of Peace and the Rise of the Younger Pitt (1782–1793)," chap. 11 in Ward, Prothero, and Leathes, eds., *The Cambridge Modern History*, vol. 6, 473–74. An added problem for Parliament at the time of the king's illness was that of discerning the political inclinations of the examining physicians. The doctors who were asked to report to the Commons on the king's capacities tended "to differ politically as well as professionally, thus adding to the difficulties of the situation" (ibid., 473).

51. Edward P. Cheyney (*A Short History of England*, rev. ed. [Boston: Ginn, 1918]) notes that "this bad custom [of parliamentary corruption] had been growing ever since the reign of Charles II, but it reached its height under Walpole. 'All these men have their price,' he once said to a friend, pointing to a group of members of the House of Commons" (548).

52. See Blum, Cameron, and Barnes, *European World*, 567–72.

53. Langer, *Encyclopedia*, 980–1120, summarizes political structures worldwide at this time. On Ethiopia in particular, see 872, 1078–79; see also Ryszard Kapuscinski, *The Emperor: Downfall of an Autocrat* (New York: Harcourt Brace Jovanovich, 1977), on the reign of Ethiopian emperor Haile Selassie (1930–36). It might be noted that Ethiopia in fact did not officially abolish slavery until 1924. Thailand's (Siam's) political system during this period is discussed in Langer, *Encyclopedia*, 906, 1104–5; see also *New York Times*, September 15, 1985, p. 2E, where "Thailand's 15 to 20 coup attempts over the last half century" are examined in light of current developments.

up and then pop down again as dictators overthrew them.[54] The three strongest countries in South America, Brazil, Argentina, and Chile, were, however, electoral and had been so for a considerable period of time.[55] The other South American countries at least paid lip service to "democracy" systems and, in fact, were electoral from time to time.[56]

Note that our definition of "electoral system" is one under which a colony owned by an electoral nation is counted as electoral. A resident of Ceylon in 1840 did not have any vote in the English elections, but the same was true of most Londoners. This can obviously be criticized, but there is a difference between Hong Kong, where the government is appointed by an elected prime minister in London, and Canton, where the governor is not. Further, by 1914 a number of the major colonies had begun to develop electoral aspects in their local governments. There were local elections in, for example, various parts of the British empire. What there was of an American empire was obviously in the process of being converted into either independent countries or self-governing parts of the United States at a reasonable rate.

The change since 1914 is, of course, drastic. All of Eastern Europe is now ruled by despotisms. The bulk of the former French, Belgian, and Dutch empires have suffered the same fate, and in the former English empire, only some islands in the Caribbean, India, and Ceylon are democratic. The former French empire no longer has any elements of democracy except (residually) in Lebanon. In South America, Argentina, Chile, and Brazil have joined the tradition in which countries are sometimes democratic and sometimes dictatorial.[57] All of this represents a significant setback for electoral systems.

54. Dupuy and Dupuy, *Encyclopedia of Military History*, 1048–50; Langer, *Encyclopedia*, 1067–69 (see also 1241–45); see also "The Generals Still Run Latin 'Democracies,'" *Washington Post*, November 10, 1985, pp. D1, D4, on current developments.

55. Shortly after this time, of course, Argentina "fell victim to both the twin evils which poison Latin America: Militarism and Politics" (Johnson, *Modern Times*, 616). Johnson continues, summarizing the problem in this region, "in the nineteenth century the military *coup* had become a standard means to change government. This disastrous practice continued after the arrival of universal suffrage. In the years 1920–66, for instance, there were eighty successful military coups in eighteen Latin-American countries, Ecuador and Bolivia leading with nine each, Paraguay and Argentina following with seven each."

56. See, for example, Langer, *Encyclopedia*, 1057–66, 1239–45. Barrington Moore Jr. (*Social Origins of Dictatorship and Democracy* [Boston: Beacon Press, 1966]) suggests in passing that "much of Latin America remains in the era of authoritarian semiparliamentary government" (438).

57. At the time this book was written there were only six dictatorships in the whole of Latin

This has been a historical account; can we do anything more than simply recount these things? Let me run through a few historical theories. The first of these is that in times when infantry is the basic arm, and when large numbers of troops are needed, democracy is apt to be the form of government. We must begin by pointing out that as a matter of fact the times in which democracy developed are all "infantry" periods. Greek city-states depended primarily on mobilizing their adult male citizenry to fight as infantry.[58] Similarly, the Roman legions were essentially infantry forces.[59] The American Revolution occurred during a period when infantry was the primary arm,[60] and the French Revolution, which introduced conscription into the modern world and won its battles essentially by throwing vast numbers of men into the gunfire of the outnumbered royal armies it opposed, was an almost perfect expression of this theory.[61]

America. This was possibly a record, but at the time of the final revision, it had risen to seven. Both numbers are low and perhaps portend a change.

58. In fact, a citizen's political eligibility for certain offices and functions was determined, at least in part, by the contribution he could make to the military needs of the state: "Since the days of Solon (594 B.C.) Athenians had been divided into four census classes, the *Pentakosiomedimnoi*, men whose estates could produce 500 measures of grain or their equivalent per annum; the *Hippeis* or cavalrymen, those who could afford to keep a horse and equip themselves for cavalry service; the *zeugitai* or hoplites, those fitted to arm themselves as infantrymen; and the *thetes*, those who could not. At first, . . . these classes had an important political significance in that membership carried with it qualification for certain offices of state. In the fifth century this was still officially the case, at least to the extent that *thetes* were barred by law from the highest purely civil office, the archonship and only *pentakosiomedimnoi* were trusted with the chief financial positions" (Forrest, *The Emergence of Greek Democracy*, 22; see also Langer, *Encyclopedia*, 65).

59. Sinnigen and Boak, *A History of Rome*, 262. See also Edward N. Luttwak, *The Grand Strategy of the Roman Empire* (Baltimore: Johns Hopkins University Press, 1976), 40ff.

60. Lynn Montross, *War through the Ages*, rev. 3d ed. (New York: Harper & Row, 1944), 417–39; Dupuy and Dupuy, *Encyclopedia of Military History*, 708–17; Marvin A. Kreidberg and Merton G. Henry, *The History of Military Mobilization in the United States Army, 1775–1783* (Washington, D.C.: Department of the Army, 1955), 1–22; Wheatcroft, *World Atlas of Revolutions*, 14–20.

61. Montross, *War through the Ages*, 450–58; Dupuy and Dupuy, *Encyclopedia of Military History*, 678ff; McNeill, *The Pursuit of Power*, 137–38, 144–206; Wheatcroft, *World Atlas of Revolutions*, 21–29; B. H. Liddell Hart, *Strategy* (New York: Praeger, 1955), 113ff; T. N. Dupuy, *The Evolution of Weapons and Warfare* (New York: Bobbs-Merrill, 1980), 154–58; R. P. Dunn-Pattison, "The General War," chap. 14 in Ward, Prothero, and Leathes, *The Cambridge Modern History*, vol. 8, 400–403.

Further, it should be pointed out that the fall of the Roman empire was essentially a triumph of mounted warriors over footsoldiers. Adrianople was the first time that the Roman legions had been ridden down by cavalry.[62] From Adrianople, for another three hundred years, Roman armies consisted primarily of armored cavalry,[63] and the restoration of infantry in the army of Byzantium[64] was not duplicated in Western Europe, where cavalry remained the dominant arm until the British bowmen and the Swiss pikemen restored the older infantry predominance.[65]

Similarly, the slide of democracy in recent years has been accompanied by the development not of cavalry, but of tanks, aircraft, etc., weapons which are not really suitable for quickly trained conscript soldiers of the levy in mass.

But having said that, there is this much truth in it; it is easy to find counterexamples too. Greece fell not before cavalry, but before the Macedonian infantry.[66] In modern times, a great many democracies have been overthrown by conscript armies following their officers rather than their elected political leaders. Colonels in Greece and the generals in Argentina are merely specific examples.[67] I think there is something to be said for this theory, but not very much. After all, historically, infantry has normally been the dominant arm simply because it is the cheapest arm. And the dominant governments have,

62. "The first great victory of Heavy Cavalry over Roman infantry came in the battle of Adrianople (A.D. 378). Emperor Valens of the East Roman Empire had assembled a large army for a showdown with the Ostrogoths and Visigoths . . . The Roman losses were tremendous . . . perhaps as many as forty thousand men were killed . . . [T]he Roman cavalry . . . did not participate in the battle, succeeded in breaking out and escaping death" (Dupuy, *Evolution of Weapons*, 39–40; see also Montross, *War through the Ages*, 86–87; Dupuy and Dupuy, *Encyclopedia of Military History*, 157).

63. See, for example, John W. Eadie, "The Development of Roman Mailed Cavalry," *Journal of Roman Studies* 57 (1967): 161–73; Sinnigen and Boak, *A History of Rome*, 426ff; Dupuy, *Evolution of Weapons*, 36–41; Hart, *Strategy*, 59–60.

64. Montross (*War through the Ages*) discusses the replacement of cavalry with foot soldiers or "foot-archers" in tenth-century Byzantium (127–28).

65. See ibid., 168–72, for a discussion of the English longbowmen, employed in England's army from the twelfth through the fifteenth centuries. On the Swiss "Halberdiers," or spearmen, of the fourteenth century, see 172–75. Both types of men-at-arms are also discussed in Dupuy, *Evolution of Weapons*, 81–89.

66. Dupuy and Dupuy, *Encyclopedia of Military History*, 43–44, gives a summary of Greece's fall to Macedonia (355–356 B.C.). As a result of King Philip's reorganization of the Macedonian fighting force, "The backbone of the army was its infantry" (44).

67. Ibid., 1341; Langer, *Encyclopedia*, 1251–53, summarizes the twentieth-century history of these practices in Argentina. On similar events in Greece, see Roy C. Macridis, *Greek Poli-*

in fact, been despotisms of one sort or another rather than democracies. It is true, as far as I know, that there have never been any democracies that depended essentially on cavalry for their defense, but granted the relative rarity of democracies and the relative rarity of cavalry predominance on the battlefield, this may simply be coincidence.

We now turn to what I call the Aristotelian theory of the overthrow of democracy.[68] Aristotle had a sort of cyclical theory of government, although it was never very obvious why the tyrannies would be replaced by oligarchies. Nevertheless, his theory of the overthrow of democracies clearly does fit at least some of the empirical evidence.

He thought that the basic reason for the fall of democracy was essentially what we would now call left-wing politics. He hypothesized a "popular" leader who succeeded in convincing the common people that he needed a professional bodyguard in order to protect himself against the wealthy. Once he had this private bodyguard, he converted it into a sort of secret police and controlled the city-state.[69] There seems to be no doubt that a certain number of Greek tyrants did indeed follow this line of development.[70] Further, both Caesar and Lenin carried out what might be argued to be a sort of modernized version.[71]

---

tics at a Crossroads: What Kind of Socialism (Stanford, Calif.: Hoover Institution Press, 1984); Dupuy and Dupuy, *Encyclopedia of Military History*, 1271–72; *New York Times*, November 21, 1985, p. A7.

68. I am here using his definition of "democracy," not mine. In his meaning of the word, the electorate was large, but not universal. Aristotle's *Politics*, book 4, in particular, discusses this problem. But see Sabine, *History of Political Theory*, 88–122, for a review and discussion of Aristotle's theory of tyranny and democracy; see also Oscar Jaszi and John D. Lewis, *Against the Tyrant: The Tradition and Theory of Tyrannicide* (Glencoe, Ill.: Free Press, 1957), 4–9 and passim.

69. See, for example, Sabine, *History of Political Theory*, 114–15.

70. Forrest, *The Emergence of Greek Democracy*, 82ff. Sinnigen and Boak, *A History of Rome*, 76.

71. On Caesar's rise to power, see Mommsen, *Rome*, 374–76. He asserts that, when Caesar became emperor, "no corps of guards—the true criterion of a military state—was even formed by him; even as general he dropped the bodyguard which had long been usual; and, though constantly beset by assassins in the capital, he contented himself with the usual escort of lictors." He admits, however, that "this noble ideal, of a kingship based only on the confidence of the people, could be but an illusion; amid the deep disorganization of the nation it was impossible for the eighth king of Rome to reign merely by virtue of law and justice. Just as little could the army which had placed him on the throne be really absorbed again into the state . . . Thou-

Having said this, however, it is, to put it mildly, easy to think of cases in which dictatorships have overthrown democracy, where they represented not the people or the political left, but the political right. Once again the Greek colonels and the Argentine generals are obvious examples. Thus, although the Aristotelian scenario undoubtedly can occur, it would be hard to argue that it is the dominant procedure. Having disposed of what I believe are the two principal theories for the overthrow of democracy,[72] we are left without very much in the way of genuine theory.

Historically, electoral systems have sometimes lasted very long periods of time. Venice was almost a thousand years old when it was finally destroyed

---

sands of swords still flew at Caesar's signal from their scabbards, but they no longer returned to their scabbards at his signal. Caesar's creation could not but be a military monarchy; he had overthrown the *regime* of the aristocrats and bankers only to put in its place a military *regime*" (375–76). Of interest is Caesar's introduction of the use of mercenaries in his cavalry, a policy innovation to which "He was driven by the untrustworthiness of the subject cavalry" (374).

On Lenin's acquisition of control, see Eric R. Wolf, *Peasant Wars of the Twentieth Century* (New York: Harper and Row, Harper Torchbooks, 1969), 82–99; G. R. Treviranus, *Revolutions in Russia* (New York: Harper, 1944), 75–140; Fitzpatrick, *The Russian Revolution*, passim; Johnson, *Modern Times*, 52ff, 66–86, 384; D'Encausse, *Confiscated Power*, 109–10. As Johnson points out, "In the initial stages of his takeover, Lenin depended entirely on the armed bands Trotsky had organized through the Petrograd Soviet. They were composed partly of politically motivated young thugs, the 'men in black leather jerkins,' partly of deserters, often Cossacks" (*Modern Times*, 65). Though on December 7, 1917, the military committee overseeing this political police force was disbanded, one section was retained, to become the "Cheka" ("All Russian Extraordinary Commission") and was "charged with combating 'counter-revolution and sabotage.' The decree which created the Cheka was not made public until more than ten years later (*Pravda*, 18 December 1927), so that Lenin's security force was from the beginning and remained for the rest of his life a secret police in the true sense, in that its very existence was not officially acknowledged" (67–68).

Stalin, of course, also employed secret police, with his political behavior becoming (from the average citizen's viewpoint) "characterized by the total absence of rules . . . [and] for this reason unpredictable. One example provides evidence. In the late forties, when the future purge was in preparation, the police, as a first step, carried out massive arrests on the periphery of the Soviet state, in the regions where prisoners who had completed their terms were confined. These former prisoners, trying to understand the logic governing their arrests, finally discovered that it was simply alphabetical; because of the first letter of his name, an individual might escape from the purge or experience [it] again" (D'Encausse, *Confiscated Power*, 41–42; see also Anton Antonov-Ovseyenko, *The Time of Stalin: Portrait of a Tyranny* [New York: Harper and Row, 1981], passim).

72. There is, of course, the very old one under which demagogues who are for some obscure reason very powerful succeed in overthrowing it. There is an equally ancient one under

by Napoléon (then a mere general).[73] Similarly, Béarn lasted a good five hundred years before, once again, the French Revolutionary troops overthrew it. Thus electoral systems can last for a long time. Some of the German city-states lasted right up to the unification of Germany in 1870.[74]

Nevertheless, that has not been the normal history of electoral systems. In general, they have fallen either because they failed to keep their arms up in peacetime or from internal causes. But the problem of developing any general theory of their fall has so far defeated me. There seem to be innumerable distinct causes.[75] There is, however, one thing that I think can be said fairly certainly: they tend to be overthrown by the executive branch of the government rather than by the legislative.

The reasons for this are, I think, fairly simple and straightforward. In general, a clear majority of the legislature would normally lose from the removal of the electoral system, whatever it is, and the substitution of a dictatorial regime. The executive branch, on the other hand, surely contains many people, including whoever is head of the executive branch, who would gain.

Note that the question of whether it is the strictly military part of the executive branch or other parts is relatively unimportant here. Traditionally, central governments have been very largely military machines. Thus, it is commoner for a military man like Napoléon to overthrow the government than for a civilian like Dr. Francia. It does not seem likely, however, that the predominance of military overthrows over civilian overthrows is any greater than the predominance of military men over civilians in the governments. Basically the executive branch is apt to be exalted by the movement to dictatorship, regardless of whether it is a civilian or military man who heads it, and the legislative branch of the government reduced.

---

which people who are simply wicked (usually soldiers) overthrow it, but in neither case is there any explanation as to why they can do it.

73. Henri Pirenne, *Economic and Social History of Medieval Europe* (New York: Harcourt Brace Jovanovich, 1937), 198–200; H. M. Vernon, "Italy and the Papacy," chap. 16 in Ward, Prothero, and Leathes, *The Cambridge Modern History*, vol. 6, 605–7; Langer, *Encyclopedia*, 238–40, 322–23, 496–97, 634–35, 700; see also Fernand Braudel, *Civilization and Capitalism, 15th–18th Century*, vol. 2 of *The Wheels of Commerce* (New York: Harper and Row, 1982), 466–67, 489–90; Blum, Cameron, and Barnes, *European World*, 102.

74. Langer, *Encyclopedia*, 715–42.

75. Such as changes in coalition formations, and in the organizational costs of forming such groups for political gain. See my article "The Roots of Order" in *Toward a Science of Politics*,

Why are, in some cases, the executives able to overthrow the electoral government and in other cases not? I must confess, I have no clear answer, but it should be said that a great many electoral systems, including those that have lasted a long period of time, have had arrangements which kept the executive very weak. The Doge of Venice, in the latter part of that republic's life, was a mere decorative figure.[76] The actual executive work was carried out by a rotating committee called the Council of Ten, members of which rarely served more than one year successively.[77] The current Swiss republic has, instead of a true president, a council of seven.[78] The rapidly rotating executive leaders of most modern parliamentary governments also have the characteristic of probably not ever getting enough power to become dictators. Still, this is a statement of condition and nothing more. I have to admit this problem puzzles me, and I would be delighted if any of the readers of this book provided a better explanation.

The reverse question is, how do democracies replace dictatorship? Here there is, for at least some cases, a fairly straightforward explanation. South America, and I suspect that this will in time develop in Africa, has had essentially temporary dictatorships; that is, dictators who for one reason or an-

---

ed. Gordon Tullock, 121–30 (Blacksburg, Va.: Public Choice Center, 1981), where I discuss this and other factors affecting the structure and stability of governments.

76. On the origins and development of the post of Venetian doge, see, for example, Langer, *Encyclopedia*, 238–40, 322–23.

77. The Council of Ten, invented in 1335, followed from a series of electoral institutions which began in 687, with the election of the first Venetian doge. In 1032, a coalition of aristocrats attempted to establish a hereditary doge, but they were defeated, and a council and senate were created instead. Later, the appointment of the doge became the council's responsibility (1171). A popular uprising (1300) was the result of moves to restrict membership on the council "in favor of a narrow, hereditary, commercial oligarchy" (ibid., 240). A more serious revolt, Tiepolo's rebellion (1310), finally prompted the formation of an "emergency committee on public safety," the Council of Ten, in 1335. "The Venetian government thus consisted of: the great council (i.e., the patrician caste); the senate (a deliberative and legislative body dealing with foreign affairs, peace, war, finances, trade); the council of ten (a secret, rapidly acting body concerned with morals, conspiracy, European affairs, finance [and] the war department, which could override the senate); the *collegio* or cabinet (the administrative branch); the doge and his council, which, sitting with the ten, made the council of seventeen" (ibid., 240; see also 238–39).

78. The origins of Swiss political institutions are discussed in W. Oechsli, "The Achievement of Swiss Federal Unity," chap. 8 in *The Cambridge Modern History*, ed. A. W. Ward, G. W. Prothero, and Stanley Leathes, vol. 11, *The Growth of Nationalities* (New York: Macmil-

other do not feel that they can remain dictators throughout the whole of their lives and pass the throne on to their sons. The reason, of course, may be that they fear that their sons would kill them if they made them their designated successors. They are also able to steal very large amounts of government money so that they can become independently wealthy.

Under these circumstances, retirement from office is desirable, but these dictators are aware of the fact that if they transfer the power to other individual dictators those dictators would have very strong reasons to have them killed, since they would always be potential leaders of opposition against them. On the other hand, if they transfer the power to a democracy, democratic leaders are likely to be grateful, and in any event, they do not have such strong motives for killing their predecessors. No doubt the democracy will eventually become a dictatorship again, but by then the dictator may be dead or will be elderly enough so that it is unlikely that the successor dictator will feel it necessary to dispose of him.

Under these circumstances, establishing a democratic government has much to be said for it. A great many South American dictators have done so. They also, of course, benefit from the fact that current democracy is intellectually in very good odor, and hence it looks as though they are behaving virtuously when they establish the democracy.

It is, of course, always possible that this kind of an arrangement will eventually lead to a permanent democratic government. So far, in South America, however, it has not done so, although the government of Venezuela has been democratic for a reasonable period of time now.[79] It is unfortunate in this regard that currently the far left, with its strongly antidemocratic traditions, is dominant intellectually in much of the underdeveloped world. Further, although the right in the United States, England, and Switzerland is firmly democratic, it is not firmly democratic in places like South America or Africa. Thus a dictator can anticipate almost immediate support from at least one large body of intellectuals. Whether these are right-wing intellectuals, as they

---

lan, 1909), passim; see also Langer, *Encyclopedia*, 714–15, 1192; Blum, Cameron, and Barnes, *European World*, 738–40; Johnson, *Modern Times*, 605–7. Current structures no doubt evolved from the introduction of "concordant democracy," under which all major political parties were given representation in the executive body (the Federal Council). The system was first established in the late 1800s following a series of reforms requiring voter decision-making in direct elections to create new legislation.

79. Wheatcroft, *World Atlas of Revolutions*, 159; see also Langer, *Encyclopedia*, 1258–59.

were in Brazil, or left-wing intellectuals, as they are with the current government of Nicaragua, their influence is equally pernicious from the standpoint of democracy.[80]

This phenomenon is not something that I think we can regard as the basic reason why democracies are replaced by dictatorships. After all, in Africa and in South America democracy never really got established. In those areas where electoral systems did become reasonably firmly established—a number of the Greek city-states, Carthaginian city-states, and for that matter medieval city-states, many of which were electoral,[81] and in Eastern Europe—the cause of the failure clearly was foreign conquest. Nevertheless, there are a number of cases in which electoral systems perished domestically. The sovereign Roman people found a more sovereign Caesar. A number of the Greek city-states and a number of the medieval city-states lost their electoral nature to a domestic dictator. Florence is, of course, the most prominent example.[82] I include the first and second French republics in this category. They were established by a country which had only the feeblest electoral tradition and were rather rapidly overthrown. At the time of the establishment of the Third Republic, however, there was some electoral tradition, and it developed to the point where as of now it seems likely that French democracy is about as secure as electoral institutions were in England in 1800. Petain was the result of a military defeat, although the Germans did not directly impose him and, in fact, to a very considerable extent, impeded the functioning of his government. De Gaulle was a rather unique phenomenon, and in any event, except in the first couple of years, he behaved like an exceptionally powerful democratic leader.[83]

80. General discussions of this problem are found in Jean-François Revel, *How Democracies Perish* (New York: Doubleday, 1984); José Ortega y Gasset, "Why the Masses Intervene," chap. 8 in *The Revolt of the Masses* (New York: Norton, 1957), 68–77; F. A. Hayek, *The Counter-Revolution of Science: Studies on the Abuse of Reason* (Indianapolis: Liberty Fund, 1979); Karl R. Popper, "The Sociology of Knowledge," chap. 23 in *The Open Society and Its Enemies* (Princeton: Princeton University Press, 1950), esp. 402–3; D'Encausse, *Confiscated Power*, 16–17; Ludwig von Mises, "The Role of Ideas," chap. 9 in *Human Action: A Treatise on Economics* (Chicago: Contemporary Books, 1963), esp. 178ff; Richard M. Weaver, "Concealed Rhetoric in Scientistic Sociology," in *Scientism and Values*, ed. Helmut Schoeck and James W. Wiggins (New York: Van Nostrand, 1960), esp. 90–98.

81. Mango, *Byzantium*, 46–59, 60, 220; Blum, Cameron, and Barnes, *European World*, 20–23; Langer, *Encyclopedia*, 155–286.

82. Pirenne, *Economic and Social History*, 204; Blum, Cameron, and Barnes, *European World*, 39; see also Braudel, *Civilization and Capitalism*, 488–90.

83. See Emile Bourgeois, "The Fall of Constitutionalism in France," chap. 2 in Ward,

It's obvious that democracies are indeed hard to overthrow if they're well established, simply because doing so requires quite a large number of people to take action following a leader, and for at least some of them, the prospects for the future will be less than if they remained ordinary voting citizens. Simple inertia may also have meaning here.

Having said all of this, however, we do still have the cases of Rome and Florence, and for that matter Syracuse, where democracy was completely removed.[84] There is also the overthrow of the Italian constitutional monarchy by Mussolini[85] a very considerable time after the Italians had begun a fairly modern electoral government.[86] It is clear that it can be done, even if it isn't exactly easy to explain. Once again, I regret to say I have no theory explaining why democracy sometimes works and sometimes doesn't. The long-run history of electoral institutions has not been one of success, but that may simply indicate that we have not waited long enough. The currently flourishing democracies may conceivably continue flourishing and gradually spread to take over the whole world.

I should, however, not conceal from the reader my own feeling that despotism is in essence the equilibrium state of human society. This does not, of course, mean that I think it is a good thing. All buildings, as physicists know, are in fact out of equilibrium and will eventually, given time enough,[87] fall down. I take it that this is not an argument for demolishing them. Similarly,

---

Prothero, and Leathes, *The Cambridge Modern History*, vol. 11, 22–42; Emile Bourgeois, "The French Republic (1848–1852)," chap. 5 in Ward, Prothero, and Leathes, *The Cambridge Modern History*, vol. 11, 96–141; Emile Bourgeois, "The Third French Republic," chap. 5 in *The Cambridge Modern History*, ed. A. W. Ward, G. W. Prothero, and Stanley Leathes, vol. 12, *The Latest Age* (New York: Macmillan, 1910), 91–133; see also Langer, *Encyclopedia*, 627–40, 679–83, 686–93, 1180–81; Blum, Cameron, and Barnes, *European World*, 480–85, 616–21, 722–29, 979–80, 1040–42; Johnson, *Modern Times*, 587–98; Fieldhouse, *The Colonial Empires*, 322–24.

84. Syracuse instituted democratic reforms in 413–410 B.C., but these were quite short-lived; in 405, Dionysius I, after winning election as one of ten generals, appointed himself dictator. His son, Dionysius II, followed him and ruled tyrannically until 345, when the Syracusans requested the political services of two foreign rulers: Hicetas, tyrant of Leontini, and later, Timoleon of Corinth. See, for example, Oman and Adam, "The Greeks of the West," chap. 37 in *Greece*, 413–338 B.C.," 407–18.

85. See Blum, Cameron, and Barnes, *European World*, 930–34.

86. See, for example, Langer, *Encyclopedia*, 700–711, 998–1000, for a summary of the development of the electoral system of modern Italy.

87. Which in many cases may be more than one million years.

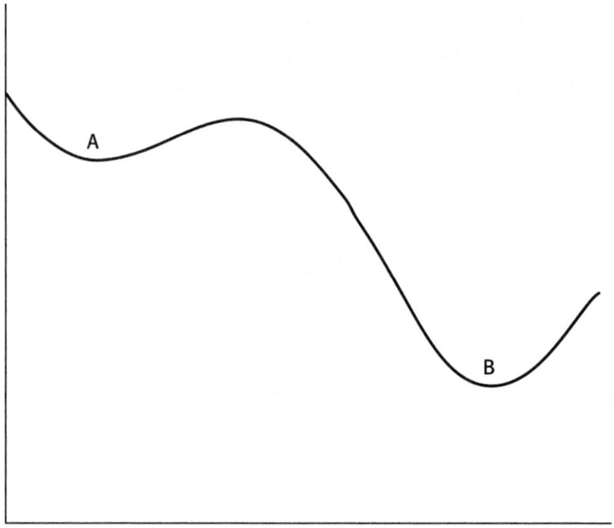

FIGURE 1

the feeling that democracy is not the true equilibrium state can be taken as an argument simply for guarding it more carefully in hopes that if we guard it carefully we can keep it or at least keep it a lot longer.

The situation is, I think, one in which electoral systems are in essence local equilibria. You can think of all possible governments as being arranged along the lines shown in figure 1. Electoral systems occupy a zone marked A, and despotism is at B. Clearly, if we have a ball on this surface it would stay in A if it were there, but if it were sufficiently vigorously disturbed, it would go over the hill and down to B. Similarly, with really vigorous disturbances, a ball which originated on B might by accident go into A.[88]

88. The similar analogy (and a figure similar in nature to my figure 1) has been suggested by Robert L. Carneiro: "Elasticity in the Capacity of a body to undergo deformation and, when the deforming forces are withdrawn, to regain its original shape . . . a force of a certain magnitude is applied to the free end of a metal rod and then withdrawn, the rod will spring back into place. If the force is increased so that it pushes the rod beyond its elastic limits, the rod will take a permanent set. So it is with human societies. Every social system has a margin of elasticity. It can be subjected to certain forces—wars, floods, famines, riots, plagues, strikes, inflation, unemployment—and as long as the magnitude of these forces is not excessive, the system will essentially return to its original conditions once the impinging forces abate. If it is not pressed beyond this margin, the society will be able to reestablish its old equilibrium . . . But if the society is subjected to forces that exceed this margin of elasticity, its existing insti-

This mechanical analogy is intended simply to indicate my view of the relationship between these two forms of government. Once again, it says nothing about their relative merits, only their relative stability. Of course, if we were trying to have a really accurate analogy, we would have a hypersurface in a multidimensional space, with some other possible forms of government, one of which certainly would be feudalism as local equilibrium.

So far, this chapter has been even less satisfactory than the other chapters in this book. I regret this and hope that some of my readers can improve on it. What I've actually done is lay out the problems rather than my solution for them. Here, however, I would like to turn to another intermediate form of government which at least arguably has been very successful. Montesquieu, in his *L'Esprit des Lois*, argued strongly for what he called constitutional monarchy, by which, roughly speaking, he meant England under George II.[89] By anybody's standard, this was indeed an extremely successful government. Not only did a country which was really not very big in terms of population, compared with the other great powers of Europe, become the dominant nation in Europe, but it also, during this period, laid the foundation for the industrial revolution and had a higher per capita income for its population than almost anywhere else in Europe.[90] Montesquieu's admiration is therefore understandable, although whether he was right in believing that the cause was the form of government is not clear.[91]

---

tutions will not be able to cope with these forces. Under heavy stress, the society will be permanently deformed, that is, it will be forced to change its structure" ("Successive Reequilibrations as the Mechanism of Cultural Evolution," in *Self-Organization and Dissipative Structures: Applications in the Physical and Social Sciences*, ed. William C. Schieve and Peter M. Allen [Austin: University of Texas Press, 1982], 111–12).

89. For example, Spearman, *Democracy in England*, 1–7.

90. See M. C. Buer, *Health, Wealth and Population in the Early Days of the Industrial Revolution* (London: G. Routledge, 1926); W. A. Cole and Phyllis Deane, "The Growth of National Incomes," in *The Cambridge Economic History of Europe*, ed. H. J. Habakkuk and M. Postan, vol. 6, *The Industrial Revolutions and After: Incomes, Population, and Technological Change*, part 1 (Cambridge: Cambridge University Press, 1965); M. Dorothy George, *London Life in the Eighteenth Century* (New York: Knopf, 1926); T. S. Ashton, *The Industrial Revolution, 1760–1830* (Cambridge: Cambridge University Press, 1962); see also Paul Mantoux, *The Industrial Revolution in the Eighteenth Century* (New York: Harper and Row, 1962).

91. I myself have argued that at least one aspect of this government was one of the major reasons for the development of modern economic systems. See "Why Did the Industrial Revolution Occur in England?" unpublished monograph, Public Choice Center, George Mason University.

Let us pause here and describe this government as it functioned, in very rough terms. Firstly, we should say that the details are matters of great controversy. Montesquieu and Namier,[92] for example, both thought that they knew as much about the government of England as possible, but their pictures are in many ways quite different. John Brewer[93] is not so convinced that he himself knows how the constitution of England operated at that time, but he does in any event present a different picture than either of the two previous authorities.

The point of this is simply to indicate that at the time, and for that matter now, the exact functioning of that government was a matter of considerable dispute. I am going to make what I think is a very general description, one which I think all disputing parties would accept. It may be, however, that this very general description is defective in that it misses certain vital details which one or more of the authorities cited above included in their studies. Nevertheless, my description, as the reader will quickly discover, fits a number of reasonably successful modern governments. These modern governments are as the English government was in the eighteenth century, governments of underdeveloped countries. Thus it may be that this is a better form of government than those we normally find in underdeveloped areas.

What, then, is the situation? Firstly, there is at the top a man who is called king in England, dictator in the more modern examples, who has undeniably very great power. There is, however, also a legislature. The exact split of power between the legislature and the dictator is not at all clear. Could, for example, George III simply appoint his own prime minister or could he not? I don't think anybody in 1776 was certain.

Secondly, if we look at the legislature itself, we find a number of rather odd characteristics. Firstly, the executive head, whether we call him a king or a dictator, clearly has a great deal of influence in determining who will hold seats in that legislature. To say he has a great deal of influence does not mean that he controls it. Characteristically, some members of the legislature will one way or another be directly appointed by him. Notably, however, even these members of the legislature sometimes oppose him.

92. See Sir Lewis Namier, *The Structure of Politics at the Accession of George III*, 2d ed. (London: Macmillan, 1965).

93. See John Brewer, *Party Ideology and Popular Politics at the Accession of George III* (Cambridge: Cambridge University Press, 1976).

When I was in Korea recently, we drove by the legislature, and as we went by, my host, a professor of economics, mentioned that one of his colleagues had been appointed to the legislature. I responded by asking, "Does he always vote with the president?" He apparently thought that I hadn't understood him and repeated that he was appointed to the legislature. I said, "Yes, but does he always vote with the president?"[94] He responded with, "I don't approve of people being appointed to the legislature by the president." I said, "I don't either, but does he vote with the president all the time?" He said, "Not always." This relationship would have been very familiar to George II or III.

Further, among those who are not put in their positions by the dictator or king, a good many have gotten there by somewhat odd means. I previously mentioned the ownership of seats in Parliament, but seats were also sometimes bought. My favorite example was a well-intentioned group of public-spirited men, of a constituency in North England, who put their seats in Parliament up to auction. The money was to be used to repair roads. Mostly, however, it was less public spirited. Once again, this is characteristic of many of the countries that I will be discussing in a moment.

Lastly, it is not at all clear exactly why this institution exists, but it is clear that it is a restriction on the power of the man who otherwise would be an absolute ruler. Let me now turn to some modern examples. Mexico is a fairly clear-cut example, as was Brazil.[95] South Korea, Taiwan, Singapore, and Thailand are also good examples.[96] Looking further back, Rome, from the time of Caesar until about the time of Severus, could be regarded as an example.[97]

94. Apparently he was under the impression that I didn't know that South Korea was basically a dictatorship.

95. Relations between Mexico's legislative Chambers of Senators and Deputies and its president are discussed in J. A. Hellman, *Mexico in Crisis*, 2d ed. (New York: Holmes and Meier, 1983), 126–28; Kenneth F. Johnson, "The Practice of Esoteric Democracy," chap. 5 in *Mexican Democracy: A Critical View*, 3d ed. (New York: Praeger, 1984), 116–59. See also Robert T. Daland, *Exploring Brazilian Bureaucracy: Performance and Pathology* (Washington, D.C.: University Press of America, 1981), 329–95, for example, on conflicts between Brazil's president and its congress.

96. Summaries of these countries' current political institutions are given in John Paxton, *The Statesman's Yearbook: 1985–1986* (New York: St. Martin's, 1985), 395 (Taiwan), 766 (South Korea), 1055–56 (Singapore), 1170–71 (Thailand).

97. Mommsen, *Rome*, 29–55. This was also true of the Spartan system. In addition to two kings, the government was controlled by "the Council of Elders, a body consisting of thirty

Further, almost all of the countries in Europe in the nineteenth century were examples at one time or another.

If we look at the older examples, they all turned out to be transitional stages. Rome, of course, moved to a complete dictatorship and eventually to a hereditary monarchy. European countries, generally speaking, moved to the modern type of constitutional monarchy where the king is a mere figurehead or to outright republics. Russia, the country in which the movement to what I'm now calling constitutional democracy was the latest, occurring after 1905, went back to a monarchy which has many resemblances to that of Ivan the Terrible.[98]

Whether this indicates that the system is transitional, and hence that the modern examples that I gave would eventually be replaced either by democracies or by monarchies, is a question which I would not like to have to answer. Just at the moment, Brazil has become a democracy, and Mexico may be moving in that direction. Developments in Thailand are sufficiently com-

---

men (including the kings) . . . chosen for life by the whole body of citizens, but only from aristocratic families. The Council tried criminal cases, and prepared matters which were to come before the Assembly. This body (the Assembly) consisted of all the citizens; it could not initiate anything, but could vote yes or no to any proposal brought before it . . . and branch of government, peculiar to Sparta. This was the five ephors. These were chosen out of the whole body of the citizens, by a method which Aristotle says was 'too childish,' and which Bury says was virtually by lot. They were a 'democratic' element in the constitution, apparently intended to balance the kings . . . When either king went on a warlike expedition, two ephors accompanied him to watch over his behavior. The ephors were the supreme civil court, but over the kings they had criminal jurisdiction" (Russell, *History of Western Philosophy*, 97). The Spartan constitution was, according to myth, due to a god named Lycurgus, meaning "Wolf-Repeller" (ibid., 97). The Spartan Assembly (or "Apella") is discussed also in Oman and Adam, *Greece*, 64.

Similar (but weaker) institutional constraints were also present in ancient Athens: "The political game was played in and around an aristocratic Council which, with the king, if one existed, was the sole organ of government. Mass assemblies might be held occasionally to show approval or disapproval of vital decisions which could lead to disaster without mass support (A declaration of war for example) . . ." Forrest (*The Emergence of Greek Democracy*), 54–55; see also Oman and Adam, *Greece*, 62–63.

98. On political events before the revolution in 1917, see, for example, Irving Werstein, *Ten Days in November: The Russian Revolution* (Philadelphia: Macrae Smith, 1967); Sheila Fitzpatrick, *The Russian Revolution* (New York: Berkley, 1982), 26–33. See also Johnson, *Modern Times*, 59; D'Encausse, *Confiscated Power*, 8–10; Wheatcroft, *World Atlas of Revolutions*, 78–95.

plicated so that it is not clear what is happening, but it could be argued that it is moving towards a democracy which would have a decorative king and hence would be the modern type of constitutional monarchy.[99]

The impressive feature of this list of countries, however, is that all are examples of exceptionally successful countries. The modern set have all done very well economically, and certainly are pleasanter places for their citizens to live in than the average underdeveloped country. Rome seems to have gone up to its peak and then slid down again under the control of this form of government, but then it had it longer than any other country. England, of course, under George II was, as I mentioned above, almost fantastically successful as a country, and the various governments of Europe in the nineteenth century had not only conquered most of the world in establishing their colonial empires, but also had a long period of rapid economic growth.

Does all of this indicate that this is a superior form of government? I regret to say, I cannot answer that question. The sample is too small. In addition, I cannot claim to know the history of all countries in detail, but for all I know, there may be other examples of this form of government where things have gone very badly indeed. I can only say I know of none. It is also hard to predict the future. None of our historic examples lasted, and the ones that I've picked out of the present world are, in general, quite young. The oldest, Mexico, is about fifty years old. This system had its attractions for Montesquieu, and for that matter for Locke, who argued for balanced governments.[100] Note, this was balanced between different forms of governments, however, not anything more strenuous. He did not argue that it was,

99. See "Thailand's Military Suffers Some Self-Inflicted Wounds," *New York Times*, September 15, 1985, p. 2E.

100. Though Locke, of course, believed that certain "just" and nonarbitrary procedural rules should be followed by any majority-rule government, he nonetheless felt that "the majority, having . . . upon men's first uniting into society, the whole power of the community naturally in them, may employ all that power in . . . a perfect democracy; or else *may put the power of making laws into the hands of a few select men, . . . an oligarchy; or else into the hands of one man; . . . a monarchy*; or and if to him and his heirs; it is an hereditary monarchy; if to him only for life, . . . an elective monarchy. And so, accordingly, of these *the community may make compounded and mixed forms of government, as they think good*." Locke goes on to stress that "*by commonwealth, I must be understood all along to mean, not a democracy or any form of government, but any independent community* . . ." (John Locke, *Two Treatises of Government*, edited by Thomas I. Cook [New York: Hafner, 1947], 186–87, emphasis added. See also Sabine, *History of Political Theory*, 534ff).

for example, particularly likely to maximize the public interest.[101] In essence, he thought that the two forms of government each had something to be said for it and that the combination was desirable. Today, most of us would feel that the dictatorship–true monarchy has little or nothing to say for it, and hence compromising democracy is not desirable. Nevertheless, this form of government does exist and, to repeat, as far as I can see, it's had a rather good historical record.

This chapter has, I think, been rather more unsatisfactory even than the previous chapters. There do seem to be some general patterns, but I am unable to put my finger on any theory which explains them. I apologize for this and hope that my readers, instead of simply repeating my own criticism of the chapter, will offer something to replace it.

101. Through, of course, the replacement of such a "balance" of political institutions by a structure desired by a single faction is not necessarily preferable, especially if it is accomplished through revolution. I discuss this problem in *The Social Dilemma: The Economics of War and Revolution* (Blacksburg, Va.: University Publications, 1974).

MONARCHIES, HEREDITARY AND NONHEREDITARY

1. *Introduction*

Most people in the history of the human race have lived under hereditary monarchies. It should be emphasized at the outset that hereditary monarchies are not regimes where the throne always passes from the beloved dying king to whichever of his children or near relatives is next in line under local law or custom. That does happen frequently, but it is also true that events like the Wars of the Roses happen too.

We tend to exaggerate the difficulties of establishing a firm line of succession to the throne, probably because the English throne was the most contested one in Europe. Thus, Anglo-Saxon history has a good deal more in the way of violent overthrow than is found in the histories of most countries ruled by monarchs.

Today there is one case—North Korea—in which a dictatorship has been made, at least for a time, hereditary. There was a period when the Somozas seemed to have a hereditary monarchy in Nicaragua, and it seems likely that the Trujillo family would have established one in the Dominican Republic had not the US government intervened by arranging not only to have the reigning dictator assassinated,[1] but also by sending in the Navy to keep his family from perpetuating the regime. Note that such ceremonial figures as Elizabeth II are not really monarchs in the old-fashioned sense.

The former European empires frequently maintained sort of semi-puppet kings along their borders, partly as a method of reducing the administrative burden, and partly because the areas were not thought to be worth a great

Reprinted, with permission, from *The Elgar Companion to Public Choice*, ed. William F. Shugart II and Laura Razzolini (Cheltenham, U.K., and Northampton, Mass.: Edward Elgar, 2001), 140–56.

1. It is ironic that shortly after President John Kennedy arranged the deaths of Diem in Vietnam, General Trujillo in the Dominican Republic, and Lumumba in the Congo, he was himself assassinated. "They that take the sword. . . ." The eventual outcome in the Dominican Republic was that Lyndon Johnson sent in the 82nd Airborne. This led to some desultory fighting in the course of which a few American soldiers and somewhat more Dominicans were killed.

deal. In these cases, although the throne was theoretically hereditary, as a matter of fact the imperial powers or their local agents could adjust lines of succession or actually remove a reigning king if there were difficulties.

Some of these monarchs are still around. There is Morocco, formerly part of the French empire, now ruled by a man who originally became king while the country was under French control. Nepal was always rather independent of the rule of the British viceroy in New Delhi. As the homeland of the famous Gurkhas, it was virtually a British ally. It retains more or less this same relationship with both Britain and India.

Along the south and east of the Arabian peninsula there is a whole collection of minor kingdoms in what used to be called the Trucial States and, of course, Kuwait. It is interesting that the British finally withdrew their last troop units from the Gulf in the early 1970s. One might speculate as to whether the 1973 oil embargo would have been imposed if the British troops had still been there.

Although these are all something of hangovers of late imperial administration, Saudi Arabia was pretty much independent. It was not true that the king would, generally speaking, take strongly anti-British positions.[2]

A special case is Trans-Jordan. That country was actually set up by the British government as a sort of gift to one of its important Arab clients. It was for some time an independent but very poor bit of desert, with the famous Arab legion commanded by an Englishman as its military forces. The current king is the great grandson of the first one. In view of his father's, generally speaking, good relations with his powerful next door neighbor, Israel, it is likely that this throne will stay in the family for a while.

All of these existing hereditary monarchies, except North Korea, are of obvious strategic importance. For special reasons they have foreign protection. A more common form of autocratic government in the world today is dictatorship, which does not at least proclaim itself as hereditary.

My own guess is that the temporary dictatorships that are around today will eventually develop into hereditary monarchies. After all, that was the history of Rome, and of the dissolution of Rome. In believing this, I am out of the mainstream. Most people think that we are moving toward universal democracy.

2. He did award the oil exploration contract to an American company rather than to a British one. This was at the time when the British needed American support in other parts of the world.

As a matter of fact, at the moment, a larger part of the world is democratic than in any previous period. Only about half of the world's population lives under dictatorships.[3] Whether this shows a long-run trend for democracy or is a temporary fillip like the ones earlier in history is something upon which there is a difference of opinion between me and the rest of the intellectual community. In any event, the purpose of this chapter is to talk about autocratic government rather than to speculate about whether it will be replaced by democracy.[4]

2. *An Aside on the Definition of Democracy*

As a digression, I should say here that the term "democracy" traditionally referred to a political system in which large numbers of people could vote. This emphatically did not mean that all adults who were not either insane or in prison were enfranchised. That type of system, the modern form of democracy, is a very recent invention. Before 1900 very few women voted, and governments where only part of the adult male population voted were not particularly uncommon.

Athens, to take one famous example, allowed all adult males who were citizens to vote. This excluded not only the slaves but also people the Athenians regarded as foreigners. These might very well be persons who were brought up in Athens of parents who had been born and brought up in Athens, and who had themselves been born of parents who had been born and brought up in Athens, but they still were not Athenian citizens. As a further problem eligible voters actually had to take the day off and go to the Pynx in order to vote.

Representative democracy is another recent development. This special kind of democracy in which a large part of the adult male population in a given city could vote if they went to the appropriate place was quite common in the Mediterranean world. Indeed the Mediterranean was surrounded by city-states of this sort, with Rome and Carthage, in the earlier days, being simply very large examples.

3. India accounts for a very large share of the people living in democracies.

4. For an earlier discussion, see my *Autocracy* (Boston: Kluwer Academic Publishers, 1987). Ronald Wintrobe, *The Political Economy of Dictatorship* (Cambridge: Cambridge University Press, 1998), is a more recent contribution to a not very large literature.

It is rather surprising that representative democracy was not invented in this period. Normally in Athens, if some decision had to be taken which was not worth turning out the entire male citizenry, representatives were not elected. Delegates to the 500-member Council (50 from each of the ten "tribes of Cleisthenes") were chosen by lot instead.[5]

Something like this limited franchise system was the way democracy worked almost everywhere until the twentieth century. It was only in 1918 that all adult males in England were permitted to vote, and not until 1930 did all adult females get the franchise. The power of England was created roughly from 1700 to 1860. The number of people who could then vote was quite restricted; the House of Lords was in those days both hereditary and powerful.

3. *Assuming Power*

To return to our major subject, dictatorships and monarchies, the important thing to remember about dictatorships is that every dictator lives under the Sword of Damocles: "uneasy lies the head that wears the crown," or so the saying goes. The adage is particularly true when the crown is not hereditary.

The second thing to be said here is that dictators are always people with greater than normal abilities. In this they differ from hereditary monarchs, who can occasionally, as a result of genetic effects, be stupid. George III and Louis XVI, for instance, were clearly somewhat defective mentally. Comparing the West and East Roman monarchies, for example, Bryce remarks that, in the latter, "the absence of regular rules of succession had the merit of giving to energy and ambition opportunities for displacing the incapable. Men of force came more readily to the top than they do in hereditary monarchies."[6] Dictators have climbed the slippery pole, and this shows great talent and ability, but not necessarily great interest in the well-being of others.

5. Samuel E. Finer, *The History of Government*, vol. 1, *Ancient Monarchies and Empires* (Oxford: Oxford University Press, 1997). Council members served one-year terms, and no one could serve more than twice. The machine used to produce these selections is still on display in the Stoa of Attalus at Athens.

6. James Bryce, *The Holy Roman Empire*, rev. ed. (1873; New York and London: Macmillan, 1904), 331. While "there was of course a tendency for the throne to become settled in a family, for an Emperor usually tried to secure the succession for his son or some other relative either by publicly destining him for power, or by associating him as co-Emperor during his

Having said that dictators are usually talented and able, I should say that this does not necessarily mean they give their countries good government, although on occasion they have. Caesar Augustus was apparently very popular, and certainly he did well except for the *Teutoburger Wald*. Of course, he set up the hereditary monarchy, and his successors were in general far inferior to him.

The combination of bright people and hereditary succession has rarely been achieved, although China's Manchu dynasty managed it for a few generations. In that case, the emperor, who had many sons, selected one to be his successor with the aid of their tutors and the High Ministers. This led to a line of four unusually able emperors.[7]

In the more typical case, this is not the selection method, and the talents of the rulers who are thrown up by the genetic lottery will tend toward the mean of the normal distribution. In those cases in which there are many potential heirs and the early Manchu system is not followed, there are usually disputes over succession, which do not help the state. Hereditary monarchs do have the advantage of training as children, but unfortunately this training usually involves how to entertain oneself while waiting for the king to die, as well as how to run the country.

The French monarchists maintained that having a king who actually owned the whole country was, from the standpoint of the citizens, a good idea because he would have no possible conflicts of interest with his subjects.[8] Indeed, although Versailles is an impressive sight, its total cost was a tiny share of the government budget, as was the imperial palace complex in China. The latter makes Versailles look like a village hut.

The French monarchists also point out that, as a result of childhood training, as long as the House of Bourbon ruled France, Germany and Italy were kept divided. It was only with the emergence of the Republic and Louis Napoleon, who ran a more or less constitutional monarchy, that Italy and Germany were united, thus greatly injuring the strategic position of France. Louis Napoleon actually took a positive role in uniting Italy.

---

own life . . . when the vigor of a reigning stock began to die out, the stock usually disappeared, and an upstart adventurer set up a new dynasty" (ibid., 331–32).

7. The fourth conformed to Chinese rather than Manchu traditions and selected the eldest son of his principal wife to succeed him. The fifth emperor was unusually poor.

8. The absence of private property had disastrous consequences for Russia. See Richard Pipes, *Property and Freedom* (New York: Knopf, 1999).

4. Holding on to Power

Let us now discuss the problem of maintaining a dictator or king in power. We shall turn later to how transitions of power can be governed. The first thing to be said is that the whole process is very risky. Further, the principal danger to the dictator is not the revolting masses, but the fact that some of his own officials may decide that they would like to replace him.

President Park of Korea, who was shot by the chief of his secret police one night at dinner, is an extreme but not atypical case. That very untrusting person, Joseph Stalin, always locked the door of his bedroom at night so that his personal, carefully selected guard could not get in. Incidentally, this may have been one of the causes of his death. When he failed to appear at the usual time in the morning, the commander of the guard was afraid to break the door down. I suppose that all of us can feel sympathy for the commander's dilemma. Hence, Stalin did not receive medical treatment until several hours later than he would have received it had he been discovered earlier.[9]

The usual procedure here is not to attempt to cultivate complete loyalty among one's immediate followers, but to keep them shifting around so that they are always a little uncertain of their positions. A well-functioning dictatorship is one in which everyone thinks that if a coup is attempted, the dictator will put it down. As long as people think that the dictator's power is secure, he is secure. If they begin to doubt, he lives at risk.[10]

Machiavelli observed that the overthrow of any prince was astonishing, because the existence of a conspiracy provided its various members with an opportunity to curry favor. Divulging the conspirators' plans is safe and

9. Interestingly enough, Stalin was at the time he died planning his own "final solution" for Russian Jews. He had begun with an attack on Jewish doctors, and it is possible that this pogrom led to his having poorer medical attention than he would have had otherwise.

10. Kinship is one margin of regime stability: "for example, the French court for most of its history was often a collection of relatives of the various noblemen. Such individuals were obliged to take up residence at the royal court so that noblemen could not rebel against the king without jeopardizing their own kin (Lee Dugatkin, *Cheating Monkeys and Citizen Bees: The Nature of Cooperation in Animals and Humans* [New York: Free Press, 1999], 162). Another strategy is to retain some of the members of the previous ruler's supporting coalition in office, diluting their power but reducing their incentives to oppose the new government (Mwangi S. Kimenyi and William F. Shughart II, "Political Successions and the Growth of Government," *Public Choice* 62 [1989]: 173–79).

certain to be rewarded, whereas siding with the organizers of the *coup d'état* is dangerous if it fails.[11]

The problem with this from the standpoint of the dictator is not that the coup may get through without his hearing about it, but that he is surrounded by people who constantly tell him that others are plotting against him. In modern times, the possibility of secret recording devices may make it easier for a person who wishes to betray a coup to convince the dictator that it is a genuine threat and not a product of the informer's ambition.

Note that I have not said anything about popular uprisings. They are rarely capable of overthrowing an established monarch. Karl Marx and Friedrich Engels both thought that a regular military force could always put down a street mob, and as far as I know, there are substantially no cases in which the military and police remained loyal to the ruler, and street rioting replaced him.

Street rioting is more apt to be either a symptom of something wrong in the government farther up or, in some cases, an incentive for the military and police to turn against the dictator because they have concluded that they can topple him. The Bastille, after all, was under attack by the mob, but it fell to a regiment of regular infantry.

Before turning to the possible overthrow of dictatorships or, for that matter, monarchies, I should pause briefly to point out that the modern totalitarian dictatorship is unlike most historical monarchies. Traditional monarchs and dictators have not striven for total control. Indeed, the degree to which the government attempted to exercise detailed control in, let us say, the France of Louis XIV was probably less than the US government does. Certainly tax collections represented a much smaller share of the national income than they do in the present-day United States. Louis's army did not recruit soldiers. Instead it rented regiments from various private entrepreneurs.

If Karl Wittfogel is right, back in the early days of history, when countries were dependent on elaborate irrigation networks to stay alive, similar types of governments existed.[12] But in modern times the usual South American dictator is far from exercising totalitarian control. Indeed, it should be pointed out that actually even totalitarian governments are not always mass

11. Niccolò Machiavelli, *The Prince*, trans. and ed. Daniel Donno (1513; New York: Bantam Books, 1981).

12. Karl Wittfogel, *Oriental Despotism: A Comparative Study of Total Power* (New York: Vintage, 1991).

murderers. Joseph Stalin, Adolf Hitler, Mao Tse-tung (or Ze-dong), Pol Pot, and Ho Chi Minh assuredly were. Slobodan Milosevic may be.

Communist states have a tendency to go in for a lot of executions, but not necessarily on the same scale. Fidel Castro apparently killed only about 30,000 people. Both Benito Mussolini and Francisco Franco killed very few people, and both of them got through almost their entire regimes without any death penalty at all.

As a general matter, the ruler, whether a dictator or king, is likely to try to keep people who appear to be too talented out of power. Gonzalo Fernandez de Córdoba won the title "The Great Captain" by long and successful campaigns for the king of Spain. Once he had been victorious, he was recalled to Spain and exiled to his estates to keep him away from the temptations of power. (This does not mean that he lived in poverty; his estates were very extensive.) Nevertheless, the king obviously thought that Córdoba's popularity made him a potential threat.

Hernando Cortés, after the conquest of Mexico, went to Spain, where he became a part of the resident nobility for a time and obviously had no power to menace the king. When he returned to the New World, the viceroy carefully saw to it that he never had a position of power. He died peacefully, and his descendants remained great nobles.[13]

The average hereditary monarch or dictator has not been a wholly nice person. But hereditary monarchs are probably nicer than dictators, on the average, because they have not had to endure the long arduous climb up the slippery pole. Nevertheless, one should not confuse the phrase "dictator or monarch" with the phrase "benevolent dictator or monarch." Some of them are; some of them are not.

Mainly they should be thought of much as the type of person who by either heredity or intrigue acquires a controlling block of stock in a corporation. The dictator is probably both tougher and more self-centered than his counterpart in the corporation, but they are of the same type. They have the success of the corporation or kingdom firmly in mind because it is, after all, their property. Furthermore, on the whole, they do not positively want to do nasty things to their citizens or their employees. When the cards are down, though, they do put their own interests above those of the individual employees or citizens.

13. Pizarro, on the other hand, stayed in Peru and apparently was suspected by the king of trying to establish an independent monarchy there. In consequence, his family was wiped out.

In both hereditary monarchies and those corporations in which the control is passed from father to son, we have the problem of the son sometimes being incompetent. This is quite a regular phenomenon in the American economy. Normally after the incompetent son has run the company down a good deal, he or his close relatives realize he is not up to the job, and he sells out at a much lower price than he could have obtained when he was first in office.

This alternative is not available to the son of a king, and normally he would not be safe if he passed the throne on to someone else. There are a few exceptions. Richard Cromwell, after failing to keep his father's protectorate, lived comfortably in England for the remainder of his life.

If we go over history, we find a very large variance among people who have inherited thrones. The same is true with people who have simply inherited noble titles. Data on the noble class of England seem to indicate that they are in intelligence, skill, and so on, above, but not far above, the average English person. There are fairly radical exceptions both ways. Louis XVI was a dunce, but the seventh Duc de Broglie (1892–1987) was awarded the 1929 Nobel Prize in physics. Charles II also seems to have been very bright and much interested in science.[14] But he was an exception.

It is likely that a collection of kings would have no higher percentage of really outstanding intellects than a collection of, let us say, college graduates. Further, the damage done by college graduates, if they turn out to be hopelessly stupid, will be minimized by competitive market forces, whereas a hopelessly stupid king may continue in power for quite some time.[15]

5. *Transfers of Power*

This raises the questions of how the actual transfer-of-power process works and why is it apparently much easier for the king's legitimate heir to seize power than it is for anyone else. For this purpose I would like to turn to some work by William Riker which dealt oddly enough with the institution of the American political party nominating convention back in the days when the nominating conventions actually did nominate the presidential

14. He attended meetings of the Royal Society. Henry VII was probably equally bright and extremely devious. Both of these kings had to fight for their thrones.

15. Louis XVI did not succeed in holding on to power, and even though George III remained on the throne, he was much less powerful when he died than he had been earlier.

candidates.[16] Today, of course, nominees are determined by a presidential primary system.

Riker pointed out that the bulk of the delegates who were at the convention, although they may have had strongly held beliefs as to whom they wanted as their party's candidate, mainly wanted to maximize the returns for themselves. These returns could be maximized by backing the ultimate winner, but not backing him too late (that is, after it was obvious to everyone who was going to win). Delay in joining the winning coalition would likely result in the nominee not offering any reward to the delegates whose support was not needed to put him "over the top."

Thus, what we typically saw was a large number of delegates carefully waiting and calculating who was going to win. Their intention was to join the winner just at the time when their vote would push him over the necessary vote threshold. Since everybody adopted the same strategy, nominating conventions experienced long periods of apparent inaction, followed by a torrent of delegates rallying around the nominee's banner. The replacement of absolute rulers exhibits much the same pattern, although perhaps not as openly.

The events surrounding a ruler's death pose a similar dilemma. Most of the people know that they have no realistic chance of being selected as the new ruler, and they had better try to make good contacts with whoever will assume power. Determining who that person is in order to back him is very important.

The problem, then, with dictatorship as opposed to a hereditary monarch is that there is no legitimate heir. For one thing, there is no accepted set of rules governing succession, but even more important there is a problem from the standpoint of the current dictator. His designated successor, if there is one, will normally be able to protect himself against charges of murder or assassination once he has assumed control. Thus, he is the person who finds murder or assassination of the dictator the safest path to power. Further, since the dictator can always change his mind, he has a strong motive to act. Once a dictator has appointed a successor, he is in danger.

Until the time of the Nixon administration in the United States, there was considerable tension between the president and the vice president. Probably this state of affairs was a civilized variant on the foregoing theme. It is notable

16. William H. Riker, *The Theory of Political Coalitions* (New Haven: Yale University Press, 1962).

that most dictators do not formally appoint a successor. There are only occasional exceptions to this rule.

If no official successor has been designated, it is still possible that some relative, preferably the dictator's eldest son, will appear to almost everybody as the likely winner. In that event, he will in fact be the likely winner unless he suffers from a really appalling lack of talent. Thus, there is a tendency for dictatorships gradually to develop into hereditary monarchies, and historically this has happened many times.

Dictators, like everyone else, sometimes want to retire. Life at the top of the slippery pole is not entirely a bed of roses. Retiring is risky, because if the dictator retires and remains in his own country, he is a standing menace to his successor, and his life is again in danger. Under the circumstances, South American dictators have on a number of occasions solved the problem by creating democratic governments and then continuing to live on their local estates. They apparently find this more pleasant than appointing a successor and taking off to France so that they increase their chances of enjoying their retirement years in full.

The reasons underlying this strategy are fairly clear, but it should be pointed out that it has recently been showing signs of change. Democratic successor regimes to dictatorships used to be grateful to the dictator for setting them up, but in the cases of the last dictator of Korea, the last dictatorial president of Mexico, and Indonesia's deposed president Suharto, new democratic regimes seem bent nowadays on finishing off or at least impoverishing former strongmen. Augusto Pinochet has not yet really been injured, but democratic forces in Chile continually campaign for his punishment. Presumably this will mean that dictators are far more likely simply to stay in power until they die rather than setting up democratic governments and retiring. Revenge is sweet, but it is also expensive.

In general, absolute rulers are deeply concerned about avoiding being overthrown, and being so deeply concerned they pay attention to the opinions of those around them. They will normally also be mildly interested in doing things that will get them public approval. They are like the rest of us and want such public approval, but also like the rest of us, the sacrifice they will make for such public approval is limited.

Hitler, a totalitarian who, one would think, was less concerned than most with such matters, had a whole branch of the secret police whose duty it was simply to find out what people were saying about the National Socialist government. People who criticized the government were not normally arrested, but notes were made as to what policies were apparently approved of and which were not, and Hitler paid some attention to these opinions in making his decisions.

It is even possible that public opinion is more likely to sway a dictator or king than a democratically elected body, because the "public opinion" that autocrats are concerned with is that of the entire population rather than just the majority.

President Bill Clinton, as a result of the Twenty-second Amendment to the US Constitution (ratified in 1951), cannot continue in office beyond his second term, but Congress can. It is somewhat ironic that a good many congressmen who were elected recently on campaign promises to vote for congressional term limits proceeded to change their minds. All congressmen worry about the next election just as all dictators worry about the possibility of *coups d'état*.

It is true that a member of Congress, although he or she may be voted out of office, is not likely to be killed. A dictator does face that possibility. Further, congressmen normally do not have elaborate bureaucracies under them, and do not have to worry particularly about the leading members of that bureaucracy deciding to launch a coup. On the other hand, on the whole, they have less control over the bureaucracy than either a dictator or a king would have.

What is the net effect of all this? What are the advantages of democracy over dictatorship? The most recent data seem to indicate that dictatorships grow about as fast as democracies, although the variance among dictatorships is greater.[17] I realize that these data are subject to criticism and that there are all sorts of unfortunate characteristics in measurements of growth, including the fact that transfer payments are frequently counted as actual production.

For example, government purchases of agricultural products at prices above market values are transfers to certain farmers, but such purchases appear as real output in the GNP accounts. The available data nevertheless seem to indicate not much difference here, and the most rapidly growing countries

17. Abdiweli M. Ali, "Economic Freedom, Democracy and Growth," *Journal of Private Enterprise* 13 (1997): 1–18, collects all of the existing studies. He sums up his findings as follows: "out of twenty-one studies . . . nine report a positive relationship between democracy and economic growth and four studies indicate a negative relation between growth and democracy. The remaining eight studies find no significant difference between regimes" (3). There are, of course, no hereditary monarchies in the sample. See also Chapters 28 and 29 of this volume.

recently were the dictatorial Asian "Tigers," South Korea, Taiwan, Hong Kong, and Singapore. Taiwan and South Korea have not been doing so well since they became democracies, but it is harder to have rapid growth when the economy has already become large than when it was still small. Undemocratic Hong Kong, which was the all-time record holder, is currently in a state of considerable disarray for external reasons. Singapore is still dictatorial and now growing quite slowly.

The average person seems to have no strong arguments for favoring democracy over dictatorship except that it is, well, more democratic. Karl Popper used to point out that in democracies, the people vote the government in, or the people can vote the government out, without resort to bloodshed. This is generally speaking true, although it should be said that, gauged in terms of casualties, the largest war the United States ever engaged in was entirely domestic—a war, it bears emphasizing, that was fought not to overthrow the central government, but for the right to secede from it. It should also be said that *coups d'état* may be rather less expensive than the average presidential election.

I should digress here briefly and point out that Mexico, from about 1930 until a few years ago, had a form of government which as far as I know was only duplicated in the Roman empire during the period of the adoptive emperors. Having no natural male progeny, emperors were succeeded by adopted sons. Marcus Aurelius Antoninus unfortunately had a son who was one of the worst emperors Rome ever had. In Mexico, until recently, the dictator ruled for six years and appointed his successor. On the whole, it seems to have worked quite well.

So far in talking about what might be called hereditary dictatorship, I have been contrasting it with democracy. I have not discussed such forms of government as the rule by civil servants that dominated China.[18] Nor have I dealt with feudalism, a rare form of government found, as far as I know, only in Europe and Japan, or said anything about the true theocracies like Utah and Tibet. I am not going to take them up now, but stick to dictatorships and monarchies.

It should be pointed out that neither dictators nor monarchs are sadists who positively want to make life difficult for their subjects. Further, they normally suspect that making anybody unhappy is likely to make their thrones somewhat less secure. Still, if the ruler makes Smith unhappy by taking his

18. There was an emperor, of course, but the officials carried out the bulk of his duties.

money away and giving it to Jones, the gain of Jones may be greater than the loss of Smith. If Smith is also killed, he is unlikely to try to overthrow the ruler.

While there are exceptions, neither dictators nor monarchs are likely to do wicked things just because they want to. Further, there is some truth in the French monarchist argument, discussed above, that the ruler has no conflict of interest with his country. He may have conflicts of interest with those parts of his country that would like to get rid of him, but the prosperity of the country as a whole is to his advantage.[19] It must be said, however, that the sovereign's interest in the prosperity of his subjects is not necessarily consistent with overall economic efficiency. One well-known model of autocracy characterizes the ruler as a "stationary bandit" whose objective is to maximize the amount of privately created wealth redistributed to himself and his supporters.[20] The interference in the economy required to achieve that goal can lead to high levels of regulation, taxation, and budget deficits as well as rent-seeking activities by individuals and groups striving to be included among the favored. Mercantilism,[21] modern *dirigiste* France and Spain, and the regimes of "Papa Doc" Duvalier, Ferdinand Marcos, and Manuel Noriega are obvious examples. But so is the Leviathan democratic state.[22]

There is a significant difference between hereditary monarchies and dictatorships, as mentioned above, which is simply that the monarch is more

19. H. Geoffrey Brennan, *The Tale of the Slave-Owner: Reflections on the Political Economy of Communist Reform*, Virginia Political Economy Lecture Series, Fairfax, Va., George Mason University, 1990; David D. Haddock, "Foreseeing Confiscation by the Sovereign: Lessons from the American West," in *The Political Economy of the American West*, ed. Terry L. Anderson and P. J. Hill, 129–45 (Lanham, Md.: Roman and Littlefield, 1994).

20. Mancur Olson, "Dictatorship, Democracy, and Development," *American Political Science Review* 87 (1993): 567–76; Martin C. McGuire and Mancur Olson, "The Economics of Autocracy and Majority Rule: The Invisible Hand and the Use of Force," *Journal of Economic Literature* 34 (1996): 72–96. "Stationary bandits are superior to roving bandits (for example, Chinese warlords) because, being stationary, they have an incentive to preserve the wealth or capital of potential victims" (Wintrobe 1998, p. 131). Wintrobe refers to such a ruler as a "kleptocrat."

21. Robert B. Ekelund Jr. and Robert D. Tollison, *Mercantilism as a Rent-Seeking Society* (College Station: Texas A&M University Press, 1981); Robert B. Ekelund Jr. and Robert D. Tollison, *Politicized Economies: Monarchy, Monopoly, and Mercantilism* (College Station: Texas A&M University Press, 1997).

22. H. Geoffrey Brennan and James M. Buchanan, *The Power to Tax: Analytical Foundations of a Fiscal Constitution* (Cambridge: Cambridge University Press, 1980).

secure and that there is not likely to be a general outburst of street fighting when he dies. "The King is dead, long live the King."

Kurrild-Klitgaard examined the history of the Danish monarchy.[23] He found that during the period when the throne was not hereditary, civil strife was endemic and kings were overthrown frequently. During the last 400 years, when the throne has been hereditary, domestic tranquility has been the norm. This was true in the days when Denmark was a genuine monarchy as well as now, when its queen is a constitutional monarch. That is only one country. Similar studies of other countries would be valuable.

Transitions of power in monarchies are not always peaceful. The ancient Persian empire, the empire overthrown by Alexander the Great, had almost continuous difficulties with the line of succession to the throne. The problem was that the emperor usually had many sons, and he tended to appoint them to administrative posts in various parts of the empire. They rarely attempted to overthrow their father, although sometimes they did, but the emperor's death usually ignited a civil war among contending heirs.

A more extreme example of this occurred in Turkey, after the time of Selim the Grim (1467–1520), who enacted a dynastic law requiring the Padashah to kill all of his brothers. As a result of this rule and other efforts to protect the Padashah, the male heirs were all confined to a palace in the safekeeping of eunuchs. When the Padashah died, a violent civil war immediately broke out within the palace walls. Normally one of the sons survived and became the next Padashah. The system did not produce very good rulers.

Most European states had a simpler rule, which was that the heir to the throne was kept close to his father in the royal capital, but not given any administrative position that might supply him a power base either to overthrow his father or to dispose of his younger brothers.[24] In general, there was a positive effort to inoculate the younger brothers with the belief that they would live well, but not become king.

Traditionally in China, where the emperor once again had many wives and children, there was a rule under which the eldest son of his principal wife was to succeed. The other sons, in essence, were pensioned off generously. Under the Ming dynasty, as a part of their pension agreement, the other sons were

23. Peter Kurrild-Klitgaard, "The Constitutional Economics of Autocratic Succession," *Public Choice* 103 (2000): 63–84.

24. Stalin seems to have done the same thing. Had he lived longer, he might well have established a dynasty.

required to move to South China, a very long way from the capital. There do not seem to have been any cases in which they attempted to overthrow their half-brother.

All of these methods worked, but not perfectly. The Wars of the Roses started when a close relative of an existing, but mentally unbalanced, king successfully replaced him.

Another solution to the succession problem, which was used originally by the Catholic Church but copied by most communist countries, is simple and seems to work in most cases. There was the Great Schism, though. In this case, the dictator, called the Bishop of Rome in the Catholic Church and the general secretary of the Communist Party in Russia, appoints a body to advise him, the College of Cardinals in Rome and the Politburo in Moscow. When the dictator dies, this group elects his successor.[25]

Transitions of power under this system did not always proceed without bloodshed, but on the basis of the rather limited experience of it in communist countries, it has worked pretty well. Perhaps the fact that almost all of the cardinals are elderly men is the reason that it has worked so well in the Catholic Church. Members of the various Communist Party politburos also tended to be elderly.

The end of the reign of a dictator who has climbed the slippery pole rather than inherited his position is rarely as orderly as that of hereditary monarchs. First, he may be overthrown by some of his colleagues or, in some cases, by

25. Electors likewise chose the Germanic monarch, and this system continued to be used after that monarch and the Holy Roman Emperor became united in one person. James Bryce (*Holy Roman Empire*) remarks "how difficult, one might say impossible, it was found to maintain in practice the elective principle" (246). While "the imperial throne was from the tenth to the nineteenth century absolutely open to any orthodox Christian candidate," the fact of the matter was that "the competition was confined to a few powerful families, and there was always a strong tendency for the crown to become hereditary in some one of these." Bryce also credits this system with contributing to the Holy Roman Empire's eventual fall: "The power of the crown was not moderated but destroyed. Each successful candidate was forced to purchase his title by the sacrifice of rights which had belonged to his predecessors, and must repeat the same shameful policy later in his reign to procure the election of his son. Feeling at the same time that his family could not make sure of keeping the throne, he treated it as a life-tenant is apt to treat his estate, seeking only to make out of it the largest present profit. And the electors, aware of the strength of their position, presumed upon it and abused it to assert an independence such as the nobles of other countries could never have aspired to" (247). In the Empire's dying days, the electors were "driven to the expedient of selecting for the office persons whose private resources enabled them to sustain it with dignity" (361).

foreign invaders. Second, as we have mentioned, he may get tired of the burden of office and simply withdraw. In any event, it is usually difficult for a dictator to control the transition of power, and the process is apt to be disruptive. There may not be anyone killed during these interregnums, but sometimes many people are.

After seizing power, dictators are apt to feel much less secure than the eldest son of the previous king. This insecurity may also cause difficulties, running from systematic executions of defeated rivals and others whose loyalty is suspect, to simply running a very weak government. On occasions the new dictator has actually had radically different ideas from a predecessor and has imposed them. Sometimes the new dictator is overthrown quite quickly because he does not have the armed support his predecessor did.

6. *Political Freedoms*

We now come to the subject of freedom. First, dictators normally object to anybody suggesting that they be overthrown, and they suppress it. Freedoms of speech, assembly, and the press may be curtailed in the process. Democracies also have a record of suppression of objectors. Socrates was in fact killed by the Athenian democracy, and Aristotle found it necessary to leave town hastily in order to prevent Athens from committing "another sin against philosophy."[26]

Democratic Germany has a very complicated set of laws that ban the expression of certain right-wing views. Most people, including myself, do not regard this as particularly offensive, although I do think they are vastly exaggerating a minor problem.

Any academic living in the United States is familiar with the problems of "political correctness."[27] Confusingly, this particular ideological movement has had grammatical effects. One is not supposed to refer to "chairman" but "chairperson" and so on.

This restriction on freedom is not only about minor language matters, though. It has led to a number of American universities wasting a great deal

26. After the establishment of Macedonian control, Aristotle returned to Athens and set up his famous academy.

27. For example, Richard Bernstein, *Dictatorship by Virtue: Multiculturalism and the Battle for America's Future* (New York: Knopf, 1994).

of money and corrupting the education of their students in order to teach certain politically correct courses. Moreover, a lot of total nonsense is being taught as "history" at the grade school and high school levels.

Restricting freedom is exactly what government, democratic or dictatorial, is about. All sorts of things one can do to injure other people are prevented by the government, it is hoped. These restrictions are not necessarily confined to ordinary crimes. The small homeowners' association that governed the area where I lived in Tucson complained about a person painting a new house the wrong color. He refused to do anything about it; the association sued and collected $7000. In this area one is not free to choose the color of one's own house. The homeowners' association thought that the value of the other houses would be lowered, and I believe that this was a correct estimate.

Altogether, the extent to which people have freedom is more or less an inverse function of the number of laws in force. In general, when I talk to people about freedom, what they actually mean is not freedom in the way I have been discussing it here, but freedom to do the things that one can now do in the United States, and not freedom to do things that are now illegal in the United States. Dictatorships have different sets of rules of this sort, and it is always possible to maintain that a given set of them is not consistent with freedom. Ulster's Irish Catholics frequently maintain that they are not free, and they sometimes even say that Ulster is not democratic. The problem here is simply that the majority disagrees with them about a number of things and proceeds to enforce its opinion.

If it is understood that freedom means the freedom to do the kind of things one can do in the United States, and not freedom to do other things one cannot do in the United States, for example, putting up a crèche on the courthouse lawn, then it must be conceded that there are more freedoms in the United States than in dictatorships. But that is not always true. I lived in Hong Kong at a time when it was run by the colonial office as a straightforward dictatorship. As far as I could see, it was a remarkably free place. More so than the United States, because the government was not attempting to enforce any of the moralistic provisions which are part of American law.

Take an earlier example. During the reign of Caesar Augustus,[28] there was substantially nothing that an ordinary free citizen of Rome could say that would get him in trouble. Ovid succeeded in irritating Caesar enough to be

28. After he was firmly established in power; when he was consolidating his power things were different.

exiled, but people without his talent would normally be left alone even if they sharply criticized the emperor.

There are two other famous examples. In one case a member of the Senate, who was a great believer in the Republic, kept going about Rome saying that he was going to kill the emperor. Caesar eventually came to the conclusion that perhaps social pressure would lead him to actually make the attempt, so he passed a special law prohibiting the man from living in Rome. Surely this was not a gigantic infringement on his freedom.

The other case, which is more amusing, occurred while Caesar Augustus was, as Roman dictators did, acting as a judge in a court. In a case originating in Spain, one party offered evidence that the other party regularly cursed the emperor. The emperor said "is that so," turned to the other party, and spent the next five minutes cursing him. He then said, "he has cursed me and I have cursed him, now let's get on with the lawsuit." It is likely that the object of the emperor's invective was not very happy while the cursing was going on.

Caesar Augustus was an exceptional ruler. Most dictators have not had this kind of freedom from deep worry which permits them to get by with this kind of thing. Hereditary monarchs very commonly have. The crime of lese-majesty is always available for a king to deal with people who criticize him, but it must be said that kings do not use it very often. On the other hand, they are not criticized very much, which may be because of the threat of retribution or simply because their subjects have little to be critical of.

7. Concluding Remarks

Much of what I have said in this chapter is contrary to the current conventional wisdom. The reader may recall that during the latter part of the nineteenth century and the early part of the twentieth century, nationalism was one of the great virtues. Austria-Hungary was broken up in its name, Germany and Italy united in it, and there are many other examples. Woodrow Wilson was a firm believer in it. That has changed. Nowadays nationalism is, on the whole, a bad word, and we have been attempting in Yugoslavia to compel separate groups of people, who do not want to live with each other, to do so peacefully. Apparently, it is to be tried in several other parts of the world as well.

At the moment, democracy has about the same respect that nationalism had in the early part of the twentieth century. Almost everybody is firmly in favor of it. For a very long time people were prepared to die, not for democracy, but for the one true king. The Wars of the Roses is a good example of this kind of thing, but there are many others. The kind of enthusiasm we now have for democracy used to be marshaled in favor of the legitimate heir to the throne. Marco Polo, who was governor of a large Chinese city, remarks that the Mongols were unpopular because the people wanted to be ruled by their own prince.

All of this is not an argument that dictatorship or hereditary monarchy is better than democracy. My view is simply that the matter has not been given much serious thought. When I have talked to people about this, they almost invariably think of Hitler or, possibly, if they are on the right, Stalin. They then turn to African countries or Muslim countries ruled by autocrats and say that democracy would be an improvement, but it is not obvious that they have good reasons for their preference. Recently, there has been a feeling rather than an argument that democracy will lead to greater economic progress. This is normally based on nothing more than the fact that people believe in democracy and in economic progress, and all good things go together. We badly need serious consideration of the matter.

Turning to my own personal feeling, I was brought up in a democracy and would be rather unhappy living under a dictatorship, although I was perfectly happy in Hong Kong. I see no reason to believe either that today's wild collection of differently organized governments that are called democracy or that the other wild collection of governments that are at the moment referred to as autocratic are the best form of government. They are both thousands of years old, and it seems to me that invention is as important in this area as in any other. On the other hand, in spite of having thought about the matter for a long time, I have no third form of government to suggest.

PART 3

REVOLUTION AND ITS SUPPRESSION

REVOLUTION AND WELFARE ECONOMICS

We shall now turn to a type of conflict that leads to the spilling of real blood. In this chapter and those immediately following, we will deal with revolutions and coups d'état. We will use new tools to analyze these phenomena, and our conclusions will be quite different from those found in the classical work in the field. The standard view of revolutions is extremely romantic in nature. Formal and large-scale use of violence is an important element in almost all romantic literature. The medieval knights did indeed engage in romantic love affairs, but all accounts of medieval chivalry also emphasized combat. Similarly, modern romantic literature very commonly involves wars, revolutions, etc. It is true, of course, that in modern times the word "romance" is sometimes applied only to love stories; but if we look at that literature which attracts people because of excitement, adventure, etc., a high percentage of it concerns itself directly with physical violence among human beings.

Why this phenomenon should exist I do not know, but it surely does. The reason I introduce it here, however, is because a particular subsection of this romantic concern with violence is important for the study of revolutions. There is probably no single topic which is normally dealt with in a more romantic way than revolution. This has led to vast misunderstandings of the subject and, in essence, to the definition of the word "revolution" in such a way that it refers to something which almost never happens. The standard concept of the revolution is that a group of poor, oppressed people rise against their oppressors. After numerous adventures and vicissitudes, the revolution is successful and establishes a new order—seldom specified in detail—which is a tremendous improvement over the old order. Perhaps the dominance of this view is affected by the way history is written. Successful revolutionaries, after all, write their own history and are apt to have a romantic view of it. Unsuccessful revolutionaries, on the other hand, have their histories written by the government they failed to overthrow; hence, they are normally listed as bandits.

There is a counterview which is equally romantic, but it is normally held by a quite different group of people. Under this view, the revolution consists

Reprinted, with permission, from *The Social Dilemma: The Economics of War and Revolution* (Blacksburg, Va.: Center for Study of Public Choice, 1974), 26–35.

of the scum of society rising, normally under the leadership of clever and unscrupulous intellectuals. After a great deal of damage and destruction, the revolutionaries establish a totalitarian state. These two romantic views differ in evaluation, but not very much in their description of what happens. In both cases, it is assumed that the same "scenario" occurs, but it is thought to be good in one case and bad in the other.

It seems to me very dubious that anything which fits this joint description has occurred in history, and certainly it has not occurred very often. If we look at those cases where a government has been removed by violence or the threat of violence, we normally find that what has actually happened is that there has been a dispute within the government—one group of officials throwing out another group, perhaps with the support of extragovernmental groups. We can divide up these cases roughly into those in which the change is mainly a few officials at the very top and those which are more radical in nature. Nevertheless, we very rarely find a government overthrown by entirely extragovernmental forces. But these issues will be discussed at greater length in succeeding chapters. This chapter is to be largely devoted to a discussion of the welfare implications of revolutions. The issues here are quite complex and require a little formal analysis. Turning, then, to Figure 5, we once again assume that the production possibility frontier is shown by *P-P*; the society is at point *A*, which in this case is on the production possibility frontier. Let us suppose some group is contemplating a revolution. Let us further suppose, as a simple first case, that the group is not proposing to have any different type of society after it takes over; hence, the only effect of the revolution on economic efficiency will be the resources used in the revolution itself. This would lower the production possibility frontier after the revolution (successful or unsuccessful) down the line *P′-P′*.

Under these circumstances, a revolution is highly unlikely if it would lead simply to some such point as *A′*; everyone is injured there. Let us suppose that instead of leading to *A′*, it will lead to point *B*. In particular, if we look at traditional historical revolution, this would mean that the people who intend to pull off the revolution—whether they are an army, the Paris mob, or some subsection of bureaucracy—propose to improve their position in the state and anticipate that this will lead to an improvement in their command over the nation's resources. For them, this can easily more than counterbalance the cost of the revolution. The fact that this is a fairly easy and probable outcome may not be obvious from our diagram. I found it necessary to draw in line *P′-P′* a good distance below line *P-P* in order to make the diagram intelligible, and

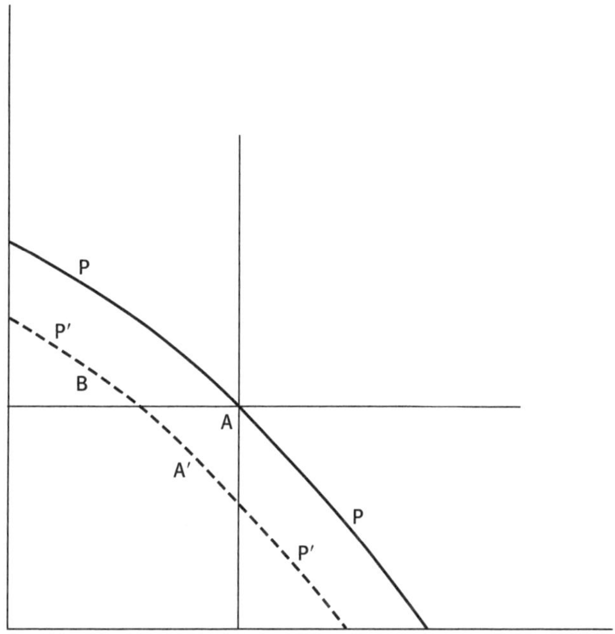

FIGURE 5
The costs of conflict

this makes it necessary to move *B* far to the left. It is a consequence of wanting the diagram to be legible, not because the real world is like that.

In actual practice, the total fall in product through a successful revolution may be quite small. Few revolutionary leaders enter into a revolution with the intention of a long and very destructive internal war, although, through mistakes, this is sometimes the outcome. With only a very modest reduction in total product anticipated from the revolution, a modest redistribution of income in favor of the revolutionaries would normally more than counterbalance the reduction in total product from their standpoint.

It should, of course, be noted that there are cases where a revolution leads to an efficiency change. It may well happen that the existing order is in some way inefficient. An obvious example would be the present Communist organization of agriculture. If one believes that the people in charge of the government at the moment are devoted to this inefficient allocation of resources for essentially religious reasons, then their overthrow may be desirable on grounds which have nothing to do with distribution. There undoubtedly have been revolutions in the past which have led to improved efficiency of the total social apparatus. However, there also have been revolutions which have led to a reduced efficiency, and there is no per se argument either for or against revolution on these grounds. In each case, we would need to calculate the probable gain in efficiency against the investment of resources in the conflict. Note the need for careful calculation. Random changes are apt to be undesirable. Thus (and contrary to the prevailing wisdom), revolutions are likely to be desirable in terms of improving efficiency only if they are carried out by cooly calculating individuals rather than hot-blooded romantics.

Most revolutions have probably not been efforts to consciously or unconsciously improve the efficiency of society. There can be no doubt that both the French Revolution and the American Revolution were initiated with this in mind, and, in fact, in both cases they did work some improvement, although whether the improvement in efficiency was worth the cost of the struggle is another question. The Russian Revolution also was an effort to improve efficiency of society, but since the people who designed it had studied economics under Karl Marx rather than Adam Smith, the net effect was a reduction in efficiency.[1] Certainly there was a permanent drastic reduction in the efficiency of the agricultural portion of the economy.

Most revolutions, however, have aimed at changing the distribution of income rather than improving the efficiency of society. Of course, the two concepts are frequently interrelated, and some individual who expects to benefit from the revolution may have great difficulty in distinguishing between that portion of the benefit which comes from society as a whole being a bit more efficient and that which comes from his improved status as a result of the revolution. Conversely, of course, people who are displaced by the revolution may have great difficulty in distinguishing between their loss in status and the concomitant reduction in their income and the possible inefficiency of the change in terms of the movement of the production frontier.

We have here a set of rules for whether or not an outsider should favor a revolution. If you anticipate that it will make a net improvement in society, and by this net improvement I am including both efficiency changes and distribution changes which you like, you should be in favor of it. If you feel that it will work a net injury, you should be opposed to it. Needless to say, most individuals in the society will be primarily interested in the change it makes in their own situation. In this respect, transfers have the characteristic that

1. Abram Bergson, "Development under Two Systems," *World Politics*, 23 (July, 1971), 579–617.

they must injure some people and benefit others. It is possible, however, to concentrate the injury on a small number of people and spread the benefits over many, with the result that the gainers will outnumber the losers even though the total gain may be smaller than the total loss.

An obvious method of doing this, of course, is to seize the property of the rich and divide it among the rest of the population. But it is not necessary that the people who suffer the injury be rich. For example, a proposal that we murder all people who have incomes under $4,000 a year would not only solve the problem of poverty as it is currently defined, but could produce material profits which could benefit the rest of us. The gain would be small compared with the loss, but the gainers would be more numerous than the losers.

Looked at in the very long run (and there is no reason why any individual contemplating revolution should look at it in the very long run), it is likely that the efficiency effects of revolution will swamp the distribution effects. The great-great-grandsons of persons now alive are apt to be benefited more by a one-fourth of 1 percent change in the rate of growth than they are by any redistribution in current income. This is partially because of the wonders of the compound interest formula, but even more because, as a general rule, great-great-grandsons will benefit little from the wealth of their remote individual ancestors almost regardless of the type of society. Thus, the present discounted value of your great-great-grandson's income is affected very little by how much wealth you have and very much by the rate of growth of the national product.

Our remote descendants, however, are only one example of a broader category. As I have mentioned, most people probably decide their attitude toward revolutions in terms of effects quite directly on them, but most people devote at least some thought to its effect on other people. Thus, changes in efficiency or in distribution may be valued to some extent for their effect on other persons than *ego*. Among participants, one anticipates this would be a small effect, but one also anticipates that it is a real one.

So far, we have been talking about individual attitudes toward possible changes in government without saying anything about whether they should participate in conflict to cause or prevent these changes. The rule for such participation is, of course, very simple: the individual should balance his probable gains against the probable cost, both suitably discounted.[2] A violent

2. See Thomas R. Ireland, "The Rationale of Revolt," *Papers on Non-Market Decision Making*, 3 (Fall, 1967): 49–66; and Gordon Tullock, "A Model of Social Interaction,"

revolution will lead to some deaths, and an individual should take this into account in making these calculations. In general, a government or revolutionary party, in attempting to attract support, should try to maximize the payoff of entry into the revolution on their side. This can be done either by offering positive rewards for contributions or by imposing penalties for not contributing. Thus, the Communists of South Vietnam have had a very large-scale policy of kidnapping or murdering leaders in the countryside who, in their view, are not sufficiently pro-Communist. This can be countered by offering large amounts of money for information.[3] One might find the same person taking an active part in the communization of his area in order to save his life, and selling information to the Americans in order to maximize his income. As long as he can keep the Communists from finding out about his second line of activity, this is quite rational. All of these issues will be discussed in detail in the following chapters.

Two essentially mythological views must be discussed before we conclude this chapter on the welfare effects of revolution. The first of these is the myth of "exploitation." Note that I am referring to the myth of exploitation and not the reality. There may well be situations in the world in which people are, indeed, exploited and in which they would be well advised to revolt to end the exploitation. There are other cases in which people are being exploited, but they would *not* be well advised to revolt to end the exploitation, because the revolt would clearly be unsuccessful and simply lead to their being killed. In addition to these real situations, however, there is the myth of "exploitation" which is probably of much greater real political importance than the real exploitation that does exist.

Assume that we have a group of people who are in charge of a government and who are interested in exploiting their subjects. I take it that the most efficient method of doing so is simply to extract very high taxes, the only services provided being those which can directly improve the subject's taxpaying

---

Mathematical Applications in Political Science, 5, ed. James Herndon and Joseph Bernd (Charlottesville: University Press of Virginia, 1971), 4–28.

3. This technique has been only slightly used by the United States. Stephen Enke, in "Vietnam's 'Other' War," Tempo Publications 66TMP-112 (December, 1966), presents a table showing the amount paid by Americans in Vietnam under a "test program" and the amount paid as a matter of regular routine by the British in Malaya. The largest payment available under the American program was $984, whereas the largest payment available under the British program was $28,000.

ability more than the cost of the service. The government will also have a heavy expense for maintenance of its internal repressive activities, but there is every reason to believe that it will be able to obtain very large profits under present circumstances. My own impression is that governments, even the most despotic, have not reached anywhere near the limit of the income which can be obtained by these methods. Perhaps, however, there are restrictions on their power which are not obvious in the present state of knowledge.

A government engaging in this type of exploitation will clearly be one its subjects would like to overthrow, but it can (by methods we shall discuss later) make the danger of revolt so great that the present discounted value of remaining subject to exploitation will be greater than the profit of the overthrow. Once again, as we shall demonstrate later, the government is likely to be subject to coups in which parts of the government apparatus throw out other parts. Protection against these coups is quite difficult.

But this is *real* exploitation. The myth of exploitation concerns a quite different phenomenon. It is not, for example, argued that the employees of the American government are directly increasing their incomes through taxes above what they otherwise would be. This is particularly remarkable because there is some recent research which seems to indicate that the civil servants and politicians are doing just that.[4] The current myth of exploitation concerns the view that certain people *outside* of the government apparatus are exploiting the rest of the population through control of the government apparatus.

There is, of course, no reason why the control group which is obtaining the benefits from government should formally be incorporated in it; but if the control group is actually doing an efficient job of exploitation, it will draw its income largely through taxes and not through other means. If we observe a group of people who seem to be well-off and who are perhaps influential in the state, but whose source of income is not the government apparatus, then we can feel fairly confident that they are not engaging in this type of political exploitation. It is possible that there is some inefficient exploitation here. Instead of drawing funds directly from the taxation process, certain people might be getting their funds by way of government protection for some monopoly rights they hold. Granted the inefficiency of this process, however,

4. See William A. Niskanen, *Bureaucracy and Representative Government* (Chicago: Aldine Publishing Company, 1971); and Raymond Jackson, "A 'Taxpayer Revolution' and Economic Rationality," *Public Choice*, 10 (Spring, 1971): 93–96.

some special explanation will be necessary. For the same burden on the rest of the economy, these people will receive a larger fund if they take the money directly from general taxation. Under the circumstances, it seems unlikely that people in control of the political process will choose this inefficient operation.

In the real world, of course, we frequently observe monopolies that are supported by the state. It seems likely, however, that these reflect relatively modest power on the part of the individuals who are profiting by them, if anyone is. If we examine the regulated monopolies in the United States, for example, they are clearly protected against competition; but, equally clearly, the result has not been any great profits for them. The returns, indeed, are no higher in the regulated monopolies than elsewhere. The cost and inefficiency of these institutions should not be confused with exploitation.

The myth of exploitation normally depends upon the existence of certain wealthy persons who are capitalists, hereditary landowners, bishops, etc., but we need not confine ourselves to these groups. All major societies of which we have any historic record have had considerable differences in the "wealth" of their members. These differences arise from a number of causes. To some extent, they are due to luck (including that special variant of luck, fortunate choice of parents), skill in activities which really have no economic value, and/or payments to the individual for being highly productive. In any given social situation, the various wealthy members of the community will normally draw their wealth from all three of these causes, and we need not for our present purposes discuss which is the significant one.

The fact is, however, that these sources of wealth are essentially extragovernmental. The government, even though the wealthy people may be influential, is not the *source* of the wealth. It does, however, provide protection. For example, if I were to come to your house, murder you, and remove your wealth (little though it may be), the government would take measures to try to make this activity costly for me. Thus it can be said the government is protecting your wealth. Surely this is indeed one of its objectives. The mythological use of the word "exploitation" involves this phenomenon. We do observe certain people who are well-off but whose income does not come from the government. The government will normally, at least to some extent, protect their wealth. Indeed, without this government protection, these people would not exist at all. This passive protection is confused intellectually with positive participation in creating this wealth. A necessary condition is converted into a sufficient condition.

The problem is particularly significant because, as far as we can see, efficient economic organization requires differential rewards. All efficient economic systems of which we have any record have used this technique to obtain productivity increases, and it will be most surprising if productivity increases can be obtained by any other method than the carrot and the stick. Thus, the view that the government is exploitative because it permitted Henry Ford to make a vast amount of money from the production of the Model T carries with it the implication that nonexploitative governments would enforce equality. This will, as far as we can tell, involve not only little inequality, but also little income.

There is a sense in which the government is aiding you to "exploit" me by preventing me from killing you and taking your property. Perhaps if you have more than I, I may even feel quite indignant about this. We should, however, keep this intellectually distinct from what I have called the exploitative state, a state which directly engages in income transfers. The current myth of the exploitative nature of Western capitalistic states is based, primarily, on bad economics and failure to distinguish between these two phenomena. Probably bad economics is the most important component in this line of "reasoning."

Our final myth is that in internal struggle, the most democratic party has advantages and normally will win. Thus the fact that one party seems to be winning or has won an internal struggle for power will be taken as evidence, perhaps only implicitly, that this party is the more democratic. In practice, this myth is so widely believed that it reinforces itself by a sort of cyclical reasoning process. Suppose we have a revolution somewhere which is winning over the government. From this fact people will, without much real thought, deduce that it is the more democratic side. If it then wins, they will use this as evidence that the most democratic side always wins. If it loses, they will put this down to its undemocratic practices, or perhaps to a loss of democratic virtue toward the end of the struggle. Thus, the myth in a sense provides its own validation.

If we turn from this mythological approach and look at the real world, it is clear that a revolution rarely leads to a democratic government. Indeed, it is far commoner for a democratic government to be overthrown by a despotism than vice versa. Consider, for example, the existing democracies. For this purpose, let us define democracies as those countries where governments are selected by voting and where opposition parties exist. If we look over this group, we observe that cases where the democracy was established by a revolution are rare. The English-speaking countries (including Ireland, although the Irish would object) developed democracy gradually over a long period of time. The development, it is true, involved a number of disputes and changes of power, but their major revolutionary struggle—the Cromwell wars—actually reduced the level of popular participation. Outside the English-speaking world, one finds either a gradual development of democracy over a long period of time, or a fairly direct copying of foreign institutions by governments which are not revolutionary in nature. France has had quite a number of revolutions, but these always ended in despotisms. The establishment of the Third Republic occurred after a foreign army had captured the emperor and after a very considerable period of gradual movement of a basically despotic government toward democratic forms. Napoleon III had, after all, been ruling through an elected legislature prior to Sedan.

There are, of course, at any given time, a number of governments which are temporarily democratic, and which are the result of a recent revolution. In South America, for example (at whatever time this book is read), there are a number of governments which have recently had a revolution and, at the moment, are reasonably democratic. These democracies, however, will mostly last only a very short time, being overthrown by another revolution which sets up some kind of military despotism. Those South American countries which have had fairly long records of democracy normally moved from a dictatorship to democracy gradually, rather than by way of an exciting revolution. There is another route to democracy which we sometimes see. This is conquest by a democratic state, followed by imposition of democracy. This particular method has worked rather well in those countries which already have some democratic roots, but in general, it has not worked well in countries which do not have at least partially democratic traditions already.

Looking at the other side of the coin, it is clear that democracy is fairly easily overthrown. Historically, for example, in 1914 practically the entire world was ruled by governments which were reasonably democratic. The regression of democracy since then has very commonly come by way of revolution. The overthrow of the Russian democratic government in October, 1917, is merely the most obvious single case. We may take as other examples the overthrow of fairly long established democratic governments in Chile and Uruguay by revolutionary movements; the suppression, by one method or another, of the democratic governments that were set up as the European empires withdrew from Africa and Asia by local dictatorships;[5] and such phenomena as the

5. This process is not yet entirely complete.

subversion of French democracy in 1958. Note that there is no strong reason to believe that these overthrows of democracy are permanent. France, in fact, is once again democratic, and may well remain a democracy for a number of years. Even confining ourselves to the continent of Europe and leaving out those areas where such democracy as did exist was suppressed by the Red army in 1945, we see democracies which have been replaced. Both Spain and Portugal were democratically ruled in 1914. Greece has been democratic or dictatorial by alternation for a long time, being in this sense very similar to a South American republic.

Looking at the matter in a longer perspective, we have had three major periods of democracy: the classical city-states, the city-states of the late Middle Ages, and the period which reached its peak in 1914. The first two ended with democracy pretty generally suppressed, although the Venetian republic, several of the Swiss cantons, and some German city-states survived from the Medieval period into modern times. The future of the present wave of democracy is, of course, as obscure as the future of anything else. What the historic record does indicate, however, is that revolutions may well overthrow democracies. Once again, the revolution is not something which brings good results per se. Revolutions have seldom led to democracy, but one can imagine a case in which they might. Careful calculation rather than acceptance of myth is necessary to decide whether any particular revolution is likely to lead to an expansion or contraction of democracy.

THE PARADOX OF REVOLUTION [1]

It is the purpose of this chapter to demonstrate that the image of revolution we find in the literature[2] is a false one. I shall also, I hope, demonstrate why this false image is so appealing to intellectuals and historians. Let us consider, for a start, a very simple situation. Ruritania is governed by a vicious, corrupt, oppressive, and inefficient government. A group of pure-hearted revolutionaries are currently attempting to overthrow the government, and we know with absolute certainty that if they are successful they will establish a good, clean, beneficial, and efficient government. What should an individual Ruritanian do about this matter? He has three alternatives: He can join the revolutionaries, he can join the forces of repression, or he can remain inactive.[3] Let us compute the payoff to him of these three types of action. Equation (1) shows the payoff to inaction.

$$P_{In} = P_g \cdot L_v \tag{1}$$

This simply indicates that the payoff is the benefit which he receives from an improved government times the likelihood that the revolution will be successful. Note that this payoff is essentially a public good. Of course, he will benefit himself from the improved government, and he may well benefit from his feeling that his fellow citizens are well-off. But in this case, he will receive no special, private reward.

The payoff for participating in the revolution on the side of the revolutionaries is shown by equation (2).

Reprinted, with permission, from *The Social Dilemma: The Economics of War and Revolution* (Blacksburg, Va.: Center for Study of Public Choice, 1974), 36–46.

1. This chapter is a revision of an earlier publication; see Gordon Tullock, "The Paradox of Revolution," *Public Choice*, 11 (Fall, 1971), 89–99. For an examination of the empirical evidence, see Morris Silver, "Political Revolution and Repression: An Economic Approach," *Public Choice*, 17 (Spring, 1974), 63–73.

2. There are only two exceptions known to me. One, Thomas Ireland's "The Rationale of Revolt," *Papers on Non-Market Decision Making*, 3 (Fall, 1967), 49, had considerable influence on me. The other, Nathan Leites and Charles Wolf, Jr., *Rebellion and Authority* (Chicago: Markham Publishing, 1970), is excellent, but had less effect on my thinking because I read it only after I had already reached my basic conclusions.

3. In the real world, of course, there are various shades between these clear-cut alternatives, but our simplification will cause no great damage.

TABLE OF SYMBOLS I

Symbol	Definition
D_i	Private reward to individual for participation in putting down revolt if government wins.
I_r	Injury suffered in action.
C_r	Opportunity cost (benefit) to individual from participation rather than remaining neutral.
L_i	Change in probability of revolutionary success resulting from individual participation in revolution.
L_v	Likelihood of revolutionary victory, assuming subject is neutral.
L_w	Likelihood of injury through participation in revolution (for or against).
P_d	Payoff to participation in revolt on side of existing government.
P_g	Public good generated by successful revolution.
P_i	Private penalty imposed on individual for participation in revolution if revolt fails.
P_{In}	Total payoff to inaction.
P_p	Private cost imposed on defenders of government if revolt succeeds.
P_r	Total payoff to subject if he joins revolution.
R_i	Private reward to individual for his participation in revolution if revolution wins.
E	Entertainment value of participation.

$$P_r = P_g \cdot (L_v + L_i) + R_i(L_v + L_i) - P_i[1 - (L_v + L_i)] - L_w \cdot I_r + E \qquad (2)$$

$$P_r = P_g \cdot L_v + P_g \cdot L_i + R_iL_v + R_iL_i - P_i + P_iL_v + P_iL_i - L_w \cdot I_r + E \qquad (2a)$$

This differs from equation (1) in two respects. First, the individual's participation on the side of the revolutionaries increases the likelihood of revolutionary victory to some extent, presumably to a very small extent in most cases. Second, the individual now has a chance of reward, perhaps in the form of government office, if the revolution is successful, and a chance of being penalized by the government if the revolution fails. Finally, he runs an additional risk of being injured or killed.

Note, however, that generally speaking the individual's entry into the revolution will actually change the likelihood of revolutionary success very little. Indeed, the value of L_i is approximately zero. Assuming this is so, then equation (2) simplifies to the approximation (3).

$$P_r \cong P_g \cdot L_v + R_i L_v - P_i(1 - L_v) - L_w \cdot I_r + E \qquad (3)$$

Approximate equation (3), however, shows the total payoff for participation in the revolution. The individual should be interested in the net, i.e., the participation in the revolution minus the payoff he would receive if he were inactive. This is shown by equation (4).

$$C_r \cong R_i \cdot L_v - P_i(1 - L_v) - L_w \cdot I_r + E \qquad (4)$$

It will be noted that the public good aspect of the revolution drops out of this equation. The reason, of course, is that we are assuming that the individual's participation in the revolution makes a very small (in fact approximately zero) difference in the likelihood of success of the revolution.

If this approximate line of reasoning seems dubious, we may go back to equation (2a), rearrange the terms a little bit, and get equation (5) which is an exact rather than an approximate expression.

$$C_r = (R_i + P_i)L_v + (P_g + R_i + P_i)L_i - P_i - L_w \cdot I_r + E \qquad (5)$$

Once again, it is obvious that unless L_i is large compared with L_v, equation (4) is a very good approximation. What we have been saying is, once again, that the revolution itself is a public good. Individuals, we have known since Samuelson's basic article, are likely to underinvest in production of public goods.

However, let us now turn to the opposite possibility—entering the revolution on the side of the government. Equation (6) shows the payoff for this activity.

$$P_d = P_g(L_v - L_i) + D_i[1 - (L_v - L_i)] - P_p(L_v - L_i) - L_w \cdot I_r + E \qquad (6)$$

Note that the individual's intervention by lowering the probability of revolutionary victory lowers the probability that he will receive the public good. Once again, assuming that the individual's participation has very little effect (i.e., L_i is approximately equal to zero), we find equation (7) which corresponds to equation (4); i.e., it is the net return from participating on the side of reaction.

$$P_d \cong D_i \cdot (1 - L_v) - P_p \cdot L_v - L_w \cdot I_r + E \qquad (7)$$

The equivalents of equations (5) and (6) could also be produced easily.

It will be noted that the approximate result we get indicates that the individuals will ignore the public good aspects of the revolution in deciding whether to participate *and* on which side to participate. The important variables are the rewards and punishments offered by the two sides and the risk of injury during the fighting. Entertainment is probably not an important variable in serious revolutionary or counterrevolutionary activity. People are willing to take some risks for the fun of it, but not very severe ones. If, however, we consider such pseudorevolutions as the recent student problems in much of the democratic world, it is probable that entertainment is one of the more important motives. The students, in general, carefully avoided running any very severe risks of injury or severe punishment, while the chance of rewards was also very slight because they directed the revolutionary activity toward such institutions as universities where little was to be gained.

If we change from our approximate equation to exact equations, it really makes very little difference. Under these circumstances, the public good remains in the equation, but has very slight weight unless the individual feels that his participation or nonparticipation will have a major influence on the outcome. Since most participants in revolution should have no such illusions, it appears that the public good aspects of a revolution are of relatively little importance in the decision to participate. Therefore, they should be of relatively little importance in determining the outcome of the revolution. The discounted value of the rewards and punishment is the crucial factor.

This is the paradoxical result which gives this chapter its title. It immediately raises a number of questions in the mind of any reasonably skeptical scholar. For example, why is the bulk of the literature of revolution written in terms of the public good aspects rather than in terms of the private rewards to participants if public good aspects are, in fact, so unimportant? Second, may we not have obtained our results by oversimplifying the situation? Third, what is the empirical evidence as to the truth or falsity of what is, so far, a completely *a priori* argument? We shall take these questions up *seriatim*.

Beginning with the question of the image of revolution, we note that this image is essentially an intellectual one. Consider a historian in his study contemplating the French Revolution. He is not going to be either penalized or benefited by participation in this revolution which happened some 200 years ago. No one will ask him to look through the little window. Under the circumstances, the only things that concern him are the public good aspects. He may have been benefited or injured by the change in society which resulted from the revolution. He surely was not benefited or injured by the system of rewards and punishments for participation in what little fighting there was. The parts of the revolution which concern him, then, are almost entirely the public good aspects. As the potential participant disregards the value of the public good generated because its value falls to nearly zero in his personal cost-benefit calculus, the historian disregards the private payoffs to participants because their values fall to zero in *his* calculus. They are costs and benefits for other people, not for him.

Similarly, the reporter filing stories on a revolution or the editorial writer in New York are affected, if they are affected at all, by the public good aspects of the revolution rather than by the private rewards or punishments which might lead to direct participation in the fighting. Putting the matter more directly, each participant or observer is interested in that part of the total situation which is of maximum importance for him. That part which is important for the observer is rarely important for the participant and vice versa.

There is one class of participants who also formally emphasize the public good aspect. A great deal of our information about revolutionary overthrows comes from the memoirs of people who have participated in them, on either the winning or the losing side. These people rarely explain their own participation or nonparticipation in terms of selfish motives. Indeed, they very commonly ascribe selfish motives to rivals or to the other side, but always explain their own actions in terms of devotion to the public good.[4] Thus, they present themselves in the most favorable light and their opponents in the least. We should not be particularly surprised by this quite human behavior on the part of these human beings, but we should also discount their evidence.

If we turn to the arguments that are used during the course of a revolution to attract support—either recruits to the fighting or, perhaps, foreign aid, we will normally observe a mixture of appeals to public and private benefits. In general the approach is much like that of the army recruiting sergeant. He will undoubtedly tell his potential customers that joining the army is patriotic, etc. He will also tell them a great deal about the material benefits of military

4. It should be noted that a somewhat similar phenomenon affects the nonparticipant observers like scholars and reporters. If they have become partisans of one side, they are apt to accuse the partisans of the other side of having individualistic motives.

service. Indeed, this is a very common practice in all walks of life. I happened one day to be walking through the Marriott Motor Hotel in Washington at a time when they were engaged in instructing new waitresses in their duties. As I walked by, I heard the woman giving the lecture explaining to the new employees what an honor it is to operate at Marriott, that the customers at Marriott Hotels are superior customers, and that the employees there are exceptionally good. This appeal to what we might call the public good aspect of employment is not uncommon in any profession.

Since the recruiting sergeants, the people asking for support for (or opposition to) revolutions, and the Marriott Hotels all make use of this appeal as well as more individualistic appeals, it is clear they have some effect. I would guess, however, that the effect is small. The army, in attempting to attract recruits, puts far more money into the salary of its soldiers than it does into propaganda about patriotism. Still, the joint appeal is sensible; people to some extent are motivated by ethical and charitable impulses.

We have thus explained why the intellectuals and other nonparticipant observers of revolutions normally discuss them almost exclusively in terms of public goods. We have also explained why the participants probably are more strongly motivated by direct personal rewards than by these public goods. I should like to emphasize here, however, that I am not criticizing the intellectuals for their field of concentration. Clearly, if we are evaluating the desirability or undesirability of a revolution in general terms, the public good aspect is the one we should consider. It is only if we are attempting to study the dynamics of the revolution that we should turn to examination of the utility calculus of the participants. Generally speaking, intellectual observers have been making judgments on the desirability or undesirability of revolution, rather than explaining the revolution. It must be conceded, of course, that in many cases they have attempted to use the public good criteria to explain the dynamics, too. This is unfortunate, but we cannot blame them too much. The public good aspect, for the reason we have given above, dominates the reports of the revolution by historians and reporters. Analysts have been misled by this dominance of public good aspects in the literature. As a result they have been led to believe that it also dominates the calculus of the participants. We should avoid this error.

Thus, if we choose to evaluate revolutions in terms of their general desirability or undesirability, we will look at equation (1). If we are attempting to understand the activities of the revolutionists and their opponents, we will look at equations (4) and (7). People planning a revolution or counterrevolutionary activity will use equations (4) and (7) in their actual planning, and equation (2) in their propaganda.

So much for our first problem. Let us turn to the second problem—the possibility that we have oversimplified the situation. Clearly our equations *are* very simple and it is possible that we have left out some important variable. First, we have assumed a very simple revolutionary situation in which a vicious and corrupt government is being attacked by a pure and good revolution. Obviously the real world is not this simple.[5] It is clear that bad governments have been overthrown by good revolutions and good governments have been overthrown by bad revolutions; but in the overwhelming majority of cases it is difficult to decide between the two parties. Historically, the common form of revolution has been a not-too-efficient despotism which is overthrown by another not-too-efficient despotism with little or no effect on the public good.

In some cases, even the historians and observers discuss revolutions in terms of the participant's personal gains. For example, most accounts of the Wars of the Roses pay little or no attention to the propaganda which was issued by both sides about good government, Christianity, ethics, etc. The only exception to this concerns the very successful propaganda by Henry Tudor about the viciousness of the man he killed at Bosworth Field.

Such revolutions constitute the overwhelming majority. If we turn to that more limited number of revolutions where there is a significant change in régime, I think it would be hard to argue that those cases in which the revolution was an improvement outnumbered those in which it was a detriment. In the judgment of most modern editorial critics, the military overthrows of the previous régimes in Greece, Brazil, Argentina, and Chile were all distinct reductions in the public welfare of these countries. Whether this judgment is correct or not is irrelevant for our particular purposes. Surely there are, in fact, many cases in which such overthrows are detriments. Further, it seems likely that the mere cost inflicted by the fighting and confusion is quite significant in most cases; hence, one would only favor a revolution for public goods reasons if one felt that the net benefit of the change of régime was great enough to pay this cost.

5. Some people seem to define "revolutions" as desirable violent overthrows of a government. With this definition, what we are to say below will not follow. Presumably they would be willing to accept some other word to mean violent overthrow of government, regardless of its moral evaluation, and that could be substituted for "revolution" in the rest of our discussion.

Thus, our equations as they are now drawn should be modified to indicate that the public good values from the revolution may be negative. If the revolutionary party proposes to put up a less efficient system—let us say it is in favor of collective farming (and we know the historically bad results of that method of organizing agriculture), then the public good term in our equations will be negative rather than positive. Again, this bit of realism does not detract from the conclusions we have drawn. The individuals will participate in the revolution or in its repression in terms of the private payoffs with little attention to the public goods. Reporters, on the other hand, will talk mainly about the public good aspects.

Another aspect in which our equations may be thought to lack realism concerns their generalist approach. The public good in our equations as we have so far interpreted it is a public good for the entire society. Note that this is not a necessary characteristic of the equations. Let us suppose that some particular group within the society has some chance of gaining from the revolution and there is some other group that will probably lose. Here the public good will apply only to these two groups. However, this will make no difference in our equations. Indeed, in this respect our equation is very similar to Mancur Olson's analysis of pressure groups in political society.[6] Following Olson, in essence we are espousing the by-product theory of revolutions.

Another element of possible unrealism in our equations is basic to most discussions of public goods. From the time that Paul Samuelson began the current interest in this field, public goods have been normally analyzed in terms of their private benefits for the individual. Thus, if we regard the police force as a Samuelsonian public good and look at Samuelson's equations, I am benefited by the police force because I do not wish to be robbed, murdered, etc. I do not necessarily take into account the benefit to other people. Clearly, most human beings have at least some interest in the well-being of others; therefore this is unrealistic. It is, however, an element of unrealism in almost the entirety of the formal public goods literature and is not confined to our analysis of revolutions alone.

This element of unrealism is not, however, a necessary aspect of the public goods literature. Further, individual scholars have avoided this particular simplification. My benefit from the police force is not entirely represented by the fact that I am protected against various crimes. I may also gain

6. Mancur Olson, *The Logic of Collective Action* (Cambridge: Harvard University Press, 1965).

something from my knowledge that other people are also benefited. Clearly, most people are (at least to some extent) interested in the well-being of others.[7] Thus my evaluation of my gain from the revolution includes not only my direct personal gain, but also pleasure or pain I receive as a result of interdependence between my preference function and that of others. In this respect, the revolution is much like any other charitable activity.

The issue here, however, is basically one of size. The scholars who have discussed public goods without paying any attention to this type of interdependence have been simplifying reality, but not by very much. As far as we can see, for most people marginal adjustment between benefit to themselves and the benefit to other people is achieved when less than 5 percent of the resources under their control is allocated to help "others." Thus we can anticipate that individuals may be willing to do something to aid the revolution for reasons of the benefit this will give other people, but probably not very much. We have here, however, a difficult empirical problem, the measurement of the degree to which individuals are willing to sacrifice for the benefit of others. The work that has been done so far is not very impressive. Still, it does not seem likely that it is wrong by an order of magnitude and it will have to be wrong by at least that much to make this particular aspect of our equation dangerously oversimplified. Indeed, the equations will not be incorrect even if it turns out that individual evaluation of the well-being of others is very high. It simply means that the public good aspect of revolutions will have a larger value than it would if the individual put little weight on the well-being of other persons.

This brings us to our third problem, the empirical evidence. The first thing that should be said is that there have been no careful empirical tests aimed at disentangling the motives of revolutionaries. The literature is overwhelmingly dominated by the "public goods" hypothesis. Indeed, so far as I know this is the first suggestion that it may be falsified. Under the circumstances, it is not surprising that no one has run a formal test.[8]

Furthermore, no one has collected the type of detailed data which are necessary to test the two hypotheses. It does not seem to me that formal statistical tests are at all impossible, although they may be difficult. The difficulty will, of course, be particularly strong in the case of unsuccessful revolutions,

7. Perhaps negatively. Kenneth Boulding has done a great deal to call attention to the role of malevolence in human life.

8. But see Silver, "Political Revolution."

since few records have been kept. Still, approximating the ex ante value of the private rewards to be expected from participation in a revolution is not impossible. It seems to me that such research is most important and I will be delighted to see someone undertake it.

It is not, however, my intention to engage in such research here. Instead I propose to look briefly at the history of revolutions and see whether it seems to contradict or support my by-product theory of revolutions. First, it must be admitted that most revolutions do have some effect on government policy. The personnel at the top is changed and normally that means at least some change in government policy. It is hard to argue, however, that in most cases this is the major objective of the revolution. In most cases, after all, the new government is very much like the one before. Most overthrows are South American or African and simply change the higher level personnel. It is true that the new senior officials will tell everyone—and very likely believe it themselves—that they are giving better government than their predecessors. It is hard, however, to take these protestations very seriously.

One of the reasons it is hard to take these protestations seriously is that in most revolutions, the people who overthrew the existing government were high officials in that government before the revolution. If they were deeply depressed by the nature of the previous government's policies, it seems unlikely that they could have given enough cooperation in those policies to have risen to high rank. People who hold high, but not supreme, rank in a despotism are less likely to be unhappy with the policy of that despotism than are people who are outside the government. Thus, if we believe in the public good motivation of revolutions, we will anticipate that these high officials will be less likely than outsiders to attempt to overthrow the government.

From the private benefit theory of revolutions, however, the contrary deduction would be drawn. A high official has, for reasons we will discuss in our chapter on coups, a very much higher probability of success in his attempt to overthrow the existing government. Further, the success of the revolution is likely to leave him in a very senior position, whereas the average revolutionary may, with luck, become a police sergeant. Lastly, the costs to him are probably not terribly great because most high officials lead rather insecure lives. The unsuccessful revolution will, it is true, deprive him of his high official position under the old regime, but he is apt to lose that through any one of a number of accidents anyway. Under the circumstances, the computation of the present discounted value of the costs and benefits of revolutions is apt to look very much more favorable from the standpoint of the high official than from the standpoint of an outsider. Therefore, we anticipate that revolutions tend to be run by prime ministers, crown princes, and ministers of war. Superficial examination of history seems to indicate that the private good theory is upheld by this empirical test. Needless to say, a more careful and exhaustive study of the point is needed.

Another obvious area for empirical investigation concerns the expectations of the revolutionaries. My impression is that they generally expect to have a good position in the new state which is to be established by the revolution. Further, my impression is that the leaders of revolutions continuously encourage their followers in such views. In other words, they hold out prospects of private gains to them. It is certainly true that those people I have known who have talked in terms of revolutionary activity have always thought that they themselves would have a good position in the "new Jerusalem." Normally, of course, it is necessary to do a little careful questioning of them to bring out this point. They usually begin by telling you that they favor the revolution solely because it is right, virtuous, and preordained by history.[9]

As another piece of evidence, Lenin is famous for having developed the idea of professional revolutionaries. He felt that amateurs were not to be trusted in running a revolution and wished to have people who devoted full-time to revolutionary activity and who were supported by the revolutionary organization. Clearly, he held a by-product theory of revolution, although I doubt that he would ever have admitted it.

Last, we may take those noisiest of "revolutionaries"—the radical left students of a few years ago. It is noticeable that these students, although they talked a great deal about public goods, in fact did very little in the way of demonstrating their devotion to such goods. Indeed, the single most conspicuous characteristic of their "revolutionary" activities was the great care that they took to minimize private cost. Always and everywhere, one of the major demands was that no private cost be imposed on unsuccessful revolutionaries by way of punishment. Further, they normally carefully arranged

9. The sample of people with whom I have talked about revolution is relatively restricted. At almost any given time, but particularly in the late 1930s and the mid-1960s, there were a number of people around universities who claimed to be revolutionaries. I knew a number of these people and talked to them at some length. My second sample consists of Chinese intellectuals who were pro-Communist in the years just before the Communist takeover in China. Being at that time in China, I met and talked with a number of them and they all fitted the pattern.

their activities in locations—such as universities—where they felt confident that no great punishment would be imposed upon them. This is in spite of the fact that it is obvious that the total overthrow of *all* the universities in the modern world would not significantly affect any government. Indeed, this may be one of the rare cases where the entertainment value of revolution is the dominant motivation.

I should not like to argue that the empirical information contained in the last few paragraphs is decisive. However, it clearly proves that the evidence is not overwhelmingly against the by-product theory of revolutions. Further, granted the fact that all previous theoretical discussion of revolutions has been based on the public goods theory, it is quite encouraging that material collected by scholars holding this point of view can be used to support the by-product theory.[10]

In sum, the theoretical arguments for the view that revolutions are carried out by people who hope for private gain and produce such public goods as they do produce as a by-product seem to me very strong. As of now, no formal empirical test has been made of it, but a preliminary view of the empirical evidence would seem to support the by-product theory. This, of course, is the paradox. Revolution is the subject of an elaborate and voluminous literature, and, if I am right, almost all of this literature is wrong.

10. Once again, see Silver, "Political Revolution."

THE ECONOMICS OF REPRESSION

As I mentioned in the last chapter, true revolutions (uprisings from *outside* the government apparatus) are extremely rare and perhaps nonexistent. Governments are usually overthrown by an internal split in which some of the high officials of the government revolt against superiors. In this chapter I propose to explain why such "outside" revolts are unusual. We shall look into the technical problem of protecting the government *against* such revolts. As will be seen, this is relatively easy. The police and army, if they are of even moderate efficiency, should be able to put down outside revolts. Having completed discussion of this subject, we will then turn to what actually happens in governmental overthrow or coup d'état to point out why it is so much more difficult for a dictator to protect himself against his chief of staff or captain of his palace guard than against a revolt of the oppressed masses. In general in this discussion we will put little or no emphasis on "reforms" in the dictator's government. We will deal with methods of repression, rather than with concessions.

In this chapter, we will deal with the repression of a revolution in its earliest stages, when there are only a few people conspiring against the state. Initially, the analysis will be presented in asymmetric terms. We will discuss the decision process of the police force and the decision process of potential rebels separately. Later I shall demonstrate that there is a symmetry between these two positions, albeit at a level which I think is not normally considered. I will also demonstrate that there are structural similarities between the police force–rebellion relationship and the relationship of the police force to ordinary crime. This should not be taken as indicating a moral evaluation of either rebellion or crime.

From the standpoint of the government, preventing revolutionary overthrow requires techniques depending upon the stage to which the revolution has proceeded. If the revolutionaries have succeeded in organizing a regular military force in the field, then defeating it is an ordinary military problem differing very little from international war, which is dealt with in our final chapters. A second form that rebellion takes on occasion is a "spontaneous" outburst of mob violence. If this outburst is indeed spontaneous and not subject to control from some central force, then unless the police force and

Reprinted, with permission, from *The Social Dilemma: The Economics of War and Revolution* (Blacksburg, Va.: Center for Study of Public Choice, 1974), 47–59.

army are quite small, dealing with it should be a fairly quick and simple procedure. A great many people may be killed, but the government should never be in danger unless the mob is actually militarily more powerful than the armed forces. Granted that the average person does not have at home any highly efficient weapons and that we are hypothesizing a lack of central control, it is unlikely that the mob *will* be able to defeat the armed forces, even if it has considerable numerical superiority. If the mob has a central control and is large, then we are back to the position mentioned before in which the rebels really have a regular armed force. Under these circumstances, once again we will defer discussion.

There is, however, a third possible state of the "revolution," which is essentially a police, rather than an army, matter. There may be an organization (or organizations) or, for that matter, individuals who are attempting to overthrow the government, but have not yet achieved enough power so that there is any prospect at all of them taking the field with a regular, organized force. They resort to guerrilla warfare of the sort in which guerrillas attempt to hide in the population, or they simply organize a conspiracy for the purpose of starting something more serious in the future. In either event, the total amount of violence these people have available is small enough so that the government could easily repress them if it knew who they were. The government's problem here is one of identification and capture of people who are not capable of directly confronting the government's force. They rely upon secrecy, rather than upon brute strength, for their security.

To turn, then, to our basic model, let us once again assume we have a government that is vicious, corrupt, etc. Let us further assume the entire populace is aware of the fact that the government is vicious and corrupt and that the entire populace would prefer to have it replaced by a revolutionary government.[1] Suppose, then, that you are a chief of the G.P.U. and you suspect that there may be revolutionary activity among the population. You may have very good reasons for this suspicion; for example, a number of high officials have been assassinated recently and pamphlets have been distributed saying that this is the first step in the overthrow of the government. On the other hand, the whole thing may be merely a figment of your imagination. Chiefs of secret police forces tend to be quite imaginative in this area. What should you do?

1. Note that the entire populace in this case would include the members of the government, except, of course, that they are drawing salaries from the government.

The first thought that occurs to you is to place guards on every potential target of the revolution, and to have your policemen go out and directly investigate in hopes of finding the revolutionaries. They can, for example, begin searching houses for concealed weapons, try to trace back the source of the pamphlets, etc. There is no doubt some payoff from such activities exists, but it is apt to be rather small while the cost is quite large. The number of your policemen is, ex definition, less than the number of the entire population. If you can get members of the population who are not part of the police force to provide information to you, you will clearly be able to deal with potential revolutionaries more rapidly than if you must depend upon the eyes of your policemen. In addition, as I shall point out below, your policemen may not be exactly vigorous in their investigations if the revolutionary forces are clever.

Since we assumed that everybody in the population favors the revolution, no one is going to voluntarily give you information.[2] They can, however, be motivated to inform you by a simple system of rewards. Suppose, then, the government offers rewards for information which might lead to the detection of rebels or potential rebels. The situation of the individual citizen who is not personally a member of the revolutionary organization is shown in equation (1),

$$P_I = R - P_g L_i - P_{u1}(L_v - L_i) - P_{u2} Z \qquad (1)$$

where

P_I = payoff for information,
R = reward,
P_g = gain to citizen from success of revolution,
L_i = change in probability of revolutionary success as a result of informing,
L_v = probability of revolutionary success if citizen does nothing,
P_{u1} = punishment for informer if revolution succeeds,
P_{u2} = punishment for informer immediately if his informing becomes known, and
Z = likelihood that informing will be known.

2. This is a trifle too strong. In practice, people who favor the revolutionary government may nevertheless feel that the cost of the revolution itself is greater than the difference between the two governments. Under these circumstances, they may be interested in preventing the revolution from getting started, and hence provide information for public good reasons. This problem can be dealt with by a special assumption, but it is probably too minor to bother with.

The payoff is equal to the reward paid by the police force minus certain cost elements. The first of these is the reduction in the likelihood of the revolution. We are, it will be remembered, assuming that each individual will gain if the revolution is successful. This factor is shown by the first term after R. There is a public good generated by the revolution times the change in likelihood that it will be successful which the release of this information to the police causes. For example, the information may reduce the likelihood of revolutionary success to 50 percent of what it had been before.

Note that generally speaking L_i is very small. As a normal rule, a person not a member of the revolutionary organization has only a rather small amount of total information. If the revolutionary conspiracy is still very tiny, this small absolute amount of information nevertheless may be enough to permit the police to completely wipe it out. Under these circumstances, L_v is small because a tiny revolutionary organization has very little chance of success; therefore L_i is necessarily small. On the other hand, if the revolution is large and well established, then L_v may be quite large, while the information given to the police by the individual is not likely to destroy the organization, but probably merely reduce its efficiency by a small amount. Under these circumstances, L_i is also small.

It should be noted that L_v, the probability of a revolutionary success given that the particular individual does not take any action, is not the same as the probability of revolutionary success provided no one informs the police. The decision of a given individual as to whether to inform or not does not control similar decisions by other individuals. This means that the value of L_v is affected by the individual's estimate of the probability that other people will inform. Thus, if something occurs—let us say a sharp increase in the reward level by the police—which may lead to an increased probability of other people informing on the revolutionary movement, this not only increases the reward the individual receives if he sells information to the police, but it also reduces the public good cost to him of so doing by lowering L_v. Further, if he anticipates that other people are making the same calculation, there is what amounts to a compounding effect.

The second cost is the probability of being punished if the revolution is successful and obtains information about informers. Note that if the revolution is successful, it probably has little or no difficulty in obtaining the names of people who have delivered information about it to the police, because it comes into control of the police records and, for that matter, most of the police personnel.

The third element of cost, represented by the last expression, is the punishment the individual may receive *now* from the revolutionary forces *if* they discover that he has informed. Discovery that he has informed in general indicates that the police were incompetent in one way or another. Nevertheless, leaks do occur. Also, the police may feel that the entire rebellion has been destroyed, and hence release his name while part of the rebellion is still in existence.

Revolutionary organizations very commonly kill informers, so P_{u2} is apt to be fairly severe, but Z is apt to be a fairly small number with even minimal police efficiency. But if the government which is subject to revolutionary attack has some judicial procedure requiring the name of the informer to become known, then the last term is automatically much larger than it otherwise would be.[3] This means that the police have to use much larger rewards in order to induce the output of information. They may also find it desirable to try to hide the informer after he has testified. Even if successful, this imposes considerable costs on the informer. P_{u1}, however, is apt to be somewhat less severe. Even here, however, the Bolsheviks killed almost every police informer they could find after they seized power in Russia, and a fairly long period of imprisonment seems to be a likely outcome.

Since L_i is apt to be small, the public good aspect of the revolution will probably play a very small part in the decision calculus of the potential informer. Note also that if L_v is much larger than L_i, i.e., the revolution has a good chance of success and the information is not likely to greatly reduce the chance of success, then the P_{u1} punishment is rather probable, and, here again, it must be offset by a very large reward. It may be, of course, that one way or another the police force offers anonymity to the potential informer even under these circumstances. If the chief of police, for example, were known to be prepared to leave the country quickly in the event of the revolutionary success, he could creditably promise to keep the informer's name a secret.

We can now deduce some things both about the problems of suppression of revolutionary conspiracies and about the operation of such conspiracies. First, since P_gL_i is fairly certain to be a small number for any potential informer who is not a member of the plot, it is likely that the public good aspect of the revolution plays very little part in his calculus. Second, it is obvious that L_v is very small in the early stages of any conspiracy. This is because

3. The principal witness for the state in the Charles Manson trial, for example, has suffered very severe reprisals, apparently from followers of Manson who are still at large. She has been beaten, suffered several murder attempts, and been robbed. *Washington Post*, 12 July 1971.

the probability of success is small. Under these circumstances, the punishment for the informer if the revolution succeeds, properly discounted, is also very small. Thus, the only parts of the equation which are likely to be large are the reward and the last term, the possibility of punishment of the informer by the conspiracy at the time he informs. These two terms are, to a considerable extent, under the control of the government. Thus, it should be possible to obtain substantially any desired amount of information from the nonconspirators by simply raising R and lowering Z.

Some governments, however, are unwilling to take either of these actions. For example, in the United States it is almost impossible to keep the name of an important informer quiet. Thus if some of the conspirators are still at large, the life of the informer is jeopardized. We attempt to deal with this by providing special protection, but so far without great success. One of the differences between the American legal system and the English is that the payment of positive rewards for testimony is of dubious legality in the United States.[4] Indeed, before the civil rights cases I would have said that it was definitely illegal. In England, it is part of standard police method, and has been carried to the point where there are people who come close to making a profession of seeking out information which can be sold to the police. This difference in attitude toward rewards for information is one of the reasons for the differential success of the British and American police forces in dealing with crime.

The American system depends primarily on the view that the average person regards the public good term as being in the opposite direction than shown in equation (1); i.e., he feels that the criminals are lowering the public good, and hence he is willing to inform. If there is an organized conspiracy known to be able to kill informers—such as the Mafia—the American government in general is unable to obtain information from people outside the conspiracy.

Turning to a somewhat wider perspective, all of the conspiracies with which I am familiar make every effort to keep their personnel from being widely known. Even in cases like Israel during the days of the mandate, where it is sure that almost every Jew favored the activities of the anti-British underground, that underground made every effort to keep its membership known to only a very restricted group of people. If the Stern gang, for

4. Payment of rewards for information on tax evasion is perfectly constitutional in the United States. Judges have argued that since the salaries of judges are dependent upon tax revenue, they should give far less in the way of "due process" to people trying to reduce their taxes than to those who have collisions with the government on other matters.

example, undertook some action like shooting Count Bernadotte, it could depend on enough public sympathy so that no one would turn them in at the exact time they committed the crime. It could not have trusted the identity of the people performing the act to any wide group of persons.

Further, even in this case, it seems likely that the reason why the activities of these anti-British guerrillas were normally not reported by people who saw them was simply that the reward system was not adjusted to such situations. The report had to have been made by the telephone and would not have been worth a vast amount of money; but in any event the British do not seem to have been prepared to make payments for such information. Under the circumstances, they got none. That the Jewish guerrilla fighters felt that putting greater temptations before their fellow Jews was undesirable is seen from the care they took to see to it that very few people knew their names or their hiding places.

Last but not least, one of the problems of use of rewards to obtain information is, of course, the possibility of obtaining false information. Great care must be taken by any police force using this method to see to it that it does not simply stimulate the production of false denunciations. Although this is a difficult problem, it is far from unsolvable; so far as I know, it has never been a major hazard to repression of revolutionary movements.

Rewards, of course, cost the government money, and most governments presumably prefer to get information without making direct payments. We can alter our equation a little bit to make this possible, but only in special cases. Suppose that the government enacts laws requiring all of its citizens to report crimes they observe, on penalty of becoming accessories if they do not do so. Further, suppose that the police or court system is empowered to subpoena any person believed to have information with respect to a crime and to question him under oath. If he refuses to answer, he may be put in jail for contempt; and if he answers falsely, he may be put in jail for perjury. Under these circumstances, in a sense the reward is the avoidance of a penalty. The cost to the government can be very small. This system, of course, is used by every government in the world for ordinary criminal work, as well as for quashing conspiracies. From the standpoint of society as a whole, it is not obvious that it is better than the reward system; but looked at only from the standpoint of the government budget, it is clearly cheaper. For a corrupt government, it has special advantages with which we will deal later.

Unfortunately, this procedure is available only under rather special circumstances. Offering rewards for information means that people who have information will seek out the police. The effort to obtain information by threatening punishment or, as we have put it, offering the reward of remission of punishment requires that you first have some idea as to who may have information. Thus, of necessity, it is less helpful than the reward system, even if it *is* cheaper. The optimal system, however, most likely would involve a combination of the rewards and the threat of punishment.

So far we have been talking about obtaining information about conspiracy from persons who are not members of that conspiracy, persons who accidentally, for one reason or another, come into possession of information about it. Of course, there will always be such persons if the conspiracy is engaging in any kind of activity at all, but their number may be small. Further, the information they have is obviously less important than the information in the hands of the members of the conspiracy. Under the circumstances, most police forces dealing with potential insurrections like to obtain information from some of the conspirators themselves. Historically, they have been quite successful in doing so.

The payoff to a member of the conspiracy who informs is shown in equation (2).

$$P_I = R + P_i(1 - L_v) + L_w I_r - P_g L_i - P_{u1}(L_v - L_i) - P_{u2}Z - P_p L_v \qquad (2)$$

As can be seen, it is equation (1) with some additional terms. The member of the conspiracy has the same motive both to inform and to withhold information as the person who is not a member of the conspiracy; but he also has some additional motives, and these are represented by additional terms. The first of these terms, $P_i(1 - L_v)$, is the probability that the informer will be punished if the revolution is not successful, i.e., the probability that he will be punished for participation in an unsuccessful conspiracy. Clearly, if he informs on the revolution, he will not run this particular risk. Secondly, there is some probability, $L_w I_r$, that he will be injured in the actual fighting of the revolution, and, once again, this risk is eliminated. These are additions to the gain which the informer will make, but there is a very important addition to the cost. Presumably he has some kind of reward in sight if the revolution is successful, and he gives this up; this, $P_p L_v$, is the last term in the new equation.

A number of things are immediately obvious from inspection of this equation. First, L_i is apt to be larger for a member of the conspiracy than for a person who is not a member of the conspiracy. Almost ex definition he will have more information, albeit maybe not very much. In general, however, those members of the conspiracy who have relatively little information also can anticipate relatively minor rewards if the revolution is successful. Thus, for the low-ranking members of the conspiracy—the people who know relatively little and who are not going to do wonderfully in the post-revolutionary world—both the public good aspect and the probable rewards discounted times the probability of success of the revolution are small. On the other hand, the police normally are willing to give them much smaller rewards than to a senior member who knows more. For the senior person, the L_i and the P_p both may be quite sizable, and, hence, large rewards are necessary to pull him into an informant's role. There is also the fact that a senior man betraying the revolution can presumably reduce P_{u1} and P_{u2} to substantially zero by doing a very good job of informing. If he can wipe out the revolution by his information, then, at the same time, he wipes out the principal costs of informing. Thus, it is by no means impossible to obtain information from senior members of the revolution as well as from junior members.

There is here a special consideration. In general, if for some endogenous reason L_v decreases, this makes it far more desirable to inform, and therefore is likely to lead to further decrease in L_v as members of the revolution begin informing on its activities.

Note again that L_v is defined as the likelihood of success of the revolution per se. One of the reasons that it may not succeed is simply that it will be informed upon. The more people who are involved in the revolution, the greater its strength in physical terms but the more likely it is that someone will be an informer. The revolution *must* pick up numbers in order to win, but L_v increases at a much slower rate than the number of members of the conspiracy. Indeed, it is quite possible that after the revolutionary group grows above a certain size, L_v actually begins to decrease because each new member of the group increases the probability of information being sold to the police more than he or she increases the likelihood of success by adding one more fighter.

Although it is probably not as easy for the police to obtain information from members of revolutionary conspiracies as from bystanders who happen to acquire information about them, historically it has not been terribly difficult. Indeed, this is the basic reason why most manuals on conspiracy recommend compartmenting the conspiracy into a series of small cells.[5] The

5. Manuals on this subject are quite numerous. As examples, see Robert Mosts, *Urban Guerrilla Warfare*, Delphi Paper no. 79 (London: International Institute for Strategic Studies), and Carlos Marighela, *For the Liberation of Brazil* (London: Pelican Books, 1971).

point of this compartmentation is to make certain that only a very few people know very much about the conspiracy. The individual conspirator who is a member of a cell of five people is not in possession of a vast amount of information to sell to the police. It is true that one member of the cell of five will be a leader and will have more information, but still the number of potential informers has been reduced by the compartmentation technique. The police should be willing to pay far more to high-level conspirators, who have more information, than to the low-level conspirators, who have relatively little information.

In discussing the receipt of information from persons not members of the conspiracy, we pointed out that R can, in essence, be changed to a remission of punishment rather than positive reward. If the police somehow find out that some person is a member of the conspiracy, they can use this technique with great profit. He can be threatened with severe punishment if he does not talk. This is, of course, part of the standard police technique in dealing with ordinary crimes in all nations. Sentences are, in modern times, mainly reduced in return for information. The ancien régime in France somewhat more logically provided that a court could, in essence, pass two sentences on a criminal: First, a sentence for whatever crime he had committed; and, second, an additional amount of punishment if the court thought that he had accomplices whose names he had not revealed. This latter punishment would be remitted if the individual gave the names of his accomplices. Of course, this is not essentially different from choosing a longer basic sentence for the crime and then giving remission. Note that although this is a sensible technique, it does require getting hold of a member of the conspiracy. This may be difficult. Once members of the conspiracy are in the hands of the police, however, this procedure is a very inexpensive method of obtaining a great deal of information.

The imposition of penalties for people who are members of the conspiracy and who are not talking is subject to certain restrictions. If the members of the conspiracy who have been captured by the police estimate L_v as fairly high, then a threat to keep them in prison for a long time will seem to be of much less importance to them than it would to an ordinary criminal. They feel there is some positive probability that they will be released by the revolutionary forces, at which point they would be martyrs and presumably have a very good position in the revolutionary government. Indeed, being in jail may be a particularly safe way of going through the revolution.

No doubt this is the line of reasoning which has led most states to impose the death penalty for conspirators against the state when the conspiracy seems to have a reasonably good chance of success. The threat of the death penalty, of course, is not subject to the discounting effect of a possibly successful revolution, unless the success is expected to occur in the next day or so. This may also be one of the reasons why torture is sometimes used to extract information from recalcitrant political prisoners. The recourse to either threats of execution or torture would be of greater value to the police the more likely the success of the revolution appeared. For the more likely the success of the revolution, the higher the discount the prisoner would put on threats of long imprisonment.

We must now turn to a final, rather special, problem, but one I think has had great impact on police activities with respect to revolutionary conspiracies in the past and, no doubt, will have in the future. It will be recalled that among the nasty things we have assumed about the government in power is that it is corrupt. If it is corrupt, it may be quite difficult for the government to use the technique of offering rewards for information, because its low-level police officials may be able to misappropriate the rewards. Indeed, very senior policemen may be tempted if the amounts of money are large.

Looked at from the standpoint of the individual police officer, paying out a reward for information is an activity that generates a public good for the entire government of which he is a member; but if he can put his hands on the money, it means that he will obtain a private good. This inverts the free-rider argument we have been using so far which indicates that revolutionaries would be likely to provide information. If I, as the chief of police in some prefecture, divert into my pocket money which could be used to purchase information and pass on to the central government some false information—perhaps executing a few people in order to give it an air of verisimilitude—I probably do not increase the likelihood of revolutionary victory by very much. On the other hand, I may increase my own income very greatly indeed. In a corrupt government, this is a very serious problem. This may be the basic reason that corrupt governments are apt to turn to the use of negative incentives (i.e., threats of imprisonment, execution, and torture) to obtain information rather than offering rewards.

In the early part of this chapter, I promised that I would demonstrate that there is a symmetry between the activities of the government and of the revolutionary organization. Let us now turn to this symmetry by considering what the revolutionary organization can do to reduce the efficiency of the government's repressive apparatus. First, it can make threats about what it will do to the police when it gets into power. The effect of such threats is not at all obvious, but at least they should have some effect. There are, however, other things to do. First, it can attempt to obtain information about police activities by offering rewards for tip-offs in advance of police raids, etc. These rewards may have to be put in future terms, i.e., as promises of good positions in the future revolutionary government; but in some cases direct, immediate payments may be possible. More importantly, however, the revolutionary movement may be able either to intrude its own members into the police force or to impose a set of negative sanctions upon certain members of the police force. Of course, the first possibility is a remote one if the police force is reasonably alert. Police forces, however, who do not carefully examine the political background of all of their recruits may be subject to this kind of infiltration. When the Gestapo set up a Hungarian subsidiary during World War II, it acquired a number of Jewish members who, although they were eventually executed, were able to markedly reduce the efficiency of the extermination campaign for a considerable period of time.

A more important procedure, one which insofar as I know was pioneered by the Tupamaros in Uruguay,[6] is the imposition of direct physical sanction upon policemen who show too great enthusiasm in carrying out their duties. The Tupamaros, when they were first organized, were very proud of the fact that no one was hurt by their activities. They rapidly changed and became quite accustomed to killing. After a while it occurred to them that the Uruguayan police force could perhaps be affected by suitably arranged killings. The head of the Uruguayan police force's special detail that dealt with the Tupamaros was living in a house which was not in any way secret or particularly guarded. He was accordingly assassinated.

As the next step, the families of a number of policemen who were thought to be a little too enthusiastic in dealing with Tupamaros were physically seized and threatened. Note that the equations we have used before for describing police activity aimed at getting information about the revolution can, in a sense, be inverted here. The Tupamaros were placing large private costs upon policemen who carried out their duty. The policeman carrying out his duty in an energetic way generates public goods, and hence the free-rider problem in this case would work to the advantage of the revolutionaries. Indeed, as far as I can see, it did. The Tupamaros rather rapidly gained considerable freedom from police investigation. The same technique has

6. For a (very favorable) account of Tupamaro activities, see Maria Esther Gilio, *La Guerrilla Tupamara* (Buenos Aires: Ediciones de la Flor, 1970).

been used by the Black Panthers in the United States. The bombing of the house of Judge Murtagh in New York is perhaps the best single example, but a number of other cases of intimidation can readily be called to mind.

Obviously, for this policy to work, it is necessary that the police force itself not take serious precautions. It must be possible to find out where the policemen live, and their homes must be unguarded. This is, of course, the real situation in most democracies. However, it is true that even in democracies a number of policemen will be detectives on undercover assignments, and, in their case, their identity may be unknown. Thus, the publishing of the names of the undercover operatives in Los Angeles by one of the "revolutionary" groups surely reduced the efficiency of the police force by making such reprisals possible. Similarly, the release of a great deal of data about informants as a result of the theft of the FBI files from Media, Pennsylvania, has acted as an implicit threat against anyone who informs to the FBI on political matters, and hence presumably has made it simpler to run revolutionary conspiracies.

If the revolutionary group is to be able to use this technique, it is very nearly a requirement that the police be restricted in the use of the countertechnique. If the police are required to follow "due process," which means that there is some elaborate procedure restricting their use of the information they receive, then they are operating under something of a handicap. If the revolutionaries, on the other hand, are not bound by due process (and, of course, they are not), then they can operate on the law of the suspected (i.e., the revolutionaries kill on suspicion), while the police can take no action until they have a great deal of information. It is then very dangerous to fall under suspicion by the revolutionaries, and much less dangerous to be suspected by the police. Revolutionaries (and the Mafia) can take advantage of this opportunity.

The Tupamaros illustrate this, since they were able to take action against policemen and their families without obtaining any real evidence that these particular policemen were indeed the people who were causing them the most trouble. They acted on the rule of the suspected and were successful. It should be noted in this particular case that it would appear that a counterforce, also acting on the rule of the suspected, developed. An anti-Tupamaro "death squad" appeared and began to shoot people who were thought to be giving aid to the guerrillas.[7] Thus, the rule of the suspected was applied

7. *Washington Post*, 1 August 1971, p. A-24.

to both sides. The army, of course, used it during the liquidation of the Tupamaros.

So far we have discussed methods of putting down the revolution which do not involve "winning the hearts and minds of the people." We might contrast these methods we have discussed with the process of making concessions. Assuming that our government is wholly bad and that the revolution is wholly good, then changes in government policy could reduce the public good gain to the citizens or the potential revolutionaries. However, we have already pointed out, and it is plain from equations (1) and (2), that changes in the value of the public good are of relatively little importance in deciding whether a citizen should inform or not. Thus, on the whole, it is unlikely that policies aimed at providing a government more in accord with that desired by the citizens will lead to the provision of much information to the government. Policy change is dominated by a system of rewards and punishments. Of course, if the government rather likes the policies proposed by the revolutionaries, it may shift to these policies with substantially no cost to itself, and conceivably this will reduce the likelihood of a successful revolution. Basically, however, repression is cheaper than reform.

This proposition, however, is subject to one very important modification. Any examination of the type of people who are normally found at the top of political hierarchies will indicate that they have very strong desires to be president, dictator, etc. However, they really have very vague ideas as to what they should do with the position. They do not appear to have very strong political preferences. For example, if one examines the policies espoused at one time or another by either Castro or Franco, you will find substantially no internal coherence except that they have always chosen policies that will get or keep power. Even Gladstone, normally upheld as an extreme advocate of principle, entered Parliament as an antidisestablishmentarianist—the extreme opposite of the political position he later held.

If this summary of the attitude held by most leading politicians is correct, then the cost to them of changing their policy is apt to be very small. Under the circumstances, they may indeed make concessions of all sorts to groups they think might be a menace to them. Franco, for example, might adopt quite a radical change in policy in order to change his prospects of remaining in power for another year from 99.9 percent to 99.99 percent. Since his preferences with respect to policy are not very well developed, the cost to him would be less than the gain. This is particularly true since the personal living standard of most rulers of nations is not greatly affected by public disasters. For most Russians, World War II was a period of disaster and near-starvation. Those Westerners who ate with Stalin during this period report a resplendent series of banquets.

In this, Stalin is not different from most rulers. He is also not different in that his life history showed devotion to radically different policies at different times. Indeed, under his rule the Communist party developed that reputation for "sharp turns" that has been with it ever since. At the center of his policy was his own power, and what he did with the power was clearly of less importance to him than its retention. In this, as I have said, he was typical. A person of this sort may offer various "concessions" on policy matters for the simple reason that the cost to him of changing a policy is very low. Reform may be cheaper than repression, simply because he has little concern about the policy his government follows. Needless to say, he is very much opposed to efforts to reduce his real power, or even to get rid of him, and in that one area he is certain to turn to repression rather than reform.

"POPULAR" RISINGS

In the mythology of revolution, the rising of the people to throw off a tyrannical ruler is the dominant theme. There is, it is true, a minor right-wing mythology in which the people, misled by vicious and corrupt demagogues, rise and throw off a benevolent ruler and put the demagogues in power, but this is a minority. Most of the mythology concerns a people, driven beyond endurance by the vicious oppression of their masters, rising up and establishing a noble and just republic.[1]

I regret to say that this myth is mainly myth. I don't want to swear that there have been no cases in history in which the people have risen and disposed of a tyrannical ruler, but I have never come across a clear-cut case. There are, however, two not historically uncommon scenarios in which the ruler is removed not by other members of his own government or by foreign governments, but by members of the local community who do not make up part of his governmental machine. I'd like to talk about these two cases before I turn to the reasons why actual popular overthrow is as rare as it is. In the latter section I will also discuss a number of cases which are normally recorded in the mythology as popular overthrows of a tyrant and point out that although they may indeed have been popular, they don't fit the myth.

Let us begin, then, with a situation which led to England having such a disturbed crown in the years before and after the Wars of the Roses. There was, in this case, a king and also local governments spreading throughout England. Local government was primarily not royal, but government by local nobles.[2] Further, when the king went to war, he did so by holding a sort of levee en masse in which all of the nobles were supposed to rally to his standard and follow him to war.[3] There was no professional army, and almost

Reprinted, with kind permission of Kluwer Academic Publishers, from *Autocracy* (Dordrecht and Boston: Kluwer Academic Publishers, 1987), 53–78. Copyright 1987 Martinus Nijhoff Publishers, Dordrecht.

1. Sometimes they establish a wise and just king, but this myth is normally placed in far-off lands and times.

2. Ramsay Muir, *A Short History of the British Commonwealth*, vol. 1, *The Islands and the First Empire* (Yonkers-on-the-Hudson, N.Y.: World Book, 1922), 174–75.

3. Actually, each noble was obligated by indenture to contract with the king to provide a stipulated number of men-at-arms; in return for these services, the king agreed to pay wages. The men-at-arms remained in the employ of the nobles, not of the king. See Richard A. Newhall,

nothing that could be regarded as a professional police force under royal control.[4] It is true that during this period the power of the king over internal policing matters gradually grew. His courts became supreme,[5] and his ability to collect taxes and uphold the peace through his sheriffs gradually increased.[6] Until Cromwell's time, however, there was no professional army, and if there was a professional navy, it was normally very weak in peacetime and depended on something roughly like the levee en masse to man ships in wartime.[7] Indeed, the English navy in time of war was largely merchant ships that had rallied to the royal standard.[8]

Under these circumstances, it was not surprising that some rival raising his standard might be able to rally as many as or more men than the king. A rebel, Simon de Montfort, Earl of Leicester,[9] is sometimes listed as the founder of the House of Commons. He summoned knights from each county and city in England. These representatives, so far as we know, did nothing except ride with Montfort to disaster at Evesham.[10]

One can, in such cases, refer to uprisings against the king, although in most cases, there was real doubt in many people's minds as to who was the

---

Muster and Review: A Problem of the English Military Administration, 1420–1440 (Cambridge: Harvard University Press, 1940), 3–4.

4. Until the reorganization of the metropolitan police initiated by Peel in 1828 created a disciplined professional force, "absurd little bodies of watchmen under a variety of different authorities . . . played with the maintenance of order" (Ramsay Muir, *A Short History of the British Commonwealth*, vol. 2, *The Modern Commonwealth [1763 to 1919]* [Yonkers-on-the-Hudson, N.Y.: World Book, 1924], 331).

5. But depended on juries composed of local notables from each district.

6. G. M. Trevelyan, *History of England*, vol. 2, *The Tudors and Stuart Era* (Garden City: Doubleday, 1953), 21.

7. Hence the name of Cromwell's military force—the New Model Army—was quite apt. See Muir, *A Short History*, vol. 1, 448.

8. Ibid., vol. 1, 218.

9. Who probably didn't speak English: he was born and spent his youth in France. This House of Commons was summoned by Simon de Montfort on January 20, 1265 (George H. Jennings, *An Anecdotal History of the British Parliament* [New York: D. Appleton, 1883], 3–4).

10. Montfort's power didn't last long enough for it to be known how he would have constituted the government of England, or whether the Parliament he summoned was any more than a congress of his loyal supporters. Prince Edward escaped from prison and led the armed opposition to Montfort. He won Evesham on August 4, 1265. See Muir, *A Short History*, vol. 1, 99–100.

king. There was not an uprising against an established governmental mechanism of force. Indeed, the established mechanism of force was, in essence, a call for people to gather together and defend the king, and it was just as easy to call for a group of people to gather together and attack the king.

A similar phenomenon, although, in general, not quite as vigorous, will be seen in the rest of Europe. As I mentioned above, the end product of this in Italy and Germany was that the central government gradually faded away. In England, France, and Spain, a firm central government was eventually established which, in the cases of France and Spain, was a despotism, and in the case of England, what we would normally call a constitutional monarchy, although this term in those days meant something radically different than it does today.[11] It is clear that one can, if one wishes, call these matters popular risings, but it is equally clear that the popular myth does not basically refer to such things as Edward IV replacing his cousin Henry VI.[12]

In England, the victory of Henry VII at Bosworth Field put in power in England a clever and cold-blooded man who decided to stop this system.[13] His method was first to kill every single person who had even a remote claim to the throne of England and, secondly, to weaken the territorial nobles.[14] As part of this weakening of territorial nobles, he moderately increased the power of the House of Commons and greatly increased the power of the royal courts.[15] These two policies were followed undeviatingly by his Tudor successors.[16] Whether it would have eventually led to a powerful central government in England we cannot say. Certainly there was no permanent regular army before the time of Cromwell. The House of Tudor, however, ran out on

11. A more general type of government, limited autocracy, which includes the old-fashioned constitutional monarchies as a special case, will be discussed below.

12. Muir, *A Short History*, vol. 1, 180.

13. Henry Tudor won at Bosworth Field (August 22, 1485) basically because he succeeded in convincing Richard III's two chief commanders to switch sides during the battle. See R. Ernest Dupuy and Trevor N. Dupuy, *The Encyclopedia of Military History, from 3500 B.C. to the Present*, rev. ed. (New York: Harper and Row, 1977), 422–23.

14. Muir, *A Short History*, vol. 1, 211–12.

15. See Ibid., vol. 1, 212–13. By the Act of 1487 Henry VII established the Court of Star Chamber with extremely broad powers, which greatly increased the effective power of the royal courts (ibid.).

16. For the continuation of these policies under Edward VI, see A. F. Pollard, *Factors in Modern History* (London: A. Constable, 1907), 476–77.

the death of Elizabeth, and the throne went to the Stuarts, who were less efficient.[17]

Now, this kind of thing will be found to have occurred fairly often in the history of the world. The Jews, in pre-Davidic times, had no central army, and, in fact, David acquired the throne to a considerable extent by raising his own army at the same time the then king Saul was raising a similar army. Saul's suicide occurred after a defeat by the Philistines, not after a defeat by David, but David's possession of a powerful band of followers is what put him in a position to succeed Saul.[18] More examples can be drawn from the history of many other countries.

All of this assumes that the central government does not have a powerful apparatus for its defense in the form of a professional army and, preferably, a well-organized professional internal police force. This is, in fact, a truthfully descriptive statement in a number of cases, but it is probably a fairly small minority of all governments of history. Indeed, it's only common in feudal societies, and, as we have pointed out before, feudalism is a rather unusual form of government.

There is a good deal of romantic literature written around the Wars of the Roses, but I don't think anybody regards this kind of thing as a likely prospect for overthrowing a modern tyrant. Indeed, after Cromwell established a regular army, there were no cases of the government being overthrown by someone landing and asking people to rally behind him. The Duke of Monmouth and two Stuarts tried it, but failed. Charles II came back to England in spite of the existence of a professional army and navy, but in his case, Parliament had neglected to pay them for a considerable period of time, and their morale was not in good condition. Furthermore, Monck,[19] the senior

17. One of the reasons it went to the Stuarts, of course, was the above-mentioned policy of killing off anyone who had a claim to the throne. The king of Scotland was able to protect himself against this activity and, hence, lived in spite of having a reasonably good claim to the English throne.

18. Shortly before the outbreak of war with the Philistines, David and his volunteer corps (of about 600) fled Judah after Saul's larger force moved against them. David actually joined the Philistines as a vassal, although his corps was apparently not involved in any direct way in the struggle between Israel and the Philistines (in which Saul died at the battle of Mount Gilboa in 1013 B.C.). See Otto Eissfeldt, *Old Testament; an introduction, including the Apocrypha and Pseudepigrapha, and also the works of similar type from Qumran: the history of the formation of the Old Testament*, trans. Peter R. Ackroyd (New York: Harper and Row, 1965), 578–79.

19. Later the Earl of Albemarle.

military officer after Cromwell died, organized what amounted to a mutiny of the navy against Parliament and in favor of the king, and the regiments of the regular army were either absorbed into a new royal army or disbanded without much difficulty. The king was, in fact, welcomed by Parliament.[20]

William of Orange entered England from outside, but he came with a sizable military machine and, once again, made preliminary arrangements so that, in essence, he had parliamentary support.[21] In the case of George I, he peacefully succeeded Queen Anne.

In connection with all of these changes after the execution of Charles I, it should be pointed out that most historians think that the House of Stuart remained more popular than the Hanoverians. It is a little difficult at this distance in time to say whether this opinion is correct or not, but in any event, it is clear there were very many people in England who favored the king across the water and that the lower classes were particularly of that opinion. Nevertheless, the fifteen and the forty-five both failed because there was a regular army to defend the king.

So much for our first scenario. The second scenario revolves around the House of Parliament which played a minor role in the last few paragraphs of my discussion of the kind of rising which led to the Wars of the Roses.

As a start, I must talk a little bit about "constitutional monarchy." The original meaning of the term "constitutional monarchy" was vastly different from its present meaning. Today we think of somebody like the current king of Sweden. He performs ceremonial, but not substantive, functions in his government.

When Montesquieu wrote the *L'Esprit des Lois* he was referring to quite a different type of government.[22] The balanced structure, which also was admired by Locke, involved a king who actually had the executive power and a

20. Maurice Ashley, *Glorious Revolution of 1688* (New York: Scribner, 1967), 201–5. Charles II secured Monck's services after offering him £100,000 a year following the Restoration (ibid., 160).

21. He was also supported by Princess (later Queen) Anne and Churchill (later the Duke of Marlborough). William of Orange landed in England on November 5, 1688, with a force of 15,000 (Arnold Temperley and A. J. Grant, *Europe in the Nineteenth and Twentieth Centuries (1789–1950)* [London and New York: Longmans, Green, 1952], 245). But even before this force sailed, the majority of English peers had been convinced to support William (Stuart E. Prall, ed., *Puritan Revolution: A Documentary History* [Gloucester, Mass.: Peter Smith, 1973], 205).

22. In 1748.

good deal of legislative power as well, balanced in part by assemblies. These assemblies were not, from our standpoint, very democratic. Indeed, the House of Lords or the Parlement of Paris which, up to Louis XIV, performed a somewhat similar role in France, were hereditary.[23] The House of Commons, while not hereditary, was, in any event, selected by methods which we would today not regard as particularly democratic. There were seats in the Parliament which were owned by individuals. The two Pitt prime ministers actually owned six.[24] Other members were elected but from very restricted franchises.[25]

Further, the method of election was what we would today call corrupt. The term is not a very good description in terms of the morals of the day. There was nothing concealed about the purchase of votes, nor was it thought to be illegal. There were actually lawsuits by people who felt that they had been double-crossed after having paid good money down.[26]

The term "limited autocracy" seems better than "constitutional monarchy" for such governments. We are going to talk about such limited autocracies a good deal below. They are a sort of compromise between autocracy and electoral systems, or, perhaps, a weak form of autocracy. Further, when we talk about methods of becoming an autocrat we will have to talk about the ways of reducing the power of such an assembly if the autocrat finds himself stuck with one. For the time being, however, we should simply note that this kind of an arrangement is by no means uncommon either historically or in the present day. To make a brief list of current examples, the Philippines under Marcos, Mexico, South Korea, Taiwan, and Thailand are all examples. In each case we have a ruler who clearly is much more powerful than any democratic

23. Christopher Hibbert, *The Days of the French Revolution* (New York: Morrow, 1980), 27–28.

24. In fact, the House of Pitt controlled a minimum of six seats; William Pitt's brother Thomas controlled three or four, his cousins usually held two, and his relatives by marriage controlled several more (Sir Lewis Namier and John Brooke, *The House of Commons, 1754–1790* [New York: Published for the History of Parliament Trust by Oxford University Press, 1964], 10).

25. J. H. Plumb, *The Growth of Political Stability in England: 1675–1725* (London and Melbourne: Macmillan, 1967), 38.

26. See Namier and Brooke, *The House of Commons*. Actually this, of course, is simply what you might call the highest development of the system, and if you went back to 1660, things were no less disgraceful from the standpoint of present-day morals but, nevertheless, somewhat different.

president. But we also have some kind of an assembly which acts in part as a check on his power.

The exact relationship between the ruler and this assembly is complex and difficult to explain or even to understand. If we look back at the England of George II, we find that the members of this legislature tended to literally sell their votes on most measures, and these votes were purchased by the king. The purchase was normally in the form of offering a job to a relative, but sometimes in other forms, of course.[27] The same kind of thing goes on in the Philippines or Mexico. Thus, we have the combination of a ruler of great power and a representative body, "elected" by rather irregular methods, which has somewhat ill-defined powers but which clearly is able, to some extent, to check the ruler. Once again, we will discuss this in more detail later. For the time being we merely wish to point out that one type of "popular" rising can be a split between the ruler and this assembly in which the normal stress and quarreling between them degenerates into actual fighting.

Splits between the king and this assembly are obviously actually a difference of opinion within an existing government. It is not the people rising against the government, but part of the government attacking another part. Indeed, the first of the major cases in which this kind of thing occurred in modern times was what we would now think of as backwards. Charles I, as we have mentioned above, left London, went to Oxford, and raised his standard against the House of Commons. The Commons retained control of the bulk of the tax revenues, and the only professional force, the navy. Charles was leading a (unsuccessful) rebellion. His eventual execution for treason was, in a way, quite merited.[28]

Something similar to this can, of course, be found in Roman history, where the republic was originally overthrown[29] by its own military officers. Consuls and proconsuls in charge of armies were the people who were dangerous to it, although, of course, there was a popular opposition to the Sen-

27. A special fund ("for secret service") was established and dispensed through the Secretaries of the Treasury for purchase of votes. On average more than £30,000 was spent for this purpose per annum (Namier and Brooke, *The House of Commons*, 195).

28. On January 30, 1648 (Muir, *A Short History*, vol. 1, 456).

29. Several times, it tended to get re-established for short periods of time after the early overthrows. Julius Caesar, the Roman Republic's chief general, successfully fought a civil war from 49 to 45 B.C., following the conclusion of which he assumed the title of dictator for life in 44 B.C.

ate which eventually led to its losing most of its power to the Assembly. Eventually both the Assembly and the Senate lost their power to the Caesars.

We've seen various other examples of this kind of thing in history, but most of the ones that I am familiar with are cases in which the representative group disposed of the monarch, or autocrat, rather than vice versa. The American "revolution" can be taken as an example of that, although by the time it occurred, the king of England was already pretty much dominated by Parliament. Indeed, in the early days of the revolution, the revolution was nominally directed against the House of Commons, and George Washington toasted the king after dinner every night in the commander in chief's mess.[30] Eventually they changed to opposition to the king also, probably because they discovered that they had a number of allies holding up military appropriations in the House of Commons.[31]

Nevertheless, looked at from the standpoint of the colonies, the government of each colony consisted of a royally appointed governor and a very tiny collection of other royal officials checked by an elected legislature.[32] Further, local police activity, and indeed, most of the local government, was carried on by local elected officials. The "revolution" consisted quite simply of the elected assemblies throwing out the royal governors everywhere there was not a large British military force present. It was part of the government, in this case most of the government, in the thirteen colonies throwing out the rest rather than a popular uprising. This does not, of course, raise questions about its popularity. There seems to be no doubt that these legislatures who were elected and who were then re-elected during the course of the protracted hostilities did represent public opinion.[33]

When I say there is no doubt about this, I should say that there is a good deal of historical opinion on the other side. In the first place, John Adams is frequently quoted as having said that about a third of the people favored the

30. James T. Flexner, *George Washington in the American Revolution, 1775–1783* (Boston: Little, Brown, 1968), 11.

31. G. H. Guttridge, *English Whiggism and the American Revolution* (Berkeley: University of California Press, 1963), 116–18.

32. The colonial legislatures controlled taxes, so they were able to effectively check the power of the royal governors, despite the fact that the latter technically had the power to veto any legislation (Jackson T. Main, *The Sovereign States, 1775–1783* [New York: Viewpoints, 1973], 102–3).

33. One historian maintains that the legislatures grew increasingly responsive to public opinion after the war began (ibid., 202).

revolution, about a third opposed, and about a third had no opinion at all. This statement was made some twenty years after the revolution and, in fact, refers not to the American Revolution but to the French Revolution. At the time of the American Revolution nobody seemed to have any doubts that it was popular.

The second reason why it is sometimes doubted that the revolution was popular is that we did not have universal adult male suffrage at the time. There were property qualifications. This was, however, a frontier society, and most of the adult male population could vote.[34] There is no evidence that it was a small minority who disagreed with a large royalist proletarian majority who ran the government at that time. I think the reason some historians tend to regard the war as having been unpopular was the extreme moderation of the statements and the eventual measures taken by the rebels. It's hard to think of George Washington as a romantic rebel. He was, after all, like Jefferson, a large-scale slave holder.[35] There was, it is true, one reasonably prominent rebel who was undeniably proletarian in his origin, Alexander Hamilton, but he does not fit in with modern left-wing prejudices very well.[36] Franklin also came from proletarian origins, but by the time of the revolution he was wealthy.

The moderation and lack of utopian dreams of the American Revolution seem to me evidence that our ancestors were smarter than the French. Utopians are apt to feel that it is not a true revolution unless blood runs in the gutters and the mobs scream for equality. I don't want to quarrel about the meaning of the word, whatever happened in the United States, it was basically popular, and it involved a change in the form of government in which the elected part of the government replaced completely the appointed part.

The French Revolution is normally regarded as a much more fitting and proper revolution than the American Revolution. The fact that the American Revolution involved almost no executions and established a peaceful and

34. Approximately 60% of the total adult male population could vote (ibid., 103).

35. Prior to Washington's arrival in Philadelphia to serve as president in 1789, Pennsylvania had provided for the gradual abolition of slavery. In order to prevent having to free his slaves, he provided for sending most of the household slaves he had brought with him back to Virginia in the event that they subsequently sought their freedom (Bernard Knollenberg, *Origin of the American Revolution: 1759–1776* [New York: Collier Books, 1961], 154).

36. Hamilton was an illegitimate child and was raised by his unwed mother in St. Croix in the Virgin Islands. He became apprenticed as a clerk at the age of eleven, and was orphaned two days later.

more or less successful government which ruled without much domestic stress for almost 100 years is, if anything, I think, regarded as a criticism of it. The French Revolution, with its bloody executions, wars with most of the rest of Europe, and rise of Napoleon is certainly a more exciting and romantic event.

Nevertheless, the French Revolution, too, was not the people rising up but part of the government throwing out the other part.[37] For a variety of reasons, most European countries, including France, had come to admire greatly the British system of government as it existed under George II and George III. Very likely, the major reason for this was simply the military success of British arms. Voltaire, in particular, was an admirer of English institutions.[38]

The Enlightenment was to a large extent an effort on the part of various Frenchmen to transmit a "misunderstood" English philosophy and system of government to France. It would appear that Louis XVI was among the people who thought that this was a good idea.

In any event, Louis organized a government which was modeled after that of England, with an elected House of Commons and a segmented upper house, i.e., a house representing the peers and a house representing the Church.[39] Louis, however, was not a very bright man, and matters very rapidly got out of control. One of the reasons they got out of control was that not only Louis and most intellectuals, but apparently most of the officers of the French army and navy, favored restrictions on the power of the king.[40] The result was a period of time in which, quite literally, the Paris mob dominated the government of France by physical coercion of the elected legislators. The end product, of course, after the temporary conquest of most of Europe by France, was the restoration of the Bourbon dynasty with a genuine constitutional monarchy modeled, more or less, after that of England.[41]

37. The best account of this, as in almost anything else upon which he wrote, is Tocqueville's *The Ancien Regime in France*.

38. Voltaire wrote a book entitled *Letters concerning the English Nation* which compared French institutions very unfavorably with English ones ([London, 1733; Oxford: Voltaire Foundation, 1979], 168).

39. Hibbert, *Days of the French Revolution*, 40.

40. F. C. Montague, *History of England from the Accession of James I to the Restoration (1603–1660)* (London and New York: Longmans, Green, 1920), 169.

41. Louis XVIII had spent most of the long period of exile in England. Herbert A. L. Fisher, *Studies in Napoleonic Statesmanship* (Oxford: Clarendon Press, 1903), 563.

The story of the Russian Revolution is much the same. After the defeat by Japan in 1905 and some rioting in St. Petersburg, the Czar decided to establish an elected legislature with a prime minister and government selected from the legislature. The Czar did not provide for universal manhood suffrage, but he did turn over the bulk of the power to the elected representatives of (a portion of) the people. His deposition in 1917, after a long and disastrous period of fighting in World War I, was carried out by that parliament.[42] It was not the people against the government, but part of that government, admittedly the part which had the greatest popular support, against the Czar.

The overthrow of the Russian republic by the Communists was essentially a coup d'état by a group of determined men opposing badly muddled democratic politicians. The vital military force was provided by the sailors of the Baltic fleet. In this case, we have absolutely conclusive evidence that it was not a popular uprising, because the coup occurred towards the end of an election campaign. In spite of the fact that the Communists were in power when the actual election was held, they lost disastrously. Needless to say, this made no difference in Lenin's plans.[43]

These are the most famous cases in which it is sometimes alleged that people overthrew an unpopular tyrant. All of them involved squabbles between different parts of the government, one of which could reasonably be called more popular than the other. They are an example of intra-governmental fights rather than an effort to overthrow the government as a whole. The overthrow of the Shah of Iran recently has become fashionable as a popular uprising against a tyrannical ruler. As time goes by, it becomes less and less fashionable because, retrospectively, the Shah seems much better than what replaced him. Nevertheless, at the time of the overthrow, the Shah was very unpopular in the West, and practically the entire Western intellectual community cheered on the revolution.

It is not at all clear what did happen here. The Shah actually departed after a good deal of street rioting, when it began to be obvious that the military would not support him wholeheartedly. He had, to a considerable extent, brought this on himself, however, not by tyrannical rule—after all, his father

42. Sheila Fitzpatrick, *The Russian Revolution* (New York: Berkley, 1982), 38–39.

43. Neither did the decision of the Russian supreme court, that his government was unconstitutional. In the November 12 election, which had been originally scheduled by the Kerensky government, the Bolsheviks won only 175 of 707 seats in the Constituent Assembly (Paul Johnson, *Modern Times: The World from the Twenties to the Eighties* [New York: Harper and Row, 1983], 64).

had been much more tyrannical than he was—but by a series of mistakes. Firstly, roughly eighteen months before his overthrow, he decided, partly as a result of pressure from President Carter, but partly apparently on his own, that his secret police should stop torturing people. In order to see that they did, he brought in the International Red Cross, and after an interval, they did stop torturing. This greatly reduced the efficiency of the secret police.[44]

Secondly, he combined inflation with a price control, which also made him unpopular with merchants, and last but not least, he was unable either to order his army to vigorously repress the rebellion or to decide to give in to it. His military officers found themselves sometimes firing at mobs and sometimes ordered not to. It's hard to tell exactly what was going on because of the extremely biased nature of the reporting of the Western press. I recall one occasion in which a general who had had some of his patrols cut off by the mob forced his way through and removed the bodies of his men. These bodies, which were severely mutilated (it wasn't clear whether the mutilation was done before or after they died), he then displayed to his troops. This was regarded by all of the Western reporters whose news stories I read as an example of unacceptable behavior on his part because it would make the troops likely to fight more vigorously in the future. None of the newspaper reporters criticized the mob for their action.

In any event, the Shah was not replaced by the people, but by government officials mainly drawn from his tame parliament. What followed was a series of rapid changes of regime, ending up with Khomeini, who, it should be said, has on the whole been able to win elections without too much in the way of cheating. He has, of course, reintroduced torture as a standard police method.[45]

This incident is very confused and conceivably does represent a popular uprising against a ruler. The weakness[46] of the ruler, his lack of skill, the fact

44. In a CBS television interview on October 24, 1976, the Shah stated that he had abolished the use of torture (Fereydain Hoveyda, *The Fall of the Shah* [New York: Wyndham Books, 1980], 94).

45. The Ayatollah had made it clear that he was going to do this before he came to power. In his book, translated to English by the Joint Publications Research Service under the title *Ayatollah Khomeini's Mein Kampf* (New York: Manor Books, 1973), he said, "God's prophet, may God's prayers be upon him, was the executor of the law. He punished, cut off thieves hands, lashed and stoned and ruled justly. A successor is needed for such acts" (15). "If we attain power, we should not be content with improving the economy and ruling justly among the people, but must make these traitors taste the worst torture for what they have done" (88).

46. The Shah was literally dying at the time.

that he had not complete control over the military forces, and last but not least, the religious aspect of the problem all were important.

There is, by the way, one other lesson we can learn from this incident. One of the reasons that the military were not well prepared for the whole thing is that the Shah had been deliberately keeping them divided. He was once before driven out of Persia by his parliament and then returned with the support of the military. He apparently drew a lesson from this, that the military were dangerous to any ruler of Persia, and hence, he had followed the policy of preventing the development of any high-level coordination within the branches of his services. As we have been saying before, weakening your army makes it less likely the army will overthrow you, but more likely that someone else will. The Shah found the truth of this.[47]

But why do we not see public uprisings against despotic and tyrannical rulers? There certainly have been enough tyrants in history, and there certainly have been many cases in which governments have been highly unpopular with their citizens. To take two recent examples, Albania and North Korea, under their early Communist governments, seem to have established almost impossible levels of public opposition to the government. In the winter of 1951, the American army, which had been beaten on the Yalu, withdrew through Korea. Almost one quarter of the population of North Korea followed them south. Further, a good many more would have gone south had transportation been available. In most cases where there were naval evacuations of troops, large numbers of these northern refugees were taken with them, but in all cases, far more were left behind.[48]

Note the situation. These were a farming people. It was mid-winter, and Korean winters are cold. Rather than come back under the control of the government which had ruled them for the previous five years, they were leaving their farms to follow a beaten army of foreigners. I can think of few more thorough votes of no confidence.

Nevertheless, in neither Albania nor North Korea has the government ever had any difficulty maintaining control against its domestic enemies. To take another collection of modern, unpopular governments, the East European countries certainly have extremely unpopular governments. In Poland,

47. In 1953 the Shah briefly sought exile in Baghdad until a coup successfully overthrew Prime Minister Mossadegh.

48. Matthew Ridgway, *The Korean War* (Garden City, N.Y.: Doubleday, 1967), 73, 95. In November, 1951, the U.S. Navy evacuated 105,000 troops and 91,000 civilian refugees from Hungnam in northern Korea. The average temperature at the time in the general area was 18 below zero Fahrenheit (ibid., 70).

Czechoslovakia, East Germany, and Hungary there have been extensive outbursts of anti-government rioting on the part of popular groups. In no case has this been anything more than an embarrassment to their Communist rulers.

Why do we find popular uprisings so rare? The answer, which I will present here, is available in much more comprehensive form in my *The Social Dilemma*.[49] It is basically a simple argument, however. Suppose that we have our common citizen in a state with an oppressive and inefficient government. Suppose also that we have a group of noble people who propose to overturn this government and set up a virtuous and efficient government. Assume that some individual believes their promises, i.e., does think they will establish an efficient and virtuous government. Should he join a popular uprising? The answer in general is no, and the reason is the simple old-fashioned economic argument of a public good.

The individual will have very little effect on the outcome. Note that I say "very little," not that he will have no effect. If he remains neutral, he will get the benefits of good government just as well as if he participates. Indeed, if he participates on the side of the government, perhaps because he is a professional policeman, and the revolution is successful, he will still benefit from the new and virtuous government. It is likely that any individual joining in the revolution, as opposed to remaining at home and cheering, will normally make only a tiny change in the likelihood of success, perhaps improving the likelihood of success from .53278 to .53279. On the other hand, his chances of being injured are greatly increased. If he compares the benefit that he will receive from participating in the revolution with its cost to him, he's almost certain to find the payoff is negative. In other words, the private costs and benefits will fall on him: the public costs and benefits are spread over the society as a whole. He will only get a small fraction of them. It is obviously very unlikely that a careful calculator would join the revolution.

This argument has dealt, of course, with the actual fighting part of the romantic revolution. The conspiracy part, which we frequently talk about in connection with undergrounds, has somewhat the same set of odds attached to it. In the first place, at the stage of secret conspiracy the likelihood of success is always very low. Secondly, the likelihood of betrayal is high because the government will presumably offer significant rewards for anyone who reports

49. Gordon Tullock, *The Social Dilemma* (Blacksburg, Va.: Center for Study of Public Choice), 26–86.

such conspiracy. If the individual contrasts the likely benefit he will receive from the success of the conspiracy, granted the success of the conspiracy is very small to begin with, and second that it is a public good, with the benefit that he could get from betraying it, it is obvious which way he would choose. When you add that if the conspiracy is betrayed, the people who did not participate in its betrayal will be severely punished, the matter becomes almost a certainty.

A number of despotic, unpleasant, and generally deplorable governments are also corrupt. Such governments have great difficulties in offering rewards for information about plots against them. The reason is not that people are opposed to corrupt governments, but that people quite correctly suspect that the corrupt police will default with their rewards. A corrupt police commander is far more likely to pay the reward money to his cousin and simply grab some people off the street as potential conspirators than to actually use it to obtain correct information. Further, if a citizen does have correct information and reports it, the money is apt to disappear en route before it reaches him.

Under these circumstances such governments normally resort to torture. A corrupt police captain is not likely to torture his nephew. Torture is a markedly less efficient method of obtaining information than simply paying for it: You have to decide whom you will torture, whereas the rewards lead people to voluntarily come in and sell you information. Nevertheless, torture, if used on a wide scale, normally works. Stalin was, of course, a clear-cut example.[50] Although the Gestapo normally preferred rewards to torture, they in fact used a mixture of the two types of incentive. Possibly Stalin's primary reliance on torture came from an intrinsic problem of any Communist state. If you give someone a million rubles for information, it's very hard for him to invest it in the Communist state in such a way that it is both even reasonably secure and will give a decent income. This, in essence, rules out the use of large incentive payments for information inside a Communist state, although the Communist apparatus has frequently used this technique outside Communist areas.

Democratic governments are sometimes unwilling to offer large rewards for information for essentially idealistic reasons. General Massu in Algiers, faced with a situation where he didn't have very much money to pay for information, resorted to widespread torture and, in fact, broke the Algerian

50. Nikolai Tolstoy, *Stalin's Secret War* (New York: Holt, Rinehart and Winston, 1981), 65–68.

Liberation Forces in Algiers.[51] All of this was no secret, in fact he talks about it in his memoirs, but it did not in any way impede his promotion. He ended up as chief of the French general staff. It is dubious that this kind of a background would have led to similar promotion in the American armed forces. In any event, payment of rewards for information undeniably dominates the use of torture. The rewards technique is certainly more in accord with our views of human rights and is also more efficient, a fortunate coincidence.

Turning to another matter, one of the problems that the government faces in dealing with a conspiracy at high levels, false denunciations, is not too important at the low levels. Firstly, people involved in these conspiracies are normally not subtle and skilled courtiers who are good at concealing their meaning. In general, they will talk openly, and frequently leave written evidence around. More importantly, however, there is no great danger to the state from simply killing everybody who has been denounced. You may get some innocent people, but you'll get almost all the guilty people, and the people that you kill are not high-ranking officials of your government, so this killing tends to weaken your government neither by eliminating potentially good officials, nor by lowering the incentives for becoming a high official. Indeed, if anything, widespread executions among the poor and powerless will increase the incentives for becoming a powerful and wealthy official.

There is an exception to all of this. There are undeniably individuals with strong public interest who are willing to take great risks or who sacrifice their lives to benefit other people. This is particularly true if religion can be brought in. If you can promise that a Mohammedan who dies fighting for Khomeini will have twenty-two concubines in the next world, or that the martyr of Catholicism who kills Henry IV will stand at the right hand of God, you are more likely to get such people than if such promises are not believed by a cynical and agnostic population. Even among religiously agnostic populations, we do find individual zealots who are willing to make great sacrifices of their own well-being for other people. It turns out that such people are fairly rare, however.[52] Most people are willing to make some sacrifices for the benefit of the public or individual other people who are in a bad way, but these sacrifices are decidedly limited. What people actually do is rather sharply at variance

51. Johnson, *Modern Times*, 500.

52. For a general discussion of the limitations on the sacrifices that people are willing to partake for the benefit of people who are not members of their family, see my *The Economics of Income Redistribution* (Boston: Kluwer Academic Publishers, 1997), 49–72.

with what they say. In analysis we should consider what they do and not what they say.

Thus, we have in this chapter three different circumstances which can possibly be referred to as popular overthrows of the ruler. They can reasonably be dealt with seriatim. Firstly, in the case in which the ruler does not actually have any professional forces at his beck and call and has to depend on some kind of levee to defend his country against both foreigners and domestic enemies, the problem is difficult. Traditionally, kings in this situation have attempted to play off different noblemen against each other and to gradually switch the situation from essentially a feudal state to a centrally controlled state. As we have seen, the kings of France and the kings of Spain were successful in doing so; the Holy Roman emperors were unsuccessful and, in fact, actually had the reverse process occur in Germany and Italy. In England, the rulers chose the rather unusual technique of attempting to create an opposition to the great nobles by turning to the lesser nobility, the squirarchy, and in the long run lost their own power to the squirarchy which, in our own days, has again lost its power to the common man. I have little to contribute to the discussion of this situation.

In the second case, where there is some kind of representative assembly which, to some extent, checks the power of the ruler, limiting the growth of power of that representative assembly is once again a matter of maneuver and devious plots. Historically, the rulers have tended to win these intergovernmental squabbles, but the success of the assemblies in the English-speaking world has probably meant, for the world as a whole, more than their loss in most other places. In modern times, as a general rule, these assemblies, whether we're talking about the Mexican or the Philippine case, have usually not had control over the forces of coercion. The army and the police force have normally been under the control of the dictator himself. This normally gives him an advantage, and there are, in recent years, no cases in which the representative assembly has succeeded in displacing the dictator, although there are a number of cases in which the dictator has been displaced by another dictator. In some cases, the new dictator has been allied with one of these assemblies. In all of the cases with which I am familiar, the ultimate outcome was no increase and, in some cases, a decrease in the power of the assembly.

The apparent reason for this difference between the present histories and the history of the development in England is, I believe, simple. The English House of Commons originally started as representatives of what we might call the lower officers of the army. The squires were not only the rulers of the local communities and the representatives in Parliament, they would also, in time of war, be the officers of the royal army. The king was dependent on them if he chose to call up troops, either to defend the country against foreigners or to defend himself against his domestic enemies.[53] Under these circumstances, if they were his domestic enemy, he was finished. In later days, potential military officers, as members of Parliament, became, if not rare, at least not dominant. All members of Parliament, however, were still closely related to military officers. The eldest son of a county family would manage the estates and go to Parliament, the second into the Church, and the third into the army. It was still true that the king could not depend on his army against Parliament.[54]

In most of the modern cases of this kind of thing, if we look around the world at South Korea, Taiwan, Thailand, etc., the officers of the army and the police are not eligible to be simultaneously members of the legislature. In those cases where a few of them may, perhaps, be in the legislature, it is just a few. Further, generally, these elected bodies have not been very favorable to increasing the wages of the military and police. Under the circumstances, the dictator has usually been able to depend on his police force and the military in squabbles with the elected legislature. The basic problem is not that the elected legislature, or for that matter the people, might rise against him, but that one of his higher officials, let us say a general in one of the army corps, may choose to overthrow him and may make temporary use of the legislature in that effort. This, as usual, means that he must try to keep his army sufficiently divided so that no general officer has that power, and that, in turn, weakens the repressive force. But all of this is another replay of what, by now, should be a familiar theme.

Our third way in which a democracy may be established after a dictatorship is essentially a retirement on the part of the dictator. Consider a typical South American dictator. He may, after a time, tire of the game. His job is dangerous and time-consuming if highly paid. Eventually, however, some dictators decide that they would rather retire, just as some heads of large businesses decide they would rather retire. Unfortunately, the dictator cannot simply ask

53. Richard A. Newhall, *Muster and Review: A Problem of the English Military Administration, 1420–1440* (Cambridge: Harvard University Press, 1940), 3–5.

54. Cromwell first emerged as the general commanding a substantial component of Parliament's army (in October, 1642) in the civil war with King Charles (R. Ernest Dupuy and Trevor N. Dupuy, *The Encyclopedia of Military History, from 3500 B.C. to the Present*, rev. ed. [New York: Harper and Row, 1977], 550).

the board of directors to elect a replacement, because that replacement would, quite reasonably, regard the retired dictator as a continuing danger to him. It would certainly be true if the dictator chose to retire and continue living in his native land, but Somoza was assassinated in Paraguay because the people who had overthrown him thought he was plotting to overthrow them.

Under the circumstances, making up a democratic constitution and electing a new government is, in general, a good idea. The new government is apt to be rather grateful to the dictator that established it and, in any event, be busy with all sorts of political matters. If the former dictator simply lives in great splendor on his hacienda, they are unlikely to bother him.

It is, of course, true, that most democracies set up this way in South America have not lasted very long, but even if they only last four or five years, that permits the dictator to age enough so that his successor is not likely to regard him as a primary danger. It seems likely that this is the principal reason that a dictatorship has some tendency to alternate with democracy in South America. There seem to be some signs of a similar development in Africa, but so far it is not well established.

Preventing overthrow by the common people is, in general, quite easy if the ruler is only willing to repress vigorously and to offer large rewards for information about conspiracies against him. If his government is so corrupt that the rewards are likely to be intercepted before they get to the actual source of the information, he may find it necessary to resort to torture. On the whole, however, this is an inferior method.[55]

In addition, he should have a military machine which is capable of repressing riots, preferably without too much bloodshed, but if worse comes to worst, a good deal of bloodshed. He should also be willing to use it. Louis XVI, Charles X, and Louis Philippe of France all flunked this particular test.[56] Louis XVI first permitted the Paris mob to intimidate him into moving from Versailles into Paris,[57] and then when there was a fight between

55. There are special cases, as even that great humanitarian Jeremy Bentham admitted, where torture might be used by a ruler who generally abhors it. They are very special cases, however, and it seems unlikely that the average dictator would torture a single person in even a long reign if he stuck to Bentham's rules.

56. Louis XVI ordered his Swiss Guard to withdraw in the face of the mob on August 10, 1792 (Langer, *Encyclopedia*, 631). Charles X ordered his troops to evacuate Paris after the mob had gained possession of the royal residence on July 29, 1830 (Emile Bourgeois, "The Orleans Monarchy," in *The Cambridge Modern History*, ed. A. W. Ward, G. W. Prothero, and Stanley Leathes, vol. 10, *The Restoration* [New York: Macmillan, 1907], 476).

57. On October 6, 1789 (Langer, *Encyclopedia*, 629).

his Swiss guard and the militia of Paris, he ordered the guard to withdraw.[58] Charles X and Louis Philippe more or less were simply unwilling to engage in large-scale fighting against their citizenry.[59]

As was pointed out earlier, the Napoleonic dynasty did not have any such scruples. The early republic was unwilling to use force against the Paris mob even when the Paris mob did use force against the legislature. General Napoleon Bonaparte received his first really high command after he had demonstrated a willingness to fire cannon into the mob.[60] The mob, discovering that rioting was dangerous, instantly ceased to be a menace to the government of France.

The second French republic, established after Louis Philippe's overthrow, was also menaced by the Paris mob, and most of the French generals refused to actually use the maximum force against it. Napoleon's nephew converted himself from Prince President of France to Emperor, to a very considerable extent because he was not only willing to use such force, but personally led a cavalry charge into the mob.[61] Once again, on discovering that rioting was dangerous and unpleasant, the rioters stopped.

In general, this is the case. The riots in Eastern Europe against Russian control vanished quickly once it became clear that the Russians were willing to kill. The dangerous situation for a ruler is one in which he kills a few people and then decides he doesn't want to kill any more. This was, in essence, what happened to the Shah of Iran. A truly ruthless leader with loyal troops and a good internal intelligence service does not need to worry very much about popular uprisings.

Popular uprisings are probably most dangerous against democracies. In general, democracies do not have to worry about popular uprisings, for the very simple reason that if the majority of the people are against them, they'll lose the next election, and hence, there is no need for rioting. If, however, there is a minority very strongly opposed to a given government, and that minority has little chance of growing to a majority, a situation which existed among college students in the Western world in the 1960s, it can be dangerous. In general, democracies are not willing to use the kind of force

58. Hence, the famous Lion of Lucerne. On August 10, 1792 (Langer, *Encyclopedia*, 631).

59. See note 65.

60. Napoleon was responsible for suppressing the Vendemiaire uprising on October 5, 1795 (Ernest J. Knapton, *France: An Interpretive History* [New York: Scribner, 1971], 76); Langer, *Encyclopedia*, 634.

61. On December 4, 1851 (Langer, *Encyclopedia*, 632).

that is necessary to put down such rioting. On the other hand, the students of the 1960s were neither centrally controlled nor clear enough in their minds so it was possible for them to take advantage of their opportunity. There have been earlier cases in which democracies have been overthrown by a somewhat similar means. The clearest example, of course, is Mussolini's overthrowing of the Italian government.[62] Lenin's subversion of the Russian republic and Hitler's conversion of his perfectly constitutional parliamentary government into a dictatorship are further examples.[63]

The reader who has followed me so far is likely to have two objections. The first of these, which is I have said absolutely nothing about legitimacy or popular support for an existing government, will be dealt with in the next chapter. The second, which is, I think, more serious, is to simply point to the undisputed fact that in the nineteenth century a great many monarchies of one sort or another in Europe and, for that matter, in other parts of the world were converted into democracies. As a rule, most of these democracies didn't last very long, but the ones in Western Europe turned out to be quite durable. Indeed, all the west European countries are democracies at the moment. The two largest democracies, India and the United States, of course, are not in Europe, and there are other democracies scattered around the world, but nevertheless, the dominant form of government east of the Elbe and south of the Rio Grande is some form of dictatorship. A quick count indicates that at the time of writing, there are twenty-eight democracies, and only five do not have their cultural roots in Western Europe. Almost all of the present dictatorial countries at one time, quite frequently at their first independence, were democracies, but democracy has lost control.

But that is a remark on the fall of democracy, not its rise.

How did it rise in the nineteenth century? The apparent explanation is a combination of the continuing great success in most spheres of England, which was regarded as a model democracy, and the fact that intellectuals of the Enlightenment admired democracy. The result was that substantially everybody in Europe thought that at least some kind of democracy, in the form, usually, of the limited monarchy, was a desirable system. The czars of Russia held out until 1905,[64] but all the other rulers set up some kind of

62. Johnson, *Modern Times*, 98–101.

63. Ibid., 283–85.

64. Fitzpatrick, *The Russian Revolution*, 27. Nicholas II agreed to create a national elected parliament named the Duma.

representative assembly. The nineteenth century was a period of internal tension in most countries, with the elected part of the government gradually gaining power. In most cases, the kings did not actually resist very vigorously, because they, too, had been convinced by the intellectuals and the example of England.

I don't want to give the impression that the change was entirely peaceful, although in most countries, as a matter of fact, it was. There was no significant internal fighting in Sweden.[65] In other places, where there was fighting, the fighting did not, in general, have immense effect on the form of government. The ancien régime was almost everywhere restored in 1848, albeit in somewhat looser form.[66] The growth of democracy was, in general (and I have to admit I do not know the detailed history of each and every country), a gradual process in which royal concessions were probably at least as important as popular pressure.

Note, however, that I have said that in many cases the rulers did not resist the democratization of their states, or even hurried it along. At first glance, this seems highly improbable because it clearly weakened their power. We will later have a chapter on this kind of mixed government which I call limited autocracy, and I will point out that it does have advantages from a ruler's standpoint. Whether these advantages are strong enough to overcome the disadvantages is not clear, but in a period of time when the dominant intellectual currents all were in favor of either democracy or constitutional monarchy, it would be very easy for a ruler to make a mistake on this matter. This would be particularly true with the hereditary monarchs who tend (a) not to be terribly bright, and (b) to be very, very confident of the loyalty of their common people to the royal household. Under these circumstances, following the advice of the intellectual community of your country to establish a constitution with elected representatives may well seem like a good idea.

Another pro-democratic characteristic of this period, however, and a very important one, is simply the composition of the armies. Large-scale conscript armies have, in the past, frequently been used by absolute rulers both to

65. There was in Switzerland, but since Switzerland started the century with an electoral system, the fight essentially was a religious squabble between the Catholics and the Protestants. It led to a quite major civil war in 1848.

66. In Italy, Germany, and Austria a new, more powerful king gained power following 1848. In France, the dictatorship of Napoléon III began in 1852. See A. W. Ward, G. W. Prothero, and Stanley Leathes, eds., *Cambridge Modern History*, vol. 11, *The Growth of Nationalities* (New York: Macmillan, 1909), 202–33.

defend their country from foreigners and to suppress rebellion internally. Indeed, the recent suppressions of democracy in Argentina, Brazil, and Greece all were done by professional officers commanding conscript armies.[67] Nevertheless, it has to be said that a large-scale conscript army does have certain democratic overtones. A ruler does have to maintain a certain minimum amount of popular support if that conscript army is to fight for him. In this respect, it is different from a professional army, which may be hired for the specific purpose of keeping the common man down.

The strength of this factor is somewhat dubious, because, historically, kings and dictators have frequently used conscript armies. Nevertheless, the late nineteenth century and early twentieth century were the heydays of the true nation-in-arms concept. Even if it is possible for a king or dictator to keep control over such an army, in the nineteenth century most of them thought they couldn't. Indeed, supporters of royal authority in the nineteenth century quite regularly were in favor of either professional armies or some very restricted form of conscription, such as that which was invented in the French monarchy after the Restoration in 1815.[68] Proponents of democracy, on the other hand, all favored an army composed of substantially the entire citizenry, who were drafted. A ruler who, in fact, could have depended on his conscripts to fire into a mob if he had ordered them to do so might have felt nervous about the matter and made concessions when he didn't actually have to. Once again, this is particularly important, granted the intellectual climate of the time and granted the fact that most of the absolute rulers were hereditary monarchs and not dictators. They were not the tough, aggressive, intelligent type we expect as a dictator, but the gentlemanly, not necessarily too tough or too intelligent type that we expect from the hereditary monarchy.

In any event, this rise of democracy has, in the twentieth century, been succeeded by a decline. In 1905 all of Europe had some sort of electoral system, mostly constitutional monarchies. Most of the independent govern-

67. On March 23, 1971, the commanders-in-chief of the armed forces deposed the president of Argentina. In November, 1968, the army high command of Brazil seized control. On April 21, 1967, a group of Greek colonels (with the apparent support of the high command) seized power in Greece (Taki Theodoracopulos, *The Greek Upheaval* [New Rochelle: Caratzas Brothers, 1978], 184–205).

68. Louis XVIII abolished the former system of conscription and replaced it with a voluntary system supplemented by a draft-via-lottery (Lady Blennerhassett, "The Doctrinaires," in *The Cambridge Modern History*, ed. A. W. Ward, G. W. Prothero, and Stanley Leathes, vol. 10, *The Restoration* (New York: Macmillan, 1907), 55.

ments of Asia had at least some electoral institutions, and the gigantic empires were ruled by democracies or by constitutional monarchies even if they were not democracies themselves. The Indians were ruled by elected officials, although they had no part in electing them. South America was, as it has been since the Spaniards left, a continent in which some states are dictatorial and some states are democratic and which changed from time to time. It was, however, true that the southern cone was both democratic and very prosperous in those days. This is, unfortunately, no longer true.

Except in South America, where much the same pattern persists, although the southern cone has now joined the rest of South America in being sometimes democratic and sometimes dictatorial, the situation has drastically changed. Firstly, considerably more than half of Europe, in terms of geography, is now firmly under an extremely strong dictatorial yoke. At any given point in time, one or two countries in Africa are, temporarily,[69] democracies. Normally, however, they are dictatorships. The same is true of the Arab lands, now that Lebanon has collapsed. Democracy never really took root in any part of Asia except Japan, and granted the current status of India, Ceylon, and Malaysia,[70] you could even say that democracy is at its high point there. Certainly, however, that high point is not very high, and granted the recent history of India, Ceylon, and Malaysia, one cannot feel very optimistic about democracy's future there.

This has been a digression inspired simply by the fact that many people feel that historical experience indicates that democracy can overcome the monarchy if it is supported by the people. These same people also think that the people will support democracy. The verdict of history is, as usual, ambiguous. But there do not seem to be any clear-cut cases of an enraged people rising up, throwing off a vicious and corrupt dictator, and establishing a pure and noble democracy.

69. Excepting, of course, the Union of South Africa, which by our definition is electoral, but not democratic.

70. And possibly, in the near future, Taiwan.

LEGITIMACY AND ETHICS

The word "legitimacy" has been given a number of meanings by various political scientists. I don't want to quarrel about definitions, and so I shall rather arbitrarily assign a very simple meaning to the term. It sometimes happens that there is popular or official support for a government, whether dictatorial, royal, or democratic, at a time when it does not seem to have a great deal of power other than that support. In other words, it is supported at a time when it does not seem to have much capacity to either reward its supporters or penalize its opponents. We will call such a government "legitimate." But the word will extend further. A government which does have power to reward and penalize will also be called "legitimate" if the public attitude towards it is such that if it lost that power, it would still have support. Obviously the second meaning is of greater empirical importance than the first. Further, this kind of "legitimacy" would be helpful to any government. How often it occurs in history is a matter to which we will turn below. Certainly there are at least some instances.

The other word in the title, "ethics," is not necessarily difficult to define. We should note, however, that its specific content seems to vary immensely from time to time and from place to place. I've recently been reading Bodde and Morris's *Law in Imperial China.*[1] This book is, to a large extent, a translation into English of a publication of the old imperial government. This publication, usually referred to as "Exemplary Cases," consists of a set of brief reports of a large number of law cases which had reached what, very roughly, we can refer to as the Chinese equivalent of the Supreme Court.[2] These cases were put together with the idea of providing guidance for future low-level courts dealing with similar cases.

Reprinted, with kind permission of Kluwer Academic Publishers, from *Autocracy* (Dordrecht and Boston: Kluwer Academic Publishers, 1987), 79–114.

1. Dirk Bodde and Clarence Morris, *Law in Imperial China* (Cambridge: Harvard University Press, 1967).

2. In fact, it resembles much more closely the adjutant general in the American army before the enactment of the uniform code of military justice. A defendant in a criminal case did not appeal his conviction, but the case was automatically sent on to the imperial court, where a body of legal officials would look at it for legal sufficiency; perhaps the emperor himself would express an opinion.

The impressive thing about this, from the standpoint of an American, is the deep concern that was given by this legal system to the status of the individuals involved and the relatively modest concern which was given to such problems as evidence and whether the person was or was not guilty. Thus, a decision might turn on whether the accused was an elder or a younger relative of his alleged victim.[3] This we would regard as a quite irrelevant, and possibly even immoral, consideration. They also provided lower punishments for officials than for private citizens convicted of the same crimes. We would regard this as corrupt and probably perverse. And last but not least, they had some rather bizarre crimes. If I, in a quarrel, called somebody some bad names and he then committed suicide, in the United States we would probably take this as evidence that he was not of sound mind. Under the Chinese code, I would be executed.

All of this, however, was, I believe, a correct expression of Chinese ethical code. The fact that it is different from ours is not remarkable. Recent readers of the newspapers have learned that under the Mohammedan ethical code, women can be severely punished for not wearing a long, shapeless garment that covers all of them except their face; for wearing makeup; and, in general, for behaving in even a moderately liberated way. This is, from our standpoint, perverse, as is the punishment for prostitution, which is stoning to death. Cutting off the hands of thieves seems to us as, no doubt, a treatment that has a good deal of preventive effect but that is, nevertheless, undesirable. Once again, this is morally acceptable in pure Islam.

One of the intriguing features of Communist practice, both in China and in Russia, is a periodic upsurge of government concern about some particular type of crime, sometimes serious and sometimes minor. Thus, if the Russian police suddenly become concerned about speeding, they will indicate their concern to the populace by killing several speeders. Similarly, when China, under Deng Xiaoping, decided that there was too much crime in the country, they began executing people for such matters as petty theft.[4] All of this is done openly and in a way which implies that the officials doing it regard the matter not so much as one of terrifying the population, but, liter-

3. Note that "elder" or "younger" here does not mean chronological age. It means status within the Chinese system of relationships in which, as a rough rule of thumb, senior members were older than junior, but where there could easily be exceptions.

4. Steven Mosher, *Broken Ground: The Rural Chinese* (New York: Free Press, 1983), 83.

ally, as something of which the populace will approve. Further, as far as I can see, the populace does not particularly disapprove and may, in fact, approve of it. Certainly, most Americans tend to think that our penalties for crime are too light, although they would hardly go to the Communist extreme.

But all of these are simply efforts to point out that morals vary immensely from time to time and from place to place. The Bible, in the book of Joshua, chronicles a war of extermination by the Jews against the original inhabitants of the land promised them by Jehovah. This was genocide and today would be regarded as very wicked. Clearly it was regarded as moral at the time Joshua was written.

The relationship between legitimacy and ethics may seem obvious to the reader, but I should like to point out that a number of governments which, I'm sure, he finds very depressing have, in our simple meaning, pretty clearly acquired legitimacy in the past. German soldiers did not begin freely surrendering even after it was clear that Hitler was beaten.[5] Even more remarkable, among the Italians who were captured in the early part of World War II or interned because they happened to be in an Allied country at the outbreak of the war, a number remained loyal Fascists right up to the end of the war.

Communists can present an even more spectacular example of this kind of thing. The foreign Communists, in particular, have been willing to follow the Communist party, originally in the Soviet Union and then in China, in the most extraordinary changes of policy. It may be, in this case, that they look forward to being officials of a new Communist state sometime in the future; i.e., they think that the current inability of the Communist state to reward or punish them will not be a permanent condition. We shall see below that this may always be part of "legitimacy" as we have defined it. But I think a lot of this, literally, is something which cannot be explained in terms of even potential rewards and punishments.

As an extreme example, Christian, after he had seized the *Bounty* and put Captain Bligh off in a longboat, proceeded first to Tahiti and then to Pitcairn. All of this time he was aware of the fact that if the British navy caught him

5. According to John Keegan, at as late a date as April, 1945, when the British and Americans were capturing 30,000 German prisoners *daily*, "those Germans still at liberty battled on, fighting and dying at every river line between the Rhine and the Elbe, counter-attacking when they could and compelling the enemy to turn into rubble every other provincial town he approached" (*Six Armies in Normandy* [New York: Viking, 1982], 323).

they would promptly hang him. Nevertheless, he always raised the Union Jack on each piece of terrain that he occupied. When the British navy finally did hunt down the Pitcairn Island remnant, the one remaining mutineer there greeted them with, "thank God you're English." As a matter of fact, they didn't hang him, but he certainly must have expected that that is what they would do. He could hardly know the changes that had occurred in England in the many years that he had been totally out of contact with civilization.

In all of these respects, this legitimacy characteristic behaves rather like specific parts of our code of ethics. There, again, you will find people carrying out ethical principles, even when there is no obvious gain to them and, in fact, where there may be a loss. Those people, and there were several in the American army during World War II who threw themselves on grenades in order to protect their comrades from being killed, were not acting out of hope of reward. Neither were the kamikazi pilots in Japan, who were, of course, immensely more numerous than Americans who were willing to sacrifice their lives in this final way. It is true that they were promised that their spirit would stay in Japan, but that, as a matter of fact, would have been true of substantially any Japanese who died at that time. They were not guaranteed a higher status in the next world.[6]

Of course, the Mohammedans, if they are believing Mohammedans, are indeed guaranteed a much superior status in heaven if they die fighting the unbelievers than if they just die. In this case, therefore, there is a reward in the afterlife for believers, which might lead them to commit suicide in the course of trying to kill American marines or heretical Mohammedans. Still, it seems likely that for many Mohammedans, other aspects of the Mohammedan legal system are followed even when there is no obvious reward system available.

The point of this discussion so far is to indicate that legitimacy is probably merely a rather general term implying that for a great many of the citizens, officials, generals, etc., of a given regime, continuation of that regime and obedience to it are part of their ethical system. "Legitimacy" is a collective

6. While it is unclear what the exact total number of kamikazi pilots who actually sacrificed their lives was, it was certainly in the five-figure range. In the period April 1 to August 13, 1945, in the Okinawa area alone there were about 2,000 kamikazi sorties against U.S. naval vessels, which sank 20 and damaged 217 ships (Richard O'Neill, *Suicide Squads* [New York: Ballantine, 1981], 169–70). The Bushido code was not the only apparent motivation behind kamikazi volunteers; collections of the last letters of these personnel reveal a wide variety of ostensible motives, including the Christian religion (ibid., 143).

term referring to the existence of a particular ethical argument in the psyche of a large number of people within that country.

If this is so, then any examination of legitimacy can best begin by looking into the problem of ethics itself. The explanation why most of us would refrain from committing most crimes, even if we thought we could get away with them, is the same explanation why most of us would probably continue obeying the American government, even if we thought that disobedience would be not only safe, but to our advantage. In both cases, note I only say "most of us," and I do not imply that we would continue on this course of action under all circumstances. Indeed, it is my opinion, and something which will be discussed below, that if the moral code or the state loses its ability to punish and reward, then, over time, its grip on the individual psyche will disappear. Faster, of course, with some people than with others.

Where, then, do ethics come from? Why do we observe people accepting and obeying ethical codes? The traditional argument in favor of ethical codes has been either that they are divinely ordained and people had better follow them if they don't want to go to hell, or that they are the result of some kind of logical deduction. A traditional Christian divine, like the traditional Buddhist, Hindu, or Mohammedan religious leader, favors the former, and the traditional philosopher, Aristotle, Plato, the latter. In, at least, the Christian tradition, the two may be combined in such a person as St. Thomas Aquinas, who relied upon both the Bible and Aristotle in reaching his ethical conclusions.[7]

I shall not engage in dispute with those people who believe that the ethical code is divinely ordained. I will, instead, permit them to continue debating among themselves. Since they are not in agreement as to who God is, or how many gods there are, for that matter, they are certainly not in agreement as to what these gods have ordained, and a simple atheist like myself can be excused for not going into their theological debates.

The philosophers are more in accord with "advanced thought." The philosophic point of view is now penetrating the churches by a somewhat odd route. No longer is it, as in the case of St. Thomas, combined with Christian religion, but Christian religion is, in fact, being bent to the philosophers.

7. In fact, Bertrand Russell claims that in most respects "[Aquinas follows Aristotle so closely that the Stagirite has, among Catholics, almost the authority of one of the Fathers [i.e., saints]; to criticize him in matters of pure philosophy has come to be thought almost impious" (*A History of Western Philosophy* [New York: Simon and Schuster, 1945], 452).

This is not the ancient philosophers as represented by Aristotle, but modern thinkers represented, in a real sense, by the *New York Review of Books.*

Thus, a disbelief in miracles is now quite common, apparently, among mainstream churches. I heard a German professor of theology argue that the resurrection of Christ probably did not occur. When a philosopher of science who is personally an atheist said that this was a challenge to the whole foundation of the Christian religion, a whole group of other German professors of theology reacted with great indignation. As the theologian said (in German), "You are ignoring the work of the theologians of the last three hundred years."[8] If I were a Christian, I would prefer St. Paul to the theologians of the last three hundred years, but since I'm not a Christian, I let the modern mainstream churches make their own decisions in these matters.

There has, of course, been a movement in the opposite direction by what are called the fundamentalists in American religion. They, in essence, go back to the pre-Thomastic view of religion depending on the Bible itself (and to some extent, Augustine) as their principal authority. This has led them into some fairly violent conflicts with modern science.

But turning to the philosophers themselves, they characteristically attempt to ground ethics in some kind of logical reasons. Normally, however, the particular ethics that the philosopher upholds depends more on his background than on his reasoning. The Chinese philosophers and the Hindu philosophers, for example, reach different ethical conclusions than do Westerners. Further, Western philosophers themselves frequently differ. Lastly, it is an intriguing characteristic of the discussions of these points that the people introducing new methods of deducing ethical principles, or attempting to argue for old methods, normally offer as evidence that their method is correct, not that the foundations of it are sound and that the reasoning is accurate, but that the conclusions drawn are those which are conventional among philosophers. This would seem to indicate that they are more accurately described as rationalizing their existing ethical code than as deducing it.

But this is not a matter of great importance for our current purposes. Philosophers clearly disagree among themselves.[9] It is, in any event, absolutely

8. The most prominent recent proponent of this view of the divinity of Christ among theologians is Hans Küng. See *Does God Exist? An Answer for Today* (New York: Doubleday, 1980).

9. "That the truths dealt with in ethics are more certain and definite than those dealt with anywhere else is a point upon which all philosophers will agree. It is, unfortunately, the only point upon which they will agree" (Anon.).

clear that most people do not derive their ethical code from careful contemplation of philosophical arguments as in favor of one or another set of regulations upon killing people, for example. The common man, then, follows an ethical code for reasons other than its philosophical coherence. What these reasons are is important to our purpose here simply because, as I have said, the feeling of the common man that you should support the government, even though there is no compulsion to do so, appears to be similar to ethical rules, and the "legitimacy" of the government depends on large numbers having that attitude.

In the case of both legitimacy and other parts of the ethical code, the performance of the code by an individual when there doesn't seem to be any concrete reason why he should, other than his feeling that it is right, may be illusory. It is possible that he has a good reason for doing so or, alternatively, that he thinks he has a good reason for doing so, as a result of erroneous calculations. Obviously, it would be fairly easy for a common citizen to mistakenly feel that the government of his country is much stronger than it is. He might feel that the existence of a military force in the capital city, which has seized the radio station and the television station, is merely an evanescent phenomenon. He may feel that the government will restore order and that if he supports this small group of military men he is in considerable danger. This calculation could be correct or it could be wrong.

Contrarily, we might have a good deal of quick change of position after such a seizure of the communication means by people who mistakenly think that the people who seized the television station are stronger than the government, and, in fact, this mistaken calculation might, if enough people made it, make the mistake a reality. This would be something which could be referred to as a loss of legitimacy by the government, although in this case, there is nothing except rational calculations. The problem would be simply that the calculations were wrong.

The reverse can happen also. People could feel that the government was strong enough so that it would come back and put down the military occupiers of the television station at a time when the government was actually weak. Once again, if enough people felt that way, the government might recover.

In these cases, if the erroneous calculations were widely enough made so that they, in essence, reinforced each other and became true, you might well think that "legitimacy" was the cause, although it would actually be irrelevant. If we observe this same phenomenon but the calculation turns out to be wrong—i.e., not enough people make the mistake—then we will observe people either supporting the government when, strictly speaking, they shouldn't, or attacking it when they should not do that. This would appear to be, by our definition, legitimacy or lack of legitimacy of the government, but the appearance would be deceptive. In this case, it would simply be rational men making mistakes. It should be emphasized that it is very difficult to make accurate calculations under these circumstances, and, hence, errors do not indicate any mental defect on the part of the people who make them.

The second reason that we might observe people apparently backing a government which is weak is, quite simply, a correct probabalistic calculation in which, however, the dice fell out wrong. Thus, it might be that there is a coup in a South American city, and I, as a junior official with some power to affect the outcome, feel that the odds are about 2 to 1 against the coup being successful. I, therefore, support the government. Assume that the odds are, indeed, 2 to 1 against the coup being successful, but that this, as it happens, is the third time. I have bet wrong; my bet was properly calculated, and I have just been unlucky. This could be taken as evidence of a belief on my part in the legitimacy of the government, although, as a matter of fact, all I was doing was making a purely opportunistic calculation.

If it had turned out that the 2 out of 3 chances of the coup failing had eventuated, i.e., it had failed, it could be argued that this was the result of "legitimacy" on the part of the government, even though everyone in a position to make decisions had made the same calculations that I had and had, in this case, simply been lucky as opposed to being unlucky.

Similar calculations can, in both of these cases, be a sort of precursor to the actual coup. A reporter visiting some South American capital may find a very large number of people who say that they think the government will shortly be overthrown and go back and say the government has lost legitimacy. The people who told him this either feel that the government is weak enough so that it won't punish them for saying it or, alternatively, that in any event he won't tell who they are. But, they have, in essence, made a calculation, which is that the next coup to occur probably will be successful. If it is true that a large number of important people have made that calculation, then the coup will, in fact, be successful.

It should be emphasized here that reporters' comments of this sort tend to be rather bad evidence as to the actual state of information among leading members of a given government. The reporters tend to talk to their opposite numbers, local newspaper reporters, and for that matter, the fringe of the intellectual community. This group is not, in and of itself, very important in making decisions and may be totally misinformed as to the attitude of the higher officials or the army.

This is particularly true because a great many of these intellectuals and newspaper reporters will regard it as a matter of virtue. In other words, if they think the government is vicious, they are likely to say it does not have legitimacy. This is a different usage of the word than the one I am using so far, although it is not incorrect in ordinary discourse. The deduction that a government which has this kind of lack of legitimacy will necessarily be overthrown is, however, wrong. Foreign armies of occupation, almost of necessity, lack legitimacy in the sense of popular support, and yet, the long history of the world's empires indicates that they are normally hard to overthrow. I doubt that any east European government would be regarded as being legitimate in the sense of having true popular support and being in accord with the local moral code. Nevertheless, I don't think there is much prospect of their being overthrown by domestic uprisings. They may be overthrown as a result of external interference, of course.

But the cases we have been discussing so far are not the cases of what I have referred to as "legitimacy"; in other words, cases in which people support the government even when it is not to their interest to do so or, essentially, reasons very similar to those of ethics. There are a couple of other situations in which this can occur. For example, suppose that I feel that the present government is likely to be overthrown but that the odds are that sometime in the not distant future it will come back. Under these circumstances, I might play a long-term strategy and support it quite rationally. I might also feel that although the present government is apt to be overthrown, it is very difficult to see what will replace it, and the best strategy under these circumstances of uncertainty is to support that government or to carry out its orders, even though I can't feel much confidence that the government will be around in the immediate future. I might, for example, pay my taxes, even if I thought the government was going out, on the grounds that whatever government comes in will probably ratify the tax rules of the outgoing government.

All of this applies also to general ethical rules. I might, if there is a breakdown of order, continue carrying out the laws as they exist, even though I know that I will not be immediately punished for violations. Even if I can make considerable gains from violating them, and this would not necessarily imply any particular ethical behavior on my part. I would be refraining from bank robberies, not because I think they are wicked, but because I think, either correctly or incorrectly, that engaging in a bank robbery is dangerous because some government will eventually punish me. This is not, I think, the basic reason why most people don't engage in bank robbery, although it is likely that if the government stopped punishing bank robbers, over time, it would become a very common occupation.[10]

But the main theme of this chapter has been why we observe this legitimacy phenomenon in some cases. And, for this purpose, I need true legitimacy, not people rationally choosing that policy which seems to have the best odds, or rationally not thinking about the matter too much and, hence, making a mistake. I am interested in cases in which people would, let us say, support a government even though, on the whole, withdrawing that support would pay more than giving the support.[11]

Recently, I heard a distinguished German biologist[12] say that human beings were "readily indoctrinable." He was, of course, pointing to a difference between human beings and most other biological species. Most of the other species can be trained to do some things, but not a great deal. Their behavior is quite heavily dependent on straightforward hereditary characteristics.

Nevertheless, presumably, the "indoctrinability" of human beings is also hereditary. In other words, we inherit, instead of a set of behavior patterns, a capacity for learning behavior patterns.[13] But learning is not all that he was referring to. We observe that people follow behavior patterns under circumstances in which, if they thought the matter over carefully, they probably wouldn't. Hence, the term "indoctrination."

We observe that different societies have radically different ethical patterns but that they all tend to accept their ethical patterns to about the same extent. Note that I say "to about the same extent," not perfectly. All known societies have deviant personalities that follow the basic ethical principles of the society rather badly, and almost every single person in any society has, at least once, violated the ethical principles of that society.

10. It would also lead to various substantial changes in the design of banks.

11. The following discussion has been vetted by a trained psychologist. The psychologist has become involved in active politics with both an increased authority in this field and a need for anonymity.

12. Hubert Markl of the University of Konstanz.

13. There may be some inherited behavior patterns too. The problem in the present state of knowledge is an unsolvable one.

If we consider the matter introspectively, assuming that all of my readers have, like myself, on occasion violated our ethical code, we note that there is a sort of policeman. We feel guilty and ill at ease after we have violated such an ethical rule. Further, we are usually driven to carry out the ethics without much thought, so that they can't really be "applied" in the sense that, let us say, I learn to apply certain mathematical rules in appropriate circumstances. They are, instead, learned in the sense that somebody learns to play golf, so that his behavior in swinging the club is almost the same as the instinctive behavior of an animal who had inherited it.

Thus, the indoctrinability of the human being means that we can be indoctrinated into a set of rules which we then follow, more or less, automatically, and for which, when we deviate from them, we feel guilty and ill at ease. Note that this indoctrination is never complete. We tend to think of inherited animal behavior as being completely dominant; that is, there is no way of deviating from it once you have the right genes. By observation, this doesn't seem to be true. Animals put in sufficiently extreme conditions will, normally, deviate from their inherited pattern of behavior, but this may simply mean that the inherited pattern of behavior carries with it a deviation in more extreme conditions. Perhaps, for example, a herbivore that normally eats only certain types of leaves, if it gets hungry enough, will begin eating random leaves.[14] It should also be noted here that this kind of indoctrinability can have much the same effect even when there is nothing ethical involved. If, for example, I have learned a certain pattern of behavior in collecting quarters to use in automatic washers,[15] if I deviate from it with the result that I don't have enough quarters, I find that my feelings about this are not just the inconvenience of not having the quarters, but a vague feeling very similar to the guilt I would feel if there was something immoral about this. Needless to say, since this is a minor matter, the feeling is very weak. If I had, however, developed a pattern of behavior in dealing with the stock market which I believed to be successful and then deviated from it, I probably would feel guilty. This would be particularly so if it led to me losing a large amount of money.

But let us temporarily stick with ethics, because I believe that the support for government is very similar to ethics rather than being very similar to these

14. The degree to which animals deviate from their inherited patterns of behavior differs, of course, from animal to animal. The insects vary little; the great apes a great deal. In a way, the human variation in this area is simply an immense extension of the trend.

15. This example is taken from life.

other types of calculations. How, then, can we explain the fact that human beings are "indoctrinable"? We could, of course, simply say this is a characteristic of human beings. There are a number of aspects of human behavior which don't seem to be explicable from an evolutionary standpoint. I put these things down to two explanations, one of which is simply that we have not yet learned enough about human evolution to be able to explain as much as we will be able to in the future.

The second explanation, however, which is probably equally unsatisfactory, is simply that the human being is not very well adapted. We grew very rapidly in terms of evolution. Our large brain was a very quick change, if we look at the rate at which most species grow. Further, during almost the entire time in which we moved from an erect ape to Homo sapiens, our ancestors were apparently dominant predators. They lived, as far as we can tell, rather like wolves or baboons today, i.e., in small tribes, and, in general, had little to fear from nonhuman predators.[16] On the other hand, the predators probably had a good deal to fear from them. As our ancestors became both bigger and brighter, the degree to which they could refrain from fearing other animals, and the degree to which other animals had to fear them, steadily increased.

Nevertheless, during most of this period of time, the principal selective pressure on human beings[17] was exerted by other human beings. What we know of animal societies, and the various primitive human societies that have been carefully examined,[18] indicates that you normally have within a society a relatively peaceful status, but occasional dominance clashes. The losers in these dominance clashes can be selected out either by actually being driven out of the tribe or by having their reproduction possibilities reduced.

The big selection process, however, was basically what we might call wars between different tribes, essentially over real estate. Like wolf packs, these groups probably had their own real estate.[19] If they did not, then the only explanation would be that the natural death rate was high enough so that they

16. Edward O. Wilson, *Sociobiology*, abridged ed. (Cambridge: Belknap Press of Harvard University Press, 1980), 290–96.

17. Leaving aside here the selective pressure of parasites such as the malaria germ.

18. They've all been carefully examined at a time when they were contemporaneous with civilized societies, and hence, the examinations may not have very much to say about our ancient ancestors.

19. See Robert Ardrey, *The Hunting Hypothesis* (New York: Atheneum, 1976), 102–28, and Edward O. Wilson, *Sociobiology: The New Synthesis* (Cambridge: Belknap Press of Harvard University Press, 1975), 565.

did not fully occupy the habitable space. This, more or less, requires some kind of predator, and except for germs, there never was one.

It should be said here that most modern scholars find that most of the primitive tribes they examined are quite peaceful. The basic explanation for this modern observation simply seems to be that the extension of various empires in the nineteenth century put down all local fighting everywhere except in Afghanistan and other parts of the northwest frontier.[20] Nevertheless, there do seem to be some cases in which, as far as we can tell, the area was quite peaceful even before the arrival of Europeans.

We have to be careful here interpreting the facts. The human species is a very slow-growing one. Tribes in a given area might well grow at the slow rate of growth which we would expect for quite a while before any tribe began realizing that the existence of neighboring tribes was reducing the resources they themselves had available. Thus, considerable periods of peace would not be surprising. The actual places which we have real knowledge of, that is, areas where a European or, for that matter, Arab or Chinese civilization expanded into a basically small tribe society, were mainly quite warlike. This was true in Africa, and certainly true in the United States and South America. Note that I am not here referring to the Aztec and Inca empires, although heaven knows they were warlike enough,[21] but to the smaller tribes who engaged in almost continuous petty raiding across their frontiers. *Under the Mountain Wall*[22] is an account of this kind of society as it existed in New Guinea before the European peace was imposed.

This description of human life before the advent of civilization implies that there was a very long period in which the principal predators to which man had to adjust himself were other men. Further, this was a period in which not only did human beings improve, but their technical equipment improved too. They began, apparently, using clubs and stones and gradually, at first very slowly and later more rapidly, improved these tools. They, apparently,

20. In both 1839–42 and 1878–80, the British attempted to establish puppet rulers in Afghanistan and each time failed in the face of Afghan guerrilla resistance. See D. K. Fieldhouse, *The Colonial Empires: A Comparative Survey from the Eighteenth Century*, 2d ed. (London: Macmillan, 1982), 195.

21. One historian summarizes the Incas' activity by concluding that "[either] the Incas were conquering new peoples, or defending what they had taken," adding that many wars "were undertaken to keep the professional army occupied" (Victor W. von Hayen, *Realm of the Incas* [New York: Mentor, 1957], 198).

22. Peter Matthiessen, *Under the Mountain Wall* (New York: Viking, 1962).

also improved their knowledge of the natural environment, and being human beings, they tended to migrate.

Thus, the environment that any given group faced was one in which their principal restricting predators were, not only other human beings, but other human beings whose physical equipment, methods of fighting, etc., were changing. Further, they probably gradually shifted locations.[23]

This slowly changing environment, together with the fact that human beings are a long-lived species and, in particular, that it is a long time from the birth of an individual until he finishes his reproductive life, means that it would take a very long time for any gene to be fixed. If we use, as a rule of thumb, a hundred generations as the time necessary to fix a gene,[24] and a generation as twenty-five years, then it would be twenty-five hundred years to fix a gene.

It seems unlikely that very many human reproductive strains would go twenty-five hundred years without suffering a fairly significant change in their environment, either through migration or, more likely, through technical improvements in the methods of warfare used by their neighbors. There would, no doubt, be backwaters where this was not true, but they would tend to get left behind in the gradual evolutionary change. It would be the humans living in the cockpits, the places where pressure was greatest, who would tend to move most rapidly towards a large brain size. As we have said, the movement was very fast by biological standards.

What all of this indicates to me is simply that human beings were evolving a combination of greater body size and strength and a very much larger brain, but that this very much larger brain could hardly be a highly specialized brain. It had to be rather general, simply because there was no environmental constant to which it could specialize. Under these circumstances, we would

23. As far as we can tell, wolf tribes or baboons do not actually remain in the same location forever. There are gradual shifts having to do with successful or unsuccessful wars on the borders, just like the shifts in the tribes across central Asia which depended on the relative success of the civilized peoples in China, the Middle East, and Europe. (See Hugo Lanick and Jane Goodall, *Innocent Killers* [Boston: Houghton Mifflin, 1971].) A very successful tribe would tend to split, with the result that a new border would be set up. All of this does not mean very much moving in a period of, let's say, fifty years, but in a period of a thousand years, a very considerable movement could be expected. A given tribe might experience quite different natural conditions than its ancestors that far back.

24. As far as I can see, biologists use this number largely because it's a nice round one. At best, it should be regarded as accurate only to an order of magnitude.

assume that the human brain would not be carefully adjusted to any particular need. Considering another dominant predator, the lion, it is clear that its behavior patterns are very heavily affected by genes. These genes, on the whole, have a high survival value. Human beings, insofar as they have hereditary patterns of behavior or drives, are probably much less tightly fitted to any existing niche, simply because there never was any relative unchanging niche during the period of our evolution.

Note here that I am talking about both specific behavior patterns and basic drives, or if you wish, basic values. Surviving species have to have some kind of mechanism which leads them to eat and which has at least some tendency to lead them to eat safer and more nutritious foods. Larger mammals, of which human beings are an example, usually have quite a wide spread of things which they can eat. Nevertheless, our taste buds lead us to avoid quite a number of readily available foods. We eat practically no tree leaves, for example. Under modern conditions, I don't doubt that we could eat tree leaves suitably processed by our food industry and get nutrition out of them, regardless of the fact that we don't like their taste.[25] Normally, if we are to reproduce, there has to be some kind of mechanism leading to sexual contact. We have to have suitable drives either in the form of a direct instinct for it or in the form of a set of built-in preferences, which lead us to move in the right direction, to avoid getting too cold, to avoid exercising too vigorously in very hot weather, and a very large number of other similar survival characteristics. As far as we can tell, in human beings this is, to a very large extent, simply a set of tastes or drives. When we are hungry we like certain types of potential foods and not others.

Taste buds, under present circumstances, probably are not a terribly good guide, because we process food so extensively. Nevertheless, I think we have to agree that the original function of the taste buds in distinguishing between pleasant and unpleasant food was to guide us in the direction of, at least, reasonably nutritious food. Since primitive humans probably moved from one environment to another, the guidance would have to be very general rather than very specific, and would also have to be designed so that if we came in contact with a new potential food source, the chances were good that simply tasting it would give us much better than random information as to whether it was safe and nutritious.

25. Or possibly have some other kind of hereditary aversion to eating tree leaves. In any event, no human group has spent much of its energy in collecting tree leaves for food purposes.

This discussion of the human preference structure which drives our behavior, is, I think, fairly noncontroversial, although the language is different from what is normally used. I don't see any reason why, in a book not intended for biologists, I should use the technical terms that biologists would use.

The important point here is that we are, to a considerable extent, an efficient animal, and that this efficiency is, to a considerable extent, the result not of our having built-in behavior patterns, but of our having a built-in set of tastes, values, drives, whichever term you wish to use. They are, of course, not identical from person to person, but they are quite similar. No one eats copper sulfate out of choice, and we all like things sweet, although the degree to which we like things sweet varies from person to person.

There are some fairly clear-cut cases of things that we do which have negative evolutionary value; that is, they reduce the number of our descendants. These are so natural to us that we have difficulty believing that they have negative evolutionary value. The one that I usually mention is our tendency to have decorations around us, e.g., pictures on the wall. This clearly lowers our number of grandchildren and great grandchildren if contrasted with using the same resources more directly for the improvement, either in number or in quality or both, of our offspring.[26] Another is the peculiar human pattern of altruism. We have no great difficulty in recognizing our relatives.[27] The economic theory of altruism, perhaps better referred to as nepotism, explains at least some gifts to our relatives. Many animals, in fact, make sacrifices for their relatives. Human beings, however, make gifts to people who are in no sense relatives. Beggars, for example. We also make gifts to household pets and to animals in the zoo.

All of these are cases where it would appear that we have a set of tastes, drives, or values, you may use your own word once again, that are not tightly in accord with the usual rules of evolution. We do not live solely in order to maximize the number of our descendants. My explanation for this is not that we are not the product of evolution, but that our evolutionary situation was

26. Whenever I mention this point, I find an outburst of rationalizations offered for pictures on the wall, etc. I shan't go through these rationalizations, but I suspect that most readers, on reading the above section, will immediately invent at least one of them. I merely suggest that you think about it carefully for a while.

27. Recent research indicates that a number of animals can recognize quite accurately a degree of relatedness too. Apparently, there is enough genetic similarity between different members of the same family so that their body odors are related. This may be true in human beings also.

peculiar. We did not adjust tightly to a specific niche, because there was no unchanging niche in existence for us to adjust to. In consequence, we developed a fairly good general-purpose computer.[28]

We also evolved a set of tastes or preferences which, granted the general-purpose computer, could tell us how to maximize survival. It is possible that in addition to this we have genuine built-in behavior patterns, but so far, there's no unambiguous case of such a behavior pattern in adults. Basically, the model which we seem to have developed is a set of tastes or preferences for things which, in fact, have survival value in the old Stone Age, together with a rather efficient computer which permits us to choose behavior patterns likely to achieve these preferences. Some of these preferences seem to lead to behavior patterns, for example, making gifts to complete strangers, which have no obvious evolutionary value. Presumably, as I mentioned above, they come from the fact that we are not tightly evolved.

The reason for all of this evolutionary background of human behavior and human thought processes may not be immediately obvious to the reader. It is, however, necessary to explain why I believe human beings are, as Professor Markl said, readily indoctrinable. We turn now to three patterns of drives or values which are characteristic of human beings and which would lead to a tendency to accept indoctrination. Note that these three could be explained in terms of evolution, which has given them to us, or in terms of our having rationally figured out a pattern of behavior and followed it, or in terms of our ancestors having rationally figured out this pattern of behavior and indoctrinated us with it while we were small children. For our current purposes there is no reason to distinguish these three possible origins. People do behave this way. But all of this indicates that there are individuals who do not maximize their own well-being in terms of careful calculations at the time of taking some action.

Note, however, none of these reasons would give a motive for an individual to take action which benefited the group that he was in while injuring himself, unless the relationship to other members of the group was close enough so that biological altruism became a feasible characteristic. This would never be true with a large group such as nations, states, or even most cities and villages. The reason that it's never to his advantage is simply that although such

28. It does have various defects. We are prone to certain types of logical errors. These errors, however, do not seem to be of the type that have great effect on the survival of a Stone Age man.

behavior would increase the survival potential of that group, it makes it likely that his own descendants will be a smaller portion of that group. Careful calculations by biologists indicate that under most circumstances the effect of the reduction in share more than counterbalances the selective effect of the increase in survival of the group. Thus, we should not expect that the rational calculating individual, making decisions which maximize preferences built into him by evolution for their survival value, would make significant sacrifices for any large group of which he happened to be a member.

But the human mind is not of infinite size. It is not possible for the individual to engage in infinitely large calculations. Further, in practice, he can't engage in very much calculation about most things he does. If you consider your daily round, you will quickly realize that although you may engage in very deep and prolonged thought with respect to some things you do during the day, most of the time you make up your mind with very little thought, and in many of the cases, you don't even make up your mind. They are habitual activities which you have put into the unconscious. I find, for example, that when I leave my house, I have to carefully think of where I am going if I am not going out to the university. If I don't concentrate on driving, I will take off for the university without thinking about the matter. This is, of course, a fairly complex set of actions, and a set of actions in which I must make many minor decisions, but I find that I can do it without conscious thought. It is a convenience, since it permits me to think about something else at the time.

All of this is simply one example of the necessary economies in computing power. The existence of a finite brain with a finite memory requires such economies. The possibility of turning certain parts of our behavior over to automatic or semi-automatic control, leaving part, of course not all, but part, of the brain free for more complex operations, is merely one example. Indeed, it is not an example which is of much use in explaining ethics or legitimacy, except that both of these have a rather distant resemblence to habit.

Another important economy is simply accepting other people's word. It is utterly impossible for all of us to learn everything about the world. Indeed, the human race as a whole does not know everything about the world. If we go back in time, human beings knew even less. Nevertheless, we do find it easier to accumulate most of the knowledge that we have either by listening to what other people say or by reading things that they have written. This is obvious, but when one thinks about it, one immediately realizes both that it is an immense economy and that there are some, at least superficial, mysteries about it.

To begin with the mysteries: one is why we tend to assume that other people are not lying, and a second is why most of the time they aren't lying. We do normally assume that people are telling the truth, but we don't always. We know that sometimes they lie. The new Soviet man, the new Chinese Communist man, the new Cuban man, to name but three examples, are all great disappointments to the propagandists who tried to create them. It turned out that the Russians, the Chinese, and the Cubans, although they could successfully be cut off from all knowledge of alternatives to what their government was saying to them, nevertheless tended to be very skeptical of it. They learned to repeat the approved slogans, indeed the Chinese were able to repeat long speeches by Mao Tse-tung by memory.[29]

This ability to repeat them did not mean that it affected their behavior very much. There were active black markets, high officials who took advantage of their official position, and low-ranking individuals who just didn't work very hard.[30] All of these are unsurprising examples of people disbelieving what they are told.

The explanation here is fairly simple and proceeds along two lines. Firstly, all of these Communist governments have simply said too many things that were known by their auditors to be false. For one example, reference to superior Russian production, when it is a sign of status in Russian society to be able to use capitalist products, is pretty hard to sell. Also they periodically make great claims as to their ability to provide various consumer goods which rather quickly turn out not to be true. Many Chinese who lived through the great leap forward remember the immense efforts put into the backyard steel furnaces and the absolute nil output.[31] Those who lived through the great proletarian cultural revolution, no doubt remember the gigantic move to have everybody write poems, and the very poor quality of the literary output. Mao Tse-tung has moved from being a god to being a villain and is now back to a sort of unperson.[32]

29. Or at least they were when I was in Communist China in 1950. I was in Korea in the later part of the war, and Chinese prisoners of war had the same ability. The speed with which they forgot one speech and learned another when the line changed was truly remarkable.

30. In China, black market operations are referred to as the "art of going in the back door." See Mosher, *Broken Ground*, 76–103.

31. More than 600,000 coke-and-coal-burning furnaces were hastily constructed in 1959, only to be abandoned six months later (Mosher, *Broken Ground*, 265).

32. When I was in Peking, his tomb was still there in the square in front of the Imperial Palace, but it was closed to all visitors. Indeed, it was, interestingly enough, quite clearly copied

Thus the first rule is that you don't trust liars, and when the only information you have are statements from a liar, you distrust it. We should not exaggerate here, however; the Chinese, Russians, and Cubans who have no access to other information are not likely to have any organized view contrary to that which their masters want them to have. It's just that they distrust what has been fed to them. In *1984*[33] the proles were fairly immune to the prolefeed which the hero was engaged in producing.

The second rule is to distrust people who would benefit from what they are saying if what they are saying were false. This is the old Latin rule "cui bono" (who gains?). The Roman jurists and, indeed, all jurists ever since have regarded testimony by somebody who has nothing to gain from it as much more reliable than a statement by a man who has something to gain. Indeed, the reverse rule is followed: a man who makes a statement which will injure him is regarded as an exceptionally accurate witness.

Note that this set of rules provides us with, at least, weak answers to both of our questions. In areas where telling a falsehood does not benefit you, it's probably less trouble to tell the truth, if you know the truth. Unfortunately, as we shall see below, what you think is the truth may simply be something that you've heard someone else say, and the origins may not be scientific research but an exercise of imagination.

When the people who utter a given statement have frequently been found wrong in the past or would benefit from your believing the statement, you would be well advised to give careful consideration to it and not necessarily accept it as true. This being so, individuals have some incentive to develop a reputation for honesty and accuracy. Still, mostly, the statements which are accepted without any question and regarded as true are those made under circumstances in which the person who makes them does not have anything to gain from lying.

Now all of this, once again, fits into our ideas of brain economy; i.e., it provides a way in which the brain can economize on its computation space.

---

from the work of the American architect who has built so many embassies. The building in which the Supreme Soviet meets in Moscow is also a copy of his work. During the period 1979–81, statues and posters of Mao were torn down, and the formerly ubiquitous *Little Red Book* was withdrawn from bookstores. In 1982, the Central Committee of the Chinese Communist Party restored Mao (mostly) to respectability, although it accused him of numerous "practical mistakes." See Mosher, *Broken Ground*, 297–98.

33. George Orwell, *1984: A Novel* (New York: New American Library, 1961).

Faced with the infinitely large collection of possible computations, it economizes by accepting as true a large number of statements made by people who do not seem to have anything to gain from lying.

The individuals who make these statements are unfortunately not quite so well restrained here. In general, there is little in the way of an accuracy check. Thus if I am asked a question to which I think I know the answer, but I really haven't done any serious investigation, I am still likely to answer. There is little or no cost to me in carrying out this pattern of behavior. Further, if there is little or no cost to me, a professor and a man who does a good deal of writing of a scientific nature, costs for many others are much lower.

Anyone who has had any serious contact with modern journalism or with the type of nonfiction which sells 100,000 copies is immediately aware of the fact that it isn't very accurate. In general, this lack of accuracy is not the result of any conscious desire to lie. Normally, it is simply that the person who is writing is economizing on his own time by not engaging in serious checking. Indeed, in the case of newspapers, TV, radio, etc., if the media did engage in serious checking of their information, it would be delayed several days at the very least, with the consequence that probably the readers would not be interested. Apparently the readers prefer to read current "news" which is, let us say, 85% correct to reading, a month later, information which is 95% correct.

All of this is presumably sensible. It's not obvious that we have any evolutionary reason for wanting to know what is going on at the Olympics or in international affairs, but if we do have some reason for wanting to know what is going on, normally we need to know what is going on now, not what went on some time ago. Henry Ford thought that history was bunk. This is not true, but it certainly is true that history normally has no great practical use in the affairs of the average man. What is going on right now is far more likely to be something to which he should adjust than what went on a month ago.

This fact, that reports in the media are not necessarily accurate, is supplemented by the existence of a genuine motive to simply make things up. This is not a motive to make things up in such a way that it benefits yourself, but to make them up in such a way that you have something to say and that that something to say is interesting. Almost all societies have at least one, sometimes several, creation myths, i.e., explanations as how the world started.[34]

34. As even a very good artificial one, see *The Silmarillion*. Greatly simplified, this myth maintains that Eru, the One, made the world by giving physical substance to music. See J. R. R. Tolkien (Boston: Houghton Mifflin, 1977), 25.

All of them, so far as we know, are false, but there doesn't seem to be any obvious reason why they should have been created at all. The explanation presumably is that the person who invented them gained credence from his hearers because he had nothing apparent to gain, and he chose to make them interesting. The gain he got was in a primitive way the same as the gain that a modern writer gets writing something like *In His Image*.[35] The human being wants to be entertained[36] and will pay for entertainment. Normally, when he is dealing with information which he finds entertaining, he doesn't check its truth. In most cases it would be extremely difficult for him to do so. *In His Image*, of course, turned out to be false, but I doubt that few of its many readers were in a position to make any judgement on its accuracy at all. Presumably, they found it entertaining and believed it to be true, but were unable to check its accuracy.

This kind of "information" is found throughout almost all societies. Further, there are a number of areas where someone has apparently made up things without very much entertainment being involved. Lastly, but by no means least, there are many cases in which people appear to have believed something, for example, most folk medicine, on the feeblest possible evidence. The witch doctor goes through some ceremony, and some of his clients recover, which is inevitable, since most people do recover from most diseases. As a result, the belief that the ceremony works is likely to become widespread. There were also, of course, a vast number of medicines which were given by doctors before the advent of modern science which we now know are worthless or, in some cases, very decidedly negative in value.

This is not a criticism of the way the mind works. It is very important that we economize on our use of the mind, because we simply cannot conceivably hope to think about everything in a finite length of time. Thus, stopping our calculations at a point where it looks like we won't get very much further, is necessary. Note my statement, "it looks like." We cannot know for certain what would happen if we engaged in further thought or further investigation of any sort. Some people are better at making these guesses than others.

What has all of this to do with our problem, first of ethics and secondly of that special subsection of ethics dealing with governmental "legitimacy"? The answer is that in my opinion these characteristics of the human mind which I have been describing help explain both of these matters. Any human

35. David Rorvik, *In His Image: The Cloning of a Man* (Philadelphia: Lippincott, 1978).

36. Exactly why is not evolutionarily obvious.

being has certainly been bombarded during his life with statements about various ethical principles which are dominant in his culture. You are trained not to take vengeance, because "vengeance is mine, sayith the Lord," or to believe that you have an absolute duty to engage in feuds if your family has been injured by other people. It all depends on the culture you're in. As far as we can tell, individuals are about as easy to indoctrinate in one of those two principles as in the other. If anything, the feuding one seems to be a little easier.

Indoctrination is not the whole of it. It is true we tend to believe things we are told, in particular, to believe things many different people have told us. But there is more to it than this. There is also the problem of stopping our calculations when it appears that nothing will be gained. This is a very well established psychological proposition. In the case of ethics and political matters also, we should stop our calculations and accept things at some point in time. In general, the motive behind this stoppage is not that it assures that our conclusion is true, but that we think that nothing very practical can come out of further consideration.

Thus, let us suppose that I am a citizen of Albania and that it is obvious to substantially everyone who thinks about it that various improvements could be made in the government. The first thing for any well-intentioned Albanian to do would, obviously, be to kill all the higher officials of the present government. On the other hand, it's equally obvious that he can't do this; they're very well guarded, and efforts to kill them would likely lead to his own death. Under the circumstances, the standard human being is likely to stop thinking about this obviously impossible solution to the problems and turn to things which are in fact within his reach. Instead of killing the local officials, he may make some effort to improve his relations with them. The first program is clearly impossible, hence it's ignored; the second program is within the bounds of possibility. It is therefore a higher payoff activity to think about methods of possibly improving your relations with the local government than to think about methods of killing some official, when, as a matter of fact, if you succeeded, he'd only be replaced by another equally bad.

Note, once again, that this could be explained either in terms of a genetic disposition, a set of calculations aimed at minimizing the amount of time one devotes to worrying about problems which one could do nothing about, or indoctrination by your parents in your early life. All three lines of reasoning would lead to the same conclusion.

There is now another characteristic of the human mind which may help explain the matter. This is the phenomenon known as reduction of cognitive dissonance. In general, people are happier about their present situation than we would normally expect them to be. Let us suppose, for example, that you are interested in buying a car. You spend a good deal of time investigating the advantages of various models. If the psychologist asks you to list those advantages and disadvantages you can do so of course. If, however, he waits until after you have actually bought the car and then compares what you have to say about the advantages of the different cars with what you said while you were still making up your mind, he will normally find that you regard the car which you in fact bought as much more superior to the others than you did at the time you were making up your mind. In other words, now being stuck with the car, you are changing your opinion so as to be happy about your choice.

Note that in this case there's no reason to believe that you have made a mistake; you may in fact have preferred the Chevrolet on the whole while you were making up your mind. Now that you have it, however, you will prefer it much more than you did before. It's obvious why human beings would be happier if something like this were built into their psyche. It means that they tend to be relatively satisfied with their current situation. Clearly, once again, they are happier with this mechanism than they would be without it. One can perhaps see the point most clearly by considering the possibility that they had the reverse reaction; that is, after they bought the Chevrolet, their feeling with respect to Chevrolet fell. This would make them, in many cases, think that they had made a bad mistake and make them unhappy with their choice.

But although it is easy to see why this particular phenomenon does make people happy it isn't exactly easy to see why this would be the outcome of any particular mechanism. Surely the point of evolution is not to make people happy, but to make them survive. As I mentioned above, it seems likely that human beings, indeed, are not tightly selected for optimal survival; so this doesn't prove that this is not genetic, but it does indicate that, in any event, we cannot argue for a genetic support. It may be genetic or not, but it clearly does not have any particular survival value.

Suppose that people thinking the matter over would like to have this particular trait because it would mean that in the future they would be happier. You can imagine people deciding that they would be better off if they felt this way than if they did not. Unfortunately, we don't have that kind of control over our own feelings. The mere fact that I am thinking about a particular trait as something desirable for me to have is apt to deprive me of it. I cannot decide that I shall make a particular logical error because it is good for me, because once I recognize that it is a logical error, I am no longer able to make it.

Thus, a decision on my part to believe that decisions I'd made in the past are better for me than they actually are would, in and of itself, probably make me unhappy because I would realize that this decision was based on something that was untrue and, hence, since I do realize that, I could not believe it.

It would, I suppose, be possible for parents to indoctrinate their children in this attitude in order to make them happier through their lives; so far as I know there's no evidence that parents in fact do so.

The result of all of this is that we undeniably have this particular trait, but there doesn't seem to be any strong reason why we should. Nevertheless, in the field of both ethics and legitimacy it is important. Once again, the citizen of Albania is apt to come to the conclusion after some time that the Albanian government isn't as bad as it seems on the surface. He may begin finding advantages to it and become reasonably happy with it. If this is so, the political scientist would say that the government had developed legitimacy.

Thus, in this case, there seem to be only two possible roots from which we could develop this feeling of legitimacy, or acceptance, of any ethical principle which is not, in fact, in our best interest. These are a genetic predisposition and parental training. In any event, we observe that human beings do act this way, and it has some effect on the retention of power by a dictator. Firstly, he may find that he is benefited by this "legitimacy," or he may find that he isn't and should do what he can to build it up.

Now, in dealing with this issue, it must be kept clearly in mind that the fact that this kind of "legitimacy" exists does not mean that the government is a nice one. Indeed, I suspect that, historically, the strongest cases of this kind of legitimacy have been hereditary monarchies in which a dynasty has been in power for a period of time. The House of Ming, in China, is notable in Chinese histories, both for its great glories and strength and for the fact that apparently almost all of the emperors were degenerate. There were generations in which the emperor never saw his high officials, dealing with them exclusively through eunuchs. One of the emperors, in an outburst of idiocy, succeeded in getting himself captured by the Mongols. The emperor was able to return to his throne because of his strong legitimacy. The junior relative who temporarily replaced him, and who certainly was as competent, was unable to hold the throne.[37]

37. The decline of the Ming dynasty began with the reign of Ying Tsung, who ruled from 1436 to 1449 and allowed himself to be captured in a minor battle on the northern frontier by a Mongol Oirat army. He was released in 1450 and began a struggle with his brother Ching

The Chinese are, by no means, unique. English history is a history of revolutions and attempts to overthrow the government. The British throne was far less secure than any other in Europe. Nevertheless, with the sole exception of Henry VII, all of these people who attempted to overthrow the crown were blood relatives. An individual might, if he was closely related to the reigning king, attempt to overthrow him, but not anyone else. Surely, these were not those Englishmen most suited to rule.

The case of Henry VII, mentioned above, is a particularly intriguing one, since his accession not only ended the very destructive Wars of the Roses, but it brought to the throne a man who had no blood connection with the royal line. The Wars of the Roses, between Lancaster and York, in essence, broke out because Henry VI went insane.[38] The result was that for a considerable period of time not Henry VI but his wife was the actual leader of the Lancastrian House, and in fact, Henry VI for much of this time was a prisoner in London.[39] The objective of the House of Lancaster was freeing him and restoring him to the throne. The importance of legitimacy is obvious here, since it is very hard to see any other reason why a lunatic should be restored to rule. Eventually, however, Henry VI died.[40] At this point, his wife, an exile in France, married a Welsh soldier of fortune named Tudor. Their son had no hereditary claims on the throne, but through his mother he was head of the Lancastrians. With the aid of the French king, he was able to overthrow the Plantagenet dynasty and establish his own Tudor dynasty.

Having considered seriously the history of England, he adopted a policy, followed by his descendants, of killing all possible rivals to the throne.[41] As

---

Ti, who had assumed the throne during his captivity. He was ultimately successful and his second reign lasted from 1457 to 1464 (R. Ernest Dupuy and Trevor N. Dupuy, *The Encyclopedia of Military History, from 3500* B.C. *to the Present*, rev. ed. [New York: Harper and Row, 1977], 442).

38. In 1453, Henry VI suffered a mental breakdown which left him in a stupor for eighteen months and from which he never entirely recovered (Giles St. Aubyn, *The Year of Three Kings: 1483* [New York: Atheneum, 1983], 39). For the complex chain of events leading to open warfare this breakdown precipitated, see Ramsay Muir (*A Short History of the British Commonwealth*, vol. 2, *The Modern Commonwealth [1763 to 1919]* [Yonkers-on-the-Hudson, N.Y.: World Book, 1924]), 177–78.

39. Aubyn, *The Year of Three Kings*, 48.

40. On May 21, 1471, Henry VI died in the Tower of London. He was probably killed on the order of Edward IV (ibid., 58).

41. Muir, *A Short History*, vol. 2, 211–12.

I have said above, the kings of Scotland were out of reach, and hence, when Henry VIII's syphilis and his children's sterility led the Tudor line to die out, the king of Scotland became the king of England.[42]

We could go on with this. Terrible governments have not infrequently been able to acquire serious support from people because of "legitimacy." However, any form of government may get this kind of support. I wish to turn to democracy below, but let me begin now with dictatorship. South America has had, in most of its countries, a record in which dictatorship and democracy are intermingled. In most of the countries, dictatorship is commoner than democracy, but there are democratic interludes. Although the dictators are, by no means, always military men, they always have military support.

The point here is that for a great many South Americans, one of the signs of legitimacy of a government is military support. This is true for democracies as well as for dictatorships. In other words, it is thought by most South Americans that not only is military support necessary for a government, but that a government which loses military support *should be* overthrown, not only *will be*. This point of view is shared by relatively few South American intellectuals, but South American intellectuals are a rather rare breed, and they also are very frequently only intellectuals by virtue of a sort of ascription process. The output of some South American universities is rather like the output of the New York City public schools.

It should be said, however, that indoctrination is also important in legitimacy, and in some cases, severe indoctrination of a particular type has tended to create a legitimacy even against the existing government. Needless to say, this occurs only when an existing government permits the indoctrination to go on.

An obvious case of this occurred in France in the reigns of Louis XV and Louis XVI. At this time, the *philosophes*, deeply under the intellectual influence of England, favored a constitutional monarchy like that of England. Apparently, this point of view was so widespread that even the last king held it. As a result, in general, the king could not depend on his army when it finally came to a showdown, and he himself clearly was in two minds about opposing the desires of the newly created legislature.[43]

42. The common man seems to feel that there is an element of legitimacy in military rule. Granted the description I have given above of the causes of legitimacy, this is understandable.

43. Note that the legislature was elected by a very restricted group of electors. Further, the early history of the French republic was very largely an effort to make sure that the royalists

The same situation appears to have been true in South America during the time when South America became independent. Most historians are[44] of the opinion that the common people were royalist and that it was the upper classes who favored republics. This meant that, of course, there was no prospect whatsoever of establishing a true republican form of government and may have been one of the reasons for South America's rapid collapse into a series of local dictatorships.

In the nineteenth century this feeling that democracy is the only legitimate form of government spread throughout much of the world, although South America always tended to be rather resistant. In the twentieth century, it has turned out that dictatorships can take advantage of this kind of legitimacy by simply announcing that they are democratic.[45] It is extraordinary how far this illusion can spread. I have had several major political scientists tell me that Russia has elections. Indeed, one of the characteristics of the modern-day world is the strong tendency to feel that socialist governments somehow are legitimate, no matter how they came into power or how apparently unpopular they are. This "legitimacy" does not seem to protect them from their own people, only from the foreign press.

But, if legitimacy has these characteristics, it surely is something that the dictator would like. Obviously, when he first comes into power, he is not in a position to claim legitimacy on the grounds that he's been around a long time. This is probably the reason that new rulers almost uniformly announce that they are firmly in favor of whatever happens to be the current mystique. The Ching dynasty, overthrowing the Ming, announced their firm devotion to Confucianism, although they had to announce it in rather bad Chinese because, after all, they were Manchus.[46] Similarly, if one looks back at the Wars of the Roses, one finds strong statements about how the previous

---

did not get a majority in the legislature. Apparently, the members of the legislature thought that although they were firmly republicans, the king had overwhelming support among the common people. Of course, the disasters of the early republic had something to do with their fear of a royalist electoral majority, and the various rather unfair measures taken to prevent it.

44. Or perhaps I should say "were"—recently Marxism has developed.

45. For example, the German Democratic Republic, the Libyan People's Republic, and the Union of Soviet Socialist Republics.

46. Although the Ching (Manchus) came from a section of what is today part of mainland China (central Manchuria), they were not Chinese. See Dupuy and Dupuy, *Encyclopedia of Military History*, 512.

government had not only been corrupt, but had failed to be respectful of the Christian religion.[47]

In recent years, dictators have usually announced that they are going to have a democratic government shortly after a few minor problems have been cleared up. Since, after a few years, the dictators are beginning to develop the other kind of legitimacy, they usually quickly forget their initial promises.[48]

Note that the dictator should, of course, try to avoid doing things which will unnecessarily annoy the people. If he is in a Mohammedan country, he should make a display of piety and avoid eating ham in public. His press should be prevented from reporting anything which might cause general distaste for him, etc. I do not think, however, that any of these things are of major importance. The really big way of getting legitimacy is simply to stay in office for a period of time. The psychological traits that I have described above will then take care of the matter.

But simply staying in office is not quite enough. He must always give the impression of being strong enough so that he will continue staying in office. Once the common man or the officials begin thinking he is in danger of being removed, this thought, in and of itself, reduces his legitimacy, although not necessarily to zero. Legitimacy is a help, and in particular a help in that it eliminates a lot of minor opposition; it is not, however, a major dependence. It is true that if a major effort to overthrow you starts, the legitimacy argument will lead a good many people to support you who, if they thought the matter over carefully, probably wouldn't. But a few defeats, and this feeling will largely vanish.

My above statement about the ending of legitimacy, of course, is primarily true of dictators. There is no doubt at all that royal families can retain a certain hold on the affections of the populace and, for that matter, the officials, long after they have been thrown out of power. Charles II was welcomed back into England; most historians seem to think that James III and Charles III were actually more popular than the Hanoverians ruling in England and were kept out primarily by the shrewd political maneuvering

47. For example, an Act of Attainder of November, 1485, under Henry VII (following the defeat and death of Richard III at Bosworth Field) accused the latter of "unnatural, mischievous and great perjuries, treasons, homicides and murders, in shedding of infant's blood" and numerous other "abominations against God and Man." See Aubyn, *The Year of Three Kings*, 242.

48. Reasons why a dictator may, in fact, be motivated to hold a perfectly free election were discussed above.

and military and police strength of the Protestant ascendancy.[49] They can be said to have retained a good deal of legitimacy right up to the ascension of George III.[50]

But, if legitimacy is of some value to the dictator, and it is, it is of more value to him in dealing with the junior officials of his regime than in dealing with the common people. The junior officials of the regime can, in the first place, cause him more damage, or benefit him more than the common people; and secondly, they are more likely to appreciate his regime, because they have, presumably, gained from it. He should also always, however, worry about the junior official who just hasn't done very well.

Penkovsky was a loyal and energetic servant of the Soviet regime, married to the daughter of a lieutenant general, and rising rapidly in the foreign intelligence branch. It was then discovered, rather by accident, that his father, whom he had not only never seen, but who was dead before he was born, was a White officer. This stopped his promotion at the rank of full colonel. At about the same time, his father-in-law, the lieutenant general, was retired and suddenly discovered that rewards offered by the Soviet Union to high officials did not necessarily apply to retired high officials. The combination led to what is, at least as far as the open literature is concerned, the most important betrayal of the Soviet Union to the West.[51]

This kind of thing can happen in any regime. Of necessity, when you promote a man from lieutenant colonel to colonel, there are several other lieutenant colonels who feel that they deserved the job. This is, incidentally, from the dictator's standpoint, the strongest possible argument for straight seniority appointments. If everyone knows it is a matter of seniority, then no one will be disappointed. Your time will come if you don't die. Seniority, of course, carries with it immense other disadvantages.

Unfortunately, legitimacy, in this meaning which I have given it, is a hard thing for a dictator to get by any means other than simply staying in power. Since staying in power is his basic problem anyway, all one can really say here

49. In fact, one historian argues that James Edward's chances of overthrowing George I in 1715 were quite good but that the Stuarts and their advisors were simply too incompetent to properly exploit the opportunity (V. H. H. Green, *The Hanoverians, 1714–1815* [London: Edward Arnold, 1965], 81–86).

50. Witness the invasion of England by Charles Edward Stuart in December of 1745—the eighteenth year of George II's reign—which generated strong support in Scotland and at least lukewarm support in England. See Green, *The Hanoverians*, 160–64.

51. Oleg Penkovsky, *The Penkovsky Papers* (New York: Doubleday, 1965), esp. 229, 394.

is that the longer he stays in power, the more legitimacy he has, and hence, the more likely he is to stay in power. Once again, power begets power.

All of this is rather different from the standard account of legitimacy. Most people have mixed legitimacy up with their own personal moral code. In practice, as I have said before, the most vicious governments have sometimes clearly acquired this kind of legitimacy. Further, it can be more readily explained in terms of certain traits of human psychology than in terms of any virtue on the part of the rulers. Nevertheless, legitimacy is of some importance to the dictator, and if he is wise he will cultivate it. Unfortunately, although if he is wise he will cultivate it, there is not really a great deal he can do about it.

So far I have said nothing about ideology, because I generally tend to think it is relatively unimportant, both in the control of the dictatorship and in the problem of legitimacy. Nevertheless, it is related to the legitimacy issue. Most dictators have taken the view that their government is not only their government but also virtuous. For this purpose, they frequently create their own set of rules for virtue. I should say that, as far as I know, there has never been a case in which these rules are particularly coherent. Qaddafi's *Greenbook* and Peron's *Justicialism* will do as examples. All of them have made strong appeals to people who are gaining from their application but have not had great impact elsewhere.

It is true that Marxism, like the other great religions—Christianity, Islam, Buddhism, and Confucianism—has had some export value. That is, people who are not directly under it have become convinced that it is true. In general, however, these are people who very much want to know the truth and aren't very critical, or people who are simply trying to get ahead. Probably the former are the largest single category. The average person would like to have some kind of explanation for the world. He is not very well informed or very critical, nor does he engage in lengthy thought about the specific systems offered to him.[52] The likelihood that he will be caught by one of these systems is, therefore, pretty good.

This is particularly true if there is a large and rather confusing literature which has as one of its themes that the system, whether it's Buddhism or Marxism, is true, but which otherwise is quite hard to understand. The Trinity, a doctrine so obscure that St. Thomas took the view that one could only

52. Margery Seldon's *Poppies and Roses* (Sevenoaks, Kent: Economics and Literacy Books, 1985) is a biography of her father, who was a particularly clear example of a man who became a Marxist for these reasons.

understand it as a result of divine guidance,[53] is probably one of the attractions of the Christian religion. Similarly, the extreme difficulty of fitting any society into the Marxist set of classes is probably one of the reasons that it works. It is awfully hard not only to fit the society into those classes but to prove that any particular fitting is improper.

Marxism has, of course, had the characteristic that it changes rapidly from time to time and, indeed, from place to place. The Ceylonese Trotskyite, the loyal follower of Deng Xiaoping, and a New York Marxist intellectual have almost nothing in common except that they will all tell you that they are Marxists. Nevertheless, they are apt to be allied against outsiders, even if they fight vigorously internally. The same can be said, historically, about Christianity, Buddhism, etc. Currently, the Islamic world is rent by a revived version of the split between Shia and Sunni.

As the reader has no doubt discovered already, I myself have little patience or interest in these ideologies. But no one who considers the growth of the Islamic empire from the time of Mohammed to the fall of the Umayyad dynasty can doubt they have been influential in human history. Further, although the Umayyads were, undoubtedly, the great spreaders of Islam, it continued growing at a somewhat lower rate and with various schisms and divisions for a considerable period of time thereafter.[54] Today, although it is no longer spreading,[55] it is clearly an extremely important influence in the lives of a large part of the human race. I think it is foolish. Nevertheless, most human beings seem to have felt a need for Christianity, Islam, Buddhism, etc. Atheists like myself are unusual.

Purely secular religions, i.e., religions which pay relatively little attention to the afterlife, such as Confucianism, Marxism, the pagan religions of Greece and Rome, and, for that matter, Judaism, have traditionally been almost as strong as those religions like Christianity, Islam, and Buddhism which offer rewards in an afterlife for a virtuous life here. Hinduism falls somewhere between these categories. It is certainly true that a good Hindu expects to go up in the caste structure if he lives a virtuous life here, but the virtue is defined in terms of whatever caste he happens to find himself in. The prospect of a

53. Aquinas claimed that reason could prove the existence of God, but not of the Trinity (or of the Incarnation or the Last Judgement). See Russell, *History of Western Philosophy*, 454.

54. The Umayyad (or Omayyad) Caliphate ruled from 661 to 750 A.D., and by 732 it controlled the Iberian Peninsula, southwestern France, all of North Africa, Arabia, the Near East (except Anatolia), Armenia, Persia, and a large bridgehead over the Indus River in northwest India. See Langer, *Encyclopedia*, 200–204.

55. Except for some missionary activity in Africa.

Brahman being reborn as a worm in the stomach of a spotted dog because he's mispronounced one word in a sacred chant once in his life seems to us excessive.

But to return to the main theme of this book, such an essentially nonmaterial motive for supporting a dictator can be very valuable to him. He can also be damaged very severely if there is such a nonmaterial motive for overthrowing him. The Muslims seem to have convinced the Byzantine governor of Egypt that, somehow or other, God was on their side. Since he was a Christian, it is very difficult to understand how he came to this conclusion, although it is true that his army had, at the time he reached this decision, lost a series of battles. In any event, this was a major step in their further success. Of course, here again, success begets the belief that you have something on your side, in this case, divine providence, and the fact that people think you have that on your side makes it more likely you will win again.

To repeat an earlier theme of this chapter, what I have had to say is not very much like the standard account of legitimacy. I have said that it is a feeling on the part of individuals that a certain government is likely to win. Not that it is in accordance with a divine order of some sort. The problem is, why do they come to that conclusion and what, if anything, can a dictator do to encourage it? Certainly, it is to his advantage if he can encourage it, and if they come to the conclusion that the reverse is true, it is to his disadvantage. But having said this, I should go on to say that I am fairly convinced that it is a relatively minor factor. In the first place, the common people and the lower officials are those who are most likely to be influenced by it. They are less important than the higher officials. Many governments thought by their subjects to be legitimate have been overthrown. The Ming, after all, were replaced by the Ching, the Stuarts by the Hanoverians; the governments of Lithuania, Latvia, and Esthonia by Russian conquests,[56] the Senatus Populusque Romanus[57] by Caesar,[58] the more or less democratic constitutional monarchy in Egypt by Nasser.[59] Legitimacy is a help to any dictator, but it is hard for him to get it in the early part of his reign, and he'll get it almost automatically in the latter part. Further, although it is a help, it is by no means a stable support.

56. See Richard F. Rosser, *An Introduction to Soviet Foreign Policy* (Englewood Cliffs, N.J.: Prentice-Hall, 1969), 188–90.

57. This chapter is dictated in Rome.

58. Who still put S.P.Q.R. on his standards.

59. On January 26, 1952 (Johnson, *Modern Times*, 488).

PART 4

THE COUP D'ETAT AND ITS SUPPRESSION

COUP D'ETAT

STRUCTURAL FACTORS

The traditional view of revolution might be represented by Figure 6. An oppressive government bears down the people. The people then rise up and overthrow it. Historically, this has rarely happened, and the theory we have been discussing for the last several chapters indicates why it is unlikely. Only the most incompetent government could be overthrown by an *outside* conspiracy. If we look at the innumerable cases in history where governments have been overthrown, we find that far from the people rising up and overthrowing the government what happens is some kind of split in the government itself. The standard South American or African uprising by part of the army, one of which has surely occurred during the month before you read this, is an obvious example. Once two groups within the government are engaged in a fight, it is possible that some extragovernmental part of the population will be drawn in. This is particularly likely if, as in the Spanish civil war in the 1930s, both sides engage in widespread conscription to fill out their armies.

The reasons why a revolution from outside the government can overthrow only the most inefficient government can be summarized under two headings. Firstly, for most citizens of the state, remaining neutral is the optimal course of action. Secondly, the state apparatus is well-equipped with organizations capable of putting down any uprising that might in fact occur anyway. To return to the coup d'état, neither of these two statements is true. In general, remaining neutral is not the profit-maximizing course of action for the average army officer, police lieutenant, etc. Indeed, if these officials tended to remain neutral in political disputes, then the state would be relatively disarmed in dealing with outside revolutions as well as with internal uprisings. But, as a matter of fact, they mainly do not remain neutral—they mainly choose sides; hence, the structure of the operation is quite different from an outside revolution.

In addition, the attempt to overthrow the government from the inside almost *ex definitione* throws the official government apparatus into disarray. There may be a well-trained and well-equipped secret police force for the sole

Reprinted, with permission, from *The Social Dilemma: The Economics of War and Revolution* (Blacksburg, Va.: Center for Study of Public Choice, 1974), 60–70.

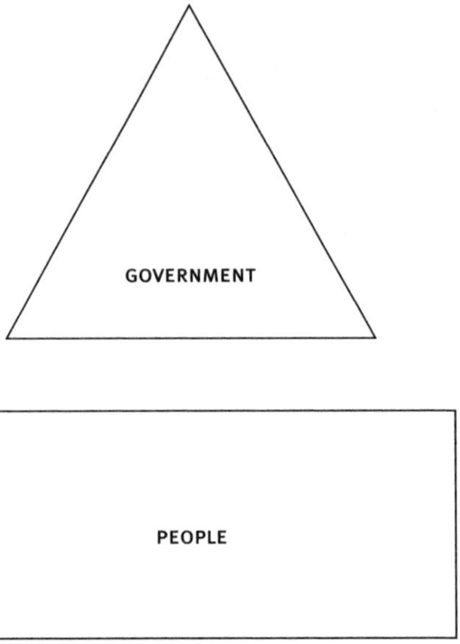

FIGURE 6
Common view of government

purpose of watching government officials, but its leader may also be the leader of the revolution. More likely, this secret police force will be split between the two sides. Under the circumstances, there is no organized, coherent structure on either side unless the organizers of the coup have miscalculated, and in that event they will not last more than a few hours. Both of these topics deserve further and more detailed discussion and let us turn to that now.

We may begin by taking the equations for individual payoffs of Chapter VI and modifying them very slightly to show the individual payoffs of officials of a government in the event a coup is under way.

$$P_{In} = P_g \cdot L_v - N_p \qquad (1)$$

$$P_r = P_g \cdot (L_v + L_i) + R_i(L_v + L_i) - P_i[1 - (L_v + L_i)] - L_w \cdot I_r + E \qquad (2)$$

$$P_d = P_g \cdot (L_v - L_i) + D_i[1 - (L_v - L_i)] - P_p(L_v - L_{i^2}) - L_w \cdot I_r + E \qquad (3)$$

It will be noted that I have altered equation (1) by inserting N_p, which represents the punishment for remaining neutral. In a way, the fact that it is costly for government officials to remain neutral in a coup attempt is the basic difference between their position and that of the individual private citizen and is also a major factor in explaining that coups work and outside revolutions do not.[1] Before discussing this aspect in detail, however, let us perform a little algebraic manipulation and then discuss certain other aspects of the equations. Instead of subtracting equation (1) from equations (2) and (3), I propose to subtract the first expression in equation (1) from all three of the equations. The individual must choose among these three possible courses of action, and we may as well eliminate the one factor they all have in common, since this can hardly have any effect on his decision process.

$$NP_{In} = -N_p \tag{4}$$

$$NP_r = P_g \cdot L_i + R_i(L_v + L_i) - P_i[1 - (L_v + L_i)] - L_w \cdot I_r + E \tag{5}$$

$$NP_d = -P_g \cdot L_i + D_i[1 - (L_v - L_i)] - P_p(L_v - L_i) - L_w \cdot I_r + E \tag{6}$$

Note that L_i, the effect that the individual may have on the coup, is not necessarily infinitesimally small for a government official. Under these circumstances, the expression $L_i \cdot P_g$ may be more significant for the government official than it is for the private citizen. This is dubious, however. Most of the junior government officials will still have very small L_i's; therefore this expression should be close to zero. On the other hand, the senior government officials, although they will indeed have somewhat larger L_i's, are also likely to receive very large rewards or very large punishments in the private sphere from the success or failure of the coup. Under the circumstances, it is likely that for them, too, the public good aspect of the coup is relatively minor.

Another feature that must be emphasized is that the participants in the coup or in the defense against the coup are officials of the government. They are that group of people who are least likely to be unhappy about the policy of the government. Further, the higher rank they have, the higher the L_i; but, at the same time, the more likely it is that they are basically rather satisfied with the existing government, except insofar as they would like to have a higher rank. Under the circumstances, public good considerations—if they are of any importance at all among government officials considering a coup—are more

1. The neutral may also run a very distinct chance of being injured in the fighting. Indeed, he may find himself being fired at by both sides, with the result that his chance of injury is even higher than if he were directly participating. I have left this out of the equation because I believe that the neutral, although he might be formally executed at any point during the fighting, would only rarely be directly engaged in the fighting. Hence, the major factor would be the possibility of punishment for neutrality, rather than the possibility of being injured in the fighting.

likely to weigh in on the side of retaining the present government than on the side of attempting to overthrow it.

Thus, public good considerations are apt to play as small a part in the decision to participate in a coup as in participation in any outside revolution. The great difference between the two situations is the existence of a cost of inaction for a government official.[2] Since inaction has a real cost attached to it, and indeed in some cases it may be a very high cost, the government official is far more likely to choose to participate in either attempting to overthrow the government or defending it than is the private citizen. Assume the private costs of entering into an attempted coup on one side or another, if the side you choose loses, are about the same as the gains you will make if the side you choose wins. Under these circumstances, choosing a side at random and participating has a higher present discounted value than remaining neutral, which carries with it a certainty of at least some cost. There is a modification to this rule, in that a period of neutrality followed by entrance into the coup may be a higher paying course of action than instantaneous entry. A temporary neutrality while you judge the odds, however, is quite a different thing from a genuine policy of neutrality.

In practice, of course, the costs of inaction or remaining neutral in a coup can be greatly varying, and, no doubt, there are some officials for whom the costs are low to nonexistent. The police captain in a remote station where there is no significant activity may be able to do nothing and end up with substantially no cost. At the other extreme, the infantry private who is suddenly informed by all of his officers that they have joined the revolution probably finds it extremely dangerous to do anything except agree with them. If he does choose to resist, it is probably safer for him to take the other side than to issue a firm declaration of neutrality. Indeed, for many government officials, the lowest cost course of action will be to simply follow the order of their superiors. In a way, this is their equivalent of inaction on the part of a private citizen.

This simple obedience to orders, however, in general is only available as a course of action for lower-level officials and not necessarily for all of them. The higher-level officials are presented very directly with a choice as to whose orders they should obey, because they will certainly receive instructions from at least two sources. Since the point at issue is who is the "government," they

2. I have counted this cost as a positive number and then subtracted it. This is in keeping with the rest of my notation, but I must admit it gives equation (4) a decidedly odd appearance.

can hardly depend on the existing chain of command as their guide in solving this problem. Some delay may have a positive payoff, as will be explained in the next chapter; but they should not plan on remaining neutral throughout the entire uprising unless their risk aversion is so extreme that they regard the certainty of the cost of failing to support the winner as less important than the chance of the costs involved in supporting the loser, together with the profits to be made from supporting the loser. For most senior officials, and all junior officials who have received orders from their superiors, it is unlikely that a policy of continual inaction would be chosen as the profit-maximizing course of action.

We may imagine a few typical examples. A cabinet minister is absolutely certain to be replaced by a supporter of the new régime, whether he has opposed the régime or remained neutral. It is likely that if he has remained neutral, the costs imposed on him will be less than if he backed the loser, but nevertheless he faces a significant reduction in his well-being. Even if no one on the winning side particularly dislikes him, they still have the problem of rewarding their supporters.

At a lower level, say a regimental commander, the costs of neutrality may be lowered, but they will certainly be real. Certainly any prospects of promotion would be blasted, and transfers to some unimportant post would be highly likely. A premature retirement is possible, and it is also possible that further penalties will be imposed. For the neutral, the slogan "He who is not with me is against me" may lead to positive punishment. More commonly, however, the injuries inflicted upon a neutral come from the need for the winning side to distribute rewards to their supporters. He is deprived of his position not because he is disliked, but because the position is needed for other purposes.

At this middle level, and even more at the lower level, simply following orders from one's superiors is in some ways the safest course of action. At this level—and, once again, particularly at the lower level—it is unlikely that the individual will have had any direct contact with the leaders of the "other" side. Thus, if a colonel follows the orders of the major general commanding his division or, at the bottom level, a private follows the orders of his platoon commander, he is probably choosing a cost-minimizing course of action. It is true that the "other" side will make every effort to communicate contrary "orders" to him. But, in general, they will be compelled to use fairly indirect and general means. The use of radio is the obvious technique, and whoever is in control of any radio station can be depended upon to transmit orders (allegedly from high authorities) to all personnel in the government, instructing them either to revolt or stand fast, depending on who happens to be in control of the radio station.

Evasion of this kind of order, however, tends to be much safer than evasion of a direct order by one of your superiors. In the first place, it is clear that whoever is broadcasting is not in a position to have you shot immediately. Secondly, in the long run, one would argue that you simply had been unable to distinguish which radio broadcast was genuine. Thus, the penalties put upon a person for simply following orders if his orders lead to him being on the wrong side are apt to be of declining importance as one moves toward the bottom of the governmental hierarchy. A declaration of neutrality, on the other hand, would be just as dangerous—or perhaps more dangerous—in the bottom levels than in the top. Last but by no means least, a decision to "revolt" against your own local structure, i.e., the infantry platoon in which you happen to be operating, would tend to be quite dangerous in immediate terms. Thus one would anticipate that the lower-level officials would tend to follow the orders of their hierarchic superiors simply because this is the lowest-cost course of action. If they did *not* follow the orders of their hierarchic superiors, they would characteristically attempt to join the "other" side. For them, neutrality would carry with it the costs of defying orders and little hope of reward.

Thus, we would find higher-level officials attempting to choose sides and little concerned with any except a temporary neutrality for the purpose of gaining additional information. Lower-level officials, usually (but by no means always) carry out the orders of their superiors. There would, of course, be no sharp boundary between these two categories of officials. In both cases, however, neutrality would be an unlikely course of action.

For our third imagined case, then, consider the police private who is ordered by his superiors to go out and put down rioting. Provided only that the police have the physical capacity to deal with the rioting, he should obey orders. Of course if it looks as though the rioters might win, then deserting the police and joining the rioters might be desirable. Even here, however, the process of desertion might be quite dangerous.

Lastly, as we have mentioned there may be junior officials in the government whose duties are such that they can avoid taking sides. The technician manning a remote meteorological survey station, for example, can afford to sit out the revolution and suffer relatively little cost. Note, however, that if he is occupying a job which seems suitable as a reward for the followers of the revolution, he is still apt to be displaced. Even in his case, neutrality carries a cost. Only if the individual who is occupying a job for which there are no rents, i.e., one which no revolutionary supporter would particularly want because the costs of performing the duties are as great as the salary in opportunity cost terms, would he really be safe. There are probably few such jobs in any government. In general, however, the less you get paid by the government, the less likely you are to be displaced by a member of the new government; hence, it is more likely that the costs of neutrality will be relatively low. There are, of course, some technicians who are hard to replace, and in their cases neutrality may well be the best policy.

Thus if we define revolutions as uprisings of the masses against the government and coups d'état as splits within the government, we see an immediate major difference. Most of the masses will be well-advised to remain inactive. Most members of the government, on the other hand, would be most ill-advised to remain neutral in the conflict. Note that this rule is one of the basic reasons why revolutions from the outside are unlikely to succeed. Most members of the mass will remain inactive, whereas most members of the government will be active partisans. Since we are talking of a rising of the masses against the government, it is clear that all members of the government would be on the government's side. Hence, the whole weight of the government apparatus deals with a rather small number of revolutionaries. The success of government would be anticipated; indeed, as we have mentioned, it is what we normally observe. It is, of course, conceivable that an uprising which starts *outside* the government (a revolution) may spread into the government ranks. It may be taken as an opportunity for people in the government who have been dissatisfied with their position in the hierarchy to attempt to improve it by joining this outside disturbance. I think this has relatively rarely happened, but giving the reasons for that belief must be deferred. The other possibility—that after a split has occurred in the government there will be a tendency to draw in extragovernmental segments of the population—is, of course, also quite possible.

To introduce another aspect, let us briefly consider three events in the recent history of Russia. The first occurred in 1953 and led to the liquidation of the chief of the secret police. Retrospectively, the winners maintain that the man who was responsible for internal security of the Communist party made an effort to overthrow the party and establish himself as a dictator but was frustrated in his attempt. Whether this actually occurred or not, I do not know. It is certainly true that Beria lost, but whether he was removed as a result of an effort on his part to get rid of his colleagues or whether they simply shot him in order to increase their own power is not known. In any event, however, it is clear that the formal structure then existing for the protection of one of the most internal security–conscious states in the world was under the control of a man who was in opposition to his nominal superiors. Further, the government found it necessary to take steps to greatly reduce the efficiency of this internal security apparatus for the specific purpose of increasing security.

The second example was the so-called "anti-party group" which in the late 1950s succeeded in obtaining a majority in the politburo and passed a resolution unseating Khrushchev. As Khrushchev later pointed out, they had an arithmetical majority but not a political majority. At the time, the Kremlin was still barred to most visitors, and the physical security of the Kremlin and the leaders living in it was the responsibility of a lieutenant general. This lieutenant general decided to go with Khrushchev rather than with the majority of the politburo.[3] Clearly, this lieutenant general was supposed to protect the politburo. Equally clearly, he chose to follow Khrushchev rather than the politburo. Whether we regard this decision as hierarchically correct for him or not, the fact remains that it could hardly be argued that he had simply carried out his orders. He had contrary orders, and his decision as to which he should follow was of great importance. Here again, a man whose sole duty was to protect the security of the central government took sides and, in part, determined the outcome of an important political dispute by so taking sides.

Lastly, we consider the removal of Khrushchev himself. We do not know how this was accomplished, but it seems fairly certain that the procedure must have involved the "defection" of part of the formal security apparatus. All three of these incidents occurred in one of the most security-conscious states in the world, and in a state which has always had at least two "states-within-a-state" for the specific purpose of maintaining internal security. One of these states-within-a-state—the party—was clearly split in all three of these cases. The other state-within-a-state—the secret police, under one or the other of its innumerable names—took an active role; but it would be hard to argue that this active role was in all cases supportive of the existing governmental structure.

The examples above illustrate the difficulties faced by a government considering the possibility of a coup. Let us assume a simple, straightforward

3. At this point, I am not attempting to explain the entire story of the operation. Indeed, not too much is known about it.

dictatorship because it is the simplest of all forms of government. It is clear that the dictator, by and of himself, has relatively little physical power. If all other members of the government unite against him, he can be removed without difficulty. Furthermore, the general promotions made possible by his removal provide for gains, albeit slight gains, for substantially the entire governmental apparatus. For reasons to be discussed in the next chapter, it is relatively rare that the entire government turns against the dictator. This is partly because the dictator tries to keep his government divided against itself, and partly because he is apt to be removed long before the entire government has become antagonistic.

There is, however, no possible way that the dictator can protect himself against *all* contingencies. In practice, the particular contingency we have been discussing so far—the uniting of the entire government against him—is impossible and most dictators have been removed by much simpler coups. It is not necessary that everyone be opposed to the dictator, but only that a fair number of high officials turn against him. Nor is there any internal structure he can produce within the government which makes this impossible. We have pointed out that the entire governmental apparatus is, by definition, opposed to what we have defined as an outside revolution. An overthrow of the existing government will injure practically everyone in it. A split in the existing government, however, is certain to benefit a good many people, simply because replacements will be needed for whoever loses in the squabble. If an effort is made to set up a sort of inner government which can be depended upon to deal with splits in the governmental apparatus in the same way that the governmental apparatus deals with opposition from outside, then the problem arises of controlling this inner apparatus. The Communist party of the Soviet Union and the Communist secret police, as we have mentioned, were both set up with this idea in mind, and in both cases have shown that they are not entirely reliable. Indeed, historically, most dictators have not depended on a single, monolithic state-within-a-state to protect themselves against a coup, but have attempted to keep the state fragmented and to have a number of different intelligence services watching each other.

Looking at the matter in the form of a very simplified model, we can consider each member of the government as having some amount of power. Any coalition which acquires more than half of this total power can remove the remainder of the government and put itself in control. It is clear that there are innumerable such coalitions and that there is no way of structuring the government so that there will not be innumerable such coalitions. Further, many such possible coalitions do not include the dictator himself or, indeed, some of his higher officials. Clearly there are profits to make by organizing such a coalition and throwing out the remainder of the government.

On the other hand, if someone begins organizing such a coalition, undeniably there are profits to be made by betraying it to the dictator. Further, once such a coalition is formed, it may be possible for the dictator to defeat it, in which case there are profits for joining the forces of the dictator. Thus, everyone is in a state of great uncertainty and a high degree of organizational cohesion is unlikely on either side.

These matters, however, will be discussed at greater length in the next chapter. Let us now turn to two special quasi–public good problems which occur in the case of the coup. Firstly, there may be some limited-scope public goods of considerable importance for the individual bureaucrat. It not infrequently happens that some particular organization gets in either the "good" books or the "bad" books of the dictator. Further, some organization may have a major role either in attacking or defending the dictatorship. It will be recalled that during the events which eventually led to the American intervention in the Dominican Republic, a very small group of military personnel who had been especially trained as frogmen played a major role in supporting the group which was eventually removed by the Americans. Clearly, someone who *happened* to be in this particular group—he happened to be a frogman—faced considerable public good problems in deciding his role in these events. It was clear that if the Bosch forces won, the frogmen were going to do very well as a group; and if the Bosch opponents won, they were going to do very badly. Since this was a rather small group, the individual put a somewhat higher value on his contribution to generating this public good than the more normal nationwide public good. Nevertheless, note that it is a public good, and the individual frogman should compute its value to him (and the value to him of taking action for it) in the same manner as the ordinary public good. The only difference is that the public good is of a much narrower scope, hence he discounts it less than a wider scope public good.

This kind of thing is quite common in a coup d'état. Normally, of course, the group which is playing such a major role is much larger; hence, the public good aspects are even stronger. Still, individuals may feel that success in the overthrow will lead to an expansion or a contraction of, say, the navy or the marine corps. Under these circumstances, they have *some* public good reasons for going along with the organization of which they are now a member.

A further reason for this type of conduct concerns the intellectual capital that individuals will have acquired by service in the government. They will be familiar with the present routines, have a number of contacts in various places, and in general have a good deal of specialized knowledge not available to other people. Drastic reorganizations greatly reduce the value of this specialized knowledge and, hence, degrade their intellectual capital. We anticipate that individuals would be opposed to such injury to their intellectual capital, although once again the public good considerations indicate that they would not fight too hard to prevent it.

There is a special consequence of this aspect of a coup d'état's or a revolution's effect on this particular type of personal capital. If there is a drastic reorganization and hence a sharp reduction in the value of knowledge of the "ropes," then much of the bureaucratic opposition to further change will be reduced. A good deal of the opposition to change we normally find in bureaucracies comes from a desire to retain this particular type of intellectual capital. Once it has been reduced in value, the opposition to further change is correspondingly reduced. Thus a sharp change in the government, imposed for purely selfish reasons, may be followed by a number of other changes which would be bureaucratically impossible under less disturbed conditions.

This chapter has been devoted to discussing some of the structural characteristics of government which are relevant to coups d'état. In the next chapter, we will discuss the actual technique of the coup, and I shall propose a theory which I believe adequately describes the data. It should be recalled that the revolution is defined as a rising of the masses against the government, while the coup is a split within the government. The private individual in both cases will (as we have found) pay relatively little attention to the public good aspects of the matter and a great deal of attention to his private costs and rewards.

With respect to the private costs and rewards, private citizens and officials face radically different situations. The private citizen is engaged in making his living by some method outside the government. He can remain calmly engaged in this activity and avoid the risks of injury, etc., connected with the civil disturbance. The government official, on the other hand, has his job on the line. Neutrality or choice of the wrong side are both likely to lead to his being considerably injured. Further, it is harder for him to take an ambiguous role because he is almost certain to receive direct orders to participate one way or another. Under the circumstances, assuming that the private citizen and the government official are much alike in their personal preferences but in different situations, one would anticipate a very high participation rate on the part of public officials and a very low participation rate on the part of private citizens. This is true whether we are talking about a revolution or a coup d'état; but it means that the revolution involves a small part of the private citizens facing the entire government, while the coup d'état involves a large part of the government facing another large part of the government with, *perhaps*, some private citizens also engaged.

So much for motives. If we look at the organization characteristics of these two types of possible internal violence, we find another drastic difference. We have defined the revolution as an outside group rising against the government. Clearly, the government of necessity will be all on one side of such an uprising. Indeed, if a large part of the government joined with the oppressed mass, it becomes—in our definition—a coup d'état. Fortunately, historically we find few if any cases of this kind of thing, although we do find many cases in which an intragovernmental split has been discussed by the historians as if it were a rising of the "oppressed."

The government structure, if it is at all normal, will have organizations the specific purpose of which is to deal with private opposition. This will mainly be part of the police force, but military forces can also be called in. Further, the small portion of either the police or the military forces which are normally devoted to dealing with possible citizen dissidence can very readily be reinforced on a massive scale by transferring personnel from the suppression of ordinary crime and defense against foreign enemies which normally occupy the bulk of these two groups. Under the circumstances, it is likely that all but the most inefficient governments will be able to nip any revolutionary movement long before it becomes well enough organized to be, in any sense, a danger. A very small, decentralized group of persons opposed to the government and willing to commit common crimes can probably engage in such activities as robbing banks, shooting policemen, etc., on a small scale for fairly long periods of time; but this is unlikely to have any significant political effect.

The split within the government, on the contrary, is not faced by a well-organized and specialized opposition force because, if the government *does* have an organized security system, this organized security system may either split between the two sides or indeed be the principal source of opposition. Thus, the factors which militate so strongly against the success of a rising from *outside* the government in general do not have much effect on the probable success of a coup. Governments must turn to other means, and in fact much less efficient means, to protect themselves against internal dissidence.

THE THEORY OF THE COUP

Let us begin with the simplest and commonest form of violent overthrow of the government: a coup, pulled off by senior officials of a despotism. For example, Peron's overthrow of the colonels' clique in Argentina and, then, for another example, his own overthrow by other military men about 10 years later. The complicated events surrounding the replacement of Sukarno as ruler of Indonesia would be another example. Indeed, such coups are extremely common. Probably three-fourths of all successful violent overthrows in history have been of this sort, and it is also probable that three-fourths of the *unsuccessful* efforts have been of this type. Assume, then, a dictator at the head of a government. The fact that such people are frequently overthrown is, I think, a well-known one. It is also true, however, that many of them remain in power for very long periods of time. Indeed, it appears to be true that the longer a dictator has remained in power, the more likely he is to remain in power for another year. The reasons why this empirical observation is in accord with theoretical expectations will be given later.

The commonplace view of how dictators get overthrown is, I think, very much like this: The head of the army, becoming unhappy with the dictator, simply takes certain parts of the army and seizes or kills the dictator. There appear to have been some real-life examples of this type of revolution in recent years in Africa. The newly established dictators in the various countries which replaced colonial empires frequently had learned politics in a colonial environment in which coups d'état were not possible. Further, if they had studied political science academically, the literature they had studied had not discussed this matter. Under the circumstances, they did not realize the grave danger they were in. They permitted the head of their very small army to remain head and in unembarrassed control of the forces for a period of time long enough so that the army developed the habit of obeying the orders of that man.

At that point, the head of the army either removed the dictator or, in a few cases, was beaten by the renewed intervention of the colonial power. For example, the present dictator of Tanzania would have been removed by his army had he not been able to call in a British naval task force to defeat the

Reprinted, with permission, from *The Social Dilemma: The Economics of War and Revolution* (Blacksburg, Va.: Center for Study of Public Choice, 1974), 71–86.

army and reinstall him in power. The dictator of Togo was less fortunate. At the moment, many dictators of former parts of the French Empire depend on the *forces d'intervention* for their continuance in office, because they fear this kind of army.

Most dictators, however, and the bulk of the African dictators after the experience of the first few overthrows, have avoided this danger by a very simple technique. It is said that one of the Greek tyrants, on being asked by his son how he should rule after his father died, took him out into a field and cut the heads from the tallest flowers. Whether the legend is true or not, the advice is good. The dictator should see to it that there is no one in the government or, for that matter, in civil life who is of great personal prominence. As we shall see later, there is now a better explanation for this policy than the one given by the Greek tyrant. Nevertheless, it must be admitted that throughout history despots have, generally speaking, followed a policy of eliminating potential rivals.

It will be noted that this policy necessarily reduces the efficiency of the government. It makes it impossible to take full advantage of the most talented members of the body politic. In a sense, the risk that a very talented prime minister may replace the dictator is greater than the benefit he gives the dictator by efficiency in running the government. Rulers have been driven out eventually because, following this rule, they kept their government too weak. Whether they would have been wiser to run greater risks of being overthrown by high-ranking appointees and having more efficient high-ranking appointees, or the policy which in fact they *did* follow is not at all clear. My own personal preference, however, would be for keeping the central government weak.[1]

The single most dangerous person to the dictator in any government is an established successor. Most dictators are aware of this and attempt to prevent any individual from being formally invested with the right of succession until very late in the dictator's life. For example, Rankovic was removed from high position in Yugoslavia because his intent to succeed Tito became obvious. The

1. President Rhee of Korea was an outstanding example of the eventual failure of such a policy. For many years, he eliminated all people with great force of character from the higher ranks of his government. Because of his military situation, he could not do this with respect to his armed forces. There he required forceful generals if he were to remain protected against the Communists. When the clinch came, his civilian government was helpless and the army overthrew him. Nevertheless, he obtained nearly 17 years of control of a very turbulent country through his policy.

elimination of Liu Hsiao-chi in China is no doubt another example of this phenomenon.[2] The successor, of course, is the one man who can safely kill the current ruler. Historically, a major cause of the death of kings has been murder by their eldest sons. The Greek tyrant we were discussing should have kept this firmly in mind as he explained his methods of rule to his son. In any event, dictators have normally taken great precautions to see to it that no successor to their own office has been formally established until they are, themselves, on their death beds.

In addition, there are two other precautions which any dictator who does not wish to be overthrown should follow. The first is what used to be called by Mussolini "the changing of the guard."[3] From time to time, senior officials should be moved in and out of office and from one position to another. The purpose of this is to prevent them from developing permanent followings within their office. There are some offices, of course, in which the power content is so low that it is perfectly all right to leave one man in charge. The foreign office, for example, is unlikely to be able to muster enough force to throw out the dictator; hence, it is possible to keep a foreign secretary in office permanently. On the other hand, a foreign office secretary's job is one of great prestige, and it may be desirable to "promote" the commander of the army or the chief of secret police to this position as a way of reducing his power.[4]

This reshuffling of higher-level personnel is, once again, a cause of reduced efficiency for the government. It is notable that in the United States where cabinet members are not politically in a position to replace the president, such

2. His successor, Lin Piao, was one of the few prominent people in China whose general state of health was worse than that of Mao Tse-tung. In this respect he is rather like the man President Rhee selected as his vice president when I was in Korea. This man was the only prominent Korean politician who was older and more decrepit than President Rhee himself. Apparently, however, not even bad health could protect Lin against Mao's wrath. With his death and with no anointed successor, Mao's life expectancy has no doubt increased. Chou Enlai's, on the other hand, has decreased.

3. A low-level variant of this procedure was and, for all I know, still is used to guard all of the important offices of the Communist régime in Russia. The guards operate under a system known as checkerboard, under which their allocation among the various guard posts is determined by a throw of dice, and they are moved from post to post at random times, again as a result of the use of dice throws. This makes it impossible for any guard or any combination among the guards to plan in advance to admit an unauthorized person to the area.

4. Recently Tito installed Rankovic's successor as the chief of his secret police—a man who had been responsible for a very large number of murders of opponents of the Tito government—as prime minister, presumably for somewhat the same motives.

reshuffling is relatively rare. In England, on the other hand, the prime minister, if he is alert, carries through such changes fairly regularly in order to keep his inferiors in line. In this case, what he fears, of course, is not a military coup but a parliamentary coup. Indeed, to a considerable extent, forceful overthrow of government maps the strategic characteristics of democratic voting.

A final protection of the sovereign is a system of giving rewards to anyone who betrays a conspiracy against him. This is, of course, the reason Machiavelli felt it was astonishing that any conspiracies ever succeeded. Clearly, the dictator is in a position to offer a highly secure and very large reward to anyone betraying a conspiracy against him. The major problem this system raises is, of course, that false warnings of conspiracy are almost as convincing as genuine ones, since in most cases the conspiracy consists of little more than oral conversations among high-ranking officials. The dictator must put a good deal of effort into attempting to prevent false denunciations from being used to eliminate a large part of his staff. It is not to be expected that the dictator will be able to differentiate false and genuine denunciations with any high degree of accuracy. Under the circumstances, he may be better advised to "punish" such reported conspiracies by transfer of the alleged conspirators to less prominent positions, rather than by actually killing or imprisoning the "conspirators."

Whether this reward system for information on possible efforts to overthrow the dictator should or should not be administered through a separate section of the bureaucracy is an open question. Some dictators have done it one way, some another. In general, there is no doubt that efforts to keep *low-level* conspiracies in hand require a special police force, simply because there are so many people who could engage in such low-level conspiracies. On the other hand, historically, such low-level conspiracies do not appear to be terribly dangerous. The high-level conspiracies which are dangerous are not necessarily best treated by a specialized bureaucracy. For one thing, this portion of the bureaucracy is in and of itself a potential organizer of conspiracies. Altogether, in this aspect the life of the dictator is not an easy one, and it is probable that he will make many mistakes.

It will be seen that the defense a dictator has against being overthrown is, indeed, formidable. We should note again, however, that these defenses contribute to the inefficiency of the régime. Indeed, it may be that one of the reasons why charismatic leaders with rapidly expanding governments—for example, Napoleon's spread over the continent of Europe—seem to do so well is simply that the combination of a charismatic leader and a rapidly expanding power offers very large rewards for everyone in the upper ranks of government and makes overthrow of the government more difficult; hence, it is not necessary to use these inefficiency-generating precautions on such a large scale. On the other hand, it should be noted that Napoleon apparently liked to keep his generals quarreling.

With these precautions, then, how can a coup be organized? It seems to me unlikely that true, long-lasting, and elaborate conspiracies have often contributed to the overthrow of a ruler. Such conspiracies are almost certain to be betrayed, and in any event can be controlled by the combination of eliminating prominent persons and "the changing of the guard." This is particularly so today when recording devices of various sorts exist which can provide definite evidence of conspiracies, even if the conspiracies are entirely oral. The problem faced by the conspirators is not to keep the secret police from overhearing one of their discussions, but to prevent one of their own members from obtaining a permanent record of it which he can then use to betray the betrayers. This is, in general, a very difficult problem; hence, one can anticipate that there will be fewer formal conspiracies now than there were in the past. Since there probably were not a great many in any event, this is not a major change.

There is, incidentally, one area in which it seems likely that something close to a long-lasting conspiracy may in fact exist. This phenomenon occurs in countries like the South American countries, Greece, and probably the new African countries in which violent overthrows of the government by parts of the army (usually associated with some nonmilitary groups) are so common that eliminating all oral discussion of them would require excessive efforts. The officers' mess of a regiment which has participated in seven coups in the last twelve years is apt to devote part of its after-dinner coffee discussion to past coups and the possibilities of future ones. Efforts to completely bar such discussion would no doubt be taken by the officers as indication that a coup was imminent; hence, it would, if anything, make the government less secure than otherwise.

Under these circumstances, it is possible for sort of protoconspiracies to be almost in continuous existence. Since there normally will be a number of different cliques of officers, each of which is looking for an opportunity to replace the government, this is not a matter with which the government need concern itself too much. It has to worry about the prospect of one of these groups growing to dominate all the others—an unlikely event, granted the fissiparous nature of such operations—or something happening of the sort we will discuss later which puts one of these groups in a position to pull off a coup. The former problem can normally be detected without much difficulty by a rather simple police organization, since it will have to be known to a great many people before it becomes dangerous.

But what, then, is the actual method used to overthrow governments? Before discussing this, let me outline a very important discovery made by Thomas Schelling.[5] Schelling has discovered that human beings are sometimes capable of solving the apparently impossible problem of reaching agreement without any discussion. Let me give you as an example a game I used to play with students. I entered a classroom and told them that I was going to repeat a statement three times; they would be permitted to ask no questions about it at all (this was to prohibit communication between them), and they were then to write down the answer to a question on paper and hand it in. The question I asked was: "Assume that a wealthy man agrees to give each of you $100 if tomorrow at three o'clock you all meet at the same place without discussing beforehand where you will meet. Where would you go at three o'clock tomorrow?"[6]

My students always gave the general impression on hearing this question that they thought their instructor had suddenly gone insane. A number of them gave the impression that they had long been anticipating this. Nevertheless, when they wrote the answer down on their sheets of paper to humor the instructor and prevent him from becoming violent, it never turned out that less than three-quarters of them had specified the classroom in which they were presently located as the place where they would meet. It also never turned out that *all* of them did so.

The Schelling explanation of this phenomenon is that, in any social situation, there *may* be what I call a "Schelling point." This is a position, argument, or what have you which is somehow more conspicuous than other positions. Thus, when people are offered an opportunity to make gains by all doing the same thing without being told what it is, each tries to anticipate what the other will do under these circumstances, and they tend to end up on these points of great conspicuousness. Schelling, who was then on the faculty at Yale, began his experimentation by asking people at Yale where they would go if they had to meet in New York without previous communication. It

5. Thomas C. Schelling, *Strategy of Conflict* (Cambridge, Mass.: Harvard University Press, 1960).

6. This was at the University of Virginia where the honor system could be relied upon, at least in a game, to prevent such discussion.

turned out, of course, to be the information booth in Grand Central Station. There are other similar examples. Needless to say, there is no rule that a social situation must have a Schelling point, and if there are several places of great conspicuousness, it is extremely difficult to predict the one to which other people will go. Situations do arise, however, in which there is a clear Schelling point and in which people in search of profit will meet at that point.

Schelling has worked out a great number of situations in the real world in which the conditions necessary for this phenomenon occur. The first requirement is that the parties not be permitted to communicate or that if they are permitted to communicate, each one of them has strong reasons to distrust what the others say; hence, there is no true communication, only an exchange of verbiage. The second requirement is that each of them know that all will make profits if they all reach an implicit agreement on action. Most of his examples are economic, but the idea has great political importance. To a considerable extent, the decision by any politician as to which nominee for the presidency of the United States he should back will depend on his judgment as to how many other people will be attracted by the same candidate. Thus everyone is attempting to guess what everyone else is going to do, and if there happens to be some obvious and conspicuous candidate, he will normally be selected. Candidates thus make strong efforts to convince everyone that they will eventually be the winner, because this is the way to become the winner. Although there is a great deal of bargaining between candidates and potential supporters, the communication value of this bargaining is relatively low because both parties realize that they cannot rely upon promises.

The phenomenon of the Schelling point provides us with an explanation of how a coup d'état can be carried out without very much in the way of advanced planning. Assume a government in which there is one dictator, some senior officials of varying rank, and a large number of junior officials. Presumably everyone in this system is interested (a) in keeping his present job and (b) in moving to a higher level. This improvement is particularly important in this case because it should be noted that the individuals will be gaining substantial rents after they acquire new jobs. The possession of a monopoly by the government is an extremely valuable resource, and it is not salable.[7] It is normally obtained, one way or another, by use of force and violence or, in a democracy, by winning elections. Thus the transfer from one person

7. Small parts of the monopoly may be salable. Sale of individual offices is quite a common phenomenon historically.

to another works a very great improvement in the wealth of the person who receives this government office with its accompanying rents, and works a very great reduction on the person who loses it. The limitations on these rents, which can be quite severe in democracy, are relatively modest in despotisms.

Assume, then, that substantially everybody in the government would like to move up and is also interested in avoiding moving down. We have briefly surveyed how the dictator takes advantage of these motives to keep himself in power. It is obvious that these motives also provide the necessary incentives for a coup. The only question is how can such a coup be organized. As a first step, it is obvious that the person who replaces the dictator gains very sharply by this change, and the dictator loses. Further, the person who gains can, at the very least, reward some other person by moving him into the job that he himself vacated, and then reward other people by successive promotions into the successively vacated jobs.[8] Clearly this technique, however, offers only rather modest rewards to those who join the coup and, I think, has only been rather rarely applied. Perhaps the replacement of Salazar by Caetano in Portugal is an example. In those cases where the government is weak enough (Salazar was in a coma) so that a very tiny coup, widely accepted by the entire government apparatus, is possible, such modest rewards may be adequate.

In the more normal case, however, it is necessary to provide more extensive and more widespread rewards. These can be done very readily by removing not only the dictator, but a number of his other officials. Thus a coup results not only in the replacement of the dictator by a man of lower rank, but in the replacement of a number of senior officials by people of lower rank. An extreme, almost comic, example was Batista's original seizure of power in Cuba. In this operation, the sergeants of the Cuban army, led by Telephone Technical Sergeant Batista, took over the government. In the more normal operation, nothing quite so drastic takes place. Let us say that half of the "cabinet" is removed and replaced, partly by cabinet ministers whose previous ministry was of less importance and partly by deputy cabinet ministers.

However, the fact that a number of people must be removed to provide rewards for the supporters of the coup means that there are a number of people

8. This assumes, of course, that the previous government was exploiting the full strength of its position. If it was not, the creation of additional jobs or the increasing of the pay and perquisites of existing jobs would be possible.

who have material motives to oppose it. Further, if the despot is able to remain in control, presumably he will remove everyone who was involved in the coup; hence, there will be a number of promotions available for his supporters. Thus, there are strong motives for participation in the coup on both sides. As demonstrated in the last chapter, neutrality is by no means a safe course of action. The dictator, if he wins, is likely to feel that any official who did not support him during the crisis lacks the requisite loyalty to keep his position, while the organizers of the coup are also unlikely to be very enthusiastic about the neutral. Thus, playing an important role in the victory of either side is likely to be highly rewarded. Playing an important role in the activities of the losers is likely to be severely penalized. Remaining neutral is also likely to be penalized, but less severely. Under the circumstances, it is very important to get on the right side. On the other hand, getting on the wrong side can have disastrous consequences. Further, a careful and protracted weighing of the alternatives is apt to be somewhat dangerous. Last but not least, calling up the two sides and asking which one can offer the most is likely to give both of them the impression that you are not particularly reliable. Thus, in the long run, *that* may pay off badly, too; although something along this line (but much more tactful) usually occurs.

It will be seen that the conditions are suitable for the development of the kind of process I have associated with the Schelling point, provided there is a Schelling point in existence. There clearly is one example of a Schelling point, i.e., the current despot. Indeed, it is likely that the strength of his position is one of the more important causes of its strength; as long as everyone thinks that he will win, he will win. Thus, the longer a régime has been in power, the more likely it is to be able to stay in power. On the other hand, if the régime is showing signs of weakness or ineptitude in one field, this may indicate that it will also be weak and inept in dealing with the coup; hence, this is reason for ambitious men to think in terms of replacing it.

On the other side, if the despot has been efficient, there will be no obvious alternative Schelling point, but there may be a person or group of men who can quickly turn themselves into a Schelling point by producing what appears to be a viable alternative to the despot.[9] The "pronunciamiento" of the South American revolution is an important example of this phenomenon. The sudden announcement of opposition by a group of high officials in

9. In some South American and African cases, the Schelling point was a man who built or maintained his image in exile; hence, he was out of reach of the current dictator.

the régime, even if the group is small, immediately compels all the other officials to decide which side they will join. If we assume that whichever side attracts the largest collection of senior officials will win, then the one that gives the best impression of being about to win will, in fact, win. This impression, of course, must not be given to the average newspaper reader, but to a group of highly informed senior officials, who are not only in possession of a number of confidential sources of information but also have subtle (not to say devious) minds. Under the circumstances, what is necessary is a "show of strength" by both parties, and this is indeed what we observe.

Normally these pronunciamientos involve not only a statement that a coup is under way, but also general statements about policy. It seems likely that for most of the higher officials, policy matters are not of first importance, and the decision to join or not to join a coup depends on estimates of the private costs and benefits, rather than public goods. Thus the really important part of the pronunciamiento is the simple announcement of the uprising, together with some propaganda as to its strength. Normally, however, these pronunciamientos contain general statements about policy as well, sometimes in great detail. The government is to be overthrown because it has made various policy mistakes.

As we have noted above, it is unlikely that people who rise to high rank in governments will pay a great deal of attention to public good considerations. Further, it is likely that they have strong preferences for getting and maintaining power. Under these circumstances, it is likely that the "policy" portion of the pronunciamiento has relatively small effect. Nevertheless, the cost of making a lengthy statement in favor of virtue and against vice is very small, and it certainly is not going to cause any great difficulties. Further, it may be that such a general statement can be so organized as to offer implicit promises of private benefits to a large number of people. Thus, the proposal to nationalize foreign investments is a proposal to hire a large number of intellectuals for jobs for which they are not really qualified, and at salaries they could not earn in a competitive environment. Still, it seems likely that the general course of developments in a coup would be little affected if these policy statements were left out. But, to repeat what we said before, the cost of making them is very low and they might conceivably do some good.

The coup may not be just a matter of attracting a majority of the officials, however. Officials can be subtracted from your opponent's coalition by killing them, or by imprisoning them, or by cutting off their communications. In particular, getting rid of the despot by killing him at the very beginning of the operation may be an excellent technique. It has the disadvantage that the new despot may feel that killing the assassin of the old despot is a good idea, either as part of the rise to power (this gives him legitimacy) or after he has obtained power, in order to make it clear that the precedent is not a good one. This phenomenon was important in the Roman polity in the first and second centuries A.D.

Killing of other officials is frequently very important. It will be recalled that the Communist coup which aborted in Indonesia did so, to a considerable extent, because, although they killed the bulk of the military high command, they did not get quite all of it. Hitler's "Night of the Long Knives," in which he destroyed a potential opposition within his own Nazi party, is an example of successful preventive measures to avoid coup. The Nazis later, in Brazil, ruined their own position by attempting to pull off a similar coup in which they were to kill the dictator. Vargas was at that time very friendly to the Fascist powers, but the plot failed, and he, quite naturally, took umbrage.

Execution is, of course, not necessary; imprisonment will frequently do as well, although it requires somewhat unusual facilities. The imprisoned official can normally make a quite credible promise to his guards that they will all be majors if they let him go. Under the circumstances, very special arrangements are necessary to keep senior officials in prison. Prevention of communication between potential opponents, either of the coup or of the dictator, is another important matter. Physical seizure of radio stations, telephone exchanges, highway intersections, etc., are methods of cutting off communication.[10]

Although more often than not, the impression that one party will win is given by the accession to it of a number of senior officials, in some cases a different route is followed. What happens, simply, is that certain military or police units who are obviously capable of winning adhere to the group that will win. The higher officials observe the balance of forces and, in essence, join the winning side after it has been determined. Here again, deception is possible and the coup group or the despot may give the impression of having far more military support than they actually do. Methods of doing this are innumerable; perhaps the simplest is a quick seizure of the capital city with a small part of the armed forces. The government of Iraq was once overthrown because a division of infantry, moving from one part of the country to the other, passed through the capital, and its general took advantage of the opportunity. The

10. Almost all of the latter considerations are discussed in considerable detail in Edward Luttwak, *Coup d'Etat* (New York: Knopf, 1969).

fact that he had relatively weak military support was not obvious until it was much too late.

In the study of the coalition process in democracies, James Coleman, and William Riker and Steven Brams have looked into the value of accession of one more person to a coalition and, hence, the maximum reward which can be given to a member.[11] The Riker-Brams formalism provides also for payoff for defection from coalitions once they are formed. It will not be any surprise to hear that these mathematical formulations include a value for remaining aloof, which changes as the coalition formation goes ahead, and a value for joining either of the coalitions (or for that matter, defecting). In the early range, the value of joining either coalition is less than the value of remaining neutral and awaiting further developments. This neutral status in this particular model does not mean that you will remain permanently neutral, but simply that you are temporarily neutral in order to get better information before committing yourself.

After a short time, however, the coalition process passes what Riker and Brams call the "take-off point." From here on, the expected value of joining a coalition is greater than that of remaining neutral. This simply means that entering a coalition *A*, you will contribute enough to its probable victory so that the managers of the coalition will be well-advised to promise you something which, discounted by that probable victory, is greater than the value you can anticipate from holding out and choosing between the two coalitions later. In general, joining the more powerful of the two coalitions has a higher payoff than joining the less powerful, for obvious reasons. Further, there is a golden period for joining. For a short time after the take-off point is reached, the returns from joining are greater than the returns which can be anticipated from waiting and making up your mind later. After a time, however, the returns fall.

Thus it is important not only to guess which coalition will win, but to do it fast enough so that you enter the coalition at a time when your entrance is still valuable enough to the coalition managers so that they are willing to reward you highly. Clearly, the intellectual task confronting the official at the time of a coup is a difficult one, and he must not only make his decision rapidly, he

11. See James S. Coleman, "The Benefits of Coalition," *Public Choice*, 8 (Spring, 1970), 45–61; and Steven J. Brams and William H. Riker, "Models of Coalition Formation in Voting Bodies," *Mathematical Applications in Political Science*, 6, ed. James F. Herndon and Joseph L. Bernd (Charlottesville: University Press of Virginia, 1972).

must conceal from everyone concerned the fact that he is wavering, and he must avoid being killed or captured. Altogether, it is not a pleasant experience, but the people who undergo it, after all, have voluntarily sought out this line of work, and we have no reason to feel sorry for them.

So far we have assumed that everyone engages in careful calculation and makes the best decision available. We have had little or nothing to say about such emotional concepts as loyalty, devotion to the good, etc. In my opinion, these concepts do play a relatively modest role in most coups. It should be noted, however, that something rather like "loyalty" is apt to be part of the make-up of any high-ranking government official in a despotism or, indeed, in a democracy. If the official is to retain his position, he must devote a good deal of time to operating his department and to improving his relations with other people who are close to the despot. Thus it is not sensible for him to continually devote time to considering the prospects of a coup. Only when these prospects rise above a certain threshold of value should he turn his attention to them. Thus, information considerations and problems of decision-time mean that the government official will, if he is sensible, behave "loyally" until such time as the prospects of successful coup seem to be quite high.

The Schelling point, together with those aspects of coalition theory which indicate likelihood of a cascade effect if coalition appears to be moving toward success, provides an explanation for a coup which does not require a long-standing conspiracy. This is no doubt the common pattern, although there are occasional examples of coups with considerable advance planning. In most cases, the coup is, of necessity, carried out without too much in the way of advance plan. At most, individual senior officials may have trusted juniors producing plans which *can* be put into effect if sufficient support materializes. In those cases in which coups are very common and therefore the armed forces are familiar with them, this type of planning may be more highly developed than in dictatorships where coups are less common.[12]

So far we have discussed why individuals would join a coup, not the decision process which might lead people to "entrepreneur" one. In essence, what happens is that a number of high officials—or in some cases low officials who happen to have access to exceptional opportunities, like the division commander passing through Baghdad—quickly take action which is intended to set off the kind of cascade effect we have described. However, the group that issues the pronunciamiento or the small unit which simply grabs can hardly

12. Luttwak discusses in some detail the nature of the plan in *Coup d'Etat*.

be making the type of calculation described above. What they do, of course, is observe a situation in which they believe that a sudden move will set off a cascade toward themselves. Since the profits of pulling off such a coup are very great (albeit the dangers of failure are also great), profit-seeking individuals might be expected to look for such opportunities. It would not be sensible to invest large amounts of time in this search, since this would tend to lead to a reduction in your position in the continuing competition *within* the despotic government; but still some attention should always be given to the possibility of such operations.

Presumably, opportunities for a successful coup occur even in the best-run dictatorships. We would assume that the possibility of a coup is essentially a random variable which, at most times, has a value close to zero. Occasionally the internal structure of the government could be such that a coup attempt would be sensible. The variables would involve such matters as the exact posts currently held by various high officials, the state of efficiency and loyalty to their present commanders of various military units, etc. General policy issues and public good considerations would, I think, be relatively unimportant in the actual decisions of the organizers of a coup. They might, however, play quite an important role in the communication process.

Let us suppose that the government has just done something which is clearly a bad mistake from the standpoint of general policy. Under these circumstances, one anticipates two effects which can then lead toward a coup. Firstly, this bad mistake is, in and of itself, evidence that the organization is not functioning at full efficiency. Thus, the possibility that the dictator is beginning to lose his grip in other areas, as well as in his policy decisions, immediately occurs to anyone who is even remotely considering the possibility of a coup. Needless to say, this would not be conclusive information but at least is suggestive.

Secondly, if the government has done something a large number of people in the upper ranks of the government regard as a policy mistake, then discussing this particular policy mistake will be far simpler and safer than any ordinary criticism of government functioning. Once the officials, army men, etc., are talking about some particular thing that the government has recently done which is thought by many to be a mistake, it becomes much easier to express criticism and to assess the likely "loyalty" of other members of the bureaucracy by noting what they say about this particular criticism.

One of the presidents of Ecuador was overthrown because he was obviously drunk at a formal dinner and said some things to the American ambassador that were injudicious. It is extremely unlikely that the people who then overthrew him actually objected to what he had said, since the point of view he expressed was one widely held in high government circles in Ecuador, both before and after the coup. It is clear, however, that a great many high-ranking officials, military and other, spent the period (and it was a short one) between the time he made this drunken display and the time he was removed making remarks about the disadvantages of having a boor and a drunkard as president. Clearly, this discussion permitted various members to assess the likelihood of success in a coup, because they could observe the fact that most government officials were making these nasty cracks about their president.

This is an extreme example; but probably the same kind of thing goes on very frequently. It is dangerous for a dictator to do something which leads to widespread criticism, not because the act itself is dangerous but because the widespread criticism provides improved information for people planning a coup; hence, the coup becomes more likely to occur.

To return to the defenses a dictator possesses, we have mentioned that he should attempt to prevent anyone from becoming too prominent and should regularly rotate his higher officials. The cost of this process to the government as a whole is, I suppose, obvious. Strictly speaking, the rulers of despotisms should attempt to extract maximum rents; hence, they should be interested in their societies running at maximum efficiency. The continued potential of a coup, which displaces the current rulers with others, is a very strong limitation on this efficiency. Once again, the prisoner's dilemma applies. If the dictator always makes decisions which maximize the net value of the state, he is likely to be replaced because somewhere along the line he will put highly competent and ambitious people into positions where they can overthrow him. On the other hand, officials who always make decisions in terms of increasing the power of the state are apt to lame themselves in terms of their preparation for a potential coup. Thus, the state does not reach maximum efficiency in exploitation of its citizens, simply because individual rationality conflicts with "group rationality." Note that there is no a priori reason to believe that the common citizen gains from this lack of exploitative efficiency, although, of course, he may do so.

So far we have been talking about the coup which is the common way in which a despotism is switched to the control of another despot. If we survey history, however, we find a number of cases in which there is quite extensive internal warfare within a country, rather than the quick change we have been describing. The commonest single cause for such revolutions is simply that the coup for one reason or another goes wrong. A group planning to overthrow the despot does not win immediately, but nevertheless feels that the prospects for victory are still strong enough so that it is worthwhile to keep the rebellion going. The despot makes a similar decision, and large-scale fighting between the two sides develops. A necessary condition for this phenomenon to develop is that the two sides each come to dominate a geographic area of the country. If the forces are intermixed, the fighting may be desperate, but it is certain to lead to a quick conclusion. Eventually, one side or the other will win. The costs of this type of operation are obviously very great.

It should be noted, however, that here again all the individuals are behaving rationally. This is particularly so since as the revolution grows more and more extensive—as the casualties mount up—the likelihood of severe penalties for the losers increases. Further, these severe penalties are likely to be put not only on the senior officials, but on their juniors, too. The private in a regiment participating in a coup can, after the coup is put down, claim with a great deal of plausibility that he was simply obeying his officers and had no idea what was going on. It is unlikely that he could maintain, after two years of civil war, that he had not realized he was opposed to the dictator who eventually won. He could not even claim with any degree of plausibility that he had no opportunity to desert. Further, the winner in the civil war is likely to have strong emotional drives to punish his opponents and to require much in the way of resources to reward his supporters for their efforts.

Nevertheless, the possibility of a composition of the differences between the two revolutionary groups or an agreement by one party to grant amnesty to the members of the other is always open. This would be a case where, once again, the prisoner's dilemma applies. The reason for the prisoner's dilemma in this case is, of course, that if one side promises amnesty and good treatment to the other in return for the second side laying down its arms, there is no force compelling it to keep its promises. Machiavelli argued that you should never tell a person to "lay down your arms so that I may kill you." Say, "lay down your arms," and then do what you wish.

On occasion, civil wars may start without any coup-type activities at the beginning. Thus, some officer or other leader who feels that the forces under his command are strong enough to conquer the government may start a civil war with the idea of winning through large-scale warfare. This was, of course, the idea of Charles I when he raised his standard against Parliament. Presumably it was also the idea in the minds of the founders of the Confederate States of America. The methods used by the despot to avoid this kind of thing are much the same as those required to prevent a coup, except that he must apply them geographically in more distant areas. In general, the pure coup can only be pulled off by people in the capital city because of the concentration of the government there. However, a civil war may start far away and, if it has the necessary military resources, still win.

A common type of civil war results from the desire of people in some particular geographical area to break away from the control of the central government. This type of civil war is, I think, more likely to be successful than that which attempts to overthrow the central government, because of the limited nature of the objectives espoused. Further, it may be possible to get a good deal more in the way of support in a limited geographical area for the independence of that area than is available throughout an entire country for the overthrow of the existing despotism. If the geographical area which is potentially revolutionary is occupied by people who are quite different from the remainder of the citizens of the country—a minority group of some sort or perhaps in some cases a majority group—then special measures may be necessary on the part of the government. The present government of Syria, for example, is essentially a very small religious sect which is in control of the officer corps of the army. In order to avoid overthrow by the rest of the country, they have had to carry out a number of careful measures to break up power of possible competing groups, including fairly extensive executions of people selected on essentially sociological grounds.

A geographically limited revolution aimed at breaking off from the main government is easier to compromise, because of the fact that it is possible for the central government to offer to the rebels a deal, in which they will remain fairly safe even if the government does change its mind. If the rebels cease fighting but retain their arms, it would, on the whole, be somewhat risky for the central government to decide to shoot all of their leaders.

In general, the odds are in favor of the existing despot and against those who wish to overthrow him. Indeed, we can say that a prudent and active despot will normally be able to prevent any coup or revolution. This may not be true in old age, partly because his powers are genuinely failing and partly because it will be obvious to all the officials of the government that he *is* going to be removed by natural causes in the near future; hence, retaining his favor is of less value.

The romantic popular uprising against a despotism has not so far been discussed because, as a matter of fact, it is a very rare phenomenon. There have, however, been some cases, and it is sensible to discuss them briefly here. First, a government may be so inefficient that it has both infuriated the population of its capital city and not provided adequate military support for itself. Under these circumstances, street rioting may lead to the physical elimination of the senior officials. There are a number of cases of this kind of thing happening in the Moslem world. Needless to say, the outcome is normally the establishment of a new despotism which, in the first few months, makes some efforts to be "popular." A second type of popular uprising against a despotism may occur through progressive loss of intellectual legitimacy. Consider, for example, Japan. From about 1000 A.D. the mikado of Japan was simply a religious figure with no political power. Political power was held by powerful feudal lords, and during the last 250 years, by the Tokugawa shoguns. The Tokugawa ran a highly totalitarian government with thought control and with a firm realization that any center of opposition might be dangerous. They included the mikado on their list of potentially dangerous people, and kept him under very close guard.

In spite of these precautions, a few years after Perry had opened Japan to the West, the emperor issued an edict removing the Tokugawa shogun, and it was generally accepted. The young man who had succeeded to the shogunate, in fact, accepted it himself. The explanation for this astonishing chain of events is simply that over the 250 years that the Tokugawa had ruled Japan, the view that the mikado actually should rule Japan and that the shogun was an illegitimate ruler became orthodox. How this happened, in spite of the totalitarian controls on thought by the Tokugawa, is an interesting subject which, so far as I know, has never been carefully studied. Once it had happened, however, almost everyone in Japan assumed that the mikado could and would win because everybody else would back him. Under the circumstances, his overthrow of the government of the Tokugawa was as easy as de Gaulle's overthrow of the Fourth Republic in 1958.

In a way, the Russian February Revolution of 1917 and the French Revolution of 1789 are examples of the same phenomenon. In both cases, it is probable that opposition to the reigning dynasty and a feeling that a change to democratic methods was desirable was commoner in the government bureaucracy than in any other part of the population. The professional civil servants and lower-ranking military officers tended to see the existing monarchial institutions as something which restrained them from very high office and which introduced occasionally totally incompetent superiors. The fact that it also gave them the particular offices they did have was not clear in their minds. Further, it should be said that, in general, they did rather well from their revolutions, although in the case of the Russians, the second (Bolshevik) revolution injured most of those civil servants who gained from the first (democratic) revolution. In my opinion, there should be a careful examination of the methods which made it possible for the bulk of the governing apparatus (as well as everyone else) within the states, which were despotic and which had rather elaborate mechanisms for thought control, to become convinced that the government should be replaced by something else.

Popular uprisings which are successful in overthrowing governments are rare historically and arise from very special circumstances. The government must be extremely inefficient. Further, in most cases, it must, in essence, either tolerate or actively encourage the organization of the "popular" forces. Here again, there is no doubt a large loss of efficiency from the government's continuous intervention to prevent such organization. Once again, however, the prisoner's dilemma applies, and such intervention is indeed rational.

COUPS AND THEIR PREVENTION

It may seem odd to begin our discussion of absolutist government not with the way one becomes a dictator but with the way one keeps the dictatorship once one has it. This is dealing with the second stage, not the first stage, of the careers of most dictators. Nevertheless, for most dictators the period which they are in power is much longer than the period in which they achieve power. There is also a structural reason. In order to understand the problems faced by a man attempting to seize power, it is necessary to have a good idea of the barriers which were placed in his way by the existing dictator. The internal history of any dictatorship is largely a jockeying for power. The dictator lives continuously under the Sword of Damocles and equally continuously worries about the thickness of the thread. His high-ranking courtiers, on the other hand, are well advised to shake their heads in order to make certain they are still firmly attached every time they leave his presence. Of course, politics in most modern dictatorships is not as bloody as that in the ancient autocracies which led to these two legends, but great personal insecurity is still part of them.

In any event, we're going to talk about how you keep power if you are a dictator or king. There are, of course, differences between the hereditary monarchy and the ordinary dictatorship. Indeed, as a rough rule of thumb, historically, dictatorships are transitory, with the eventual switch to hereditary control being likely. The Duvalier "presidency" of Haiti, which lasted two generations,[1] and the apparent establishment of the Kim dynasty in North Korea[2] are, I believe, merely the precursors of what will, with time, become the normal procedure. The situation in Singapore is less clear, but apparently

Reprinted, with kind permission of Kluwer Academic Publishers, from *Autocracy* (Dordrecht and Boston: Kluwer Academic Publishers, 1987), 17–34. Copyright 1987 Martinus Nijhoff Publishers, Dordrecht.

1. François Duvalier was dictator of Haiti from 1957 to 1971 and was succeeded by his son, Jean-Claude. Both proclaimed themselves "president for life." Although the son was eventually overthrown, he was ruler for a longer period than his father.

2. The North Korean dictator Kim Il Sung has publicly designated his eldest son, Kim Jong Il, his successor and has taken the precaution of ordering the state-controlled press to print numerous stories concerning the son's infallibility ("So This Is Paradise: North Korea Will Be More Perfect When the Great Leader Meets His Maker," *Washington Post* October 31, 1982, p. c1).

the throne will be hereditary.[3] Enver Hoxha, the dictator of Albania, 1945–1985, actively promoted his son as his successor,[4] but the son failed to take control when his father died.

The Somoza family governed Nicaragua through three generations, and Trujillo would probably have been able to pass the throne on to his son if the American navy had not intervened. Looking over the long reach of history, the usual situation is a hereditary succession interrupted from time to time by dynastic overthrows.

But there are differences between the hereditary king system and the dictatorship. Firstly, the change of dictator is apt to be a fairly disturbing event; occasionally large numbers of people are killed. There are some technical ways of avoiding that, which I will discuss later, but normally transmission from one dictator to another is a rough period. The succession in the royal dynasty usually is not, although quarrels within the ruling family, or between it and other families, can cause a good deal of bloodshed.

The second major difference here is that the kings, through the accidents of gene selection, can be fairly stupid and inept people. Louis XVI, of course, is a good example. Dictators, on the other hand, although they may not be nice people, are pretty invariably talented. They tend to be intelligent, tough, and aggressive. They also tend to be much less secure than a hereditary monarch. Napoleon is sometimes quoted as having said that a hereditary monarch could go out every summer for ten years and lose a battle and then return to his capital and live quite happily, but that he (i.e., Napoleon) would be finished if he lost one battle. This is a slight exaggeration, but it does point in the generally correct direction.

In this chapter I'm going to talk mainly about dictators rather than hereditary monarchs, mainly because they are much commoner in the present-day world. Having said that I'm going to talk about how dictators stay in power, I must now once again confess that I do not have a general theory of dictatorship or a general theory of how dictators stay in power. I've been concerned about the problem of dictatorship for almost as long as I've been interested in Public Choice. Indeed, my first work on what now is thought of as Public Choice was undertaken while I was in Communist China, and I was

3. Prime Minister Lee Kuan Tew, the dictator of Singapore, appears as of this writing to be grooming his son Lee Hsien Loong as his successor, *Wall Street Journal*, October 8, 1984, p. 31.

4. James Dunnigan and Stephen Bay, *A Quick and Dirty Guide to War: Briefings on Present and Potential Wars* (New York: William Morrow, 1985), 78.

thinking more of the government there than I was of democracies. The reasons that my writings have mainly been concerned with democracies is simply that dictatorship turns out to be a very difficult subject.

Theoretically, the problem of maintaining power in a dictatorship is really very similar to that of maintaining a majority for redistributional purposes in a voting body. It is easily demonstrated, of course, that it is always possible to build a majority against any particular program of redistribution by offering something to the "out's" on the original program and fairly high payment to a few of the "in's."

The situation in a dictatorship is similar. It is always possible, at least in theory, to collect a group of people which is more powerful than the group supporting the status quo. This group will be composed of important officials of the regime who could benefit from its overthrow and their concomitant promotion. The reason that this is so is that the rewards now being received by the supporters of the status quo, and it should be kept in mind that the dictator himself usually is very well paid, are available for redistribution to their successors.

As an example, which doesn't really fit most dictatorships, but nevertheless may be familiar, suppose that Reagan is a dictator in the United States and that his cabinet is in complete control. The ambitious secretary of state, shall we say, offers to the undersecretary of defense a promotion to secretary of defense and makes similar offers to other officials. Since the dictator himself and his prominent supporters are to be removed, there is clearly plenty of room for the promotion of other people. This is like the circulating majority problem in a democratic voting body.

It should be said here that it's something of a mystery why the voting bodies do not behave in the highly unstable way that the Arrow Theorem would imply they should. Indeed, I have been conducting a long debate on this subject under the title "Why So Much Stability" in my journal.[5] The purpose here, however, is not to contribute to that debate, but to discuss the dictatorial counterpart.

How, then, does the dictator avoid this problem? The first thing to be said is that most of them don't avoid it permanently. There have been many dictators who have died peacefully in office, and over time the tendency for rulers to pass the throne on to their sons has been strong. Although there have been many such dictators, the number who have been overthrown is much larger. Thus the problem I have stated, although successfully solved by some dicta-

5. *Public Choice.* It has now lasted three years and shows no sign of ending.

tors, has not yet been solved by all. Even those who are overthrown, however, have usually a number of years of success before the overthrow occurs.

Traditional discussions of dictatorships rarely bring this matter up. The problem, however, surely dominates the activities of the dictator. To quote an American euphemism, "In order to be a great Senator, one must first of all be a Senator." Similarly, if you are to do anything as a dictator, you must first of all be a dictator.

I am not here discussing the overthrow of the dictator by popular forces. If the police and army are even reasonably efficient and willing to shoot to kill, that won't happen. Indeed, I'm not positive there is any clear-cut case of a popular overthrow of the government. Generally speaking, it is a fight within the government itself, although the government may have democratic aspects. In the United States, for example, the local legislatures and sheriffs of the thirteen colonies were already elected.[6] These elected legislatures threw out the royal governors. This was clearly a fight within the government rather than a rising against the government. I believe that most other cases of what is claimed to be democratic overthrow of dictatorial regimes will be shown to have the same pattern, although I cannot claim to have made a careful study of all of them.

Characteristically, however, the overthrow of the dictator simply means that there will be another dictator. This second dictator will normally announce that he has popular support, and for that matter, he may have it at the beginning. Basically, however, it is one dictator replacing another, and the policies they follow will probably not be radically different. If we look at the world, we quickly realize that these policies will not be radically different from those that would be followed by a democracy either.

Here we must point out once again that the modern totalitarian dictators, Hitler, Stalin, Mao Tse-tung, Pol Pot, are exceptional and unusual people, and I'm not talking about them here. I suggest that the reader think of Francisco Franco, a more normal dictator, even though he originally maintained that he was a follower of Mussolini and Hitler. It's hard to find any policy other than keeping power which he followed throughout his reign. Although he, of course, prevented centers of opposition from developing, his government was not violently oppressive.

As mentioned before, during most of his reign, Spain had no death penalty. The reinstitution of the death penalty in his last year came after extremely severe provocation in which his political opponents had "executed" something

6. Bernhard Knollenberg, *The Origin of the American Revolution, 1759–1766* (New York: Free Press, 1961), 49–57.

like one hundred of Franco's supporters. Even here, when they murdered his prime minister, instead of striking back hard he chose to make concessions and selected as the new prime minister a man who was thought to be more acceptable to his opponents. All of this is not intended to argue for Franco's regime; in fact, I think it was a very poor government. Nevertheless, it was not a violently repressive regime. Franco in no way compares with Pol Pot.[7]

But this has been a digression. Let us return to our main topic of how the dictator holds his power, in spite of the fact that he will inevitably be in a position where a coalition of, let us say, the commander of his army and the chief of the secret police could jointly remove him while benefiting themselves.[8] Hume pointed out that although a ruler could rule the people by the power of his police and army, he could not rule the police and army by that power. As he put it, rule depended on opinion.[9]

It seems to me that this insight of Hume, like most of Hume's other insights, was an extremely good one. Hume did not, however, properly describe the opinion. I should like to repair this deficit and say the opinion which a dictator must maintain among the people around him is not so much that he is a good, just, or God-ordained dictator, but simply that if it comes to an effort to overthrow him he will win.

A more modern social scientist than Hume, Schelling, has pointed out the situation in which people can agree without discussing the matter in advance. If there are a number of people, all of whom will gain a great deal if they make the same choice and all of whom will lose if they do not make the same choice, there may be certain characteristics of the environment which act as cues and lead them to, in fact, make the same choice. On the other hand, of course, there may not.[10]

7. John Trythall, *Franco: A Biography* (London: Macmillan, 1970).

8. It's very hard to tell who will remove you. Batista was a mere sergeant when he staged his first successful revolution. He and his fellow noncoms removed most of the regular officers of the army and appointed themselves in their place (Paul Johnson, *Modern Times: The World from the Twenties to the Eighties* [New York: Harper and Row, 1983], 619; Hugh Thomas, *Cuba, or the Pursuit of Freedom* [London: Macmillan, 1971], 639). The current dictators of Surinam and Liberia did somewhat the same thing (on Surinam, see *New York Times*, February 26, 1980, p. 5; on Liberia, see *New York Times*, April 13, 1980, p. 1).

9. David Hume, *Essays, Literary, Moral, and Political* (London: Ward, Lock, 1870), 23.

10. Schelling's first example involved two people who would be highly rewarded if they met in New York without prior consultation. He (at the time a professor at Yale) reasoned that each would independently go to the information booth in Grand Central Station.

For a political example, let us consider the Brams and Riker view of what happened in American nominating conventions back in the days when the convention was not a mere puppet of pre-existing primaries. All of the people attending the convention were professional politicians who hoped very strongly to be rewarded because they had provided support for whoever was nominated as president. On the other hand, usually they didn't know when they arrived who was going to be nominated. There was then a cautious feeling out of the situation, with individuals moving to the support of whoever they thought was, in fact, going to win. The early movement tended to give more information to others, and very quickly everyone was rushing to get on the bandwagon of the winner. Those who waited too long, of course, were not rewarded, because their vote had not been necessary. Further, those who failed to get on or who pushed too hard for one of the losers would not be rewarded. The result here is a combination of Hume and Schelling. The opinion which counted here was opinion as to who was likely to win. The decision had to be made while it was still uncertain who was going to win, because if you waited too long, you would get no reward, and the result was at first caution and then a cascade of people rushing to join whoever they thought would win.

Efforts to overthrow a dictator have somewhat the same structure. The basic difference is that everything is much more concealed than it was at a convention, and secondly, if the dictator himself will win as he usually, but not always, does, the thing may proceed so rapidly that we don't even see the early stage at all.

The basic problem can be seen in figure 1. The top panel has on the vertical axis the probability that a dictator will be overthrown, and on the horizontal axis, the strength of opposition against him. Note that the individuals would have different lengths along the axis, with a private in a provincial garrison taking up very little space, and the chief of staff a great deal.

The extreme example of this disproportion was the events in France in 1958. Before de Gaulle decided to overthrow the government of France, there was substantially no chance of it being overthrown; as soon as he made up his mind, the government collapsed.[11] In essence, he himself occupied a space on the horizontal axis which perhaps extended from point A to point B.

11. The French army was a critical factor in the overthrow, and support from the army coalesced around de Gaulle following his decision (Bernard Crozier, *de Gaulle* [New York: Scribner's, 1973], 453–78).

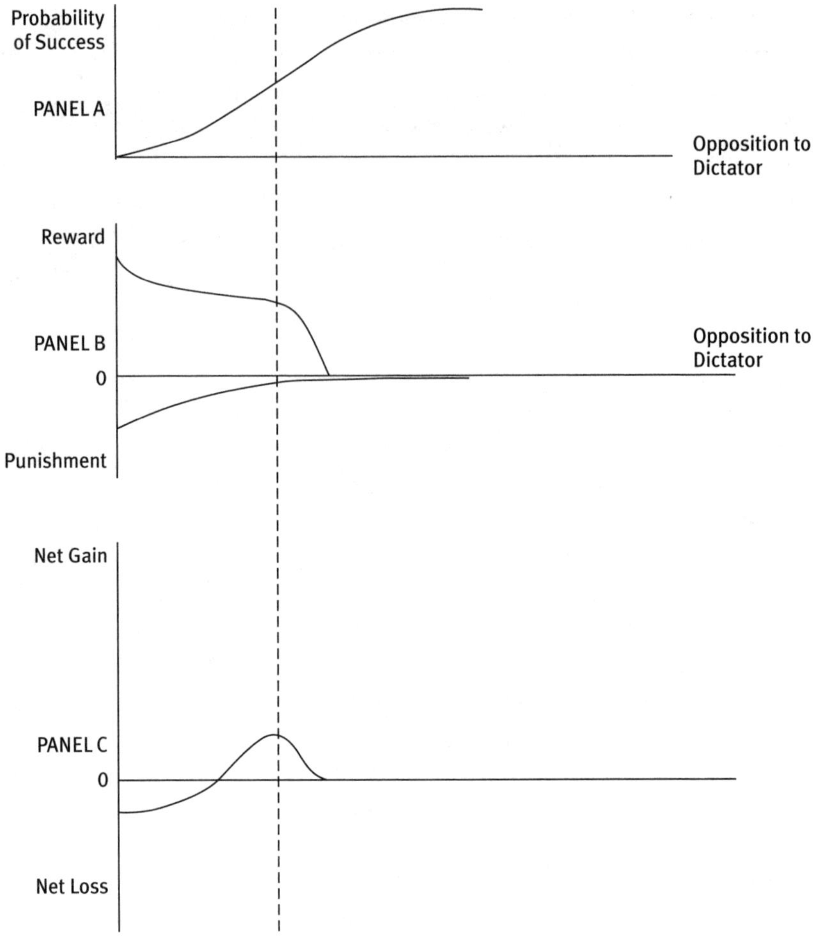

FIGURE 1

The vertical line which extends from the top panel through all the other panels cuts the curve on panel A at a point where the probability is 50/50. In other words, anything to the right of that line has a better than even chance of overthrowing the dictator; anything to the left has a worse chance.

On panel B, we continue the same horizontal axis, but the vertical axis is the reward from successful participation, with the reward from the overthrow of the dictator above the line, and the penalty for failure to overthrow the dictator below the line. Note that I have drawn these lines not on the basis of empirical evidence, but more or less the way I think they should be. The reader is invited to experiment with other lines if he doesn't like these.

The lower line, which is actually on the second quadrant of the Cartesian axis of panel B, shows the punishment which the individual is likely to receive if he joins the revolutionary effort and it fails. The bottom panel simply shows the net present discounted value of joining the revolutionary conspiracy for some individual contemplating such an action. It is computed from the first three lines. The problem of the dictator is making certain that everyone thinks that he is in the negative payoff portion of this diagram. The problem of the person attempting to organize conspiracy is to convince people that the present discounted rewards of joining the revolution are positive.

This rather simple set of diagrams is, of course, intended for heuristic purposes and is not intended as an empirically accurate measure of probabilities, etc. Nevertheless, it does, I think, represent quite accurately the type of calculation that must be undertaken under these circumstances.

Suppose, then, that the commanding general of the Third Army Corps suddenly announces that the government is corrupt, wicked, etc., and that he will save the country from these depraved rulers. He tries to make this announcement as convincing as possible, and what he is trying to convince people of, in general, is not that he is good, just, etc., but that he is strong and will win. Of course, there is no reason not to claim virtue, and he no doubt will, but this is less important. He will try to obtain control of communications—under present circumstances, this means the television or radio stations—because he wants his message, which is "I am strong and will win!" concealed under "I am virtuous," to be transmitted and the current dictator's message not.

At this point various other people in the country, particularly the higher officials, are presented with a difficult problem. Is it better for them to jump on the revolutionary bandwagon or join with the dictator in suppressing the revolution. Further, it's very dangerous to show hesitation. This is particularly so if you think that the dictator himself might win, because he is likely to regard hesitation or neutrality in these cases as treason. Strength comes from an appearance of strength, but strength also gives an appearance of strength.

This discussion of how dictators are overthrown is extremely brief. I have not, for example, even dealt with the not particularly uncommon situation in which the attempted overthrow is strong enough so that it seizes part of the country physically and there is then a protracted civil war. Here again, the real point of the civil war is to convince people that one side or the other is going to win.

But how does a dictator prevent this kind of overthrow? He must always have as one of his primary objectives the presentation to the world of a picture of strength. Note here that the world is not the average citizen, although the dictator should try to convince them too. The world is actually his higher officials. An impressive-looking but actually hollow armed force may frighten the citizenry, but it's not likely to frighten the higher officials who know how hollow it is. On the other hand, the hollowness of this force may mean that the officials feel they cannot rely on it in an effort to overthrow the dictator.

The dictator must prevent subversive coalitions from forming. His basic rule in preventing them from forming is convincing people that they will be unsuccessful. Since there is always the possibility, both in theory and in practice, of a successful coalition against him, a coalition of people who will gain from overthrowing him and who have power enough to do so, he cannot rely on the low possibility of such a coalition at any point in time. What he must try to do is make it appear to anyone contemplating either starting a conspiracy or joining a conspiracy not that any conspiracy against the dictator is impossible, because that is absurd, but that that particular conspiracy will fail. In essence, he has to interrupt communication among potential conspirators by making communications dangerous.

In order to attract potential conspirators into a given conspiracy, it is necessary to offer them rewards in the form of promotion, etc., inside the hierarchy. It is hard to do this while keeping matters a secret. Once the revolutionary coup is announced, of course, such promises can be made with no difficulty.

How does a dictator deal with this? A precaution that he normally will take is stringent enforcement of the law against treason. Any conspiracy, even discussion of overthrowing a dictator, is apt to be severely punished if the dictator finds out about it, and he'll make every effort to do so. His reasons are, of course, simple. Things which indicate his strength are plainly visible. He has guards, police, and the military, to say nothing of possible public demonstrations. People involved in these various activities are apt to feel that the other people involved in the same activity are loyal to the dictator unless they have some positive information to the contrary. By making it illegal to even discuss overthrowing a dictator, the dictator makes it difficult for such positive information to develop. Thus the dissatisfied lieutenant in the dictator's personal guard is apt to feel that his dissatisfaction is a limited phenomenon and not realize that there are a great many other people who'd be delighted to overthrow the dictator. On a more cold-blooded level, if the lieutenant in the dictator's guard realized that it must be true that there are a large number of people who could benefit by overthrowing the dictator and moving upward themselves, he is unable to safely communicate with them and hence insure his own future in the revolutionary movement.

This prevention even of discussion of overthrowing the dictator is an important precaution which any sensible dictator will take. It has, however, a serious defect. Machiavelli said that it was astonishing that any overthrow of a prince ever occurred, because, of necessity, the conspiracy was risky and there was a safe alternative, which was to betray the conspiracy to the prince.[12] The prince would then, naturally, reward highly the person who had betrayed the conspiracy and take care of those members of the conspiracy that had not informed.

In general, Machiavelli correctly identified the phenomenon. He overlooked, however, another problem here. One of the ways of rising in the entourage of any dictator, Machiavelli's "reward," is to denounce a conspiracy. It's not necessary that there actually be a conspiracy there to be denounced. The dictator is apt to be surrounded by skilled and subtle courtiers, all of whom are trying to convince him that all of the others are disloyal to him. Their reason is simply a desire to rise in his favor. Thus the dictator has very strong motives to suppress conspiracies against himself and to reward highly people who inform him, but the reward system, in and of itself, tends to generate false alarms.

All of this makes life difficult for the dictator and indeed is by no means the only thing that makes it difficult.[13] He can neither trust his officials not to conspire against him nor necessarily trust reports of these conspiracies. It should be said that in recent years the development of very small recording devices has made it somewhat easier for the person who wants to betray a genuine plot to do so. Unfortunately, most of the people who are in a position to plot (i.e., the higher officials) are rather subtle individuals who are accustomed to communicating by allusion and indirect methods, and hence, recording their conversation is not all that helpful. A general conspiracy may not sound like it, and casual conversation may possibly be interpretable as a conspiracy.

But if the ruler cannot prevent subtle conspiracies among the people of high rank around him, he pretty surely can prevent any widespread conspiracy

12. Niccoló Machiavelli, *The Prince*, trans. Luigi Ricci (New York: New American Library, 1976).

13. Xenophon is largely a discussion of these difficulties. He exaggerates some, but not a great deal.

from developing. Thus, higher officials may feel that there are enough of them antagonistic to the current dictator so that a conspiracy would work, but there is no way that they can assure themselves that their subordinates will follow their orders. It was, of course, this problem that stopped coups and attempted coups by the German military against Hitler.[14]

Firm enforcement of the law against treason is certainly highly desirable for the dictator, but he will find it very difficult to do, and it is certainly not a solid final reliance. In practice, dictators tend to respond to reports that one particular official is conspiring against them, not by killing the official, but by appointing him ambassador to some far-off place. He can then be brought back later. Stalin, of course, followed the policy of simply killing, and it must be admitted that he was extremely successful.

Let us now return to the positive methods that the dictator has for demonstrating strength, for convincing all the people around him that in the event of any effort to overthrow him, he will be successful in supressing it. The first of these, of course, is simply seeing to it that any group of people that he particularly suspects are kept physically from doing anything about it.

The current king of Morocco has suffered several efforts by military men to replace him. In consequence, at the moment, the army is almost entirely kept out of Morocco proper and engaged in a war against the Polisaro. When they are in Morocco, they are not permitted to leave their base without police permission and are escorted by the police whenever they do leave the base. This offers a good deal of protection against the army, although the possibility that it might decide to march into Morocco cannot be totally ruled out. It doesn't offer any protection against the police.[15] The current dictator of Syria has chosen to balance matters. Not long ago his brother commanded a special very well equipped military force which, in essence, guarded the dictator. He has since been exiled to Switzerland and then brought back. The dictator does not permit any force to get large enough so that it could independently overthrow him. The Special Defense Companies, formerly commanded by his brother, were matched (and watched) by the Special Forces of the same size. Neither could safely take on the current dictator and the

14. In this case, the army major commanding troops sent to arrest Goebbels allowed the latter to talk him out of it (Constantine FitzGibbon, *Denazification* [London: Joseph, 1969], 210).

15. *Washington Post*, January 27, 1984, p. 19. The army further has no minister of defense or chief of staff and has only one active general for 170,000 men (*Time*, September 24, 1984, p. 44).

army.[16] Such balancing is more common than the kind of thing the king of Morocco is doing.

The problem here is that in a real sense a dictator lives in a state of nature. He is not the owner of important assets in a well-run state. There is no overwhelmingly powerful state which can protect him. What he needs to be protected from are parts of the state. All of this makes his life dangerous and in some ways unpleasant, but presumably the dictators regard the advantages to be greater than the disadvantages.

The situation is analogous to a very typical Public Choice problem: the self-enforcing constitution. It's fairly easy to design a constitution for a state which would lead to at least a reasonably good government. The problem is designing this constitution in such a way that it enforces itself. How do you, to give but one example, prevent a supreme court from deciding that it should be supremer than the designers of the constitution intended? At the moment, we don't have very much of a solution to this problem in democratic politics, and the dictator must face it every day.

The Gang of Four in China lost their position of power because the commander of their guard force chose to arrest them rather than guard them.[17] Arevalo, a dictator of Guatemala, was assassinated by one of his own guard while he was walking towards the dining room of his house with his wife.[18] President Park of Korea was shot by the head of his secret police.[19] But this problem can to some extent be mitigated in a dictatorship by attempting to enforce the law against treason and by a variety of other techniques to which we will now turn.

The first of these is simply preventing others from getting positions of firm power. The dictator should practice what Mussolini called "changing of

16. Hafez al-Assad's brother Rifaat is the colonel in command of the elite Special Defense Companies. His rival, General Ali Haidar, commands the Special Forces (of similar size); the two organizations spend a lot of time watching each other (Dunnigan and Bay, *Quick and Dirty Guide*, 57). At the time this page was actually written, Damascus was an armed camp, with different military factions pointing their guns at each other and occasionally engaging in light gun fire (*Washington Post*, February 9, 1984, p. 7). This is a more overt expression of the normal situation in the Syrian dictatorship or, indeed, in any dictatorship. Normally it is better concealed.

17. Andres D. Onate, "Hua Kuo-feng and the Arrest of the Gang of Four," *China Quarterly* 75 (September 1987): 562.

18. *New York Times*, July 28, 1957, p. 1.

19. Park was shot to death during a dispute between KCIA director Kim Jae Kyu and his chief bodyguard (*New York Times*, October 27, 1979, p. 1).

the guard"; i.e., he should move his high officials around so that they never develop a firm personal following in whatever job they hold. This is particularly important in the case of the army and police force, and it is, of course, in those areas where most modern states rotate higher officers with regularity. Firstly, this shifting around demonstrates the power of the dictator. Any individual knows that at any time he can be removed. Secondly, it provides a way of quietly rewarding services.

The dictator, if he's well advised, not only will rotate people from one military command to another but will, at least occasionally, remove individuals from command totally and then a few years later bring them back. It should be said here that in Mexico the Institutional Revolutionary Party originally was simply a coalition of military men. The conversion of a rather disorderly state to one which is rather orderly, as dictatorships go, largely involved imposing on the higher military officials, all of whom were in fact bandit chiefs with their own little armies, rotation, with their troops not going with them.[20]

There are many cases of this. When Mao Tse-tung seized control of China, he actually was the head of an organization in which there were in essence five armies, all of which had been built up by one leader from practically nothing and which were, to a considerable extent, loyal to that leader. Mao might have been able to deal with this by ordinary methods, but the Korean War gave him a wonderful opportunity. He, in essence, drafted from each of these armies specific units to send to the Korean War. These units were then rotated back to China on a regular basis, but were not returned to their original army. As a result, at the end of the Korean War the five major armies had been melded into one. Mao Tse-tung was then able to remove the four most important generals from their positions of personal power.[21]

One thing that most dictators should at least give careful thought to is personal command of the army. At the least, the dictator must devote a lot of attention to who commands it and, if possible, should fix it so that there is no true commander, but a number of officials with titles such as Minister of

20. On the history of the Institutional Revolutionary Party (PRI), see Peter Smith, *Labyrinths of Power: Political Recruitment in Twentieth-Century Mexico* (Princeton: Princeton University Press, 1979), 11–20.

21. On the five field armies, see Stanley Karnew, *Mao and China* (New York: Viking, 1972), 68–69. For the rotation policy and postwar reorganization, see John Gittings, *The Role of the Chinese Army* (London: Oxford University Press, 1967), 294–99. It should be said that I believe that I am the actual source of this idea. So far as I know, a secret dispatch written by me to the Department of State from the Korean embassy was the first mention of it.

War, Chief of Staff, etc. He can, however, take direct command himself, and this frequently is very helpful in retaining power.

Another technique is collegial control (i.e., putting a board or commission at the head of almost everything). The lords of the Admiralty are an example of this from the present day.[22] Cabinets and councils are others. A group of this sort cannot effectively conspire, because somebody will talk, nor is any individual likely to be able to use it to build up a personal following.

Another technique, a very traditional one, is "cutting off the head of the tallest flowers," disposing of people who are rising in power and influence.[23] When the Great Captain returned to Spain after having won most of Italy for the king of Spain, he was almost instantly exiled to his estates and prevented from having any influence in the government of Spain.[24] Khrushchev disposing of Zhukov right after Zhukov had made Khrushchev a success in the "Anti-Party Plot" affair certainly is another example.

As a minor, but nevertheless possibly important, aspect of keeping power, a lot of pompous ceremony surrounding the dictator is a good idea. It should be said here that I suspect that the dictator also enjoys it. It is particularly helpful if the dictator can arrange to have himself surrounded by a great deal of pomp and ceremony while putting on an appearance of being a very simple man himself. Lord Montgomery, during World War II, insisted that all of his staff officers be absolutely perfectly dressed, with shoes shined, etc., while he himself wore less than perfectly tailored uniforms. His public relations officer made quite a bit out of this contrast.[25] This kind of thing frequently pays off for a dictator.

22. Originally established under Henry VIII, the Admiralty (composed of five lords commissioners) was in charge of Royal Navy operations until 1964. After this date, the Admiralty became the Navy Department, within which the Admiralty lords still exist, although their functions are undefined.

23. Thrasyboulus was said to have given advice on how to be a tyrant to the young Periandros of Corinth, "taking his messenger for a walk by a cornfield and thoughtfully lopping off with his walking stick the head off any stalk that looked superior to the average" (A. R. Burn, 126).

24. El Gran Capitan was Gonzalo de Córdoba, whom Ernest Dupuy and Trevor N. Dupuy (*The Encyclopedia of Military History, from 3500 B.C. to the Present*, rev. ed. [New York: Harper and Row, 1977]) describe as an "organizational and tactical genius" (488). He was recalled to Spain following his spectacular successes and never given another opportunity to command "due to the jealousy of [King] Ferdinand" (ibid., 470).

25. See Correlli Barnett, *The Desert Generals* (New York: Ballantine, 1960), 269, 280. Interestingly, it was only after taking command of the Eighth Army in August, 1942, that Lord

There is another important aspect which is that the dictator should always get his way. In order to always get your way without making a lot of mistakes, the dictator has to be careful. Machiavelli said, "a dictator should continuously solicit advice, but never take unsolicited advice."[26] This is still a good bit of advice for any dictators if they're willing to accept an unsolicited suggestion from me. Secondly, the dictator should normally make up his own mind late in the discussion of any particular problem. And lastly, if he runs into a particularly difficult problem, he should push the whole thing off on an inferior. He can blame the inferior if things work out badly. Once he has taken a position, however, in general, it is dangerous for him to change. A dictator can get away with this sometimes, but not frequently.

The basic problem here is one which has been discussed in connection with nuclear war, "escalation dominance." The dictator should be surrounded by people who feel that opposition to the dictator has less chance as it proceeds to a higher level. In other words, the individual courtiers should believe there is no point in starting a serious argument with the dictator, because the dictator will win; that if he tries to arrange a coup, the dictator will win; and that if he actually starts a civil war, the dictator will win. As long as every courtier thinks all of these things are true, the dictator is safe.

These problems are clearly very difficult for the dictator, and it is also clear that the solutions that I have suggested are incomplete. This is, of course, characteristic of the real world. Dictators do not, on the whole, keep their power permanently. Further, the lack of true intellectual precision of my discussion here, I believe, also reflects the real world. The dictator is faced by a set of very difficult problems, and his solutions to them are, generally speaking, not the neat mathematical solutions that we would like to find.

When I discuss matters of this sort, I normally find that I get two reactions. The first of them is that this is obviously absurd, and the second, sometimes from the same person a little bit later in the conversation, is that everybody has always known these matters. I believe the second is, in fact, correct, at least when we are talking about dictators themselves. Although I think most dictators have been, on the whole, aware of the kind of problems I have been

---

Montgomery began dressing eccentrically (most notably wearing outlandish headgear); until then his dress had been quite orthodox (ibid.). In Montgomery's *Memoirs*, he admitted that this reflected a conscious policy (Bernard Law, 1st Viscount Montgomery of Alamein, *The Memoirs of Field-Marshal the Viscount Montgomery of Alamein* [Cleveland: World Publishing, 1958]).

26. Machiavelli, *The Prince*.

discussing, and for that matter the kind that I will be discussing in the next two chapters, they have rarely spoken about them. This is probably because they regard any open discussion on these matters as likely to weaken their power.

Political scientists, when talking about dictators, have tended to pay little attention to these problems. The existing literature on dictatorship is sparse and, in my opinion, very poor. It is very heavily dominated by moral considerations and, in fact, to a considerable extent, consists of simple attacks on the whole idea.[27] These attacks can be rather restricted. It's an intriguing characteristic of Communism that it does not have any political science at all for its own governments (which are, of course, always dictatorships), but that it does have an elaborate attack on other governments. All of them are accused of being dictatorships, and this accusation is apparently intended to hurt. But even there, they have no theoretical structure.

If we turn to the few things that I can find in Western sources, Machiavelli is perhaps the most informative. A mixture of moralistic attacks on dictators, moralistic advice to dictators (i.e., they're told to be good), and occasional discussions in terms of the class structure of the dictatorship are almost all we find. In my opinion, all of these things are beside the point. Dictatorship may indeed be immoral and wicked, but we should try to understand it. Further, offering moral lectures to dictators is not likely to be much help.

27. See those by John J. Johnson and Hugh M. Hamill Jr. for examples.

PART 5

THE ECONOMICS OF WAR

INTERNATIONAL CONFLICT

TWO PARTIES

We now turn to formal international warfare. The analysis will be somewhat briefer than our analysis of revolution, principally because there is less to be said in a purely formal way. However, I must begin by stating my view of why people normally go to war. In my opinion, gain (or avoidance of loss) is the common reason for undertaking warfare. This is not the conventional view. Generally, if I understand current intellectual discussions of war, attacks on other people are thought to be motivated by various irrational motives, such as an aggressive drive. Defending your own property or your own nation does not apparently qualify as irrational; hence, the desire to avoid loss is accepted as one of the standard motives for present-day warfare.

If wars are undertaken for irrational means, then, of course there is little that can be said about them. I do not think it is possible to read history with care, however, without realizing that at least some wars were undertaken for perfectly rational reasons, albeit the people making the decisions may have miscalculated. Businessmen frequently make investments that turn out badly. This is not because they are not motivated by a desire for gain or because they are irrational, but simply that the problems are very difficult and it is easy to make a mistake. The problems of war and peace are equally difficult and mistakes are equally likely.

When, then, can wars be profitable? Most people seem to believe that defensive wars are normally and automatically wars that are sensible to fight. Whether we accept this proposition or not depends on individual calculation. Certainly in some cases countries have quite voluntarily and quite rationally chosen not to fight when attacked (for example, Czechoslovakia in 1938, 1948, and 1968); and in other countries and other cases, countries have chosen to fight. It is not clear that either of these choices is irrational per se; calculations in which the likely cost of war, the likely cost of being conquered, and the probable outcome if some degree of resources are committed to fighting would be necessary before we could say. Surely, however, we can all agree that there would be some cases in which countries would be well-advised to fight when attacked.

Reprinted, with permission, from *The Social Dilemma: The Economics of War and Revolution* (Blacksburg, Va.: Center for Study of Public Choice, 1974), 87–106.

The same general line of reasoning applies for countries that might undertake an attack upon another country. If the country subject to attack is militarily weak enough and rich enough, then the present discounted value of the military operation would be positive. This would be true regardless of the technique of war. Nuclear war is sometimes said to be an impossible alternative. The people who make this statement, however, are implicitly assuming that the war would be somewhat equal, i.e., that great damage would be inflicted on the victor, also. This may be true, if we are contemplating a war tomorrow between the United States and Russia; but it is by no means an inevitable characteristic of nuclear war. Indeed, the current nuclear treaties take so seriously the possibility of nuclear war under one-sided conditions that the major nuclear powers are pledged to go to war to protect non-nuclear powers against nuclear attack by second-rate nuclear powers.

But even if cost-benefit analysis of some particular war—whether offensive or defensive—would indicate that the nation would be unwise to take the warlike alternative, it may nevertheless be sensible for the government. Suppose there is some dictator in fairly secure control of country A. Nearby there is another country, B, which is well armed and which the dictator believes will fight hard if attacked. The dictator feels that if he undertakes a major attack upon country B, about one-third of the national wealth of each of the countries will be destroyed, and he has a nine out of ten chance of emerging from the war victorious in the sense that he will be in complete control of both countries.

It is clear that this is an extremely bloody and destructive war and, looked at from the standpoint of the entire citizenry of the two countries, undesirable. Looked at from the standpoint of the dictator, however, it has a positive discounted value. If he is successful, he will have made a $33\frac{1}{3}$ percent increase in the resources he controls, and he has a nine out of ten chance of being successful in this sense. He may, of course, be risk-averse and, hence, not feel that even this gamble is desirable; but clearly not all national rulers have been risk-averse. Surely you could not say that his desire to undertake an attack under these circumstances was contrary to his material interests or not motivated by hope of gain. Similarly, a decision to resist attack might be rational for a dictator even if it is irrational for his country.

I do not argue that all wars have been caused in this simple, straightforward desire to achieve gain. It is true that I think a great many of them have been and that the modern discussion of wars in terms of basically irrational factors is misleading. Nevertheless, people who believe that many wars are the result of irrational factors—in fact, even people who believe that all historic wars were the result of irrational calculations—would still have to concede that there is a finite chance of wars in which gain can be made. It is to this type of war that we shall now turn. Wars, if any there be which are essentially irrational in their motivation, can also be analyzed by the same apparatus. This simply requires our putting into their preference functions whatever are the irrational desires of the individuals concerned in making the decisions and, hence, taking that type of gain into account, i.e., the likelihood that they will get whatever it is that they desire. Implicitly, however, my models are all fairly straightforward gain models, and I make no discussion of how the gain is derived.

The reader may or may not agree with me on this matter. However, unless he feels that selfish desires have no significance whatsoever in war, he should be willing to read the next chapters where some consequences of this assumption are worked out. From the idealist's standpoint, these chapters will seem gloomy. The fact that wars and threats of war can be profitable, that the less a nation prepares for war, the more likely that an attack upon it will be profitable, and that bilateral disarmament increases the likelihood of war are all propositions which will make the conventional student of foreign affairs unhappy. There is little I can do to dispel this gloom except to point out that it is better to act in knowledge than under the influence of a myth. We may not be as satisfied in the short run if we realize the nature of the world, but the long-run prospects are better if our actions are based on truth than upon an attractive falsehood.

I can, however, offer a little bit of cheer. The next chapters will be particularly gloomy because they will simplify the international situation by assuming conflict between two parties. After dealing with this simple situation, we will turn to discussing the situation where there are more than two nations, and we shall see that under these more realistic circumstances the situation is more cheerful. Finally, in the last chapter of the book, we will look into the general problem of minimization of the costs of conflict. Unfortunately, although this may be still more cheerful, we shall find that there are very distinct limits on the amount of minimization which can be successfully achieved.

War is perhaps the best example of scale economies. In general, an increase in the resources devoted to combat will make a more than proportional increase in the likelihood of success. In Figure 7 we show, on the horizontal axis, some nation's probability of victory in conflict; on the vertical axis, we

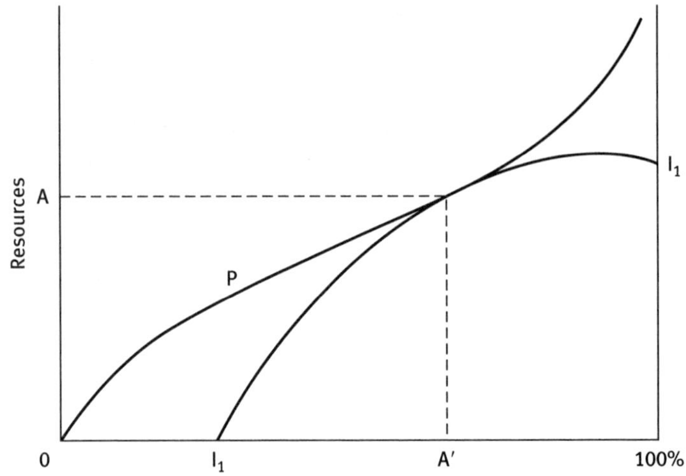

FIGURE 7
The welfare effect of arms

show the resources which the nation devotes to that conflict. Line *P* shows the probability of victory "purchasable" with varying amounts of resources.

The victor, in this case, is not defined as being better off after the war but simply as having won the war, even though the physical damage inflicted may be much greater than whatever it is that has been won. This distinction is, of course, particularly important in nuclear war; but it is certainly true that England and France were on the winning side in World War I, but were much worse off in 1919 than they had been in 1914.

In order to keep our initial model simple, we will make a special set of simplifying assumptions which will be gradually relaxed as the chapter continues. We ignore the difference between peacetime preparation for war and the actual use of resources in fighting. Thus, this line can be taken as indicating either the probability of victory in an actual war, or the probability of victory in a potential war. Further, we assume that the opponent has a constant resource commitment. These assumptions will be relaxed shortly.

Economies of scale are shown throughout almost the whole of the range by a continuing declining cost of purchasing each additional increment of probability of success. The upturn at the end may or may not be a real phenomenon. It is certainly true that small armies have sometimes beaten very large ones. It may, therefore, be true that it is very expensive indeed to acquire certainty. It may be, however, that some other factor compensated for the small size of the weaker army. The Macedonians may actually have

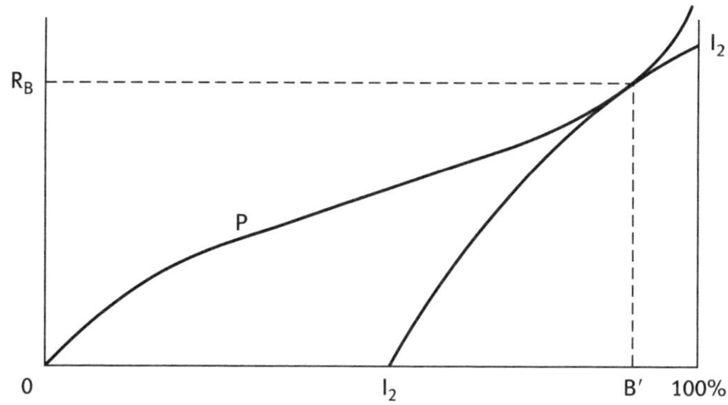

FIGURE 8
Payoff to power

had more resources on the field at Arabella than the Persians, because they had Alexander, and the real value of his services may have been much greater than that of hundreds of thousands of Persian infantrymen.

It might be thought that all countries would expand their commitment of resources until they had a reasonable certainty of victory. This is impossible. At the beginning of any conflict, at least one of the two parties must have a 50 percent or worse probability of success. It may be that the two parties' individual estimates do not show this, i.e., that their individual estimates of success would add up to more than one. However, it is probable that even subjectively the probability of success must seem small in many wars. For example, Finland, facing the Russian invasion in 1939, can hardly have calculated a very high probability of success. She could hardly even have thought she had a very high probability of the limited success she did achieve, in which she lost only about one-fifth of her inhabited territory and her second largest city. Nevertheless, most countries do not invest in military capacity up to the physical limits. The reason they do not, of course, is simply that the investment in military resources reduces investment in other matters and thus pushes the last unit of other things purchased back up the demand curve. This implicitly increases the opportunity cost of defense.

Since the objective of the population would be certainty of victory at no resource cost, the peak of the indifference mountain is in the lower right-hand corner, and *I-I* is an indifference curve. The citizens would choose to spend *A* to purchase *A′* probability of winning. A large country contemplating war with a small country may face the situation shown in Figure 8. The likelihood of success is once again shown by the line marked *P*. The commitment of

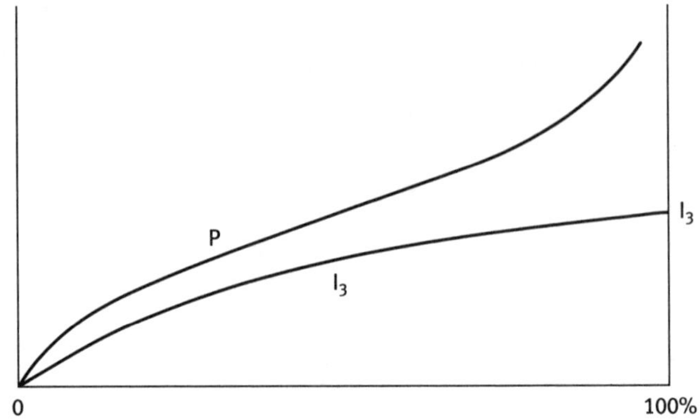

FIGURE 9
The wages of weakness

resources to this war is a small proportion of the resources available to the country. Thus, the per capita cost will be much lower, and indifference curves will be of the shape shown. This is particularly true if the country concerned normally maintains a military establishment much larger than is needed for any particular minor war; hence, the opportunity costs of committing overwhelming resources to the war are slight.

The decision by Victoria's First Lord of the Admiralty as to how strong a squadron to send to chastise some South American government which had been impolite to Her Majesty's minister, would be a decision of this sort. Similarly, the American invasion of the Dominican Republic is an example. The force sent was trivial by American standards but strong enough so that if it had been used vigorously the Dominicans would have had substantially zero chance of success against it. In practice, it was used in a somewhat timid manner, and the particular Dominican group which objected was able to resist its politically restricted efforts for a short period of time.

What of very weak countries? On Figure 9 we show a weak country facing potential war with a strong country—roughly the situation that Finland faced in 1939, and Czechoslovakia in 1939, 1948, and 1968. Under these circumstances, the cost of purchasing any likelihood of success may be so great that the indifference curves would have the shape of I_3 on Figure 9. Sometimes countries do choose not to fight. The Czechs in 1939, 1948, and 1968, the Danes in 1940,[1] and the British in Hankow in 1926 are examples.

1. The Royal Guard put up a token resistance in which two were killed.

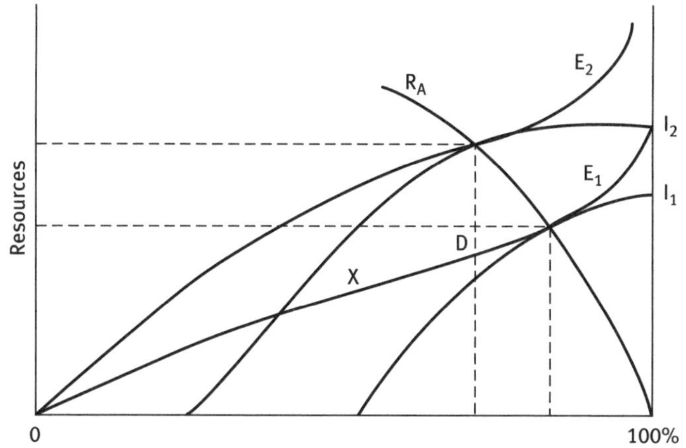

FIGURE 10
Adjustment to different arms levels

So far, we have discussed the situation in which some country adjusts its defense budget without considering the reaction of its opponent. This is most unrealistic. Let us now consider two countries adjusting to the changes in each other's activities.[2] In Figure 10, then, we show country *A* and indifference curves I_1 and I_2 are a pair of its indifference curves. E_1 and E_2 are the production functions for the probability of victory with different resource commitments, granted two levels of resource investment by country *B*, the potential enemy. For each of these levels of resource investment by the other country, country *A* has an optimal response of its own, and the locus of all such optimal responses is shown by the response line, R_A. The shape of *R* shows that, as security becomes more expensive, we choose to buy less of it. On this particular diagram, the demand for security over most of the range is inelastic.

It will be observed that this analysis has a structural resemblance to the work of Louis Richardson.[3] It is my opinion that this resemblance is almost entirely structural. The motivating forces in the Richardson model are essentially emotional, rather than rational, efforts to obtain gain or avoid loss.

2. The model can be used for more than two countries by lumping several together as "the other side."

3. L. F. Richardson, *Statistics of Deadly Quarrels*, ed. Quincy Wright and C. C. Lienau (Pittsburgh: Boxwood Press, 1960).

This leads to some rather drastic differences between the results of our reasoning and the results of his. In particular, it is always rational to start a war if your enemy is both rich enough and weak enough.

We anticipate that the reaction curve has this general shape, except at the extreme ends. At the right end, where, as we have said, it may be that the increasing marginal returns on investment in security cease to apply, it is possible that a rise in the budget of the opponent, small enough so that it does not drown out the effect of this reversal of the economies of scale, actually reduces the amount of resource investment in defense. In the late 1950s, the United States had an extremely powerful long-range bomber force capable of devastating the Soviet Union, and the Soviet Union had substantially nothing in the way of a long-range bomber force capable of hitting the United States. The development of antiaircraft equipment and improved fighter defense, however, began to make it look likely that bomber forces could not get through. Hence, a switch to ballistic missiles, which at that time were believed to be immune from interception, was sensible. The United States, therefore, built a missile system, retaining the bombers only as a supplementary force. Although exact comparisons are difficult, it appears that we chose to spend less for missiles than we had previously put into our bomber force. Certainly it is true that we made no effort to maintain the kind of superiority over the Russians in missiles that we had in bombers. Instead of about a 20-to-1 superiority, we settled for about 4 to 1 in 1964–65. There was a significant reduction in deliverable tonnage. Developments after that date will be discussed later.

Another region of elasticity of a sort exists at the left end. A country whose resources or determination are such that its indifference curve is tangent to the production function near the far left of the horizontal axis, may, if its opponent increases its resources, reduce its investment. In general, however, one anticipates that increases in the resource commitment of an opponent leads to a decision to purchase less security, but to spend a larger sum in purchasing that security as in the R_A curve.

Response curves of two countries are shown on Figure 11. This figure uses a somewhat unusual type of space, and it may be useful to discuss it. *A*'s resource commitment to military activity is shown on the horizontal axis, and *B*'s on the vertical. Both zeros are in the lower left corner. The straight lines marked 75 percent, 50 percent, and 25 percent show the relative probability of *A* winning with different amounts of comparative resource commitments.

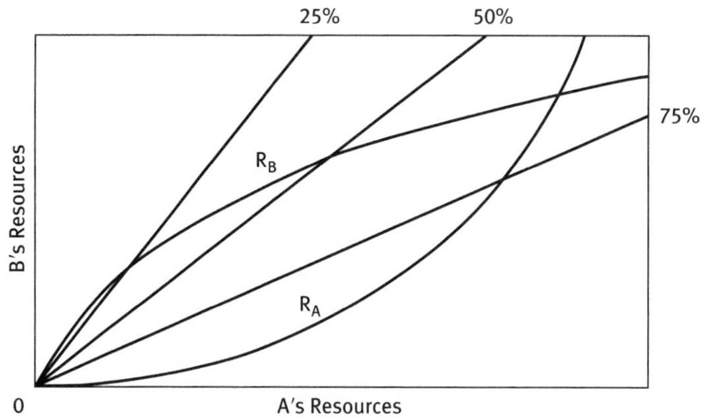

FIGURE 11
Armament equilibrium

The straightness of these lines indicates an important aspect of military matters. What counts is not the absolute size of military forces, but their relative size compared with that of an opponent. Having twice as big an army as your opponent is of about as much use if your army consists of two men and his consists of one[4] as if yours consists of 20 million and his consists of 10 million.[5]

The *A* axis in Figure 11 is longer than the *B* axis to indicate that country *A* has more total resources than country *B*; hence it can, if it wishes, readily outbuild its opponent. Whether it will take advantage of this opportunity, of course, depends on the shape of its indifference curves. The United States, with a national income of at least twice and probably four times that of the Soviet Union, currently is inferior to the Soviet Union in long-range deliverable weapons, and a very powerful political group apparently would be quite satisfied to see a pronounced Russian superiority.

The response curve of Figure 10 can be mapped over into Figure 11 and is shown, as is the equivalent response curve of country *B*. The general shape of these curves reflects simply the fact that as the cost of purchasing another 1 percent probability of victory goes up, i.e., as the size of the opponents' force goes up, each country chooses to purchase more arms but with less

4. Of the same size and capacity, of course.

5. This is a slight oversimplification owing to organizational and logistical problems which may lead to economies or diseconomies of scale.

likelihood of winning. Both of these lines come out of the origin tangent to their respective axes and then gradually bend away.[6] They can never bend farther than vertical to their own axis, because this would imply an inefficient region. The two lines must cross, and at the point of intersection, there is an independent adjustment equilibrium. At this equilibrium which, let us say, corresponds to the tangency between I_2 and E_2 on Figure 10, a decision by *B* to lower his resource commitment by some specified amount would lead *A* to also lower his resource commitment, but at the same time to increase the probability of *A*'s success in a war. This would put us at some such point as *X*, which would not be a point of tangency between an indifference curve and the existing production function for *B*; hence, *B* would increase his military machine. The outcome would be a return to the equilibrium point. As we shall see later, however, by agreement the two parties might achieve a solution which is very much better than the independent equilibrium adjustment.

My reaction curves are a trifle simpler than those in the real world. *A* responds to *B*'s resource commitment, and *B* responds to *A*, but neither, in this present simple model, takes into account the likely reaction of the other from his increase or decrease in armaments. In order to take this into account, we could go back to the earlier figures in this chapter and replot the production function to include probable reaction on the part of the other party to changes in resource commitments. This would lead to reaction curves somewhat different from those shown on Figure 11, but with the same general shape. The consequences of taking into account probable reactions of the other party to your changes in resource commitment will be discussed later in this chapter and in the next chapter on disarmament.

We must, however, pause here to point out a characteristic of the resource commitment which is not obvious from Figure 11. The resources committed in this case are total resources, including anticipated resource expenditures in the future. Thus, it may well be that a sharp increase in current resource expenditures, followed by a successful war, would lead to a reduction in total resource expenditures. A reduction in armaments of one side, which appears to the other side to give an opening for a potentially decisive blow, may lead the other side to increase its military budget. On a less extreme note, if there is a reduction in current armaments expenditure which appears

6. Strictly speaking, the two lines bend up just before they reach the origin. Both parties would prefer the certainty of victory with a very small resource commitment to 50-50 chances with zero resources. The refinement, however, would be microscopic.

to come from a change in the preference pattern of the country making it, this may also lead to an increase in armaments expenditure on the other side. If country *A* appears to have reduced the value it will place on a given probability of victory, this means that the cost of achieving an increase in probability for country *B* has fallen. Under the circumstances, *B* may choose to purchase an increase.

It would appear that the United States has undertaken a maneuver of this sort with respect to Russia. Before 1963–64, American military policy called for maintaining a nuclear force that was vastly superior to that of the Russians. It was, during all of this period, substantially impossible to imagine a Russian war plan for an attack against the United States. Russia might have had some ability to injure the United States if the United States suddenly attacked, but it was clear that Russia could not afford to initiate such an exchange. Beginning in 1963–64, parity between the United States and Russia began to be popular in the United States. It became particularly popular in certain high circles of the Department of State and the Secretary of Defense endorsed it.

Under these circumstances, it would appear to the Russians that the current situation of the American defense establishment was such that they could very greatly increase their comparative military standing without an American response. In essence, the American military leaders were saying that their preferences had changed, and that they now put less negative value on a change in comparative strength. Under these circumstances, it became comparatively very cheap for the Russians to move from a position of crushing inferiority to a position of approximate parity. Naturally, they took advantage of the opportunity.

Before this period, it had been obvious that not only was it not cheap for Russia to move from its position of crushing inferiority to a position of parity, but it was impossible. The United States had such a large advantage in economic resources that Russia could not even play in the same league if there were an arms race. Therefore, Russia had very sensibly (from 1945 to 1964–65) never really engaged in an arms race, although on occasion they had undertaken propaganda campaigns, sometimes backed up with the production of small quantities of hardware, which gave the impression that they were competing.[7] With the change in American attitude, however, the

7. There is one possible exception to this generalization, which is the attempt by Khrushchev to approximately triple his deliverable missile strength by placing short-range missiles in Cuba. If the deliverable capacity of American ballistic missiles was less than he would have

Russians faced a very low price for improving their relative position. Further, they may well be able to obtain a marked superiority over the United States.

Certainly, no one examining American public opinion at the moment would be sure that they could not. America did not respond to the very large, well worked out civil defense mechanism of Russia with its elaborate shelters, although American intellectuals have regularly said that a shelter program in the United States would increase the likelihood of war. We also did not respond to the introduction of a fairly sizable antiballistic missile defense system around Moscow, although we eventually began construction of our own system for different motives. We have permitted the Russians to neutralize our carrier air force by placing a trawler directly behind each carrier which keeps its location known to Russia so that it could be eliminated at the beginning of war. It would not be surprising if Russia felt that long-run resource commitment could be minimized by an increase in resources investment now.

It is by no means certain, however, that this would be a correct calculation. It may be that the present American attitude would change sharply if the Russians moved from their present modest advantage to a great superiority. Since the United States can very easily overtake the Russians, and since we *might* begin a large-scale buildup if it looked likely that the Russians were achieving a position of heavy superiority, the Russians would lose from such a development and would be better off staying at their present relative position. This, however, involves guesses as to future reactions, and any further discussion of them had better be put off until we have turned to the very unpleasant analysis of nuclear exchange below.

I live in Blacksburg, Virginia, and read the *Roanoke Times*. Recently on the front page of the *Roanoke Times* there was a long article headlined, "U.S. Deeply Puzzled by Soviet Expansion of Military Power."[8] The "puzzlement" came from the fact that the author of the article, and indeed many politically important American intellectuals, had not considered the real consequences to Russia of a policy of arms restraint by the United States. A decision not to expand our ICBM force, even if the Russians build up to and beyond it (decisions which were made with a great deal of publicity so that the Russians

---

after the Cuban missiles had been erected and his antiaircraft defenses could deal with American bomber forces, this might have given him a temporary parity with the United States. Apparently he proposed to use this parity to seize West Berlin.

8. Fred Hoffman, "U.S. Deeply Puzzled by Soviet Expansion of Military Power," *Roanoke Times*, AP story from Washington, D.C. (3 June 1969).

could hardly avoid knowing about them), immediately greatly cut the cost of improving Russia's military situation. With such a reduction in cost, it was to be expected that they would choose to improve their military power. In 1960, the cost of achieving nuclear parity with the United States must have seemed very nearly infinite to the Russians. Certainly it was beyond their resources. In 1964–65, the cost of achieving even superiority must have seemed to them relatively modest. It is not surprising that they chose to purchase far more deterrence at the lower price than they would have purchased at the earlier higher price.

If unilateral disarmament or unilateral development of an antimilitaristic temper is likely to lead to these unfortunate consequences, how about an agreement? This problem will be the subject of the next chapter, and any lengthy discussion must therefore be deferred. I would, however, like to anticipate conclusions of that chapter. In general, *fair* agreements to reduce armaments bilaterally, or to reduce the scale of violence in war, or to compromise a war rather than fighting for unconditional surrender, are Pareto optimal in the simple sense. Unfortunately, individual parties may gain either by appearing reluctant to enter into such agreements or by cheating on the agreements once they have been signed. Once again, we are in the social dilemma.

Returning, however, to a straight conflict situation without disarmament agreements or negotiated compromises, the two-nation situation, in general, is an extremely unfavorable configuration. Fortunately, as we turn later to more than two parties, we will find that life gets somewhat more cheerful. We will assume that we are in a nonprogressive economy; i.e., the total product in the next year cannot exceed the product this year. As an implication of this assumption, if part of the capital equipment now in existence is destroyed, this reduces the output of the society permanently. This nonprogressive assumption is here solely for simplicity. An assumption of any other rate of growth would be equally useful, but this particular rate is the easiest to manipulate, and leads, mainly, to the same conclusions. It does have one rather obvious defect, however. From the time of John Stuart Mill to the present, economists have regularly noticed the rate of growth *after* physical devastation is very high. A country which has a base rate of growth of 5 percent will, after it is badly damaged by war, earthquake, etc., temporarily have a rate of growth at 10 to 15 percent until it gets up to its original trend line. This factor will be introduced into our reasoning later.

Assume the reaction curves shown on Figure 12. Country A has more resources than B and has chosen to purchase a better than 50-50 chance of

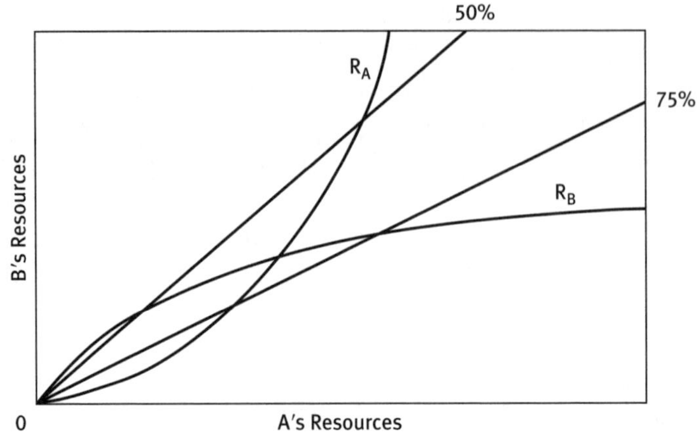

FIGURE 12
Lower expenditure

success in war against *B*. *B*, on the other hand, has bought a less than 50-50 chance. Should either or both of them initiate a war? If the answer were "certainly not!" for either country, then the other country would, of course, be well-advised to threaten war in order to achieve its ends. If, for example, country *B* with a less than 50-50 chance of victory is unwilling to fight under any circumstances, then *A* can obtain the full benefit of a war, i.e., *B*'s complete and unconditional surrender,[9] very cheaply by simply sending a note which indicates that they will fight if *B* does not surrender.

Note that there is a slight oversimplification in the ordinary use of the English language. We normally say that any country *can* start a war, but it is always open to the "invaded" country to refuse to fight. During the wars of the French Revolution, the French armies not uncommonly encountered minor countries, like Hanover, that put up large signs along their boundary saying "neutral territory," and then when the French invaded, simply surrendered unconditionally. This is always open to any country and will, of course, attract invaders.

Assume, however, that country *A* does not feel assured that country *B* will immediately surrender should they attack. We can, for that matter, consider whether *B* should attack also, since, historically, small countries have not infrequently attacked and conquered larger countries. It seems likely, however,

9. It might, of course, remain necessary for *A* to do a little bit of active fighting in order to convince *B* that it meant what it said.

that in those really very numerous cases where tribesmen on the boundaries of powerful empires have conquered the empires the investment of resources in military preparedness was probably higher in the small country than in the larger, in spite of the very much greater real resources of the large country. The small tribe, in which all the members had spent their entire lives learning to fight and fighting against other small tribes, has very nearly all of its resources available for fighting. The powerful empire has only a fraction of its resources available for war. If this fraction is small enough, the tribesmen may well be in a position where the physical odds are in their favor.

There are, of course, cases in which a country may be well-advised to start a war, even if the chances for its success are less than even. If the country feels that the chances of success are, let us say, one in three now but that the passage of time is changing the balance against it and that it is almost certain to be attacked in four or five years with a one-in-six chance of success, it may be well-advised to fight now. Even more commonly, the leaders of some country may be well-advised to take that country into war, even though there is relatively little chance of victory. A dictator who feels that his power is slipping domestically and that a foreign war would strengthen his domestic situation, may feel that he has, shall we say, a one-in-ten chance of being in control of the country a year from today if there is no war. If there is a war, his country has a five-to-one chance of losing; but if it does win, he will stay in power. Thus his present discounted value of starting a war would be positive. It is, however, on the whole unlikely that very many dictators have made this particular calculation. Starting a foreign war which you are very likely going to lose is less attractive than starting one which you are very likely going to win, and it seems probable that dictators looking for a foreign war have always tried to get into the second situation.

But to return to our initial question: should country *A*, the more powerful country, start a war? The first thing to note is that, on the diagram, country *A* has slightly better than three chances in five of winning the war. If we assume that the war will lead to total victory or total defeat for one party or the other, and that is a suitable simplifying assumption with which to start, then *A* calculates whether the present discounted value of a gamble, three to two, for the whole resources of the area in which their own current resources are put up as the wager is worthwhile. In this connection they should notice, of course, that the actual fighting will lead to a decline in the total amount of resources. As we have pointed out again and again, conflict aimed at working a transfer consumes resources, and war is an extreme example. Thus, if *A* initiates the war, it is sure that the total amount of resources available for *A* plus *B* at the end of the war will be less than at the beginning. But it is quite possible that *A*'s share will increase enough to more than compensate *A* for the war.

If *A*'s initial military appropriations were such that the odds were, let us say, 80 to 90 percent for *A*'s victory and the amount *A* would gain is as great (compared with his own national income) as is shown by the length of the two resources lines *A* and *B*, it seems likely that *A* would be well-advised to start the war. On the other hand, if *B* has succeeded in putting enough into her military machine so that the spoils of victory by *A*, i.e., the total value of the entire product of *A* and *B* after war damage discounted by the probability of loss for *A*, is less than the present discounted stream of continuation of the present situation, *A* would not be well-advised to fight. In a way, *B*'s decision on armaments is the crucial one here. There surely is *some* military budget for *B* that is small enough so that war would be attractive for *A*. The smaller *B*'s military budget, the more likely *A* is to win and the less damage there will be in the fighting.

It should be noted that there are two aspects of this decision which are frequently ignored. If *A* conquers *B*, in the future it will be unnecessary to put any significant amount of resources into arms. Thus, in a sense, the total product available for consumption will go up. Even if there is a reduction in the total product of *A* plus *B*, it may well be that the resources available for nonmilitary expenditures after the war will be higher than they were before the war. The second frequently overlooked aspect is, of course, that the quicker and less destructive the war, the more there is left at the end of the war; i.e., spoils of victory are likely to be greater if *B* is unable to defend herself, partly because that will mean that she has spent more on nonmilitary matters and, therefore, is wealthier, and partly simply because there is less resource consumption in conflict.

The last consideration implies that mutual disarmament should increase the likelihood of war. Suppose that the United States and Russia today reduced their ability to injure each other to 1 percent of its present magnitude. Let us also assume that the reduction is proportional so that the probability of success for the two countries is not changed. Either country would face exactly the same likelihood of success in war that it had before the disarmament, but the war itself would be vastly less destructive. Surely with the product to be purchased—victory—more valuable because there would be less physical destruction and with part of the cost—physical destruction—much lower, there would be more likelihood that people would choose to start wars. This is simply a special application of the well-known principle that when something's price is cut, people buy more of it.

Thus, in our simple model as it now stands, *A*'s decision whether or not to attack *B* in hopes of conquest depends partly on *A*'s military appropriation and partly on *B*'s. If *B*'s military appropriations are large enough so that the discounted value of the war to *A* is negative, *A* should not enter the war. If *B*'s appropriations are smaller, then *A* should. It should be noted in this case that it is not entirely *B*'s appropriations, but also its determination. If *B* had a very powerful military force but there was reason to doubt that she would use it in the event of war—let us say there was a powerful pacifist current in its society—then the probability of an easy victory by *A* would be improved by whatever the likelihood that *B* would, in fact, choose not to use its existing military resources. The resources put into deterrence are simply wasted if potential enemies do not believe that there is a determination to use them. During World War II, in French North Africa there was quite a powerful army which the Allies thought was unlikely to oppose their landing. In consequence, they invaded. The Japanese decision to invade Thailand *en route* to Singapore raised somewhat the same issues. For contrary cases, we may take Sweden and Switzerland, who showed great determination to fight the Germans if invaded.

These decisions whether or not to go to war can be expressed by the inequality shown as (1).

$$A_R \cdot (1 - A_A) < (A_R + B_R)(1 - D)(1 - A_P)V_A - A_R \cdot (1 - A_A)(1 - V_A) \quad (1)$$

$$V_A = V(A_A, A_B) \quad (2)$$

$$D = D(A_A, A_B)$$

where

A_A = resources committed to arms by A (%),

B_R = B's resources,

A_B = B's armament expenditure expressed as a fraction of the national income,

A_R = A's resources,

D = destruction from war,

A_P = arms after successful conquest, and

V_A = probability of victory by A.

Equation (1) shows on the left the present discounted value of peace (assuming, of course, that *B* does not attack) and on the right the discounted value of the war. The "nonwar" situation is the resources *A* has multiplied by a discounting factor which adjusts for that portion that will be put into military expenditures if *A* does not attack *B*. The outcome of the war is, if *A* wins, possession of the sum of *A*'s and *B*'s resources discounted by the destruction, the postwar military expenditures, which should be smaller than the arms *A* is now acquiring, and the probability of victory of *A* minus the loss that *A* will suffer if she loses. The latter is her present income multiplied by the probability of loss. A risk-aversion factor might also be put in, but it is frequently not at all obvious which course of action is the least risky in the real world. As is shown by equation (2), the probability of success by country *A* is a function of both her own armaments expenditure and that of country *B*. Damage is also a function of armaments. Country *B*, if she wishes to avoid a war and is not thinking of attacking, would try to choose a value of A_B such that, granted the armaments being purchased by *A*, V_A would have a value which would make the inequality in (1) go the other way.

So far, we have been assuming that the only outcomes of the war are the total conquest of one party by the other. As a slight, but important, modification we might assume that the weaker party *B*, because of its limited resources and/or its lack of interest in winning, has no possibility of conquering *A*, and, therefore, the outcome can only be a conquest of *B* by *A* or a failure to conquer *B* by *A*. Under these circumstances, the portion of equation (1) to the right of the minus sign outside the parentheses disappears, and it becomes equation (3).

$$A_R \cdot (1 - A_A) < (A_R + B_R)(1 - D)(1 - A_P)V_A \tag{3}$$

It is now much harder for *B* to provide a military budget which guarantees against an attack by *A*, but it is not impossible. Further, this situation has a very good analogy in the present-day world.

It seems to be accepted by many policy makers in the non-Communist part of the world that war should be one-sided. Thus, the North Vietnamese attempted to take South Vietnam and we defended it. Apparently no consideration at all was given to the prospects of conquering North Vietnam. We, in fact, continuously reassured the Communists on this score. Nor is this the only example of this same policy. The guerrilla war in Greece, the efforts by Cuba to start guerrilla wars all over South America combined with the United States Coast Guard's vigorous efforts to prevent the starting of an anti-Castro guerrilla war in Cuba, and, for that matter, the latter half of the Korean War are all examples. Most of the time, indeed, we went even further. North Vietnam in many years did not suffer any domestic destruction from the war. The cost of the war to North Vietnam was thus limited to those resources they voluntarily commited to the fighting in the South. There is now no cost to them which they do not completely control. Thus, D becomes extremely small, which makes it hard to make the war undesirable from the standpoint of the North Vietnamese.

We may draw another instructive lesson from the Korean, Greek, Cuban, and Vietnamese affairs. During most of the fighting in all of these cases, the United States' power was vastly greater than that of their opponents.[10] Nevertheless, the United States has chosen to commit only a small part of its forces and, in general, those forces in which it has no particular advantage. It has also put very great restrictions on the damage inflicted on its opponents. Under the circumstances, it has provided a situation where equation (1) becomes equation (3) and where equation (3) is very likely to show the inequality that leads to war. The Communists, being quite rational in this respect if not others, have chosen war.

Let us once again broaden the coverage of our model in order to consider negotiations for peace once war has begun. We are apt to think that major wars are fought to the finish, but this is not normally the case; most wars have ended with a compromise. Even in World War I and World War II our opponents made repeated efforts for compromise which were rejected by the Anglo-Saxon powers. Let us suppose, then, that a war is being fought and a proposal is made to terminate it. Presumably, the termination will involve some decision on the resources the two countries will maintain, and an agreement that the fighting shall stop. Since the fighting is destructive and therefore the total amount of resources available between the two countries after further fighting will be less than the amount now available, it would appear that there would always be a Paretian bargain that would put the parties in a better situation than the continuance of the war. In history, however, we find that wars *have* frequently gone on for some period of time. Anyway, our Paretian argument would imply that such an agreement could have been reached before the fighting began.

10. As a partial exception, at the end it was not obvious whether American nuclear power was greater than that of the Russians, but it was also not at all obvious whether Russia would choose to defend North Vietnam, and surely our power was greater than North Vietnam's. Further, we were surely much stronger than the Russians in 1965–66.

We can deal with this problem in a very simple way using the equations we already have. We can assume that each day the parties decide whether or not to continue the war. As long as for both parties the portion to the left of the inequality in equation (1) or (3)—whichever is applicable—is less than the part to the right, they will continue fighting. If the parties had exactly the same estimate of the situation in the future and there was some way of making certain the agreement reached between them would be kept, they would always make peace immediately. Historically, of course, the parties frequently have overestimated their own strength, and there is no doubt that there have occasionally been groups who liked fighting or even got pleasure out of destruction. Nevertheless, it seems to me that the basic reason for continuance of war under these circumstances is the final condition: the requirement that there be some way of seeing to it that the treaty is kept.

For example, assume that *A*, the more powerful country, is discussing with *B* whether a war should be started or whether it should be continued. Both parties feel that the probable cost of the war is such that *A* will end up in a situation where its total resources bear a higher ratio to those of *B* than they do at the moment. Under these circumstances, an agreement between the two parties almost certainly involves a transfer from *B* to *A*. In a domestic law system with a court to enforce a contract, it can, nevertheless, be optimal. Internationally, however, there are no courts and no way of enforcing contracts. Once the transfer has occurred, the two parties once again build their military machines up to the point which corresponds to their new resources and desires, and we find that country *A* is spending a smaller percentage of her national income to purchase a higher probability of victory, and that country *B* is spending a larger share of her national income to purchase a lower probability of victory. At this point, it is wise for country *A* to once again raise the question of war, and the conditions for *B* are even more unfavorable than before. It is clear that a series of acts like this eventually leads to the elimination of *B*. *B* can only avoid this sequence by making the costs of forcing a transfer upon her greater than the transfer is worth.

The normal way of robbing a bank is to point a gun at the teller and tell him that you will shoot him if he does not give you the money. There is, however, another method sometimes used, in which instead of a gun the robber carries a bomb. He informs the teller that if he is not given the money, he will set off the bomb, thus killing both the teller and himself. This is an inferior method of robbing a bank, but clearly it can work. The point of this little story is that, from the standpoint of the weaker power, defense really depends on this bomb technique. The weaker party says, in essence, "if you wish to seize part or all of my territory, I will fight in the full knowledge that the damage inflicted on me by the fighting will be at least as great as and probably greater than the damage inflicted on you; but the damage inflicted on you will be great enough so that if you are rational, you will choose not to fight." Thus, in this case, the weaker party, if it is rational, will choose to fight even though the present discounted value of fighting in the short run is less than that of a compromise. The stronger party may feel that, after some fighting, the weaker party will recognize the advantages of surrender, and, therefore, the stronger will start the war.

Nuclear war frequently raises problems rather like this. The declared policy of the United States is to undertake nuclear war under certain circumstances—i.e., a Russian invasion of Western Europe—in the full knowledge that it would cause the destruction of the United States. Indeed, we have made little preparation to even limit the destructiveness of such a war. As long as we can convince the Russians that we will, in fact, do it, Western Europe is safe from invasion. If, however, they begin to feel that we would behave rationally in the event of their invasion, they would be well-advised to invade. Thus, a rational defense of the United States under present conditions requires that we give the appearance of irrationality. It has sometimes been said that Hitler made it clear to his opponents that one of them must behave rationally and that it would not be Hitler.

In a way, our present foreign policy has this characteristic.[11] To return to our example of a war between *A* and *B*, with *A* being the stronger party, in general *A* should always be willing to end the war, in return for a suitable gain from her original position, because this will give her an opportunity for a future war under still better conditions. *B*, on the other hand, should be motivated to fight to the end, with the idea of making it clear to *A* that war is an extremely painful business. The successful defense of Finland during World War II is an example. As we shall point out later, when there are more than two countries concerned, we do not have this desperate pure opposition of interests.

Let us now further weaken the restrictive assumptions with which we began this chapter. Let us consider a situation in which *A* and *B* are not

11. Note that I refer only to the present, i.e., 1967–74 foreign policy. Our foreign policy before 1967, owing to the fact that we had overwhelming superiority over the Russians, did not have this irrational element.

currently at war and are contemplating a disarmament pact. In the next chapter, we will discuss the countries' motives to cheat on such agreements, but for current purposes, let us assume a disarmament contract which neither party violates. As was pointed out earlier, such a disarmament pact should make war more likely because it reduces the destruction component of equations (1) and (3) without changing the odds or the spoils of victory. In fact, it actually increases the spoils of victory slightly, because the countries will have been putting less money into armaments and, hence, will have more nonmilitary wealth.

Such a disarmament pact is, however, of particular advantage to the stronger nation. The weaker of the two parties is unlikely to choose a policy of aggressive war. It will realize that its best situation is not to fight and that its second best situation is to fight a successful defensive war, but that it has really very little chance of conquering its opponent. The more powerful nation really has two alternatives: an attempt to conquer the weaker nation, or peace. A joint reduction in armaments, which leads to probable victory in wartime at the same level as before but cuts their cost, benefits both parties if they choose a peaceful policy. However, to repeat, it makes it more likely that the stronger will find that a war of aggression would be desirable. The cost of the war has gone down, and the spoils have not. Thus, disarmament treaties may be to the disadvantage of the weaker party. It may be that the Russian objection to disarmament agreements before 1967 reflects this fact, although I am inclined to feel that it is based on a feeling that the Russians can depend on the Western powers to partially disarm even without an agreement.

A disarmament agreement in which the stronger party disarms more than the weaker party might be of equal benefit to both parties. It would not be as beneficial to the stronger party as an equal reduction in strength, but if the weaker party were unwilling to buy an equal reduction in strength, it might be that the stronger party would be well-advised to enter into an agreement in which the advantage of the stronger party was reduced. An accurate calculation of the appropriate ratios would be extremely difficult, and the advantages of cheating are so great that it seems to be unlikely that this solution would be reached in the real world, but it is at least theoretically possible.

Let us now turn to agreements that have nothing to do with war or arms. Normally, there are many areas where agreements between countries can lead to real gains in the net efficiency with which they use their resources.

Normally, also, these gains are relatively modest.[12] These treaties, however, have military overtones. There are two reasons for this. First, many of them will give an advantage or disadvantage to one of the parties militarily as a by-product of the economic gains. An integrated communications network, for example, may not only be more efficient than two separate communications networks, but it may be so arranged that an aggressor would be in a good position to temporarily jam the communications of his victim at the beginning of a war. But I believe this particular type of military advantage is normally small and probably plays a relatively small role in decisions as to whether or not to enter into such agreements. It may play quite a significant role in the negotiations of the details.

The second, and more important, effect such treaties might have on the relative war-making power of the two states comes from the fact that almost by definition any individual treaty will benefit one party more than the other. Further, there is normally a bargaining range, and by holding out for the maximum terms, a nation improves not only the profit of the agreement, but also its future military position by increasing future resources. Thus, an apparently innocuous proposal to develop some resource jointly may have very real, if small, military overtones. This is, of course, one of the reasons that international agreements are hard to negotiate. In my opinion, such agreements generally do not have more than minor military overtones, but small advantages can be obtained from them. Further, if there are a great many such treaties between two countries and one of them regularly obtains an advantage in the negotiations, the sum total of these advantages may be significant.

12. There is one area where such a gain possibility exists in the real world where it would not exist if the countries were engaging in rational calculations, and that is trade agreements for reduction of tariffs. Since rationally maximizing countries would have revenue-only tariffs, these agreements can only be entered into if the countries have already made a mistake in their policy. Granted the commonness, however, with which this particular mistake is made, such an agreement might give an advantage to both countries, and in this case the advantage could be very great.

AGREEMENT AND CHEATING

The outcome of individual adjustment being, on the whole, disappointing, it is sensible to look into the probability of improvement through mutual agreement among the parties. We shall mainly discuss disarmament agreements, although other agreements to limit conflict also fit our analysis.

To return to our diagrams, from the standpoint of both parties, the equilibrium point shown on Figure 11 would be inferior to any point on the ray connecting it with the origin. If both parties reduce their military expenditures proportionately, they retain the same probability of success and save resources. A movement down and to the left of this ray would correspond to a vertical downward movement on Figure 10. Assume, for example, that the point of tangency between E_2 and I_2 on Figure 10 corresponds to the equilibrium point on Figure 11. A joint agreement to reduce resources might then move party *A* to point D on the E_1 production curve. Clearly, this would be a sharp improvement in the well-being of country *A*. Country *B* would, of course, make an equivalent improvement. It is the obvious possibility of this kind of joint gain that is the motive for mutual disarmament efforts. The independent adjustment equilibrium shown on Figure 11 is clearly inferior to the adjustment the two parties could reach by agreement.

Before turning to the difficulties of disarmament agreements, we must point out that any disarmament agreement is inferior to a simple agreement not to fight, provided the two parties are of about the same size and the equilibrium position is somewhere on the order of a 50 percent probability of victory for each side. Neither party has very much to gain from the initiation of hostilities under these circumstances, and the saving, both in the risk-avoidance and in resources, that either party obtains by abandoning their military force *and* achieving security against attack more than pays for this probability of winning a war. Needless to say, this does not apply for a party which has an overwhelming probability of victory. Even with a 50-50 probability of victory, a small poor country may find war attractive against a large wealthy country. A binding agreement not to resort to war at any time in the future has the great advantage that there is no need to pay any attention at all to your

Reprinted, with permission, from *The Social Dilemma: The Economics of War and Revolution* (Blacksburg, Va.: Center for Study of Public Choice, 1974), 107–25.

opponent's military force. You can simply adjust your own military force down to whatever you think is necessary for internal reasons.

The obvious reason that countries do not enter into agreements not to fight and then abandon their military forces, or, to be more precise, the reason why countries do indeed enter into agreements not to fight and then not only retain their military forces but eventually get into wars, is simply that under international conditions you cannot trust the other party. There is no court or other process that will give you protection against violation. If country *B* enters into an agreement with country *A* under which they will never again engage in warfare and then reduces its military to a strictly domestic force, country *A* would be in a position to totally eliminate country *B* with very little difficulty. Clearly this is a highly profitable operation for country *A* and history seems to indicate a high probability that country *A* takes advantage of it. Thus, country *B* is not likely to reduce its military force just on the word of country *A*. Normally it requires some other evidence that its safety is not being reduced.

An agreement to mutually disarm under conditions in which each country can inspect the armed forces of the other may be sensible. For example, consider the 1922 naval limitations agreement. For reasons that are not clear to me, this agreement has had bad press, but it was successful. There was a very sharp reduction in naval appropriations of the major powers, with very little change in their comparative strength. It may be that the reason almost everyone was unhappy can be seen from Figure 10. Assume that an agreement reduces a country's appropriations to point D. Clearly this is not an equilibrium point for that particular country, granted the military expenditures its potential opponents are making. It would prefer to move up and to the right until indifference curve I_1 is tangent to the production function E_1. This would improve its well-being. The only reason for not doing this is that, if other countries know you are making this move, they will respond in kind, and you will eventually return to the individual adjustment equilibrium which is inferior to point D. Nevertheless, a continuing dissatisfaction with point D and the obvious fact that the country can improve its state of well-being quite easily may, over time, lead to a feeling of dissatisfaction with the treaty.

In practice, the 1922 naval conference agreement was kept quite strictly by all parties, although there are numerous allegations on the part of everybody that the other members of the agreement were cheating in one way or another. When we look into these allegations, we almost uniformly find not that the alleged cheater was actually violating the agreement, but that they were doing something which was not banned by the agreement but which increased their level of security. The Japanese, for example, objected to a rebuilding of the engines of American battleships which added a half knot or so to their speed. There was nothing in the agreement that banned this. Similarly, the United States objected to the Japanese construction of a large number of light cruisers in the 1920s and the early 1930s. Again, the agreement did not restrict this.

If we turn to matters that were actually covered by the agreement, there seems to be no evidence of any other than accidental minor violations.[1] The reasons for this rather strict adherence to the agreement are, I think, fairly simple and straightforward; it is extremely difficult to conceal a battleship. Further, the battleship must proceed to sea for maneuvers if it is to remain efficient. Thus, it was very difficult to conceal any violations of the agreement, and hence a movement from D to the tangency solution would normally be detected immediately and would lead to immediate reprisals from the other countries concerned. Further, all of the countries who entered into this agreement (except Italy) were democracies.[2] Democracies are not necessarily any more peaceful or any less likely to violate treaties than are dictatorships. In fact, it is possible to make a good historical argument that the converse is true. But democracies do find it much harder to keep secrets than dictatorships. Thus, the successful evasion of the treaty in secret would have been hard for these governments. The Italian failure to evade can, I think, be put down simply to the inefficiency of Mussolini's government.

To discuss the problems of evasion, though, we must begin by pointing out that the potential savings by disarmament are great enough so that some evasion may be acceptable. To clarify the situation, suppose that there is no genuine evasion, but that it is hard to compute the relative effect on the strength of two powers of some particular reduction in their budgets. Let us suppose, for example, that one country very largely depends on a conscript army and the other on a professional army. Under these circumstances, a reduction in the budgets of both countries would probably leave the conscript

1. Individual ships may have exceeded the tonnage limitations by a ton or so, owing to the designers' efforts to come as close as possible to the maximum weight permitted, and to the inexactness of naval designing.

2. The fact that Japan was a democracy before World War II has been well obscured by wartime propaganda. We may not regard it as an ideal government, but the fact remains that there were elected governments with opposition parties, cabinet changes, and newspapers which were highly critical of the government.

army more powerful than the professional army. On the other hand, if the budget reductions are matched with some reduction in the number of conscripts taken, then the exact match is a matter upon which it would be hard to make exact calculations. We can, then, imagine that each of these countries (again represented by Figure 10) instead of finding itself at the point shown by D, finds itself at some other point. It will be noted that even if the error is quite sizable, both countries could be better off than at the original point, although one would, of course, make a larger gain than the other.

The same principle applies to cheating. Suppose it is thought that one party is likely to cheat and the other is not. Under these circumstances, they negotiate an equal reduction in arms, but one party, in fact, cheats by not making all of the promised reductions. The one who keeps the agreement will face a production function which is not as much below the original production function as that faced by the country which has cheated. Both may well be better off than they were originally, but it is clear that the country that has cheated will gain more than the country that has not. Obviously, if the cheating is extensive enough, the country which does not cheat will be worse off than it was before.

Note that the country which does not cheat has only one way of retaliating: it breaks the treaty itself and thus moves back to the original point of equilibrium. Thus, its only threat is that it may injure itself as well as its opponent. Under these circumstances, the potential cheater may not feel there is a very high probability that his cheating will lead to any very bad consequences, even if it is detected. It may be that those people in the United States who argue strongly for disarmament agreements with Russia, without very much concern about determining how much the Russians actually disarm, are following a line of reasoning of much the sort we have specified. They feel that the net effect of the United States keeping the agreement and the Russians cheating will still be an advantage to the United States, although, of course, there will be a very much greater advantage to Russia. These people are implicitly saying that they are willing to let the Russians cheat to a certain extent but still hope to make a gain.

Let us assume that the noncheater would not abandon the treaty and return to independent adjustment *unless* the amount of cheating detected were some particular amount "A." Note that A must be the amount of cheating which is detected, not the amount of cheating actually undertaken, because the noncheating country, of course, only knows what it knows; it does not know what it does not detect. Under these circumstances, the cheating party can plan to cheat some amount larger than A, let us say A + X. This cheating is relatively easy because the country does not have to make any great effort to conceal the A portion. It will only conceal that portion of its cheating which is greater than the amount of cheating the noncheating country will tolerate without returning to an all-out arms race. If the amount of cheating, "A," which will be tolerated is the maximum amount of cheating which will still leave the noncheating power better off than in the arms race, then it follows *ex definitione* that "A + X" will leave the noncheating power in a worse condition than it would be in the arms race.

Since X can be arbitrarily small, it is fairly easy under these circumstances for the cheating power to keep the noncheating power in a real situation worse than at the time of the arms race, but in a slightly better apparent situation. Of course, it is not certain that this is the optimal policy from the standpoint of the cheater. The cheater's indifference curves may have a relationship to the production function specified by the noncheater's budget such that the point of tangency involves an amount of cheating less than A + X. However, the cheater would probably cheat the amount of A + X.

This conclusion means that the complying country can never feel any high degree of certainty that the detected cheating is the *total* cheating. Thus, the detecting country cannot put any "confidence" in the policy of the other country if it detects any cheating at all. The amount it detects may be all that is being undertaken, or it may be that the amount it detects is simply a part. Under these circumstances, it seems sensible to devote the remainder of this chapter to cheating and its consequences.

We shall start with the prisoner's dilemma model we have previously used. Let us assume that two countries are contemplating mutual disarmament. Once the treaty is completed, each country will have to consider whether to keep the treaty or cheat. For both countries, not keeping it is equivalent to not entering into the treaty, except for the expenditure of resources in negotiating. However, let us assume that the treaty has been concluded and the two countries are considering whether or not to keep it. On Figure 13, *A* and *B* are shown with *K* (for Keep) and *NK* (for Not-Keep) strategies available to them. The payoffs are in the usual prisoner's dilemma form. For each country, the best of all possible worlds is one in which they cheat and their opponent does not; the second-best world is one in which both parties keep the treaty; the third-best is that in which neither keeps it; and the worst of all is that in which they keep it and their opponent does not. Put differently, you favor most a situation in which you can easily conquer your enemy; secondly,

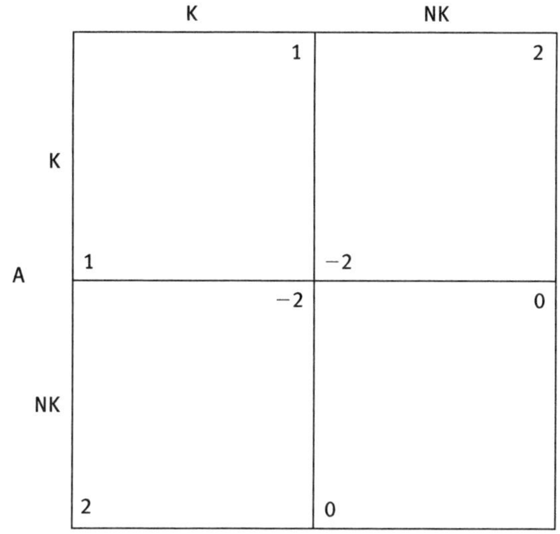

FIGURE 13
The armorer's dilemma

a cheap standoff; third, an expensive standoff; and fourth, a situation in which your enemy can easily conquer you.[3]

Let us begin by assuming that the individual contemplating such a treaty has some idea as to the probability of the different parties playing varying strategies. Under these circumstances, it is easy to deduce the payoff of the game to, let us say, party *A*, and the result of the somewhat tedious operation is equation (1).

$$\text{Payoff to A} = P(A_K) \cdot P(B_K) - 2P(A_K) + 2P(B_K), \qquad (1)$$

where
P = probability,
A_K = A keeps treaty, and
B_K = B keeps treaty.

3. A pacific country might not be interested in conquest, and hence would be indifferent between the first and second alternatives. For such a country, the number I have shown as 2 in Figure 13, would be 1. The country would still be better off cheating on its agreement, but the motives for such cheating would, of course, be weaker than if the values are as shown on Figure 13.

Assume that party *A* proposes to carry out the contract strictly if it is negotiated, and therefore $P(A_K) = 1$. Under these circumstances, equation (1) reduces to equation (2); *A* gets a positive discounted value from the contract if he believes that the probability that *B* will keep the contract is better than 2 out of 3.

$$\text{Payoff to A} = 3P(B_K) - 2 \quad (2)$$

On the other hand, if he feels the probability that *B* will keep the contract is less than 2 out of 3, the payoff to *A* is negative.

Suppose, on the other hand, that *A*'s sole motive in entering into the contract is to cheat *B*, and *A* does not intend to carry out the contract. $P(A_K)$, then, is equal to zero, and equation (1) reduces to equation (3).

$$\text{Payoff to A} = 2P(B_K) \quad (3)$$

Under these circumstances, clearly *A* should reach agreement on the treaty, regardless of his assessment of the probability that *B* will keep it, unless he feels that the actual cost of negotiating the treaty (not included in our matrix) is greater than the expression in equation (3).

The rather simple line of reasoning shown in our three equations offers a neat explanation for the fact that countries who are by no means interested in keeping their treaties frequently are in favor of disarmament agreements. They have nothing to lose. On the other hand, countries who favor keeping their treaties (and who in fact commonly do) are apt to be very reluctant to enter into disarmament treaties. Thus, one's attitude toward disarmament treaties is less affected by the desire for armament or disarmament than by the desire to cheat.

Let us, however, convert our present line of reasoning to a somewhat more general form.[4] Assume that party *A*, at the time of the treaty, is not certain whether he himself will carry it out. This might be because his decision in this matter will be determined by events that occur in the future, including the possibility of violation by the other party, or simply because he finds his own behavior difficult to predict. Under these circumstances, he should make an estimate both of the probability that the other party will keep the treaty and the probability that he will. We can use equation (1) to compute those joint probabilities of keeping the treaty which have the same payoff to

4. The following paragraphs are based on H. Edwin Overcast and Gordon Tullock, "A Different Approach to the Repeated Prisoner's Dilemma," *Theory and Decision*, 1 (June, 1971), 350–58.

party A in anticipated terms as the 0,0 which is equivalent to not having a treaty. This is an indifference line and is shown by I_A on Figure 14. Note that the high point of A's indifference surface is in the lower left corner of the diagram; hence, this particular indifference curve bends the wrong way. It does not lead to a corner solution, because each of the parties has control only of movement on one of the two dimensions. Therefore, it raises no problems for the usual theorems. In a sense, it is an intellectual curiousum. All other indifference curves for party A can be drawn in by similar calculations and will show the same general shape.

The particular curvature of the line I_A is, of course, the consequence of the values in the matrix. For a more general solution, let us turn to Figure 15 where the payoffs have been represented by the four letters W, X, Y, and Z. Assuming some probabilities for K_A and K_B, the payoff for A is shown by equation (4).

$$\text{Payoff for A} = P(K_B) \cdot W + (1 - P[K_A]) \cdot P(K_B) \cdot X$$
$$+ (1 - P[K_B]) \cdot P(K_A) \cdot Y + (1 - P[K_B])\,(1 - P[K_A]) \cdot Z \qquad (4)$$

Multiplying and collecting terms leads to equation (5).

$$\text{Payoff for A} = P(K_B)\,(X - Z) + P(K_A)\,(Y - Z)$$
$$+ P(K_A)P(K_B)\,(W + Z - X - Y) + 1 \qquad (5)$$

It will be noted that the curvature of line I_A comes from the final term before the +1. If $W + Z > X + Y$ as it is in the matrix of Figure 13, then the curvature will be as shown. If $W + Z < X + Y$, the curvature will have the normal shape and, if they are equal, the indifference curves will be straight lines.

Returning then to Figure 14, I have also drawn in the indifference curve for party B passing through the 0,0 point as I_B. A is only interested in disarmament treaties if his assumption as to the probability of the treaty being carried out, both by himself and by his opponent, indicates an outcome to the left of I_A. Since A can always achieve the no-treaty or no-compliance point by himself, he need not accept any outcome to the right of this line. Similarly, party B is only interested in treaties to the right of I_B. It should be noted in this connection that any party violating the treaty will always be either at the joint no-compliance point or at a point which is better for him than the joint no-compliance point.

However, if we assume that neither party feels that he can deceive the other, then a disarmament treaty will only be signed if the joint probabilities of keeping the treaty by the two parties lie within the space bounded by the

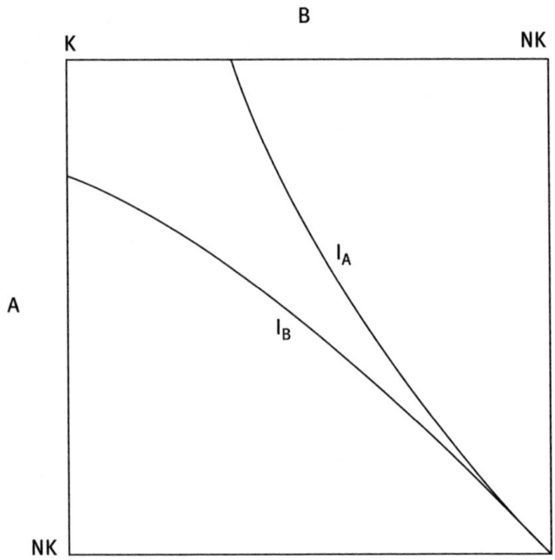

FIGURE 14
Continuous space game

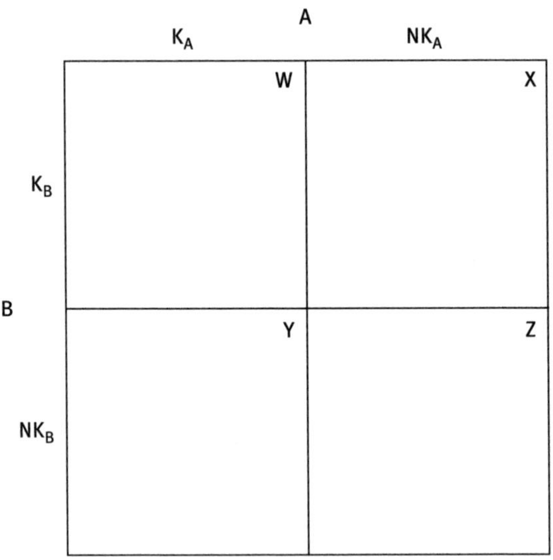

FIGURE 15
Abstract matrix

two indifference lines shown on Figure 14. This is true regardless of whether or not the gains from the disarmament treaty taken by and of itself are large or small. Indeed, it is more likely that small gains may be obtained than large gains. The advantages of cheating on an agreement for minor disarmament are much less than those for cheating on a major disarmament, and there are usually minor areas where policing is easy.

So far, we have assumed that the parties are entering into treaties without the use of any resources to avoid cheating. The establishment of a police force which enforces all agreements, of course, would eliminate the prisoner's dilemma problem as we have pointed out before. In international affairs this is not likely to be an attractive solution, because it involves giving to a third power the enforcing mechanism, the power to compel both of the parties of the original treaty, and it is likely that this third power will use this power for other objectives as well. It involves deliberately placing yourself in the −2 position on a second matrix in which the enforcing apparatus is the other party.

It might be thought that this conclusion could be avoided quite readily by simply giving to the enforcing authority not the full power to enforce the agreement but the power to keep the balance between the two existing countries. The problem with this solution is that if one of the parties chooses to violate the agreement, it is unlikely that the other parties would regard that as a *causus belli*, if they did not regard the nonsignature of the treaty itself as a *causus belli*. Thus, the effect of violating the treaty, if it were detected, is merely that you are back to the situation which would have existed before the treaty was drawn.[5] People contemplating breaking civil contracts in the United States would be delighted with this alternative to having the courts enforce their contracts. Nevertheless, it is possible to use resources to reduce the likelihood you will be cheated. For example, both parties can set up arrangements under which it will be fairly easy for them to detect cheating. If it is immediately detected when one party cheats and the treaty ceases to have any application, then it is less likely that either party will cheat.

There are two problems connected with this particular situation. The first of these is that the situation provides a wonderful opportunity for one of the

5. The civil equivalent would be if the sheriff's office enforced contracts by sending a deputy who would assist you in fighting if you chose to fight. The deputy would, let us say, be a small, relatively weak person who was not capable of winning the fight by himself but who, in most cases, would carry the balance of power in the fight. Clearly, a great many people would choose not to go to law if the only outcome of a successful suit was an opportunity to personally engage in combat with a better chance of winning.

parties to cheat the other by proposing methods of detection of violation which are, in fact, inefficient. If there are efficient and cheap methods of detecting violation, it is unlikely that anyone would violate. If, however, one party can convince the other that methods of detecting violation should be used which are expensive and uncertain, then, in the first place, the parties will choose to make less use of these expensive methods, and secondly, detection will be less likely. Under the circumstances, there may be very strong motives for cheating. In practice, of course, the countries which argue against the use of efficient methods of detecting violation are characteristically those countries who themselves propose to cheat. Naturally, they do not say this; they make remarks about national sovereignty, the wickedness of spies, etc., but basically their motive is simply to impede detection of their own cheating.

The second problem in the use of resources to prevent cheating is simply that resources, of course, are expensive and that it may well be that the expense of this use of resources is greater than the advantage of the disarmament treaty. I must say that I think this would only be true in those cases where the two parties did not choose the most efficient method of enforcement. The most efficient method of enforcement, which was invented long ago, is to repeal all laws against espionage. Both parties would then offer large rewards for information (including information on punishment of people who are engaged in espionage). It would be extremely difficult, if not impossible, to evade this type of surveillance.

If, on the other hand, detection depends on such things as the use of satellites, seismic detectors in vast arrays at long distances from the potential violation area, etc., and if these methods are not only expensive but of somewhat uncertain effectiveness, then the opposite conclusion may emerge. This is particularly true if the aspects of your opponent's military machine you are interested in detecting are certain tests that he may or may not choose to undertake. It seems unlikely that under present circumstances anyone would feel it really essential to test a hydrogen bomb. *Scientific American* has explained how hydrogen bombs are built. With a little knowledge of physics and the appropriate article in *Scientific American*, it is possible to produce a design which no physicist would have many doubts about. One could then build a very large number of such hydrogen bombs without ever testing one, and thus have a major military force. There would be some small chance that the bomb would not work; however, this could be tested by setting off a bomb in some part of your own territory two minutes before you plan to launch your attack. If it failed to go off, you would have done nothing that could be

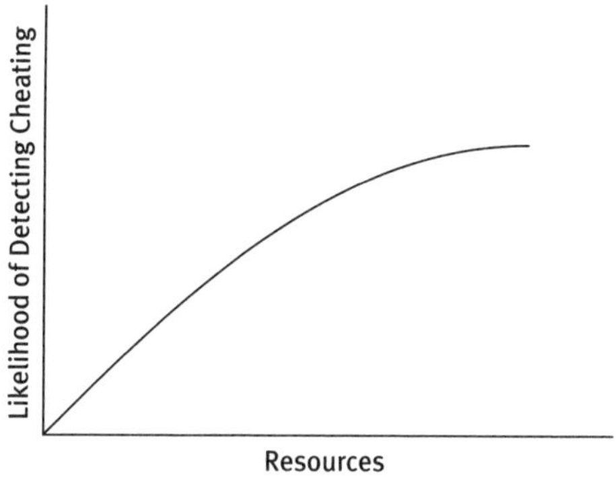

FIGURE 16
Returns to cheating

detected, and you could stop your attack; if it did go off, the detection would do your opponent no good.[6]

Let us, however, turn to this problem of investment of resources in detecting cheating in a slightly more formal way. On Figure 16, we show on the horizontal axis the resources put into detection, and on the vertical, the protection obtained. Note that I have drawn in the usual declining marginal return. A function like that in Figure 16 will be available for both parties. One can think of the two parties as playing a differential game in which zero resources by both parties was in the upper left-hand corner of the matrix and increasing commitments of resources by the two parties ran along, respectively, the horizontal and vertical axes away from it. This will be a prisoner's dilemma–type game, since both parties (on this game only) will prefer zero commitment of resources. It is also not at all obvious in this case that one can, strictly speaking, refer to the system as a matrix. *A*'s decisions as to how much he will invest in detecting possible cheating by *B* are in no way involved in *B*'s detection or nondetection of *A*'s cheating. Nevertheless, for each player we can take some function which has the same general shape as shown in Figure 16, and the equations we have already developed for the indifference levels of the parties to the agreements. We can thus obtain the optimal amount of resources to invest in protecting the parties against being cheated. In general,

6. There remains, of course, the possibility of "fizzle," i.e., some kind of nuclear reaction which would not be usable as a weapon. Presumably, if the fizzle was feeble so that the "hydrogen bomb" would be of no use as a weapon, then if the tests were underground, it would be undetectable.

the two parties will have a joint gain from the use of more efficient methods of protection against cheating, and individual gains from successful cheating with less efficient means of detection. We anticipate the usual prisoner's dilemma.

And how will we protect ourselves against being cheated? If we look into ordinary business bargains, we find that businessmen have a wide variety of methods. The first, and perhaps the commonest, is simply to refuse to deal on a credit basis with people who have been unreliable. We can refuse to enter into otherwise apparently desirable contracts since the desirability depends, to some extent, on the trustworthiness of the person with whom we are making the agreement. In consequence, many agreements which are desirable on their face, are undesirable because of the problem of enforcement.

This is particularly true in international agreements, since the alternative of court enforcement is not present. In general, countries are very reluctant to enter into agreements with other countries on major matters where the other country can easily cheat and obtain an advantage. The problem can perhaps be illuminated by a strictly commercial example. In the 1820s and 1830s, the importation of opium to China from India was largely dominated by three major firms, two of which were Charles Dent and Company and Jardine Mathieson and Company. Quick communication between the main offices of these firms in Canton and their buying agents in the opium market at Calcutta was important and, generally speaking, was facilitated by a cooperative arrangement under which all of the companies in the trade transmitted their mail by the ships of all the companies. Thus, if a Dent and Company ship happened to be leaving Calcutta on the seventh of January and no Mathieson ship was leaving until the fifteenth, the Dent and Company ship would carry all the mail for Canton.

The reason this arrangement is important is that on one occasion there was a very sharp fall in the price of opium in Calcutta. The Jardine Mathieson ship, which left Calcutta with the mail to Canton, as usual was met at the bar by a Jardine Mathieson agent. After looking over his own mail, he instructed the captain to hold delivery on the mail to the other companies for one day. During this day Jardine Mathieson sold enough opium at the old price to Dent and Company to permanently cripple Dent financially. Jardine's would never have thought of cheating Dent on a minor matter. They were aware of the fact that, over the long run, maintaining their credit with Dent was more important than minor gains. However, given the opportunity of dealing a crippling blow to Dent, they took the chance and made a great deal of money by doing so. Situations like this arise relatively rarely in commercial life, but international relations are full of them. This is particularly true with respect to disarmament treaties.[7]

Thus, one way of investing resources in reducing the likelihood of being cheated is to simply refuse to enter into otherwise profitable contracts because the contracts might lead to your being cheated. The two characteristics would have to be laid off against each other and we could, in the usual manner, find an optimum strategy. A second procedure is to design the contracts according to the principle of "simultaneous performance." A "simultaneously performed" contract is a contract in which at no time can any party make any great gain by discontinuing the contract because, at any given time, discontinuance of the contract by either party will not make much difference.

As a commercial example, a person who buys the furniture for his house on the installment plan is in a situation where the refusal to pay the installments would leave him with the furniture and the installment company with a lawsuit. In the absence of courts to enforce the contract, it is very doubtful that furniture companies would enter into this kind of contract. On the other hand, a joint agreement between someone who wishes to furnish his house and a furniture company under which the furniture will be provided piece by piece as it is paid for, according to some prearranged program which permits the realization of economies, would involve simultaneous performance and there would be relatively little risk on the part of either party. Since there are no great gains from violating the contract, one would anticipate that there would be little tendency to so violate. A disarmament contract with very good arrangements for detecting cheating would, more or less, fall in the category of the second type of arrangement; whereas a disarmament agreement with poor arrangements for detecting cheating would fall in the first.

Once again, it is obvious that signing only treaties with "simultaneous performance" rules out many treaties which, if it were not for the possibility of cheating, would be desirable. The final method of attempting to avoid being cheated is simply to try to arrange for some very good detection system, so that you will know the moment the cheating occurs. Needless to say, this is

7. Laurence W. Beilenson, *The Treaty Trap: A History of the Performance of Political Treaties by the United States and European Nations* (Washington, D.C.: Public Affairs Press, 1969), is a survey of substantially all of the significant political treaties entered into among the Western nations in the last 300 years. His general conclusions as to the value of these solemn undertakings by a group of more than usually respectable nations is perhaps indicated most clearly by his title.

only relevant in those cases where simultaneous performance has been arranged by treaty. If an arrangement were made under which, let us say, the United States was to disarm today and Russia was to disarm next year, the fact that we were able to detect absolutely perfectly that they had not disarmed would do us very little good.

Thus, this method again means that many otherwise desirable contracts are not feasible. There is, of course, an excellent way of eliminating all of these problems, which is to provide some powerful organization to enforce the contract; but this is difficult in the international area. The problem of *quis custodiet ipsos custodes* immediately arises. If we establish a monopoly of force internationally which means that we make ourselves defenseless before it, in general, we would be in jeopardy. One can, as a possible example, consider the situation of Israel if the United Nations were a powerful organization capable of enforcing its decisions.

For minor matters, however, there is a sort of enforcement mechanism implicit in what we think of as "credit." Let us suppose that we as a nation anticipate that in future years we will have many occasions on which contracts between ourselves and other people will be mutually profitable, that none of these contracts will be of such importance that a person violating them could obtain a definitive advantage over the victim of his fraud, and that in many of these contracts a simultaneous performance arrangement will not be optimal. Under these circumstances, we may decide to enter into such contracts and keep them strictly. However, we could follow the strategy of refusing to enter into any further contracts with countries that had broken their agreement. This is rather the way merchants using credit bureaus behave. Each country realizes that violating a contract right now will give it an advantage, but will make it impossible to enter into a number of advantageous contracts in the future. As long as the advantage to be gained from violating a contract right now is less than the cost of reducing the likelihood of contracts in the future, they will keep contracts even when gains are available from breach.

Note, however, that this procedure requires, as part of its apparatus, that the countries concerned *do* penalize parties who seldom keep contracts by refusing to enter into further agreements with them. If the only result of country *A* violating a contract is that gain accrues to country *A*, this motive for honesty on the part of country *A* evaporates. This can occur if country *B*, its victim, wishes to have further contracts which country *A* can then either violate or not, as it chooses. It seems that one of the reasons for the general difference between the behavior of the Russian government in dealing with democratic governments and with businessmen is a consideration of this problem. The Russian government cannot be compelled to carry out a contract with a foreign country. It also cannot be compelled to carry out a contract with a foreign businessman. In practice, however, the Russian government's record for keeping contracts with foreign businessmen is respectable, if far from perfect. However, their record for keeping agreements with democracies is extremely poor. The explanation for this seems fairly obvious: Breaking agreements with businessmen would make other businessmen unwilling to enter into agreements in which "credit" was extended to the Russians. Since the gain to be made from breaking any given contract is usually small and the cost of having one's credit reduced in the future is quite large, it is seldom sensible to break contracts of this sort.

Contracts between the Russian government and dictatorships raise somewhat the same problems because dictators also are likely to respond to the reputation of a country for keeping its contracts. Treaties with democracies, however, do not seem to raise these problems for a potential welcher. Democracies have notoriously short memories, and in all Western democracies the public tends to think that agreements are good things, per se. Thus, over many years the Russian government has been able to enter into agreements with democracies—which it then does not carry out—without making it impossible to enter into other agreements. It must be admitted, of course, that the democracies are not total gulls and in negotiation do not treat the Russians in quite the same way they would treat, say, Switzerland. Still, the effect is there. It is ironic but true that if the democracies were more reluctant to enter into treaties with the Russians, if they tended to penalize the Russians for violating one treaty by not being willing to enter into "credit-type" treaties with Russia for a number of years thereafter, it is likely that the Russians will be motivated to keep their contracts better. Contracts which under current conditions would clearly be foolish, would become sensible.

A special problem in connection with cheating has to do with the advantages of secrecy. For many activities, there is a distinct efficiency gain if some or all portions of the activity can be kept a secret. The obvious case, of course, is a purely military operation where generals always attempt to keep secrets from the enemy. Clearly, providing the force who planned to invade Europe in the spring of 1944 with a complete set of totally uncensored reporters with full access to all data including plans would have handicapped Overlord. Fighting in Vietnam was, in fact, greatly hampered by the press. I myself knew about the "Fishhook" operation 24 hours in advance because I read the

Washington Post. The efficiency advantages of secrecy run throughout political activity. Diplomacy works better if your opponents do not know what your minimum terms are, etc. In many cases, governments are interested in keeping things secret from their own citizens and are aware of the fact that foreign nations will break this secrecy if the foreign government learns about it. We will develop some other examples of secrecy efficiency below.

For the moment, however, let us simply point out that secrecy, like suicide, cannot be punished. Attempts at secrecy and attempts at suicide *can* be punished; but in either case if the operation is successful, no punishment can be imposed. Thus, if I wish to gain the benefits of secrecy with respect to something or other, there is no cost to me from this secrecy unless it is unsuccessful.[8] The problem, then, is that the secrecy may not be successful; it may be only an attempt at secrecy. In deciding whether or not to attempt to keep something secret, I should weigh the likelihood of the secrecy being penetrated against the penalty, if any, to which penetration of secrecy would lead against the likelihood the secrecy will be successful and the benefits which would be drawn from that.

Bacteriological warfare research can be carried on relatively inconspicuously, while testing hydrogen bombs is much more difficult to hide. But there are other aspects. It is much easier for a totally closed totalitarian society to keep secrets than it is for an open society. About half of Russia, for example, is currently barred to foreign visitors. The existence of this situation in which half the country is off-limits makes it much easier to hide a given installation than it is in the United States, where almost the entire country is open to casual inspection; therefore, an area in which travel is prohibited automatically attracts attention. The unsuccessful Israeli effort to camouflage their atomic plant as a textile mill illustrates the difficulties which a relatively open society has not only in concealing things, but in concealing the fact that anything is being concealed.

Disarmament treaties normally concern matters for which secrecy is important. Our military units will function more efficiently, regardless of their size, if their location and battle plans are kept secret. Secrecy with respect to

8. It is possible, of course, that the secrecy might be only partial. Thus, for example, let us suppose that I wish to keep secret the design of a new type of biological weapon but do not wish to keep secret the location in which research is proceeding on it. Under these circumstances, it would be readily possible for anyone who wished to find out that I did, indeed, have a secret. If I conceal both the results of the biological studies and the fact that I am undertaking them, I would be immune to this particular type of difficulty.

their state of training is also an efficiency improving factor. Last but not least, secrecy as to their weapons will greatly improve their efficiency. This last secrecy is partially because we may not want our opponent to copy weapons which we develop, a subject which will be discussed later, and partly because our opponent would be able to prepare his military forces to deal with an American unit whose equipment is known. Thus we are motivated to try to keep secret a great deal of information about our military machine, simply because keeping it secret is a very cheap way of increasing the efficiency of that military machine.

Disarmament agreements, then, must contend with these special motives for secrecy. Reducing the secrecy of our army is in itself a reduction in its strength. On the other hand, assume that we have decided to reduce our military force to some particular level and, in fact, that we loyally keep this promise. Under these circumstances, we will have the strongest of possible motives to try and keep the exact characteristics of our military force, its current location, those details of its equipment which are not strictly determined by the treaty, and its state of training and readiness concealed from the potential enemy. We anticipate that he will feel the same way. Thus, per se, efforts to keep military matters secret do not necessarily indicate an effort to cheat.

On the other hand, once we accept the fact that our opponent will be permitted to keep certain aspects of his military machine a secret, it becomes easier for him to cheat. Since both parties can obtain a greater military capacity very cheaply by secrecy, refusing this particular economy to the two parties of the potential disarmament treaty may mean that they will find it necessary to spend considerably more on military preparedness than otherwise. The compromise between these two factors clearly will be an uneasy one.

Let us now turn to secrecy in weapons development. We shall begin with the problem of secrecy in science in general, and then switch to weapons later. Suppose two countries, which we shall call *Small* and *Big*. *Small* devotes $1 million to scientific research in each year, while *Big* equally regularly devotes $10 million to this end. Assuming that all of this research money is put into patentable research, there are no particular problems raised other than those involved in investments of any sort. The individual country should put money into the research until such time as the marginal cost of the resources invested, and this may well work out to our $1 million and $10 million figures. Note, however, that the benefits of the research (other than the payment of royalties) accrues jointly to the two countries. The fact that some invention happens to have been made in *Small* does not mean that it cannot be used in *Big*. The benefit which accrues from the research by way of the patent royalty goes to the country where the research was done originally. The other benefits which may accrue as a result of research are spread between the two countries, roughly in accordance with their economic potential.[9]

Assume, however, that some of the inventions are kept secret in one country. The result of this is, first, that the country which keeps them secret loses part of its royalties. Second, the other country loses part of the benefit it could obtain from using those patents. Perhaps the more important result of this, however, is that advance in science is somewhat retarded because the scientists of the country that does not have access to this particular secret development may be spending their resources either in attempting to reinvent or attempting to develop something that would be easier to invent if they knew the scientific principles of the secret invention. This disadvantage is not only a disadvantage for the country that is not privy to the secret, but is also a disadvantage for the country that is keeping the secret, in that certain inventions that would be of use to it will either not be made or be made more slowly by the other country. The effect will be to reduce the total world product while, at the same time, working a shift in the percentage of the product received by the two countries toward the country that is keeping the secret. Normally—but not in military goods—this type of restriction would be irrational.

Let us now turn to the pure science case and assume that *Small* and *Big* are spending their money solely to encourage pure or unpatentable research. Under these circumstances, a discovery by either *Small* or *Big* is utilized by the scientists in *Small* and *Big* together. In other words, the creation of any given invention increases the knowledge thoughout the area. *Small* benefits from an increase in *Big*'s research efforts, and *Big* benefits from an increase in *Small*'s research appropriation. We have here private production of a public good, and the usual general public benefits. There are also the usual problems in the generation of a public good, but we will ignore them for the purposes of this book.

Let us suppose that one of the countries proposes to keep its pure research a secret. Assume, for example, that *Small* keeps all of its research secret. The result of this will be that the scientists in *Small* are better informed than the scientists in *Big*. They have access to all the work done in *Big* and, in addition, the work done in *Small*. The scientists of *Big*, on the other hand, only have access to work done in *Big*. In consequence, the scientists in *Small* should be able to keep somewhat ahead of the scientists in *Big*. Note again, however,

9. Some patents, of course, might be particularly useful to one country or the other.

that this advantage for *Small* is purchased by retarding the total development of scientific knowledge. Surely, some scientists in *Big* at any given time will be attempting to make discoveries that have already been made in *Small*; and in some cases things that have been discovered in *Small* will never be discovered in *Big*, with the result that certain further developments will never occur. This retardation of the rate of growth of science in *Big* reduces the total scientific knowledge of *Small*, since *Small* has access to all of *Big*'s output. Thus, again, one nation acquires a relative advantage by choosing a smaller amount of new knowledge. Again, leaving aside military matters, this would be irrational.

If we assume that the research funds of the two countries are mixed between patentable research and pure research, the same general results follow. Once again, secrecy gives the country which maintains the secret a comparative advantage, but retards the development of science in general, including the development of science in the country which retains the secrecy.

As we have said, this type of secrecy is, leaving military matters aside, generally irrational. Unfortunately, when we talk about military science, it ceases to be irrational. In designing a military force, it is important to have weapons—if possible—more advanced than those of competitors. Granted the choice between the war in which my army has longbows and my opponent has crossbows, or a war in which both parties have equally efficient machine guns, I would prefer the former. There is no reason why any country should be concerned with the absolute level of development in arms. What they are interested in is whether their arms are more advanced than those of their possible opponents.

Given that the countries are only concerned with the comparative efficiency of their equipment, then secrecy in military research immediately becomes important. Note that this secrecy can be carried to the extent of providing a good deal of secrecy in research which may have nonmilitary applications, too. The gains in improved efficiency of the military apparatus may well more than counterbalance the losses in reduced efficiency in the rest of the research apparatus. Thus, we have again an area where secrecy is an efficiency characteristic in military affairs. Abolishing all research secrecy would, in itself, reduce the efficiency of the military machines using that research. Hence, a disarmament treaty should lead to a higher net budget for the two parties if there is no secrecy than if there is. And, once again, the laying-off of these two characteristics against each other is not easy.

THREE OR MORE COUNTRIES AND THE BALANCE OF POWER

The concept of the balance of power was developed in the latter part of the Enlightenment, and David Hume's discussion of it still is the best in the literature.[1] The point of this chapter is not to replace Hume, but to present his thoughts in more modern dress and to elaborate on their implications for the present. For this purpose, we shall begin by considering a three-nation system, then proceed to larger numbers. At first, we shall assume we are in the pre-atomic age without disarmament agreements. Later, we will add nuclear weapons and potential disarmament contracts.

Before discussing the balance of power, however, an essentially false issue must be eliminated. The balance of power was an important topic in discussions of foreign policy for most of the 19th century. During this long period, however, a subtle change occurred. The balance of power, as described by Hume and the other thinkers of the late Enlightenment, had nothing to do with peace. Indeed, it could be said to have guaranteed the persistence of war as an institution, since it ruled out the development of a "world empire." In the 19th century, however, people gradually began to refer to the balance of power as a mechanism for insuring peace. Since, in practice, it has not and, in theory, *could* not insure peace, this gave the concept a bad name.

Putting the matter in "modern dress," however, assume that we have more than two countries and that no one of them has enough power to conquer all the rest put together. Further, assume that these countries, or the people running them, wish to retain their independence and that they have certain elementary abilities to foresee obvious dangers in the future. The last assumption is a little vague, but, as we shall see, it is also very modest.

For a specific example, assume we have three countries, *A*, *B*, and *C*, and that their military forces are in the ratio, respectively, of 7, 5, and 4. It will be observed that no one of these countries can conquer the other two, although there is considerable disparity in their power. Suppose that country *A* attacks

Reprinted, with permission, from *The Social Dilemma: The Economics of War and Revolution* (Blacksburg, Va.: Center for Study of Public Choice, 1974), 126–38.

1. Hume's thoughts on the subject have been collected in *The Anglo-American Tradition in Foreign Affairs*, ed. Arnold Wolfers and Laurence W. Martin (New Haven: Yale University Press, 1956), pp. 63–77. The most prominent modern proponent of the classical balance of power is, of course, Morton A. Kaplan, who has written extensively on the subject.

country *C*, with the objective of annexation. Clearly, *A* has a high probability of success. Equally clearly, if it so succeeds, it will produce a joint country *A-C*, with a total military force which, after recovery from the damage of the war, will be equivalent to 11. Even if the war damage and, perhaps, efforts by the inhabitants of *C* to break away reduce its power, still the new *A-C* country would be easily able to conquer *B*. *B*, having a certain amount of foresight and wishing to be independent, realizes that the consequences of *A*'s conquest of *C* are likely to be disastrous. Hence, it will come to the aid of *C* if *A* attacks. Since *A* is incapable of defeating both *B* and *C* together, this means that *A* cannot annex either one of them.

It appears, at first glance, that although no one power is willing to let the other conquer the third, a partition may be possible. Thus, for example, *A* and *B* might partition *C*. First note that such partition involves a larger transfer of *C*'s territory to *B* than to *A* if *B* is not to find itself in a position of hopeless inferiority after the war is over; the jackal must get the lion's share. If *B*, for example, gets three-quarters of *C* and *A* gets one-quarter, then *A* and *B* will be equally powerful. It may be hard, however, to meet this requirement, because, at the immediate termination of the war between *A* and *B* on one hand and *C* on the other, *C*'s military forces will be in a state of disruption, and *A*'s military forces will be larger than *B*'s. Clearly this is a time of great danger for *B*.

However, even if this difficulty can be overcome and *A* and *B* can barbecue *C* quietly, it should be noted that both *A* and *B* will find that their security is reduced. As long as there are three countries, any country can assume that if it is losing a war, someone will come to its aid. Thus, if we assume that the countries are more interested in retaining their own independence than in, say, a 50 percent increase in their total size (which seems quite reasonable), they will be unwilling to engage in this kind of partition. Partitions, however, are ruled out only to three-nation systems. If there are more than three nations, partitions may be possible. It must be said that they are very rare, probably because of the great difficulty of negotiating them in such a form as to benefit each of the partitioning powers.

This line of reasoning, once again the product of the Enlightenment, explains rather neatly the sometimes shockingly quick change of side we observe in history. Suppose, for example, that *B* attacks *C* and appears to be winning. *A* then enters the war on the side of *C* in order to preserve *C* and prevent itself from being confronted in the future with a country *B-C* with a power of 9. With the defeat of *B*, however, immediate danger arises that *B* will be extinguished and that *A* will obtain enough of *B*'s property so that it will be able, eventually, to conquer *C*. Under these circumstances, a sudden shift of *C* to alliance with its former invader against its rescuer is to be expected. Perhaps the most famous case of this historically is the alliance between England, France, and Austria-Hungary against Russia, which was negotiated as the first bit of business transacted at Vienna. Ostensibly the allied powers—Russia, Austria-Hungary, and England—had gathered to impose a treaty of peace upon their defeated enemy, France.

Still, such quick changes must be expected, and we do observe them frequently. It should be noted, however, that we have so far assumed that countries in our model have foresight. Historically, they have not always had such foresight. The United States and England, for example, did not realize the risk that Russia's movement into Central Europe posed for them until well after Russia was established there. Similarly, the danger in destroying the German and Japanese military machines was totally overlooked by the Western allies. Looking back into earlier history, we can see a number of cases in which balance of power systems have collapsed because a clever and aggressive nation had succeeded in outwitting its opponents. Ch'in Shih Huang Ti unified China thus ending a long period of balance of power politics. Rome overcame the four other major powers in the Mediterranean basin—Antigonid Macedonia, Selucid Syria, Ptolemaic Egypt, and Carthage—and established a "world empire" in that area. Similar mistakes may lead to similar results in the future. The assumption that countries have foresight is usually correct, but not always.

Let us, however, expand the number of nations to five. Let us assume that *A* has a power of 9, *B* of 7, *C* of 6, *D* of 5, and *E* of 4. Note, in this set, that *A* is perfectly capable of defeating either *D* or *E* all by itself, and can, with a 50-50 chance of success, take on both of them together. Under these circumstances, the same general principles apply, but their application may be more complicated. The conquest of one of the nations by another will not necessarily be disastrous to the rest. It is true that the conquest of *B* by *A* means that the resulting *A-B* country will be more powerful than all the rest put together, but this is the only conquest which will have that effect. One anticipates that *C*, *D*, and *E*, any one of which can in alliance with *B* defeat *A*, will rapidly come to *B*'s assistance if *A* attacked *B* and appeared to be winning. The conquest of other countries, however, will not produce such a "monopoly" of power.

Thus, let us say that *A* attacks *E*. *D* might immediately come to *E*'s defense or, on the other hand, *D* might reason that it is safe to wait. *D* might feel that once a new nation, *A-E* with a power after recovery of 13, has been established, any attack by this new nation *A-E* upon *D* will immediately lead *B* and *C* to come to *D*'s assistance. Thus, *D* might feel that the investment of resources in defending *E* right now would be ill-judged. For example, for some time I have thought that, on the whole, it would be to the advantage of the United States if China were to occupy Burma and Thailand because of the effect on India.

D will have other problems; it will realize that if it entered the war on *E*'s side against *A*, there will be a real possibility that either *B* or *C* will enter on *A*'s side with the idea of sharing the spoils. The problem of eliminating the balance of power by reducing the number of nations to two would not arise. It is true, of course, that in general any country would rather have more than three countries in existence, because of the insurance it gives against accident; still, this is not anywhere near as strong an incentive as those raised by the problems of the movement from three countries to two.

If we add more countries, the same general principles continue to apply. The more countries there are, the less the independence of any one particular country is protected by the balance of power; but, on the other hand, the world is a surface of a globe and the situation in any given area normally does not involve a large number of competing countries. Thus, let us suppose that Germany attacks the Netherlands. Strictly speaking, only those countries which border on Germany and Holland will be directly concerned with this matter, and there are only five or six countries that meet this requirement. Probably all of them will regard this as something they would like to prevent, although they might not feel strongly enough about it to declare war. Any strengthening of one country by the conquest of another country or, for that matter, by economic development, is a cause for concern on the part of other countries and may lead to defensive coalitions.

Thus, the end product of the balance of power reasoning is rather simple. A country which appears to be increasing its power automatically accumulates enemies because other countries realize that this increased power is dangerous to them. It is not even necessary that this improvement in power come from conquest, although this has been the common cause. Admiral Byng destroyed the Spanish fleet without declaration of war, thus giving a precedent to Admiral Yamashita, because the Spanish government had come under the control of an efficient prime minister. England feared that the great resources of the Spanish empire, if efficiently utilized, would be a danger. The war was continued until the king of Spain agreed to dismiss his efficient prime minister and return the government of Spain to its customary muddle.

The balance of power makes it unlikely, although not impossible, that one country will succeed in conquering all the others because a career of conquest automatically develops counteracting coalitions. This, of course, does not eliminate war, but it does mean that war will seldom be vital. Wars will be fought about relatively minor matters with shrewd statesmen attempting to weave a pattern of small acquisitions into a position of power which may eventually permit them to break through the chains of the balance of power. This is not impossible, because, as we have pointed out, people do make mistakes. The Seleucid king failed to realize that the Roman campaigns against Carthage and Antigonid Macedonia were to his disadvantage. He received the payment for this inattention at Magnesia.

The balance of power, then, does not totally prevent world conquest by one power; it simply makes it unlikely. Indeed, if everyone plans with even moderate ability, no one country will be able to conquer all of the others. It should be noted, however, that one of the requirements for this system to operate is that no single country be more powerful than all the rest put together. If power is acquired by conquest, then the balance of power itself is likely to insure this particular condition. Where power is acquired by internal development, however, this may not be so. The power of the Ch'in was, to a considerable extent, the result of internal development rather than conquest, although they exploited it for purposes of conquest. Similarly, a country out on the edge of civilization may be able to expand away from the other powers and not arouse suspicion. In a sense, the early development of Rome followed this pattern and the expansion of the United States to the west, Russia to the east, and Spain and Portugal beyond the seas did so, also.

In two cases, countries rose to great power entirely through internal development. Athens rose to a position where she came close to dominating Greece essentially because of a superior economic system. Similarly, the United States rose to being the overwhelmingly dominant economic power in the world, and could have made use of this power to produce military power, which in turn, no doubt, would have made the conquest of the world reasonably simple. Indeed, in the years right after World War II, the United States actually *did* have the necessary military power for world conquest, but lacked the will to make use of it. It is possible in the case of the United States that our failure to develop an efficient military high command, with the result that our resources are normally used very badly (as illustrated in Vietnam), may be another internal characteristic which would have made it impossible for the United States to conquer the world anyway. However, it seems likely, in the case of the United States that the fact that our living standard has always been markedly higher than that of anyone else's is an important reason for our failure to embark upon a career of conquest. Until the development of nuclear weapons, at any event, American dominance of other countries would have required large garrisons; and it is, on the whole, unlikely that most of the countries of the world, with their relatively low gross national product, could have yielded enough in taxes to pay for garrisons at American rates.

So far we have discussed the balance of power without any reference to modern weaponry. As we shall see in a few moments, nuclear weapons actually reinforce the functioning of the balance of power. Before turning to this issue, however, let us consider another rather remarkable characteristic of the modern world. There is one country which is allied with a number of other countries which are very much weaker. Further, these other countries feel confident that the major country is not likely to attack them and, with less confidence, feel that the major country will not abandon them. This confidence is what makes the recent situation unique. Historically, alliances between large and small powers are quite common, but the small power rarely feels that the large power is really committed to its interests. Hence, the small power remains armed. Assume, however, that the small power does feel confident that the big power will, in fact, fight to defend it and will not attempt to seize it. Under these circumstances, the degree of security the small power will achieve through its alliance with a major power is vastly greater than the change in that security it can achieve through its own efforts. The security production function on our diagram (see Figure 6) comes very close to a straight vertical line, and the small power is apt to choose to purchase no security through its own efforts. It is a classic corner solution.

There seems to be no doubt that most of our allies have felt that this situation existed during most of the last 20 years. They were, therefore, reluctant to arm. Further, for obvious reasons they were most reluctant to do anything which might offend the United States. The result of this was an odd situation in which they built up some military force, not with the idea of contributing to their security directly, but because the United States expressed a desire that they do so. It is notable that in recent years as the reliability of the United States as an ally has begun to be questioned, these countries have begun to show some signs of actual interest in defending themselves. The end product may be a more normal world in which we do not have numerous totally helpless countries dependent upon one great master power. Granted the type of military equipment now available, this may not be an improvement.

Leaving aside this special circumstance, we must next address ourselves to a common error which is that small countries are not able to produce much in the way of military forces and, hence, are basically defenseless and should not waste resources on arms. The error in this line of reasoning is, of course, solely in the latter portion. Small countries can, in general, make very little military contribution to an alliance of which they are a member or fight long if they are attacked by a major power. Nevertheless, they can often successfully defend themselves. The reason is that the benefits to be obtained from conquering a small country are normally small, also; hence, if the cost is driven up, major powers will choose not to conquer it. In World War II, Finland retained its independence, although twice attacked by Russia. Further, Switzerland, Sweden, Turkey, and Spain all succeeded in remaining neutral, essentially because they were heavily enough armed so that no one thought the advantage of invading them outweighed the cost.

On the other hand, Denmark and Norway were invaded, although the advantages the Germans could obtain were modest, but they were weak enough so that a tiny invasion force was suitable. The Allied landing in North Africa was another example. If the French armed forces in North Africa had been capable of fighting hard for the defense of the area, the Allies would most assuredly have decided to attack elsewhere, instead of passing through this particular neutral area as part of their attack on the Axis. In this case, the French military forces in North Africa were large, but, for political reasons, it was known that only some of them would fight.

Small powers, of course, may find themselves involved in war, regardless of their armament. The Netherlands and Belgium were of such strategic importance that they were invaded in spite of the fact that they were well armed. Given their military strength, however, they would never have been invaded for reasons of simple conquest. In general, armies quite commonly invade a neutral country as part of their military operations against one of their major enemies. The North African landing, the passage through Belgium in both World War I and World War II, the Japanese landing in southern Thailand preliminary to their invasion of Singapore, and the Ho Chih Minh trail through Laos are all examples. Needless to say, this particular type of operation will seldom be undertaken if the small country is well equipped to defend itself. The original Schleifen plan involved an invasion of both Belgium and Holland. In the years before World War I, however, the Dutch built up their armed forces. In consequence, the Germans decided to alter their plan and pass only through Belgium, which, at that time, was very weak. Aggressive small countries can also obtain a positive payoff from their arms. It is not that they will become major military powers, but that the contribution they can make is proportional to the land they wish to add. Serbia was an aggressive small power in the years before World War I and, as a result of World War I, was able to almost double its land area.

Let us now, however, turn to the balance of power under more modern circumstances and assume a nuclear capacity. For this purpose, let us assume certain very general characteristics of nuclear weapons which seem to have been true at all times in the last 20 years. These technical characteristics are simply that nuclear weapons are essentially a one-shot arrangement.[2] Thus, for example, we now have approximately 1,000 land-based Minutemen. If we use them to attack Russia, we would have zero at the end of this period. If we decide to use only half of them, we would have only 500, and it would be some time before the deficit could be replaced.

In general, this has been characteristic of nuclear forces, although during the early days, when the United States depended upon night bombers for delivering the bombs to Russia, and when the Russians had substantially no antiaircraft defense against them, it may not have been true. At that time, we may have had many bombs, although I doubt it. My impression is that during this period we had a genuinely limited number of bombs. This, of course, is no longer true, since the number of warheads or potential warheads we have on hand is in excess of the number of delivery vehicles. Nevertheless, the assumption I am making is that nuclear war involves preparation for what we may call a very short war in which a very large part of the force used will be destroyed—either because it is fired at the enemy and destroys itself or because it is destroyed at its base. I do not think this is a great distortion of reality.

For simplicity, let us assume that this force we are now discussing is a single-warhead rocket system. Note that the rocket system could be composed, to a considerable extent, of antiballistic missiles. They also have the characteristics of destroying themselves in use. If we fire a certain number of antiballistic missiles and successfully intercept and destroy the incoming warheads, we nevertheless have disposed of those antiballistic missiles we fired and will be that many short until the deficit has been made good (which may take considerable time). Here again, under normal development, the weapons will for the most part be used very quickly. The non-nuclear armies provided

2. The use of multiple warheads does not basically change the one-shot characteristic of the carrier. A shotgun may be single-shot.

a large volume of cheap ammunition to be used over a long period of time and expensive guns which were hardly degraded at all by use.

Once again, let us assume we have three countries—*A*, *B*, and *C*—and that each has long-range rockets in its silos: *A* having 500, *B* having 400, and *C*, a lesser power, only 150. Ignoring any possible desire on the part of the rulers of these countries to save their subjects from suffering or to save their physical plant from disaster, let us assume that they are simply interested in increasing the relative power of their country and that they are careful plotters. Under these circumstances, how would a war go?

Suppose, for example, that country *A* decides to attack country *C*. The initial attack consists of 150 rockets with the objective of destroying *C*'s 150 rockets.[3] It is widely believed that rockets would automatically be aimed at enemy cities. There are some special circumstances where this would be desirable, but in general destroying your opponent's military equipment, with the result that he cannot destroy your cities, is a higher-paying activity than destroying his cities and then letting him destroy yours. After you have destroyed your opponent's military force, it may be sensible to threaten the destruction of his population; and, indeed, if he is stubborn, it would be sensible to carry out this threat. Forces in existence are vital for success, however, and should be attacked first. The principal exceptions to this rule are the circumstances in which for one reason or another you cannot attack his forces: perhaps your rockets are too inaccurate or you do not know where his rockets are located.

In any event, if this attack was successful, *A* ends up with 350 rockets and *C* with zero rockets. *A* can then threaten *C* with further destruction of *C*'s cities unless *C* surrenders. At this point, however, *B*, realizing its interests are concerned, will presumably interfere. Even granting my extreme assumption that every rocket fired hits its target and that, hence, one can destroy one's opponent missile force by use of only one of your own rockets for each missile

3. Throughout the following models, I shall assume a quite improbable perfect accuracy of the rockets. More realistic assumptions would complicate the reasoning, but would also strengthen the conclusions. We also stick to our single-warhead rockets. In part, the reason for this is simply that I did this work originally some time ago when this was the existing equipment, and it is still the basic equipment of both the Russian and the American rocket service, although it may not be by the time the reader sees this book. Primarily, my reasons are simply that it is much easier. If the reader is interested, he can substitute multiple-warhead rockets and some level of accuracy other than perfection into my model and get the appropriate results for that level.

he has, it is clear that *A*, under these circumstances, cannot afford a war with *B*. Indeed, it appears that *B* will be well-advised to immediately attack *A*. It can eliminate *A*'s 350 rockets and remain with the only 50 rockets in the world, which should be enough potential blackmail to cause a surrender of both *A* and *C*.

I can, of course, assume technologies different than I have assumed so far, but the general rule will follow. Under nuclear conditions a very large part of the military force is designed to be self-destroying in use. This means that the mere act of going to war leads to a very sharp reduction in the military forces available to the belligerents. Thus, the third party, a noncombatant, immediately gains by war between any two of our three countries.[4] Only if one country has a marked advantage over all the potential belligerents put together, as the United States had up to about 1966–67, is war likely to be successful in conquering the world, even granted a lack of interest in preventing destruction in your own country.

It should be noted, of course, that any country which achieves this kind of superiority is subject to very great temptations to immediately use it, because it is unlikely that the superiority will be permanent. If Russia succeeds in obtaining a "kill" superiority over the United States in the 1970s, it would on the whole be sensible for them to make use of it, because the likelihood of retaining it permanently would be low. The argument against this, of course, would be the likelihood of physical destruction; but this, again, is a matter of technology. If the Russians feel confident that they would eliminate the bulk of the American force in the first blow while still retaining a large force of their own, they would probably also feel confident that the United States would not dare use their remaining forces to reply in view of the terrible punishment the Russians could inflict upon the United States. But these are speculations for the future and not part of the current model.

Note that the reasoning we have been presenting so far would not be particularly altered if the countries also had antiballistic missile defenses. Only if these antiballistic missile defenses were of a sort (lasers) which were not degraded by use would they make any significant difference.[5] It is, however,

4. Note that his gain is entirely in power terms. There are some by-products of nuclear warfare which might cause injury to the third party. This would, however, be little or no consolation to the two primary parties; hence, the balance of power would work as expected.

5. The steady increase in the power available from lasers, if continued much longer, could totally revolutionize the nature of war. Instead of long-range attack with nuclear weapons, war

probable that if each of our countries had a choice between antiballistic missiles and offensive missiles, and all of them chose some antiballistic missiles, then the likelihood of war among them would be reduced because of the reduction in the first-strike capacity. Thus, if we assume that the forces consist of *A* with 250 rockets, *B* with 200, and *C* with 150 and that each has an antiballistic missile system which will eliminate one out of every three incoming rockets, then *A* will literally not have enough rockets to completely knock out *B*'s rocket force, even in a single attack, and her disadvantage *vis-à-vis B* after having attacked *C* will be even greater than in our previous example.

Thus it would appear that the balance of power is an even stronger restraint upon world conquest in a nuclear world than in a non-nuclear world. Again, however, this is an example with three parties. If we add countries *D*, with 250 rockets, and *E*, with 200, to our example and, once again, drop the antiballistic missile and assume that a rocket can be fired to knock out a rocket on the ground with absolute probability of success, then as was true when we moved from three to five in the earlier example, the problem becomes more complicated, and the possibility of a successful attack on one of the smaller powers becomes greater. If, for example, *A* attacks *C* under the conditions we gave before and loses 150 rockets in the process, it is unlikely that *B* will be in a position to immediately attack *A*, because the use of enough of her rockets, to eliminate the remaining rockets of *A*, will leave her naked before *D* and *E*. Thus the extinction of small powers, which is unlikely in a three-power world, becomes possible in a five-power world. Note that this tendency will, in general, not lead to conquest by one country, because as soon as *A* has acquired *C* and, let us say, after a few years has replaced and built up so that she now has 650 rockets, she will immediately pose a major menace to the remaining three countries. They will form some kind of alliance to respond immediately if the *A-C* country proceeded to attack some other country, let us say *E*.

One special characteristic of this type of nuclear warfare, however, is the possibility of cheating your ally. In conventional warfare, if *A* wishes to help *B* defend herself against *C*, she must actually commit forces to that end. In nuclear war, however, it will be possible for *A* to in fact refrain from firing her rockets during the first exchange. There is such a short time involved that her

---

would become a matter of completely horizon-dominated operations with almost perfect accuracy in "gunnery." It is not at all obvious that this would give the defense or the offense an advantage, but it certainly would totally revolutionize present technological conditions for warfare.

ally will probably not realize this has happened. Thus, she will be in a very superior position for the second round. This particular type of treachery was not possible with old-fashioned arms. Clearly, in appropriate circumstances, it could be highly profitable.

It should be noted, however, that although the balance of power applies (in fact in many ways works better with nuclear weapons than without), once again it does not rule out warfare. It simply indicates what we might call major wars of conquest are not likely to be successful. In the great days of balance-of-power politics (1600–1800), major war was normally not undertaken by countries who understood what they were doing. The characteristic war was an effort to seize some small piece of property, with the idea that after many years one might obtain enough property so that world conquest became possible.

In the nuclear situation, this is still possible. In the first place, the nuclear forces are not the only forces available. The use of obsolete weapons (à la the present fighting in Vietnam or the fighting in Korea) for the purpose of grabbing a small piece of real estate which can then be exploited to increase power in the future will still be possible unless some of the countries choose to regard it as a cause for nuclear war. Indeed, we have seen a great deal of this in recent years. It is possible to use nuclear weapons for minor wars, also. A demand for some small, international concession—say a border province—backed by a threat of nuclear weapons, might very well be acceded to by a country which believed the threat. Firing your rockets if the province was refused might lend credibility to future threats.

Suppose, then, that *A* has some quarrel with *C*, a quarrel which does not involve (in the immediate future) the continued existence of *C* but, let us say, the transfer of the Himalayan foothills from India to China. *A* threatens nuclear war unless *C* agrees, and when *C* refuses, believing that *A* is bluffing, *A* fires 50 rockets, thus reducing her power from 500 to 450 and *C*'s from 150 to 100. She also announces that if *C* responds, she will wipe out *C*'s nuclear force and also destroy a large number of *C*'s cities. It is unlikely, under these circumstances, that *B*, *D*, or *E* will enter into the fight until, at any event, there has been a further exchange between *A* and *C*. *C* faces a very difficult situation. If it fires, let us say, 50 rockets at *A*, it will reduce *A*'s rocket force to parity with that of *B*, but will not protect itself at all from further reprisals by *A*. It is unlikely *B*, *D*, or *E* is deeply enough concerned about one province to be willing to intervene unless it sees a probability of gain for itself; under the balance of power, it is unlikely that it will do so. For example, suppose that *A* uses 50 more rockets to eliminate the remainder of *C*'s rockets. *B* can now, by use of 350 of its rockets, eliminate *A*'s rocket force, but will leave itself substantially defenseless against *D* and *E*, something it probably would not want to do. A lesser commitment of rockets by *B* against *A* will again degrade *B*'s combat capacity. Altogether, it seems unlikely that anyone will come to *C*'s assistance as long as the demand by *A* against *C* is small enough not to jeopardize the interests of the other countries. Indeed, *B*, *D*, or *E* may decide to take a piece itself.

So far I have been assuming rather narrowly defined nuclear weapon capacities. In practice, of course, many different types of nuclear weapons are available and the technology regularly changes. Nevertheless, it does seem likely that the special characteristic I have included in my models—that the bulk of the equipment will be eliminated in the early part of any war—will remain true of wars in the future. Whether there are now three countries capable of acting as part of the balance of power—for example, Russia, the United States, and China—is not clear. It is not known, for example, whether the United States and Russia have very close to the same nuclear capacity or not. It is not even clear which one has the lead. If this is a difficult problem, the question of the power of the Chinese nuclear force is even more so. Nevertheless, it is certainly possible that China's nuclear force, at the moment, is equal to the difference between the military forces of the other two powers.

Let us, however, turn to a discussion of disarmament. Suppose, again, we have *A*, *B*, and *C*, and they have, as before, 500, 400, and 150 nuclear weapons. Let us assume that keeping these weapons up is a costly process; hence, savings could be made by reducing the weapon power. Suppose, then, a proposal is made that each reduce its nuclear weapons by half to 250, 200, and 75, respectively. As we have seen, this is a mutually advantageous proposal if the countries do not fear that their opponents will cheat. On the other hand, as we have also seen, there are very strong motives for cheating.

Under our present model, however, the motives for cheating are less strong than they would have been under a two-country model. Assume that any country feels that it has the prospect of building 20 percent more rockets than it has agreed to without being detected, but that a higher percentage than that will raise unacceptable risks of detection. With two countries, it is unlikely that an agreement for disarmament can be negotiated under these circumstances. In the three-country model, however, this might nevertheless be sufficient. Suppose, for example, that *A does* succeed in producing 50 additional rockets without anyone knowing the difference. She still does not have more rockets than *B* and *C* put together. On the other hand, it might be easier to get away with violation under these circumstances. That is by no means certain, but it is at least conceivable that violation will be easier, simply because it is of less importance to the other countries. *B* is less menaced by a small increase in *A*'s rockets if *C* continues to exist than she will be if *C* does not exist. Hence, she chooses to use fewer resources in attempting to detect such a change, and the consequence may be that the amount of cheating possible in a three-country system is greater than in a two-country system. If so, this might more than offset the advantages which the three-country system has in being able to adapt to a larger absolute amount of cheating.

It also should not escape notice that the example I just gave depended on the exact numbers of rockets I have assigned to the different countries. If *C* had only 110 rockets, then the 20 percent increase in *A*'s rockets would have given *A* a superiority over both parties, although she had a very slight inferiority before the disarmament treaty.

If we move to five countries—*A* with 500 rockets, *B* with 400, *C* with 150, *D* with 250, and *E* with 200—as usual, we find that the situation is not quite as satisfactory for the individual country as with three. There are certain advantages here, however. It will be extremely unlikely in the three-country model that *A* and *B* will be willing to accept major reductions in their armaments if *C* does not go along. That *A*, *B*, *D*, and *E* will accept major reductions in their armaments without *C*'s participation, however, is far from impossible. *C*'s capacity is just too small, compared with those of the entire rest of the five-country group, to be a menace. Countervailing this, of course, is the fact that cheating would be easier in the five-country system than in either the three- or two-country, simply because it is less vital to the interests of the countries that would be attempting to detect the cheating.

Although the fundamental situation we discussed in two-nation models continues to apply in the many-nation model, it is in many ways much less desperate. We have a game in which significant but not fatal costs are imposed upon the parties. It is even possible, in the nuclear case, that the only costs which will be imposed are those of maintaining nuclear weapons that will never, in fact, be used. This is particularly likely if the countries retain the capacity to tell who has used a nuclear weapon against them. This does not seem to be a terribly difficult requirement, since the only motive for using such a weapon is gain, and it will normally be possible to determine who gained.

EPILOGUE TO *THE SOCIAL DILEMMA*

THE ECONOMICS OF WAR AND REVOLUTION

In a way, it is fitting that the final substantive portion of this book concerns the problems of nuclear strategy. The book as a whole is far more gloomy than most. Although it does not indicate that the world is doomed, *à la* much modern ecological discussion or that the population boom will drive us into dire poverty, nevertheless it does indicate that certain utopian dreams are indeed utopian.

By now I take it that the reader is thoroughly convinced that the investment of resources in conflict is frequently rational from the standpoint of individuals, but leads to net waste from the standpoint of society. Whether the investment of resources in obtaining transfers from other persons takes the form of attempted robbery, fraud, bargaining maneuvering, lobbying for legislation, war, or defense against any of these activities, it will normally be sensible for the individual to invest at least some resources in this activity. Since people will be making such investments on both sides, there is net social loss regardless of the outcome of the efforts to obtain or prevent transfers. This is the social dilemma.

Unfortunately, I have little to suggest in the way of reducing these costs. In individual cases one can think of suitable methods. The police force, for example, reduces the costs which would be imposed by the possibility of certain types of transfer. Unfortunately, the police force itself is a costly institution; hence we only reduce but do not eliminate the costs by this method.

Similar institutions exist to minimize costs in other fields. Unfortunately, in the area of government activity, this does not seem to be true. In general, lobbying to obtain or prevent government income transfers would appear to be something we cannot control in a democratic state. In the exploitative state, intrigue for power is similarly an essentially uncontrollable phenomenon. Lastly, of course, no effective methods of controlling international conflict exist. These somewhat gloomy conclusions are based only upon present knowledge. It may well be that some of the readers of this book will be able to solve problems that have escaped my grasp.

Reprinted, with permission, from *The Social Dilemma: The Economics of War and Revolution* (Blacksburg, Va.: Center for Study of Public Choice, 1974), 139–40.

One of the strongest doctrines of the Enlightenment was belief in the perfectability of human institutions. It is the argument of this book that a great many institutions will always remain somewhat imperfect. Nevertheless, this does not mean that they cannot be improved upon. It merely means that the best we can do will fall short of our dreams. The truth may not make us free, but it should improve our efficiency. If we abandon the search for utopia and turn to a more modest quest for amelioration, we can hope for genuine improvements. Continuing to believe in utopias and acting as if they were possible may mean that we will achieve far less than can be obtained with a more realistic view of the world. In this, as in so many other areas, the best is the enemy of the better. If we abandon dreams of the conflict-free world and turn toward understanding and controlling conflict, we may achieve a world which, if not perfect, is nevertheless an improvement.

INDEX

References to bibliographic information appear in italics.

The typeface used for the text of this book is Galliard, an old-style face designed by Matthew Carter in 1978, in the spirit of a sixteenth-century French typeface of Robert Granjon. The display type is Meta Book, a variant of Meta, designed by Erik Spiekermann in the 1990s.

This book is printed on paper that is acid-free and meets the requirements of the American National Standard for Permanence of Paper for Printed Library Materials, z39.48–1992. ♾

Book design by Richard Hendel, Chapel Hill, North Carolina
Typography by G&S Typesetters, Inc., Austin, Texas
Printed and bound by Worzalla Publishing Company, Stevens Point, Wisconsin